VIZ GRAPHIC NOVEL

X/1999™
SONATA

BY CLAMP

This volume contains the X/1999 installments from Animerica.Anime & Manga
Monthly, Vol. 4, No. 7 through Vol. 5, No. 1 in their entirety.

STORY & ART BY CLAMP

ENGLISH ADAPTATION BY FRED BURKE

Translation/Lillian Olsen
Touch-Up Art & Lettering/Wayne Truman
Cover Design/Viz Graphics
Editor/Julie Davis

Editor-in-Chief/Hyoe Narita
Publisher/Seiji Horibuchi
V.P. of Sales & Marketing/Rick Bauer

Printed in Canada

Published by Viz Communications, Inc.
P.O Box 77010 • San Francisco, CA 94107

10 9 8 7 6 5 4 3
First printing, January 1998
Second printing, December 2000.
Third printing, March 2002

X/1999 GRAPHIC NOVELS TO DATE:
Prelude
Overture
Sonata
Intermezzo
Serenade
Duet

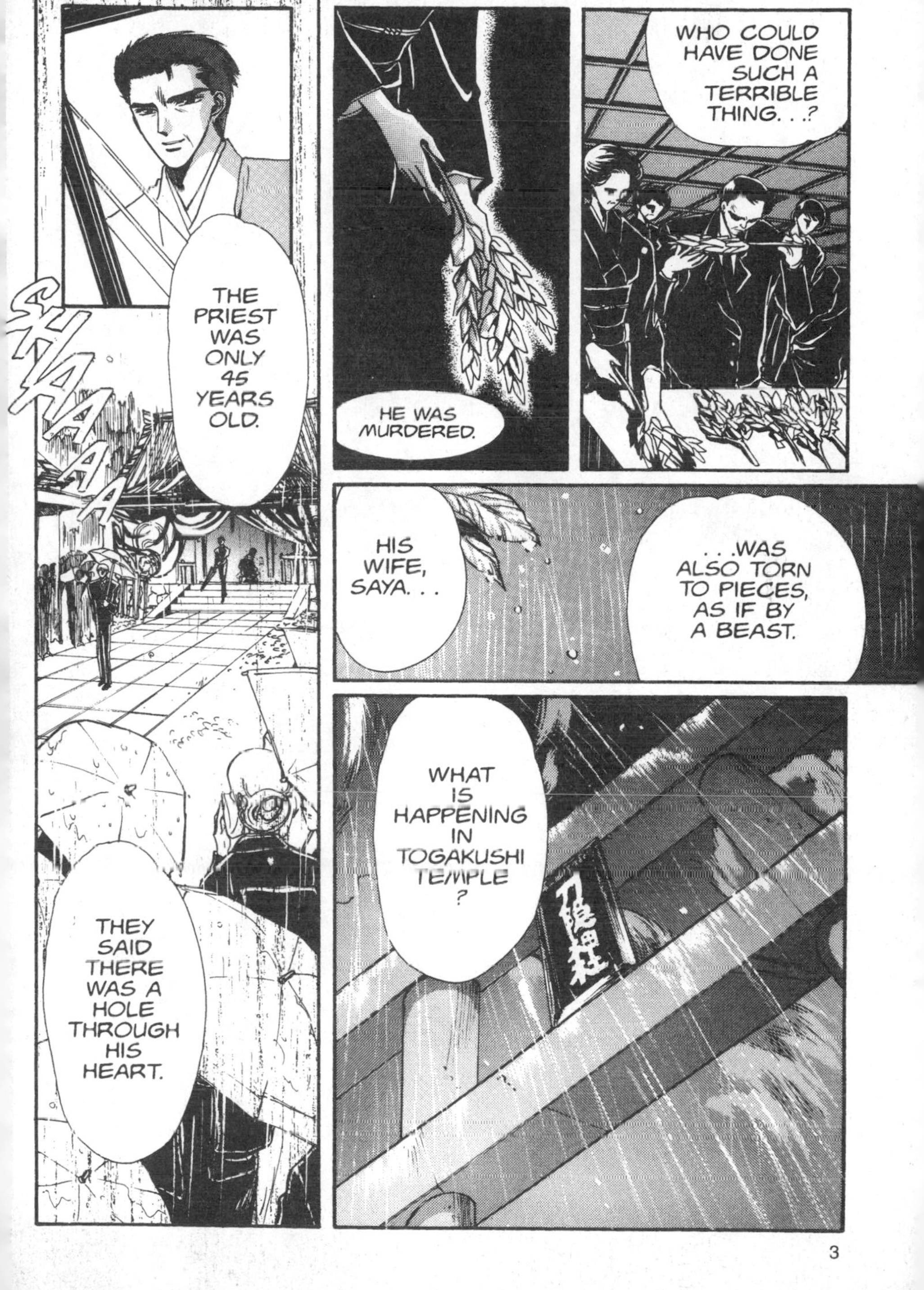

THE PRIEST WAS ONLY 45 YEARS OLD.
SHAAAA
THEY SAID THERE WAS A HOLE THROUGH HIS HEART.
HE WAS MURDERED.
WHO COULD HAVE DONE SUCH A TERRIBLE THING. . .?
HIS WIFE, SAYA. . .
. . .WAS ALSO TORN TO PIECES, AS IF BY A BEAST.
WHAT IS HAPPENING IN TOGAKUSHI TEMPLE?

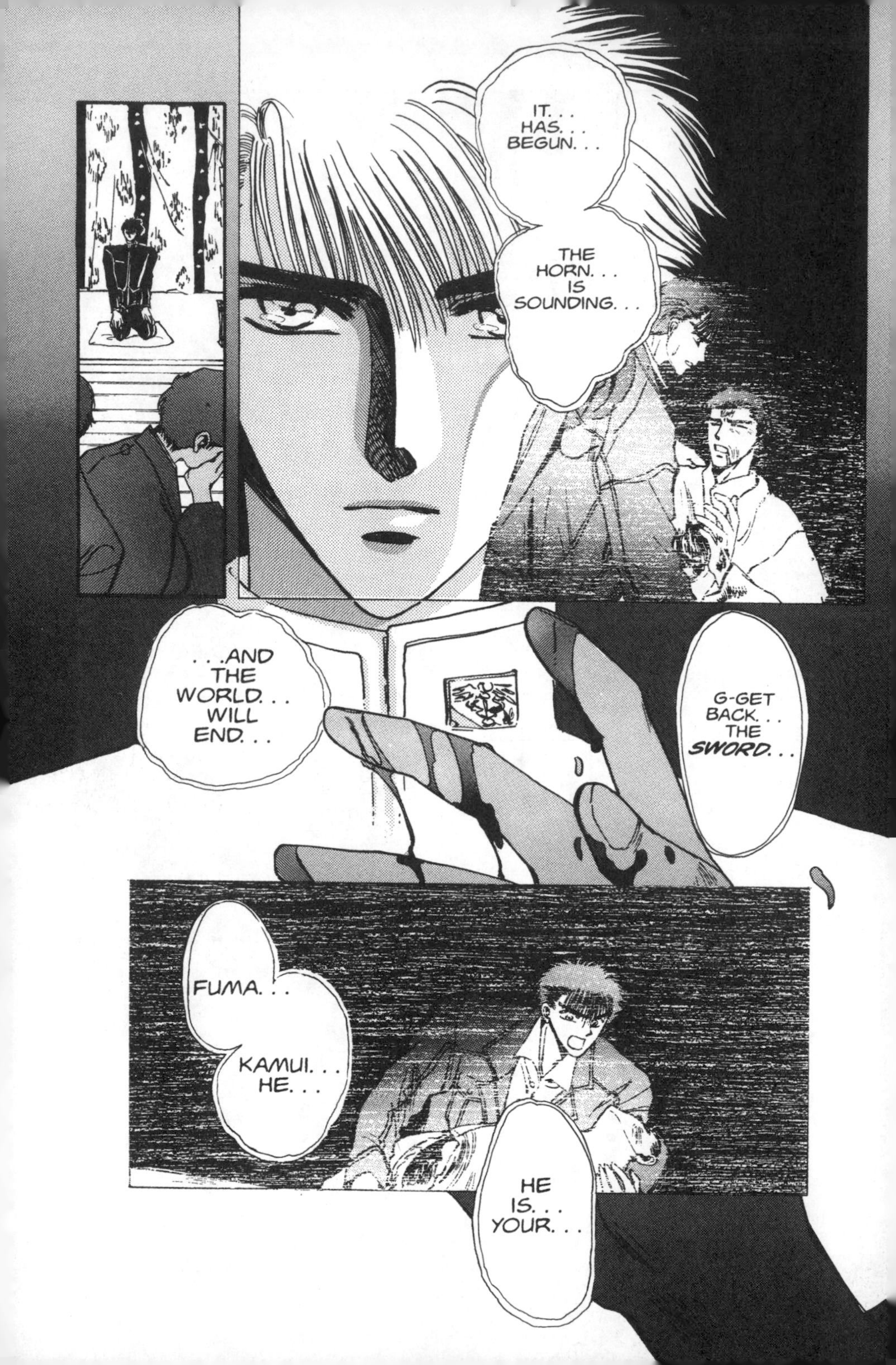
IT... HAS... BEGUN...
THE HORN... IS SOUNDING...
...AND THE WORLD... WILL END...
G-GET BACK... THE SWORD...
FUMA...
KAMUI... HE...
HE IS... YOUR...

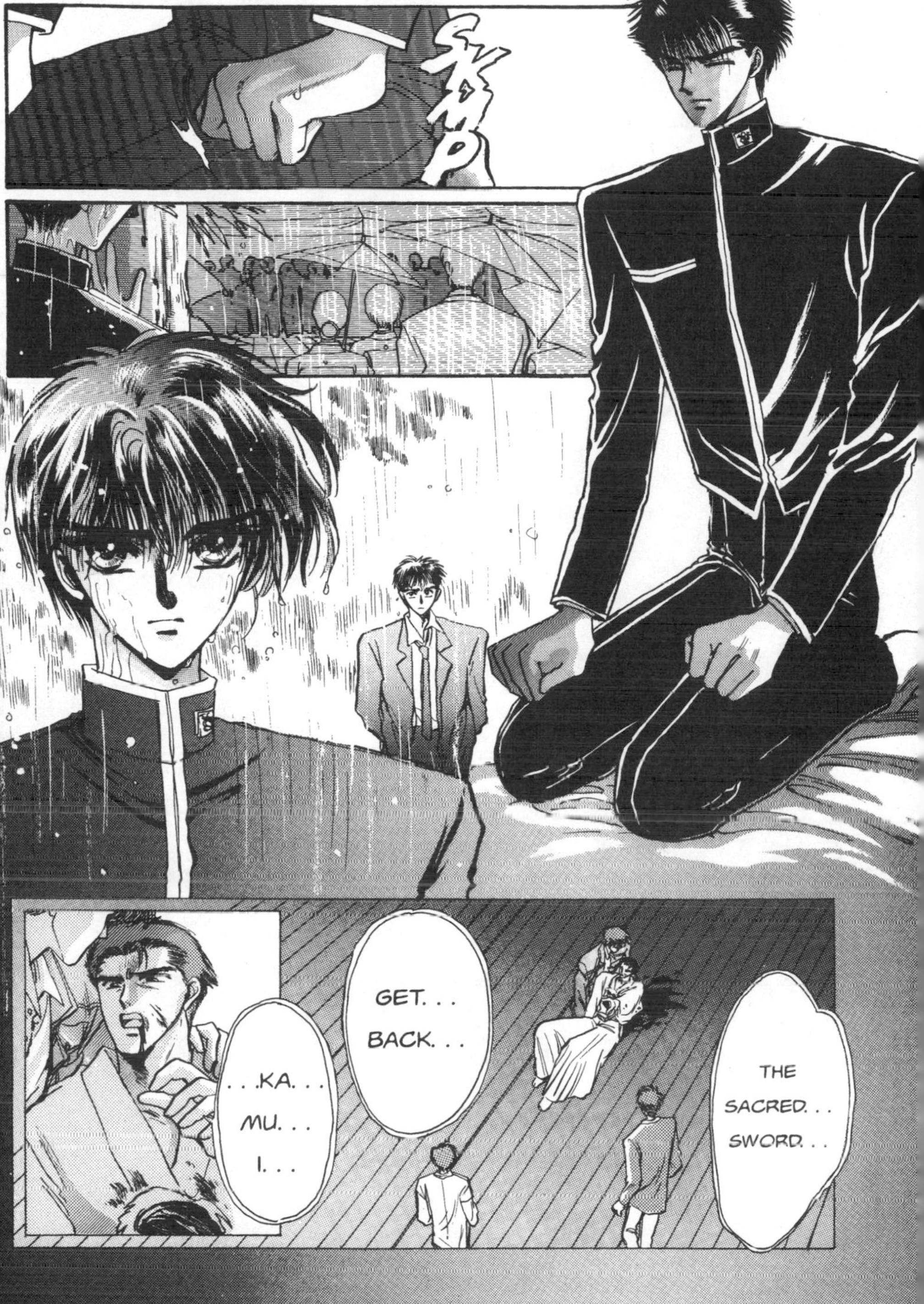
. . .KA. . . MU. . . I. . .
GET. . . BACK. . .
THE SACRED. . . SWORD. . .

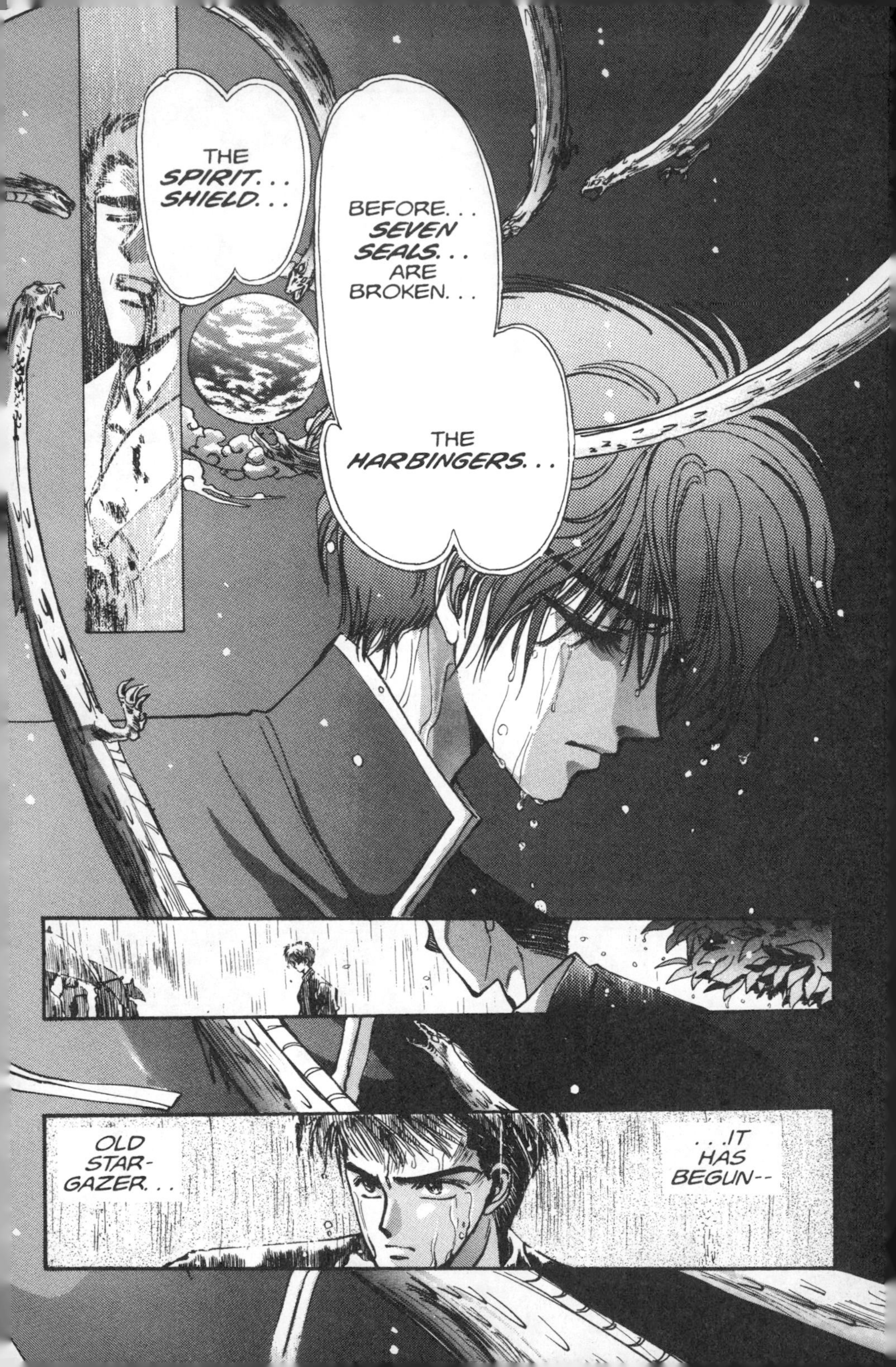

THE *SPIRIT*... *SHIELD*...
BEFORE... *SEVEN SEALS*... ARE BROKEN...
THE *HARBINGERS*...
OLD STAR-GAZER...
...IT HAS BEGUN--

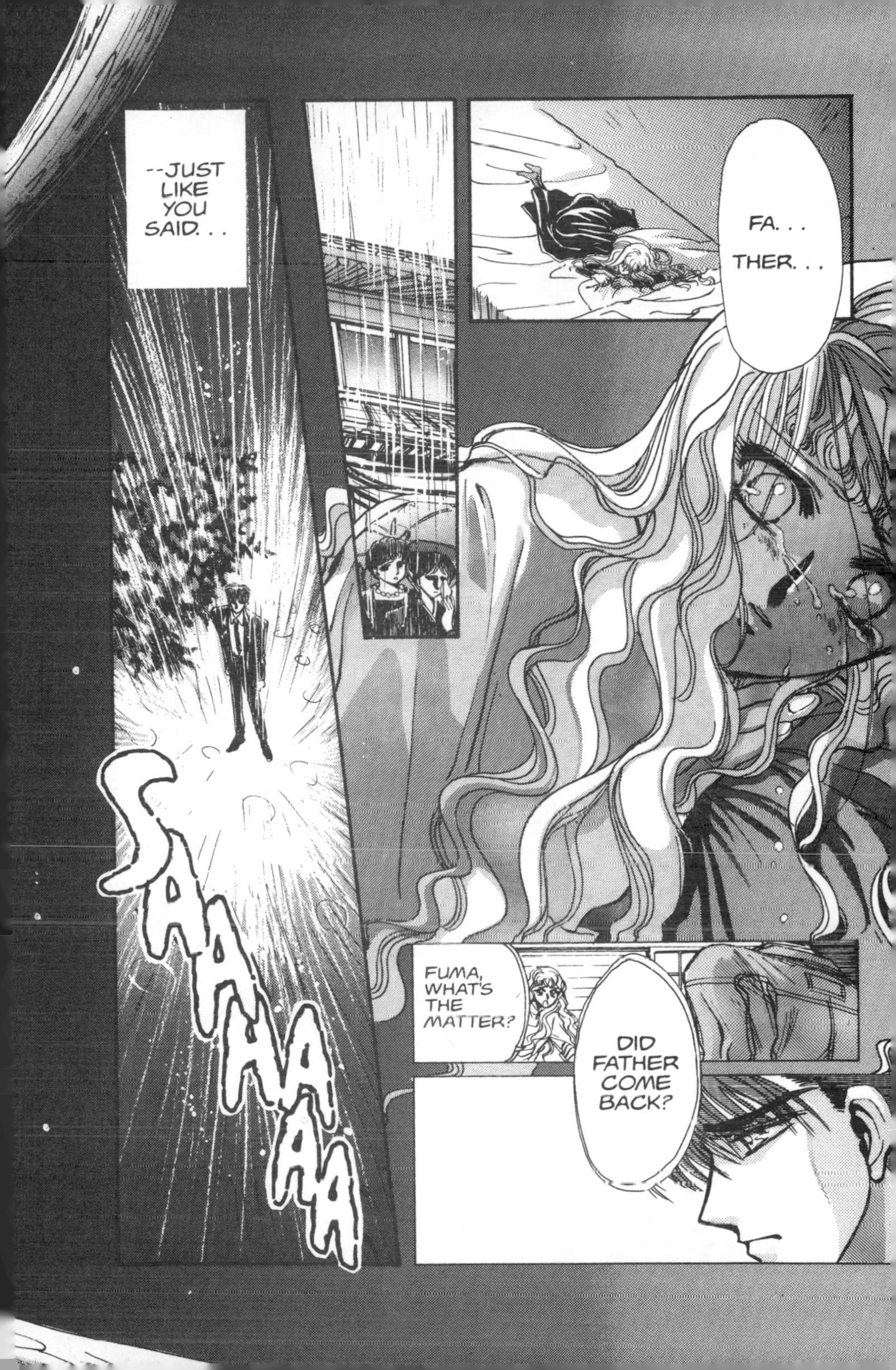
--JUST LIKE YOU SAID. . .
SAAAAAA
FA. . . THER. . .
FUMA, WHAT'S THE MATTER?
DID FATHER COME BACK?

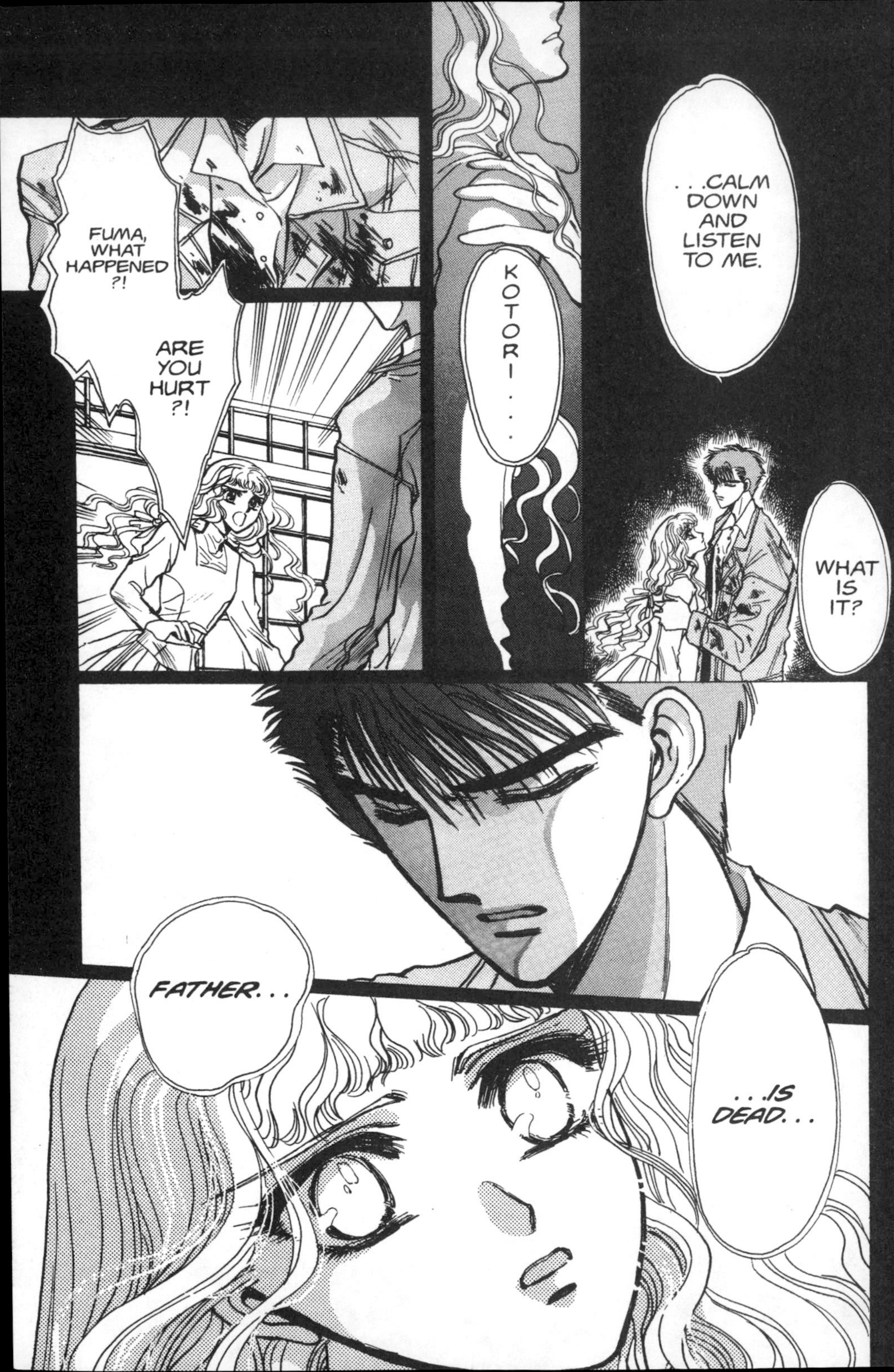
FUMA, WHAT HAPPENED ?!
ARE YOU HURT ?!
KOTORI . . .
. . .CALM DOWN AND LISTEN TO ME.
WHAT IS IT?
FATHER. . .
. . .IS DEAD. . .

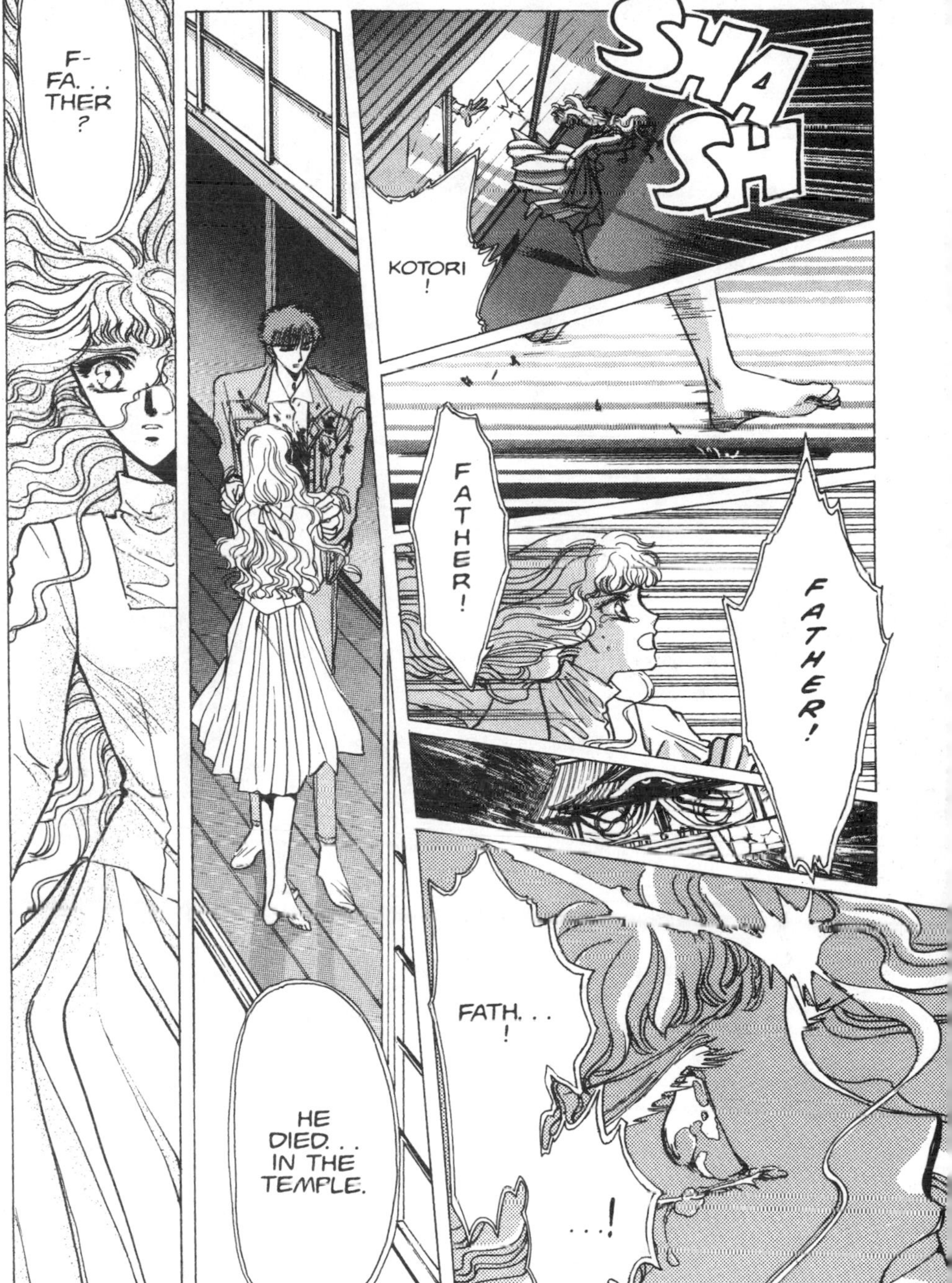
F- FA. . . THER ?
HE DIED. . . IN THE TEMPLE.
SHASH
KOTORI !
FATHER!
FATHER!
FATH. . . !
. . .!

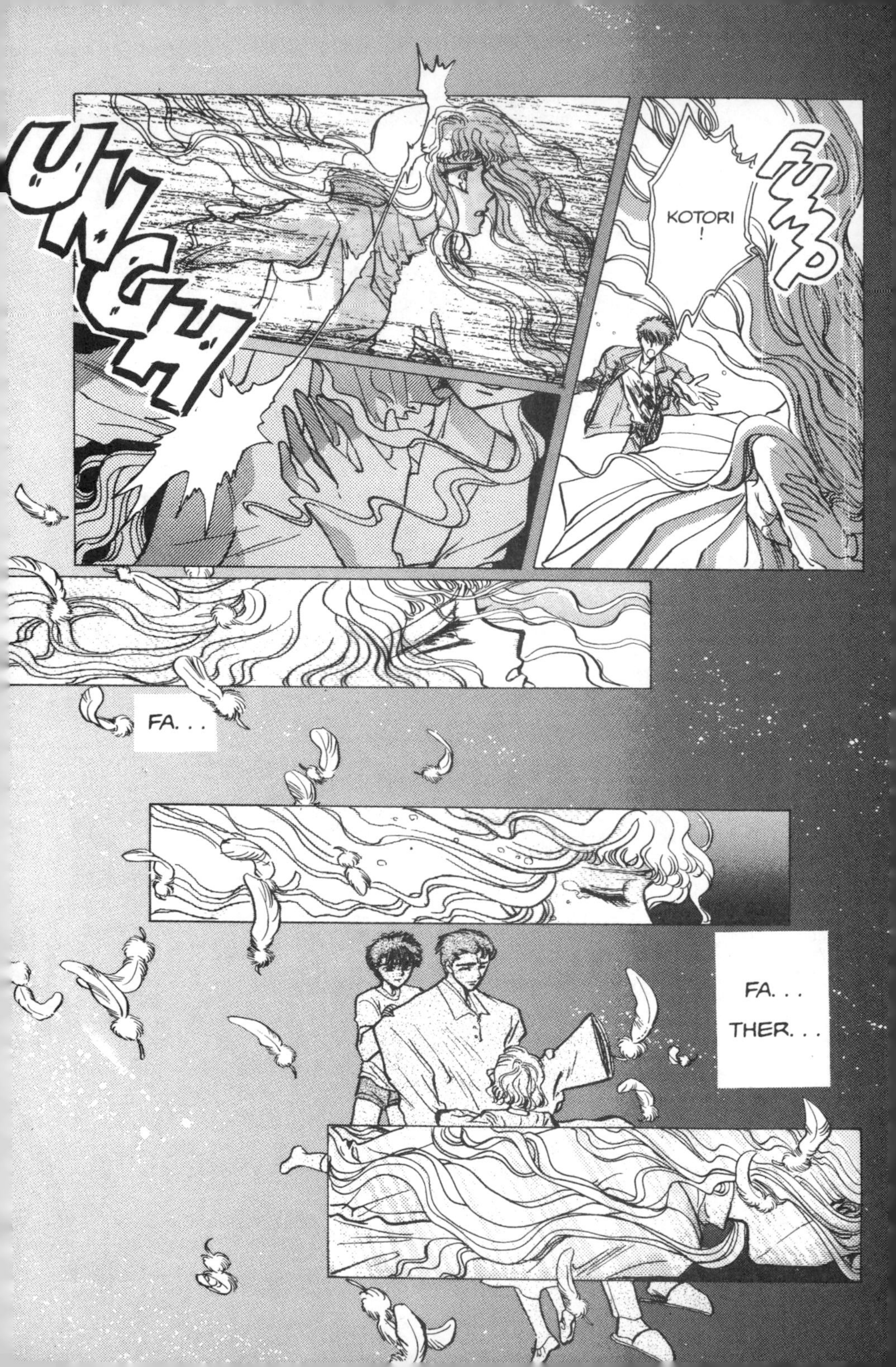
UNGH
KOTORI!
FUMP
FA. . .
FA. . .
THER. . .

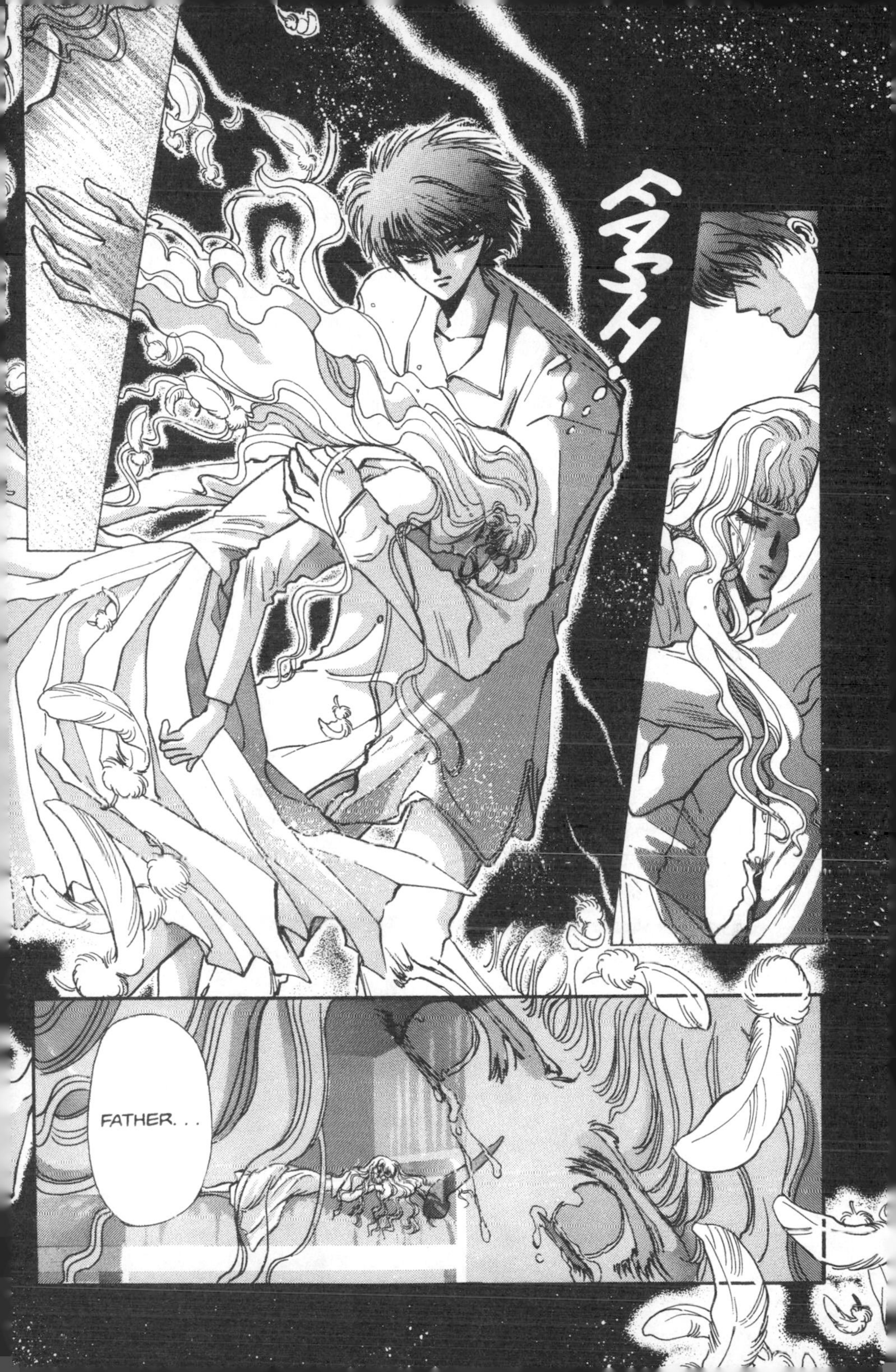
FASH
FATHER. . .

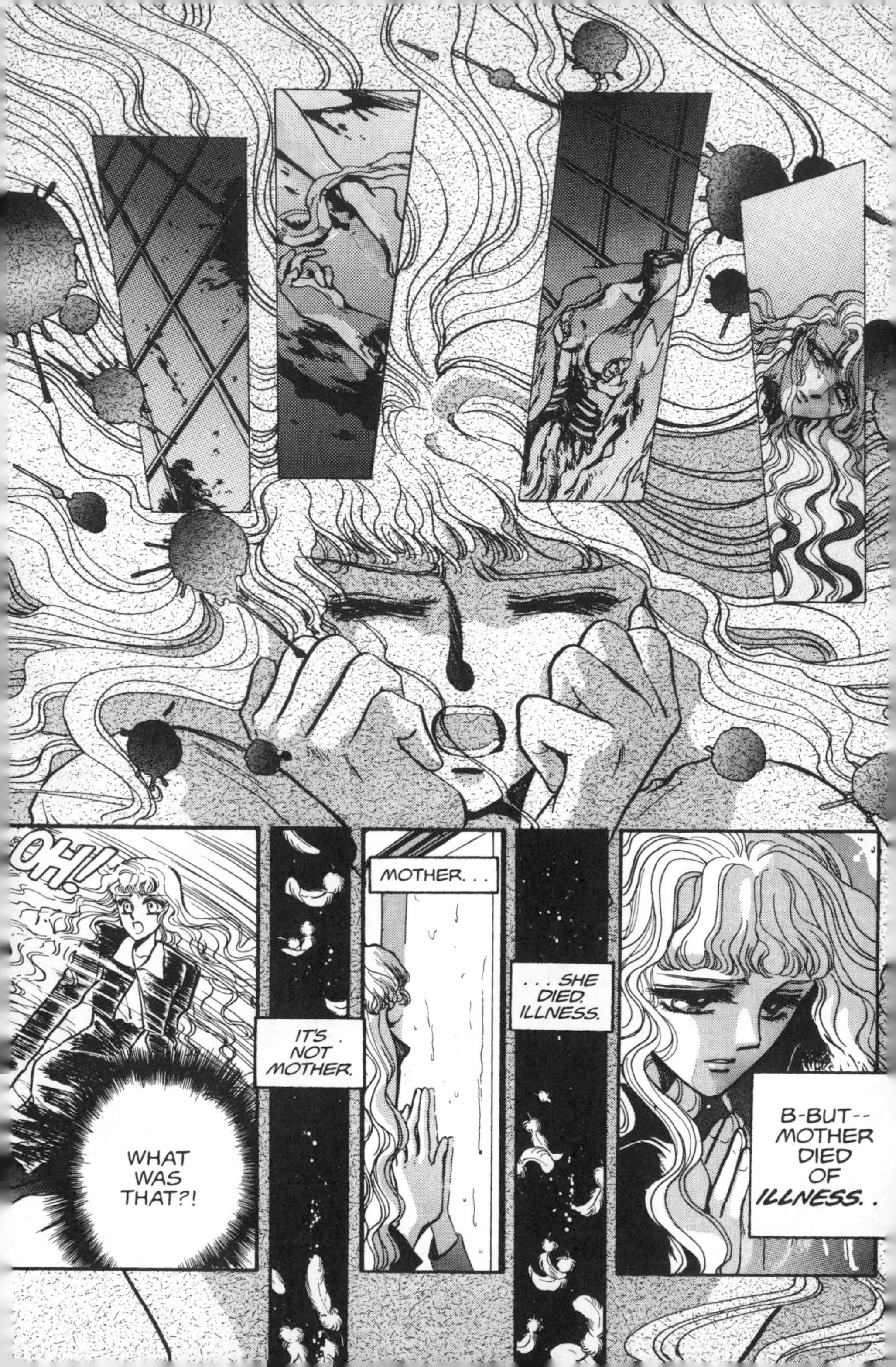
OH!
WHAT WAS THAT?!
IT'S NOT MOTHER.
MOTHER. . .
. . . SHE DIED. ILLNESS.
B-BUT-- MOTHER DIED OF ILLNESS. .

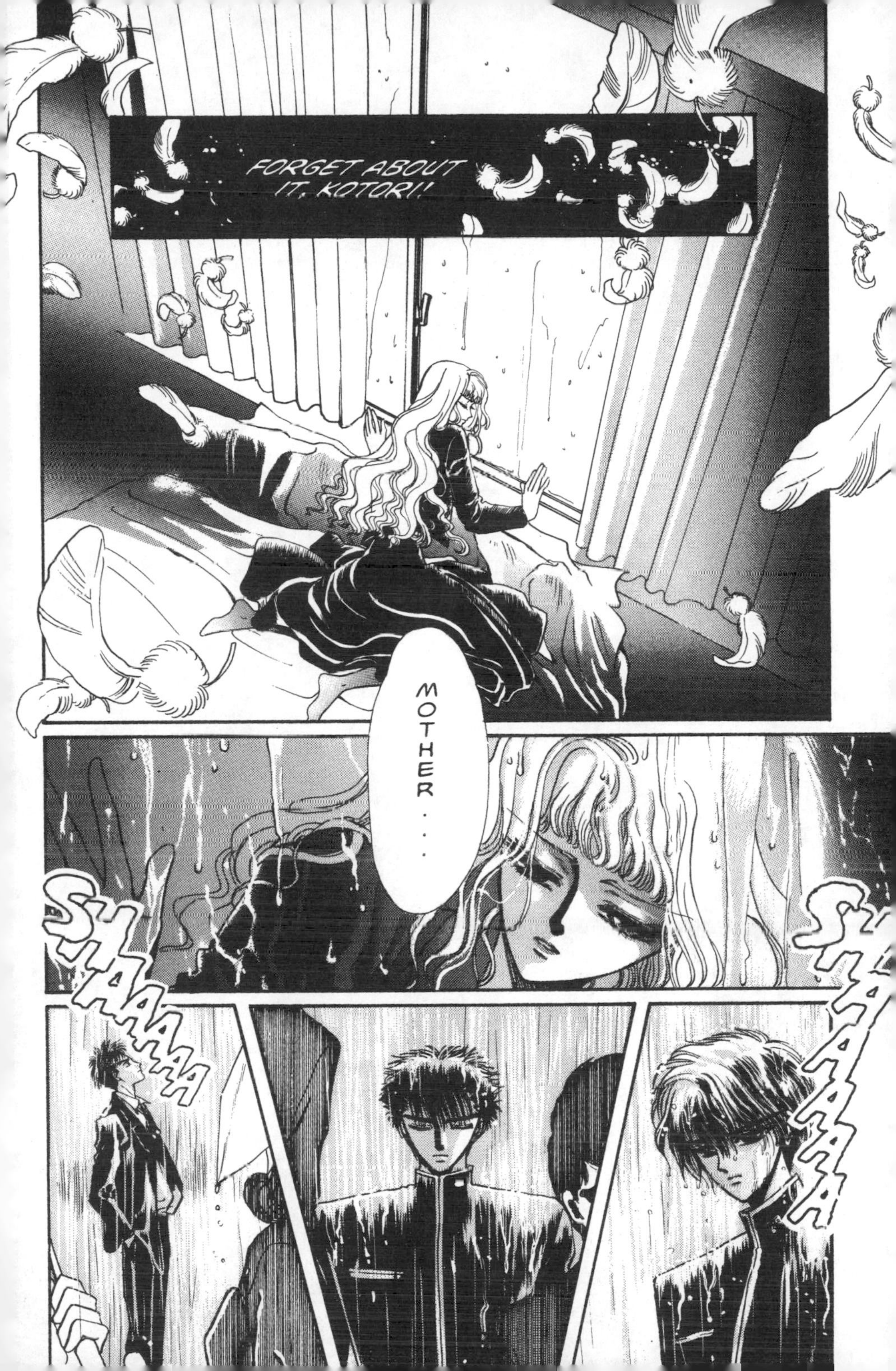
FORGET ABOUT IT, KOTORI!!
MOTHER . . .
SHAAAAA
SHAAAAAA

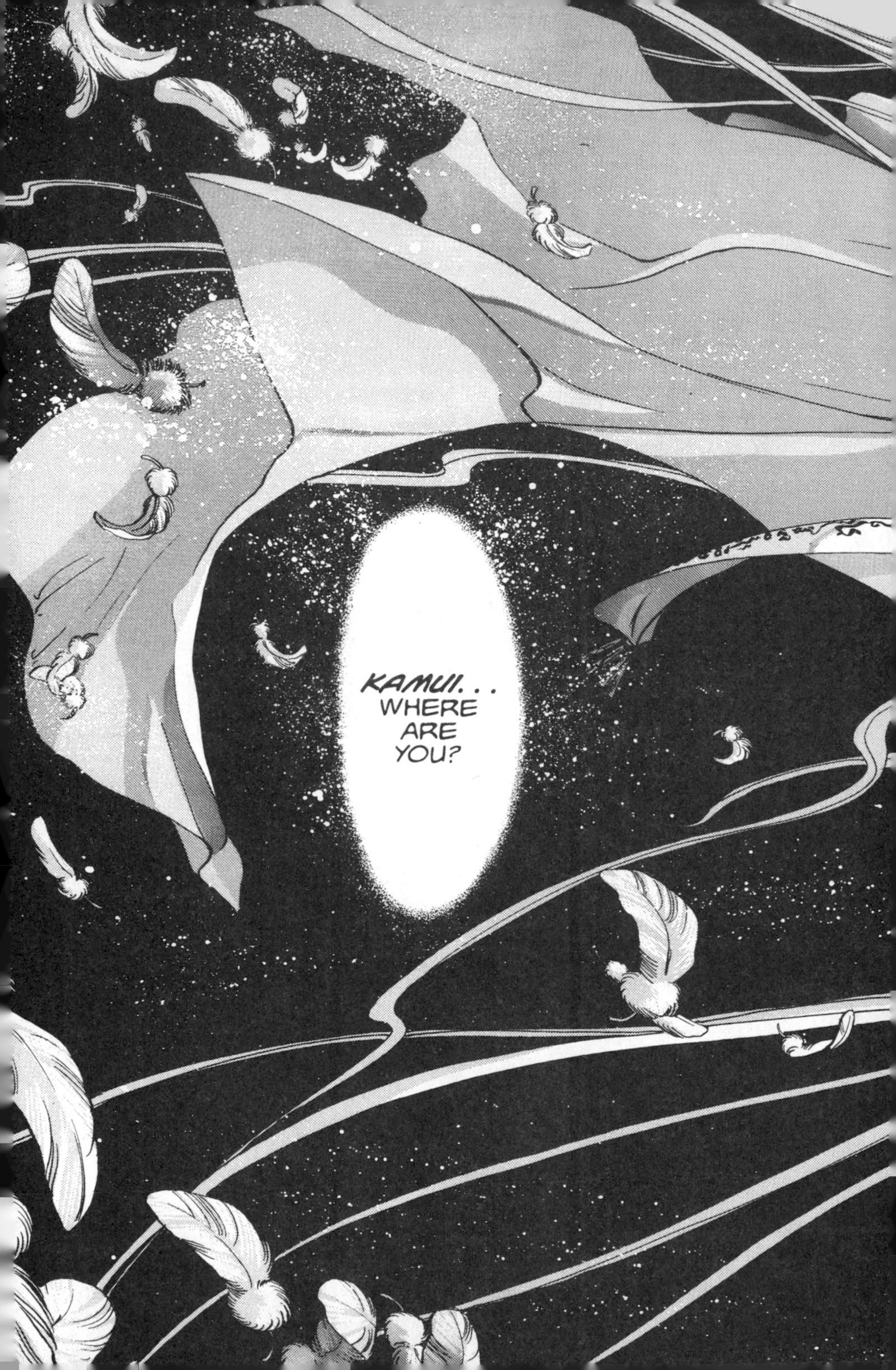
KAMUI. . . WHERE ARE YOU?

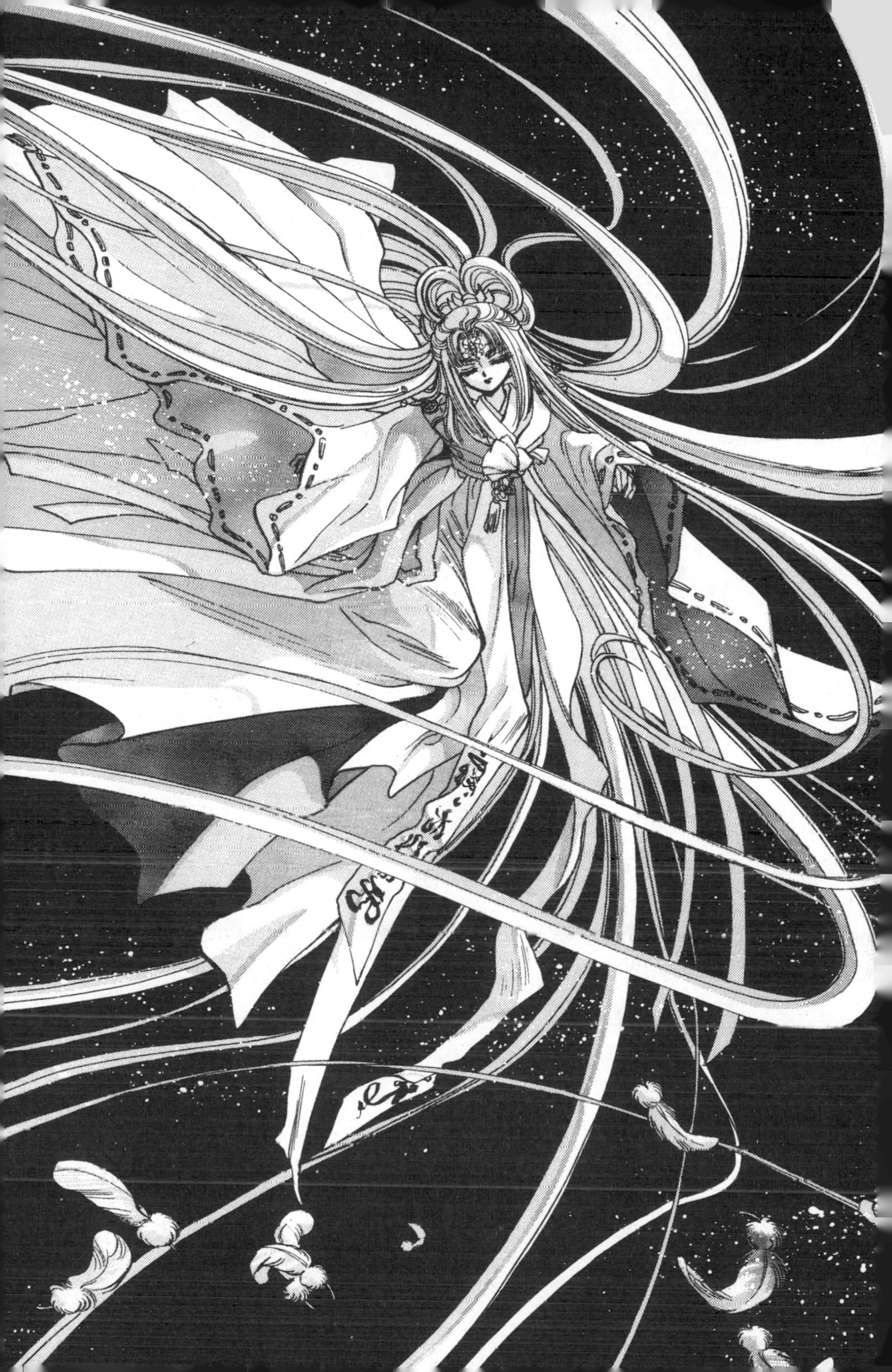

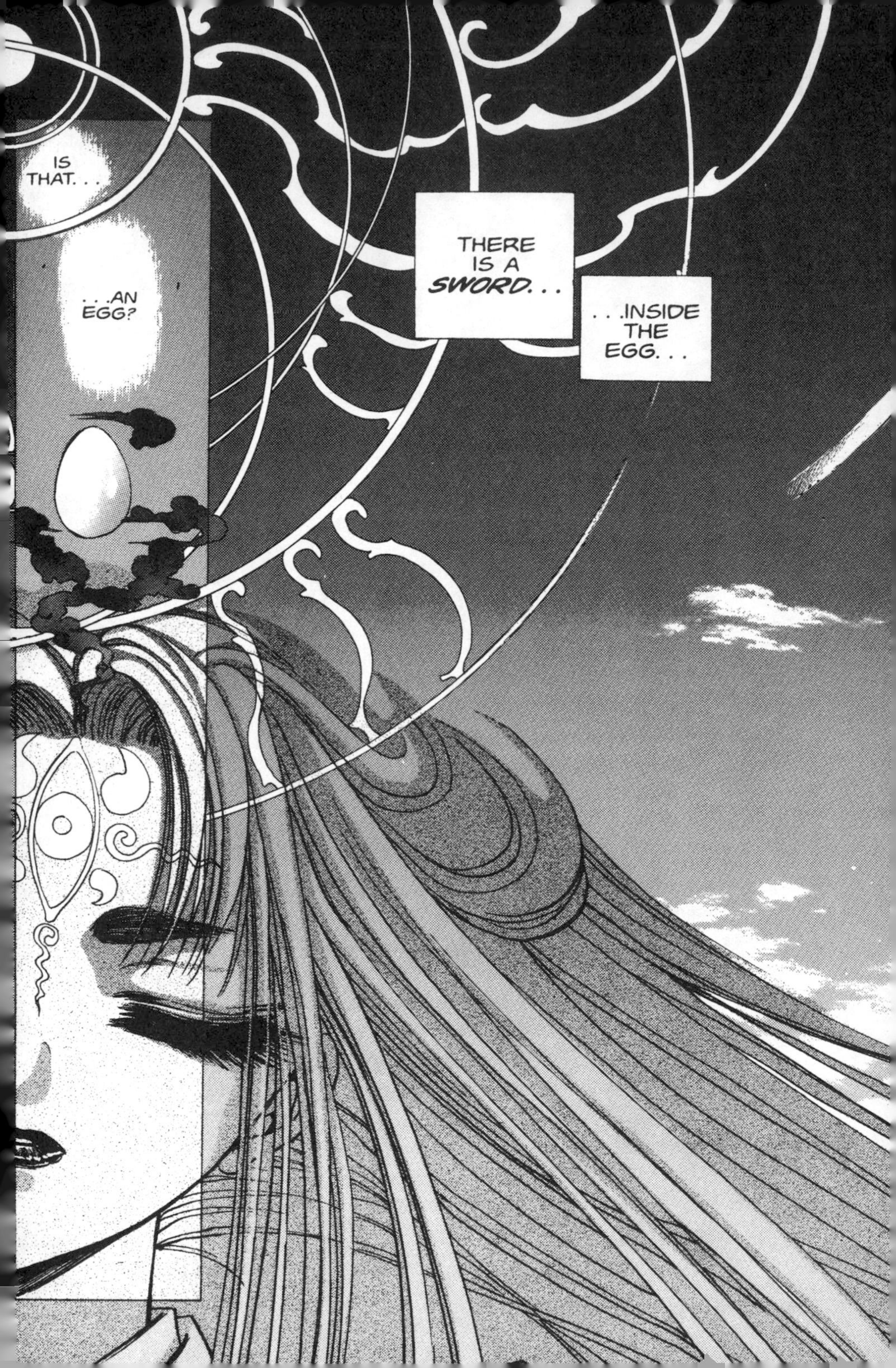
IS THAT. . .
. . .AN EGG?
THERE IS A SWORD. . .
. . .INSIDE THE EGG. . .

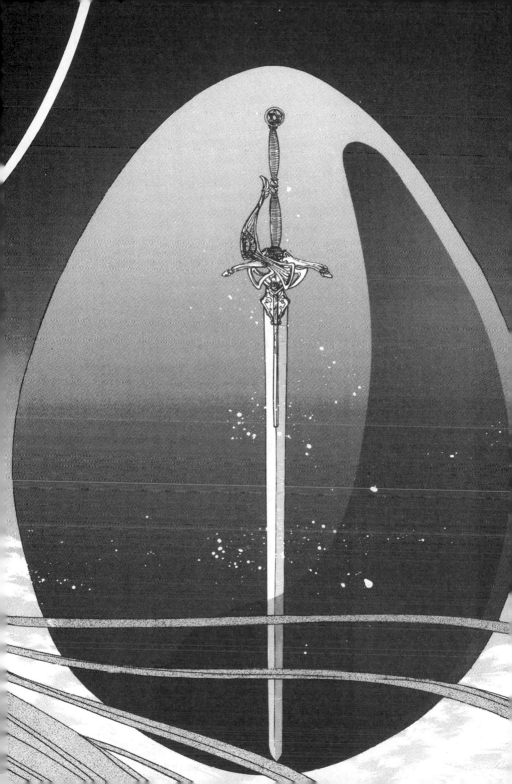

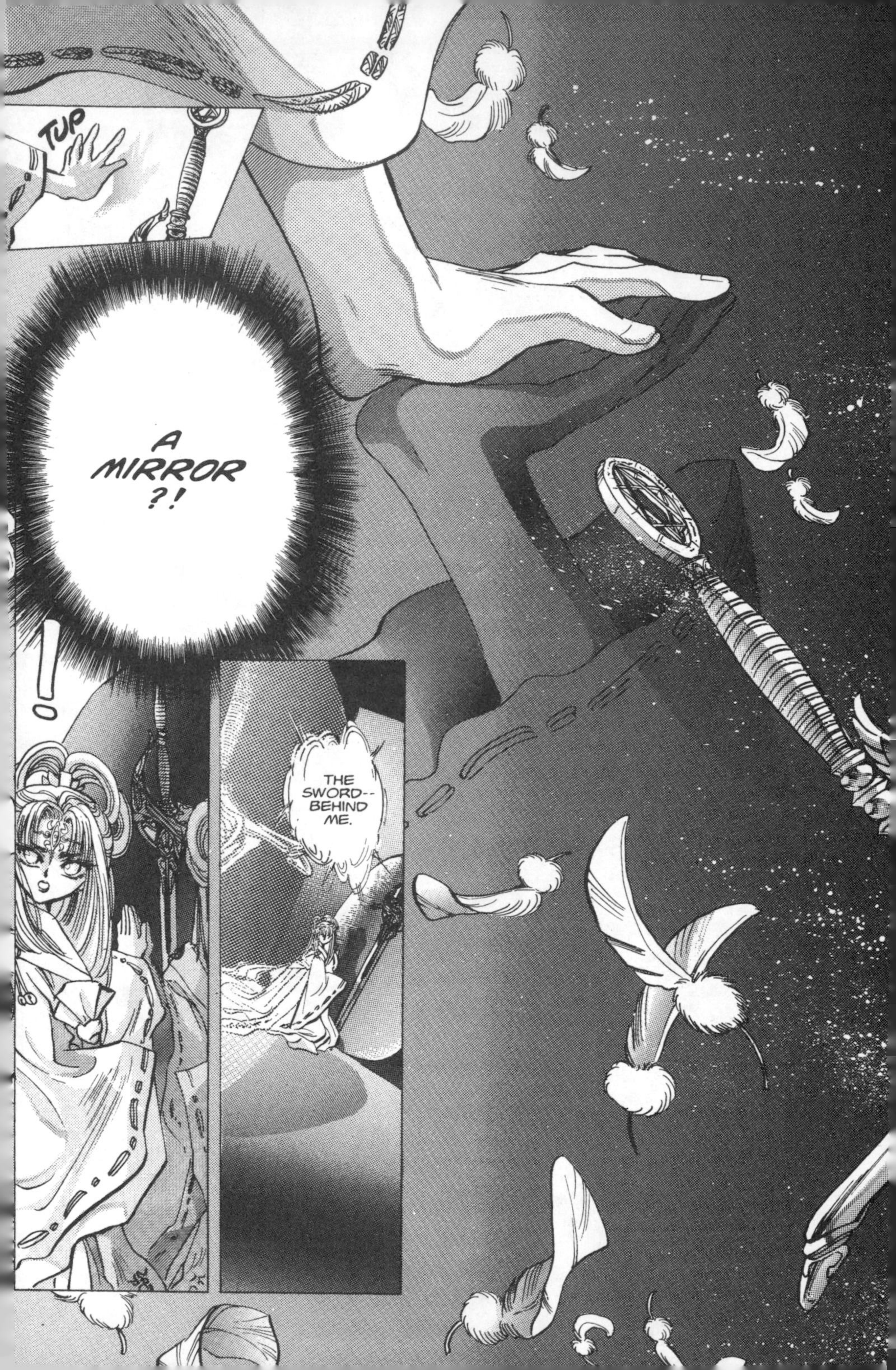
TUP
A MIRROR ?!
!
THE SWORD-- BEHIND ME.

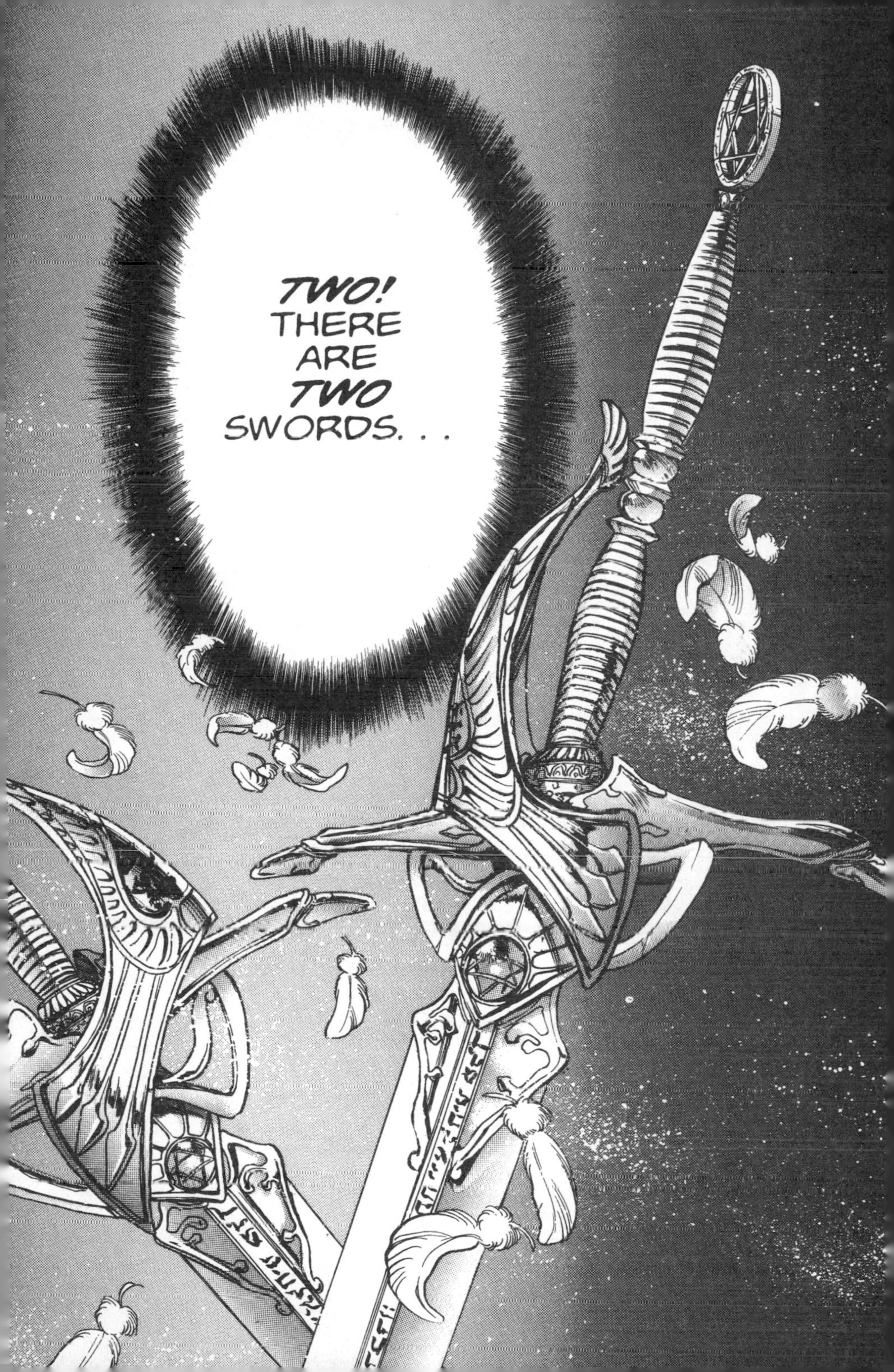
TWO! THERE ARE TWO SWORDS. . .

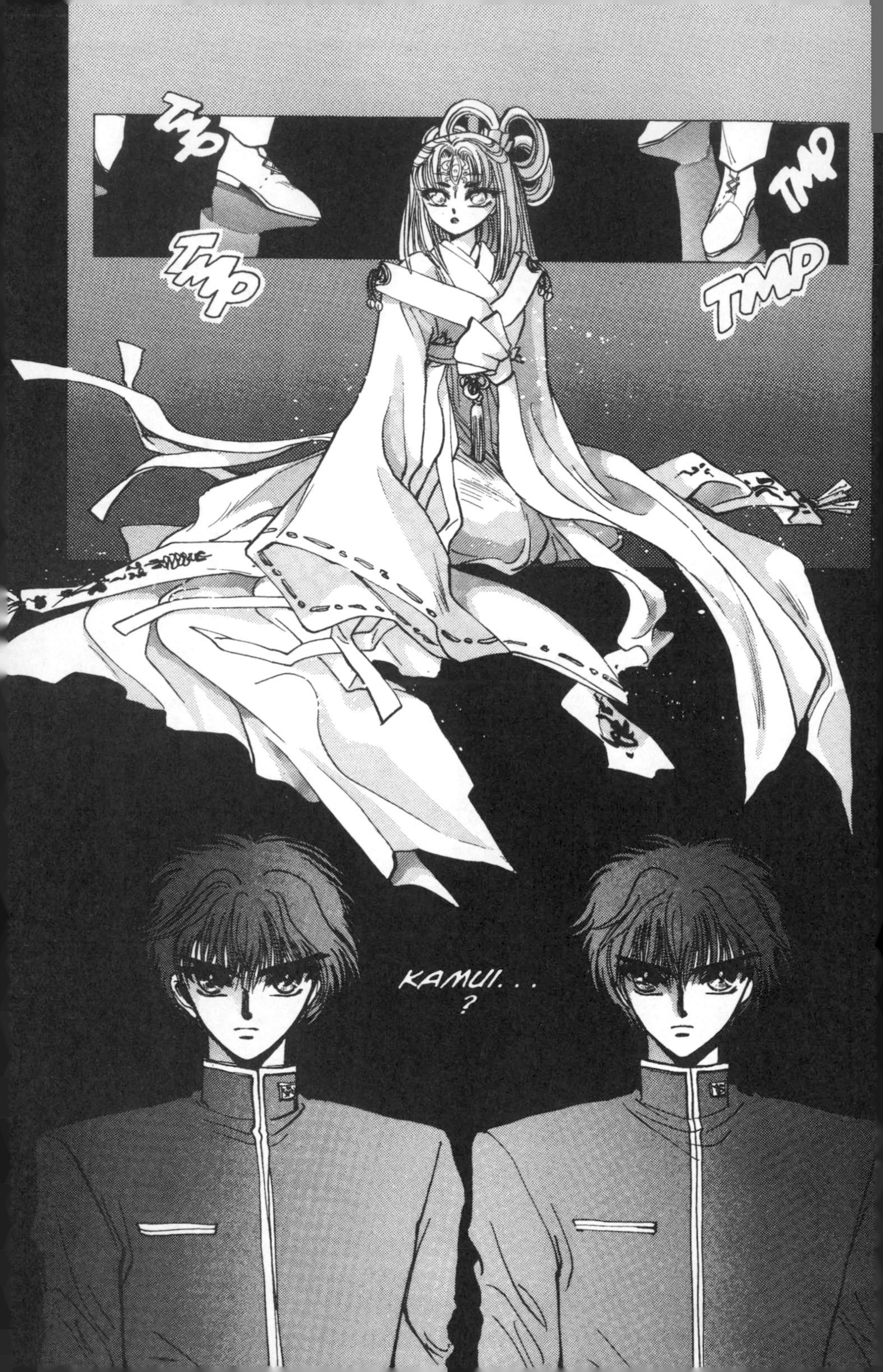
TMP
TMP
TMP
TMP
KAMUI...?

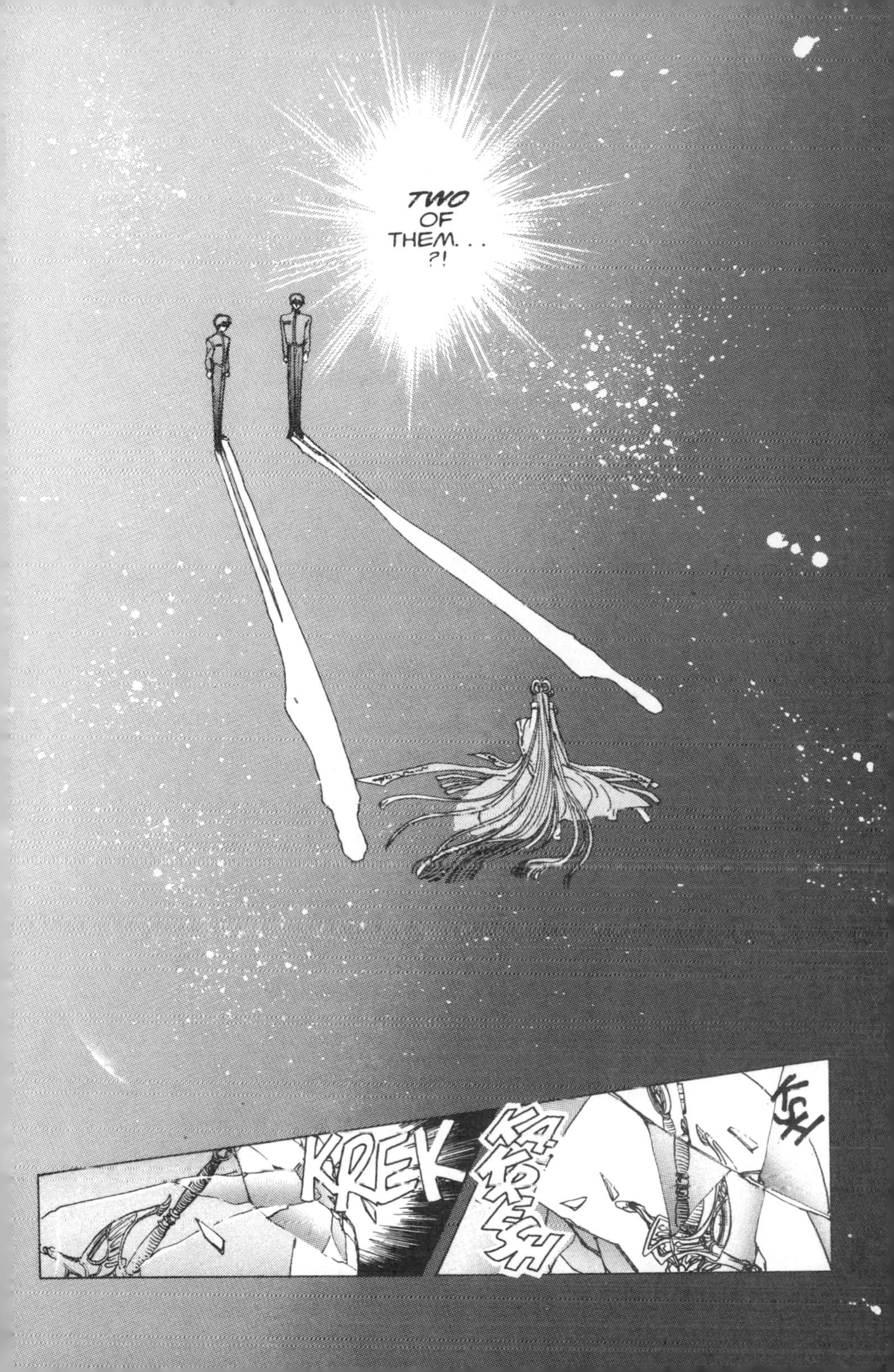
TWO OF THEM. . . ?!
KREK
KA KRECH
KSH

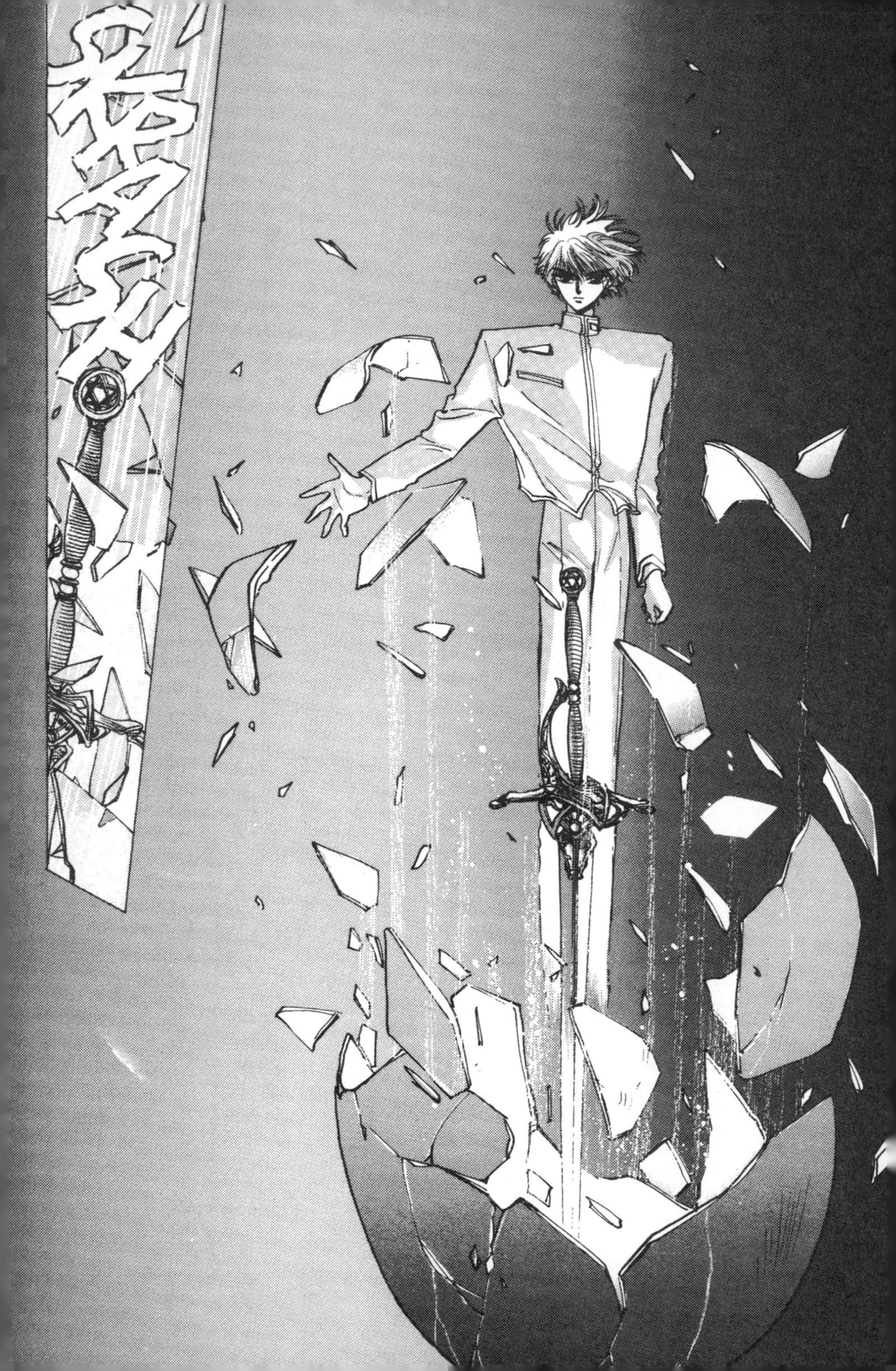

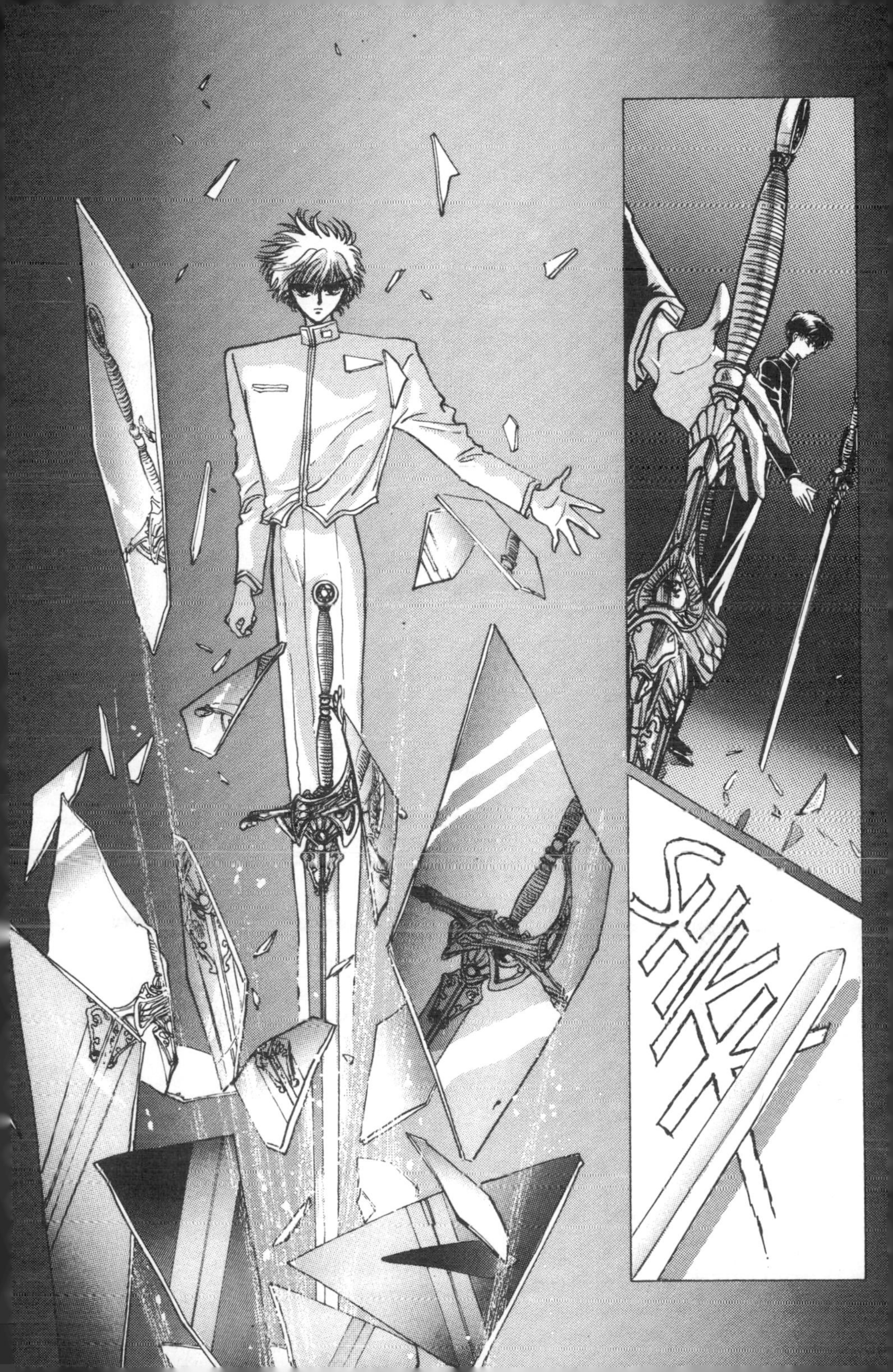
SHINK

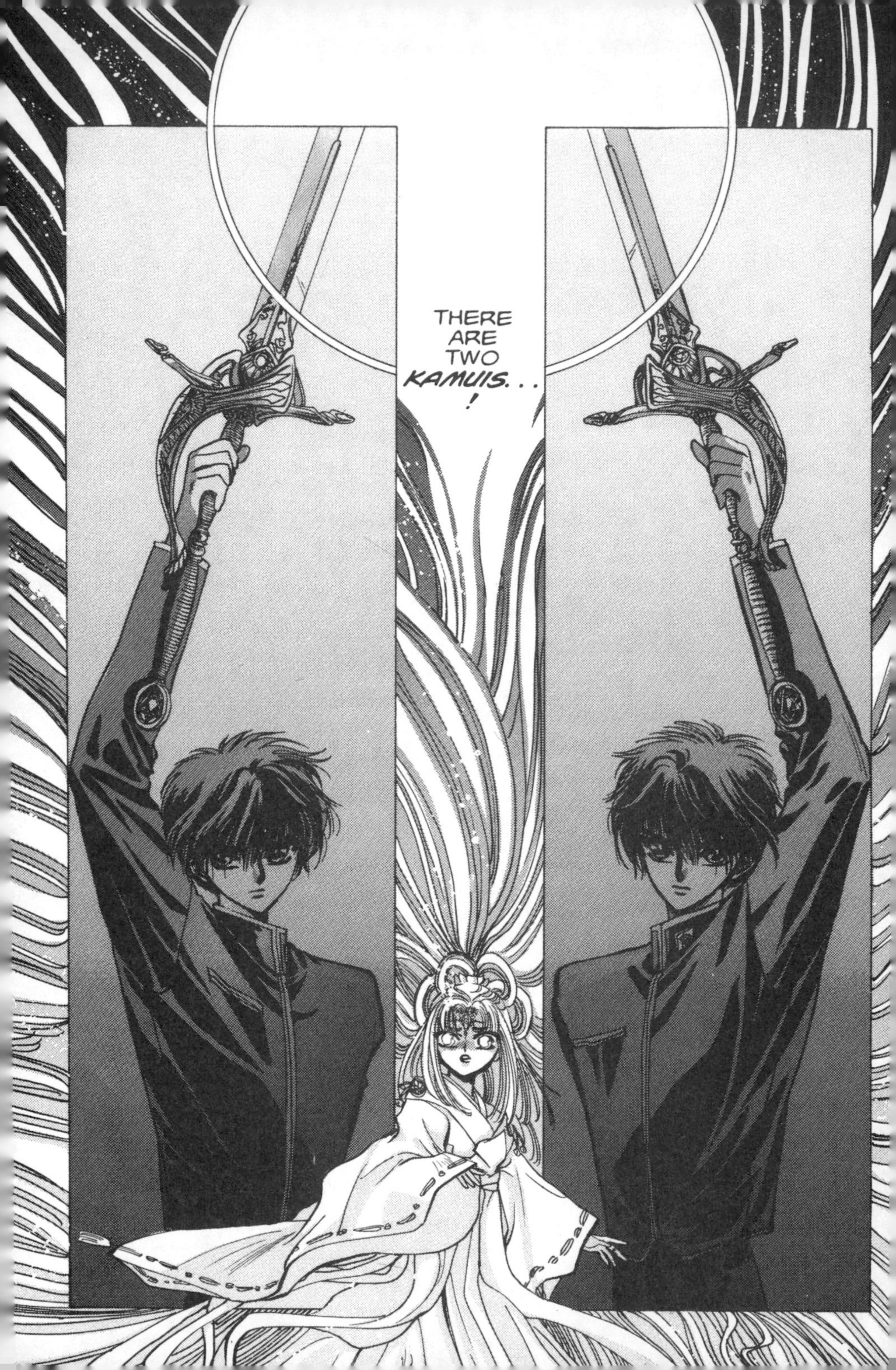
THERE ARE TWO KAMUIS...!

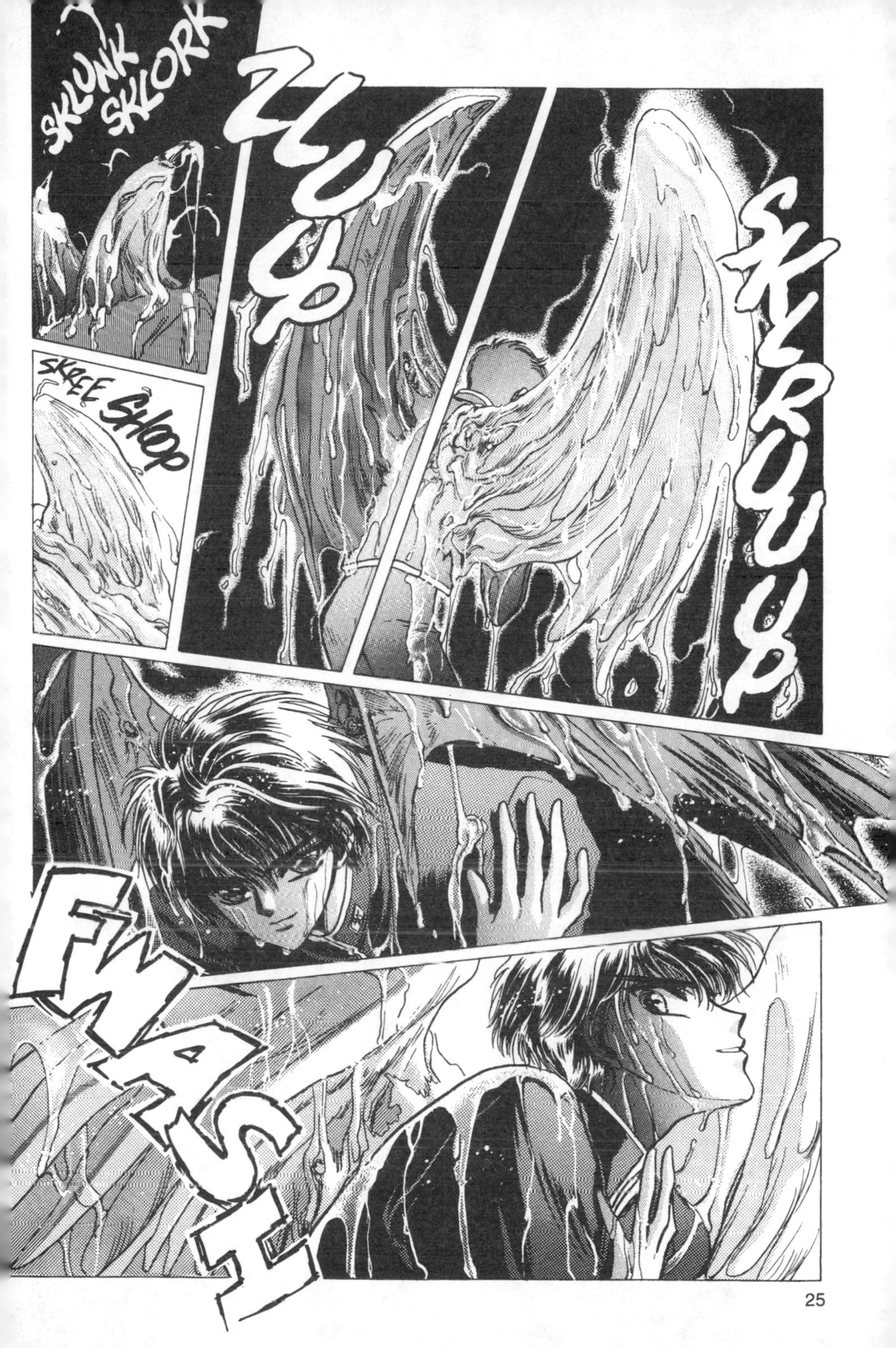
SKLUNK SKLORK
SKREE SHOOP
FWASH

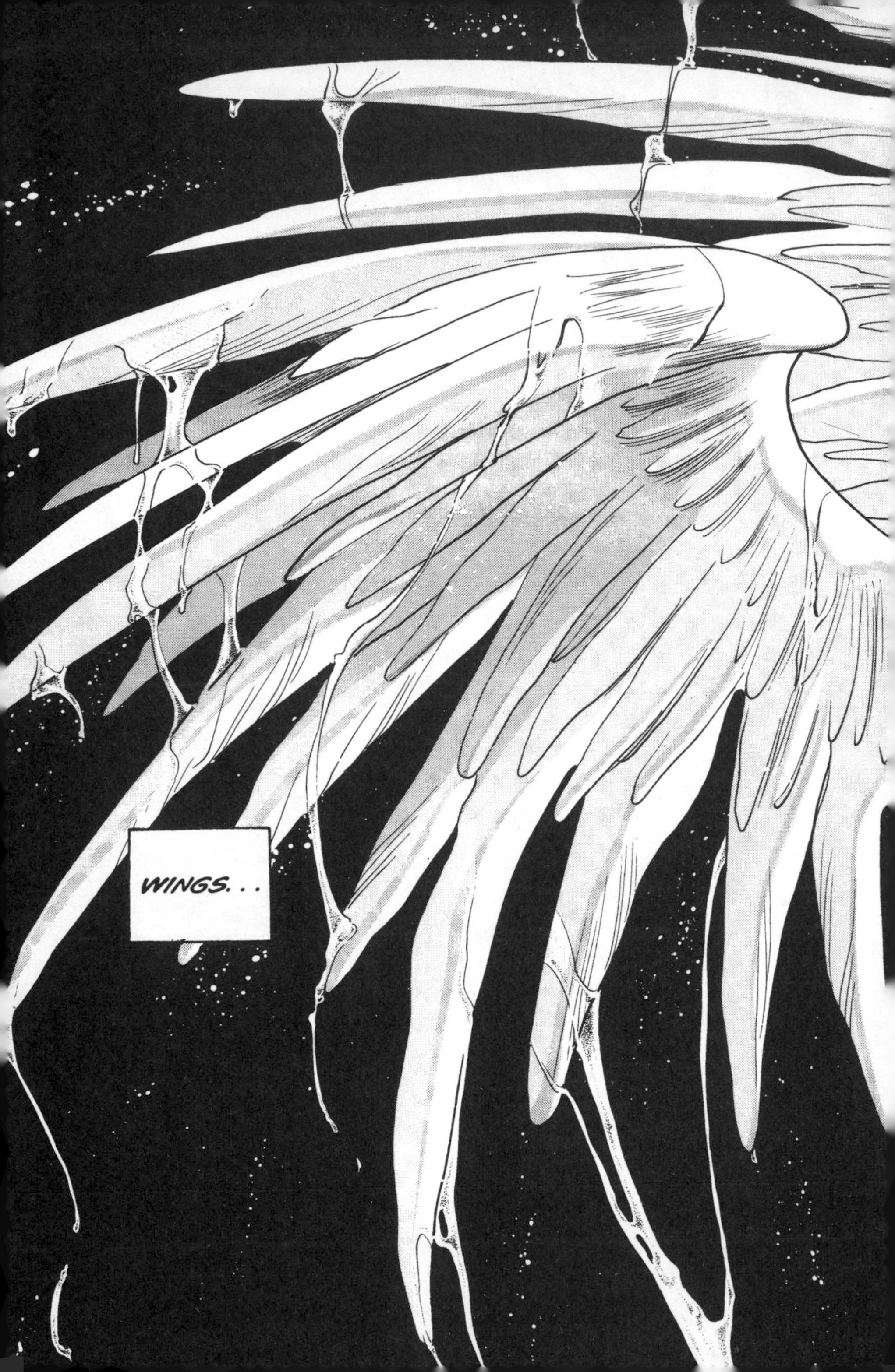
WINGS...

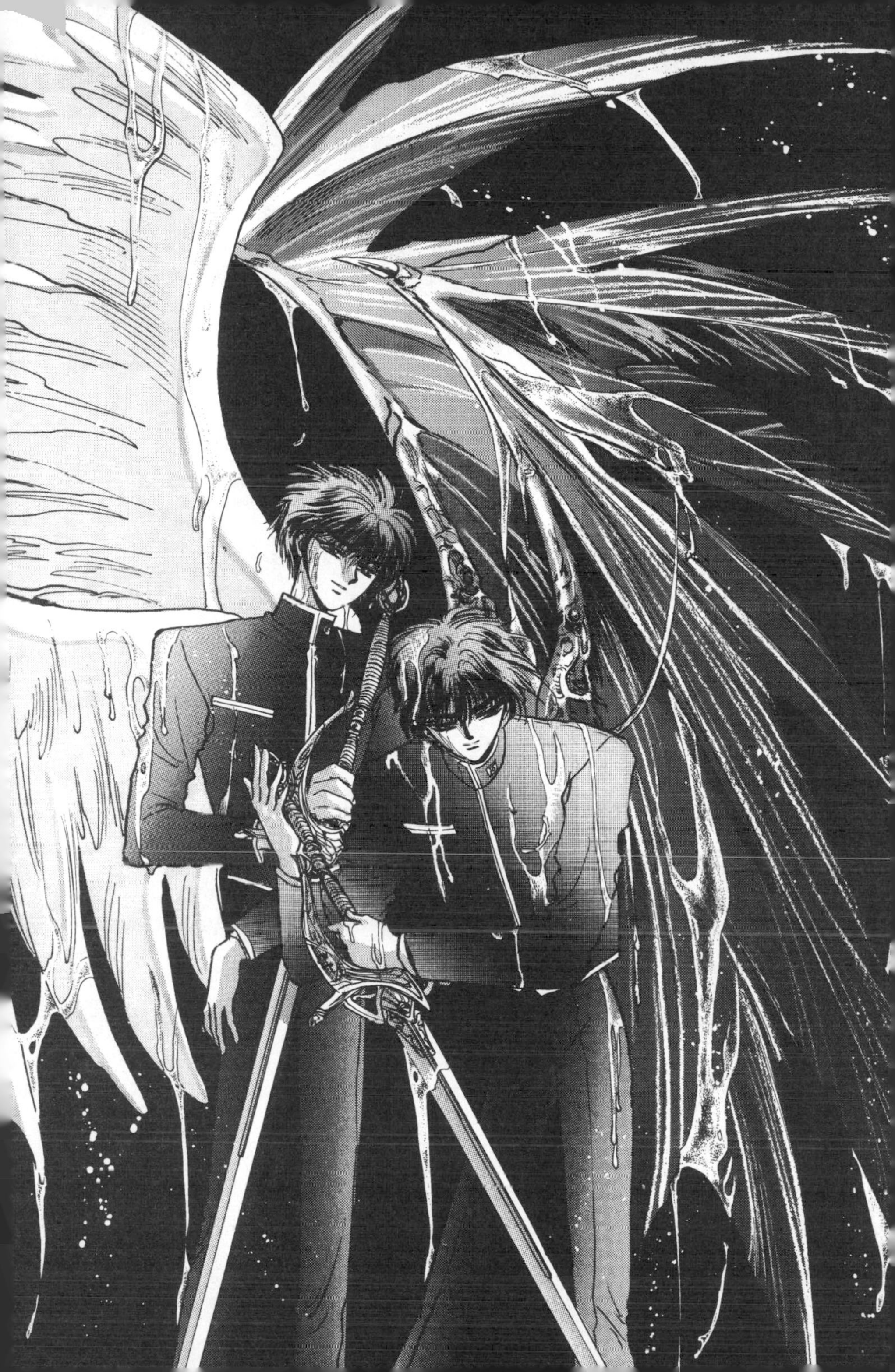

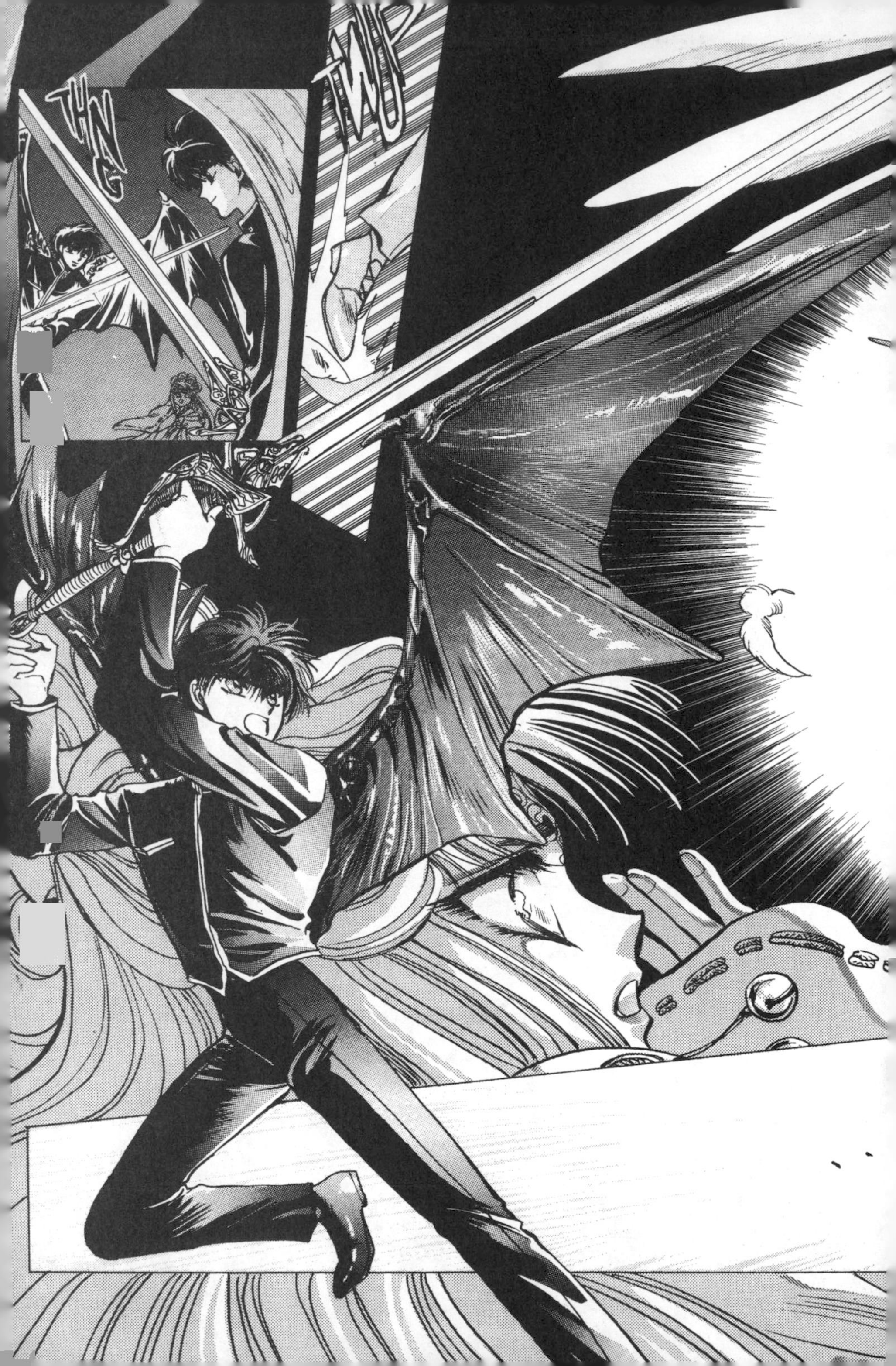
THNG

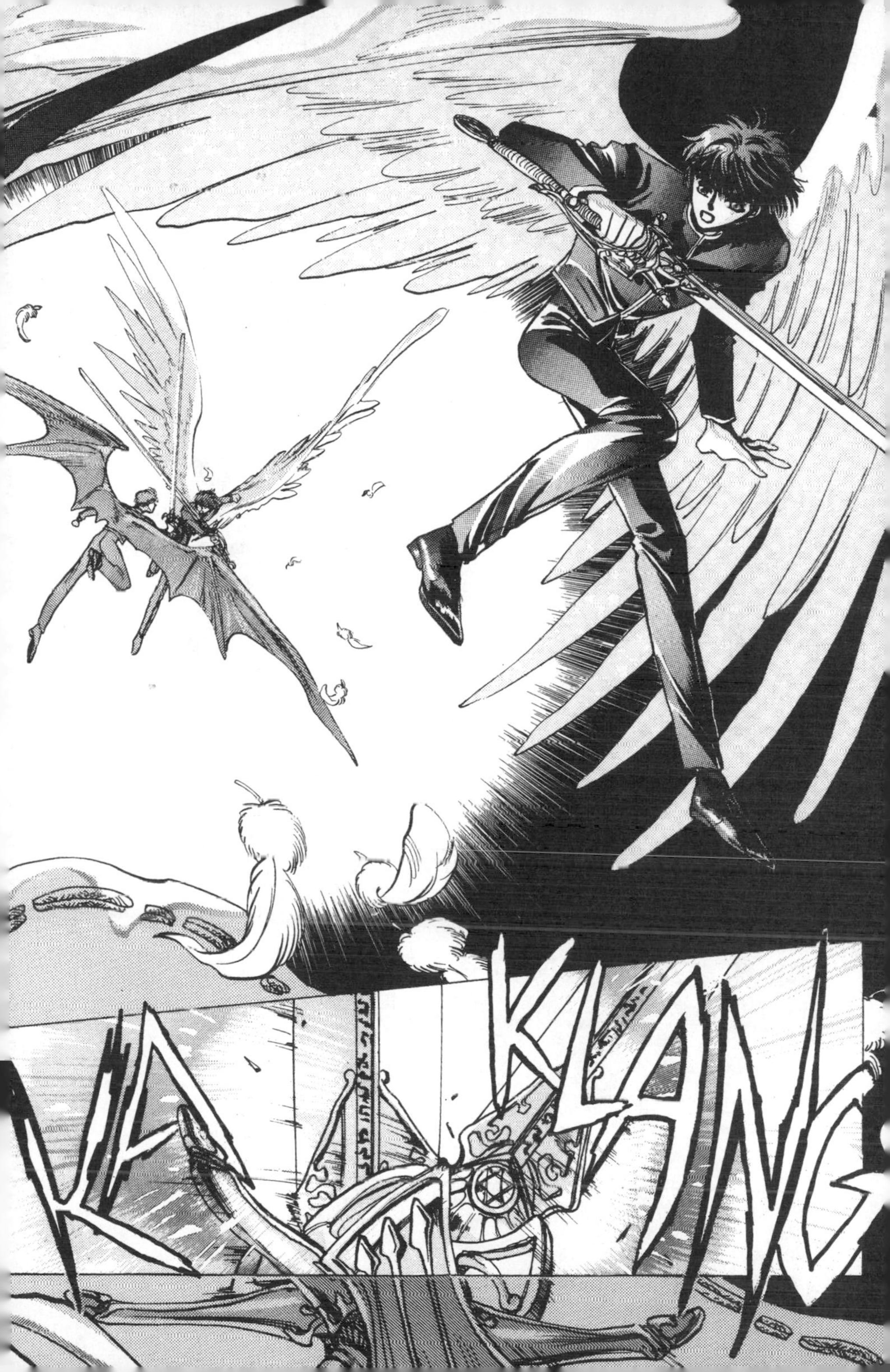
KLANG

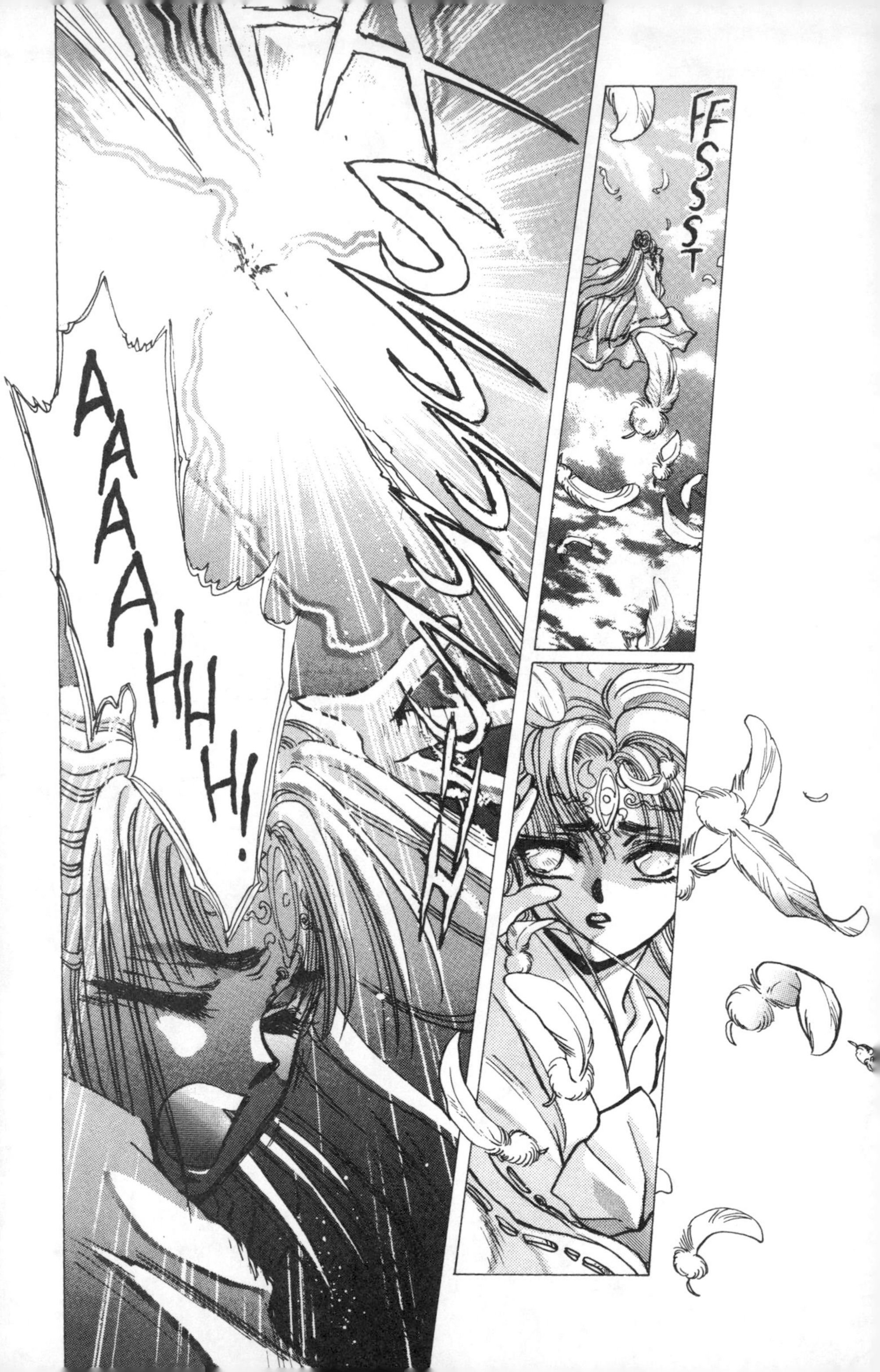
AAAAHHH!
FFSSST

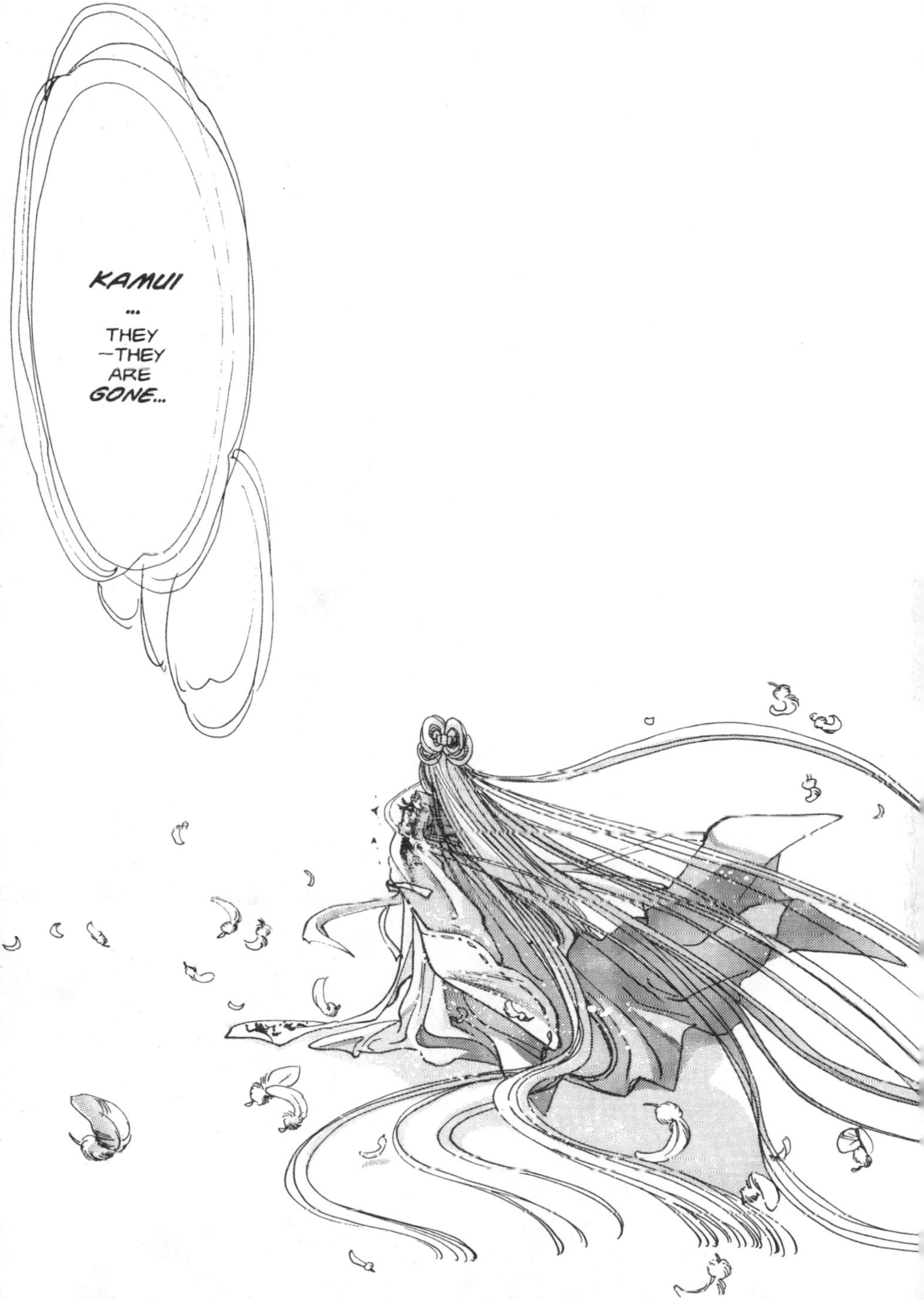
KAMUI ... THEY —THEY ARE GONE...

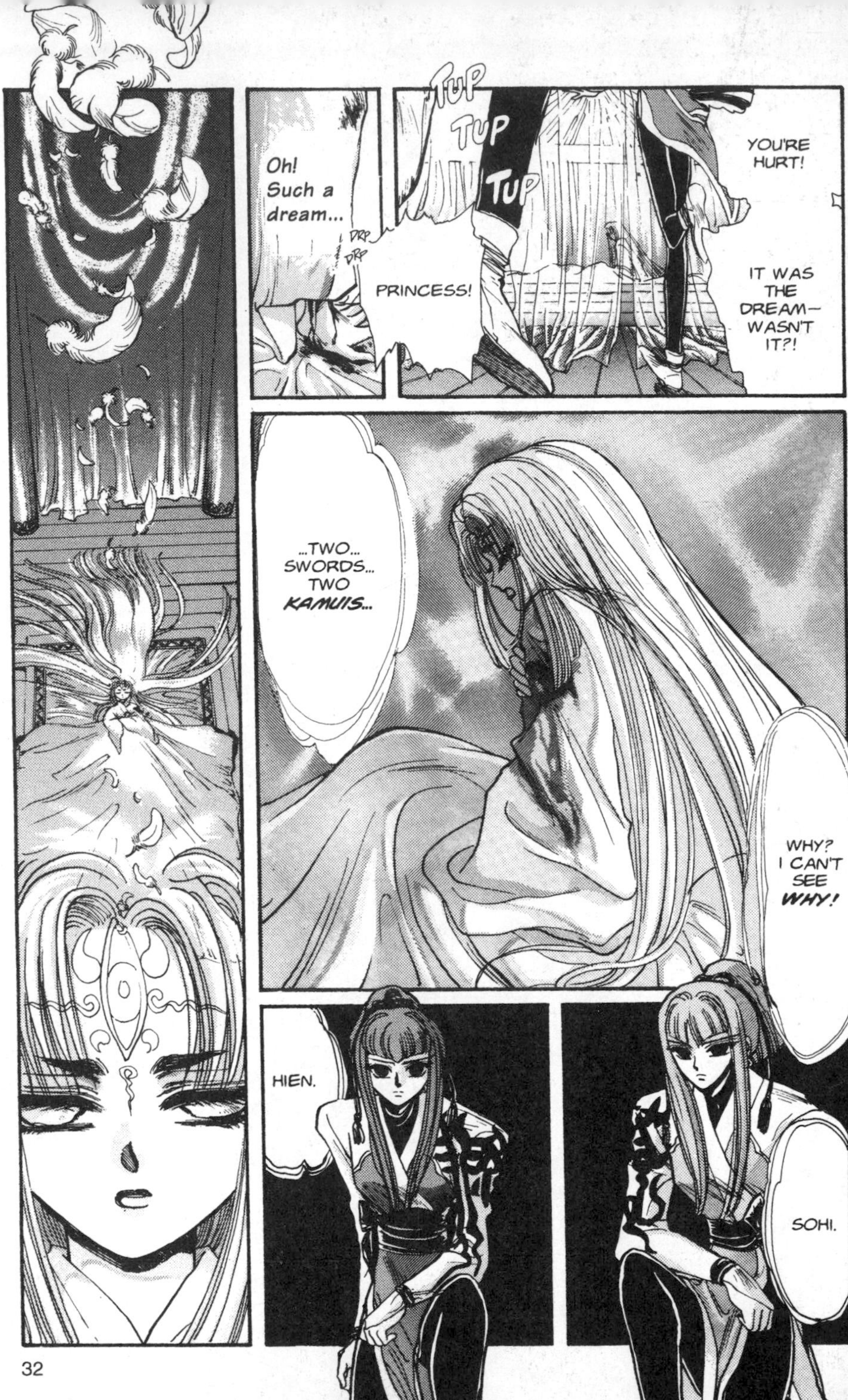
Oh! Such a dream...
DRP DRP
PRINCESS!
TUP TUP TUP
YOU'RE HURT!
IT WAS THE DREAM—WASN'T IT?!
...TWO... SWORDS... TWO *KAMUIS*...
WHY? I CAN'T SEE *WHY!*
HIEN.
SOHI.

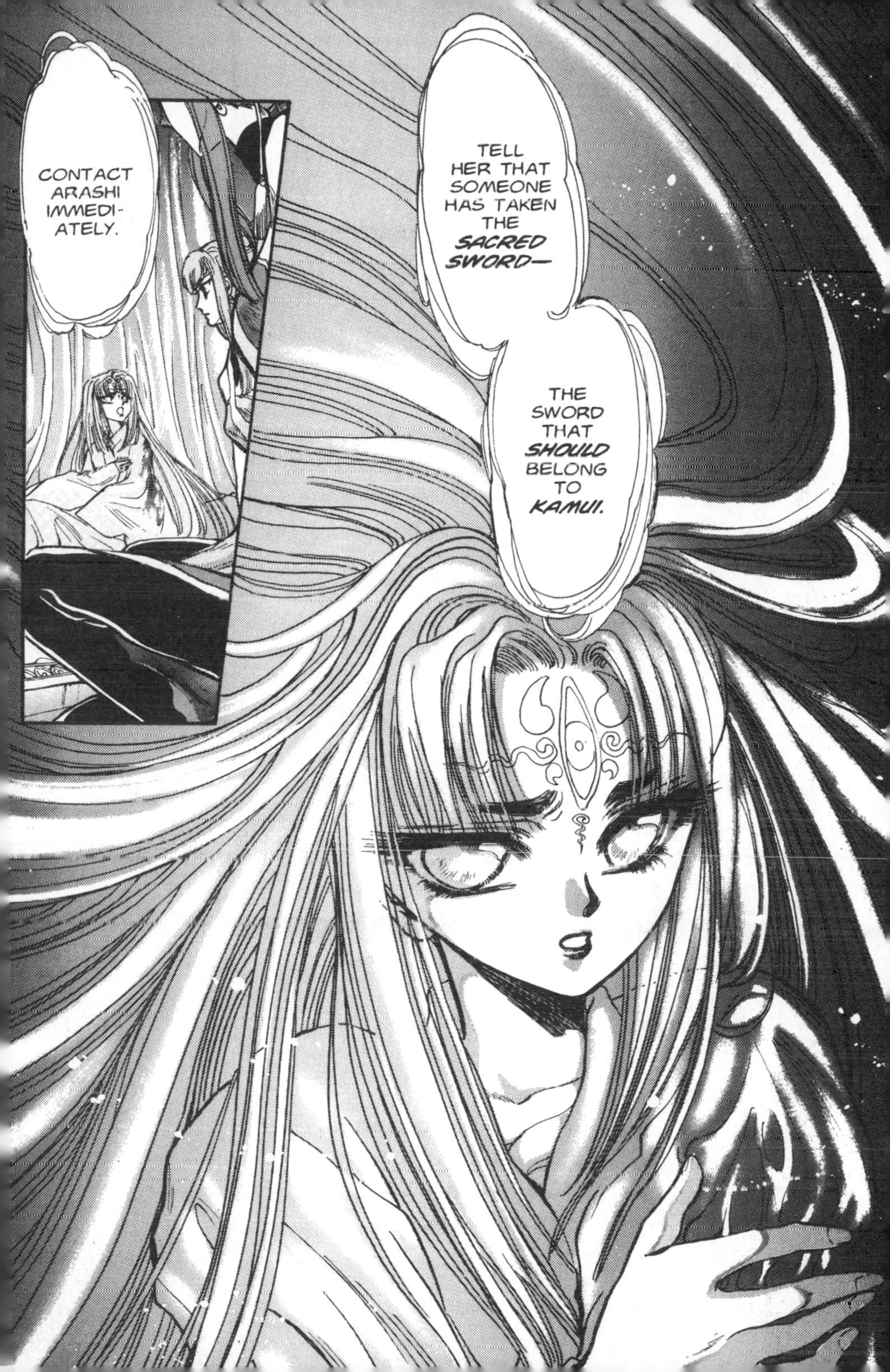
CONTACT ARASHI IMMEDI-ATELY.
TELL HER THAT SOMEONE HAS TAKEN THE *SACRED SWORD*—
THE SWORD THAT *SHOULD* BELONG TO *KAMUI.*

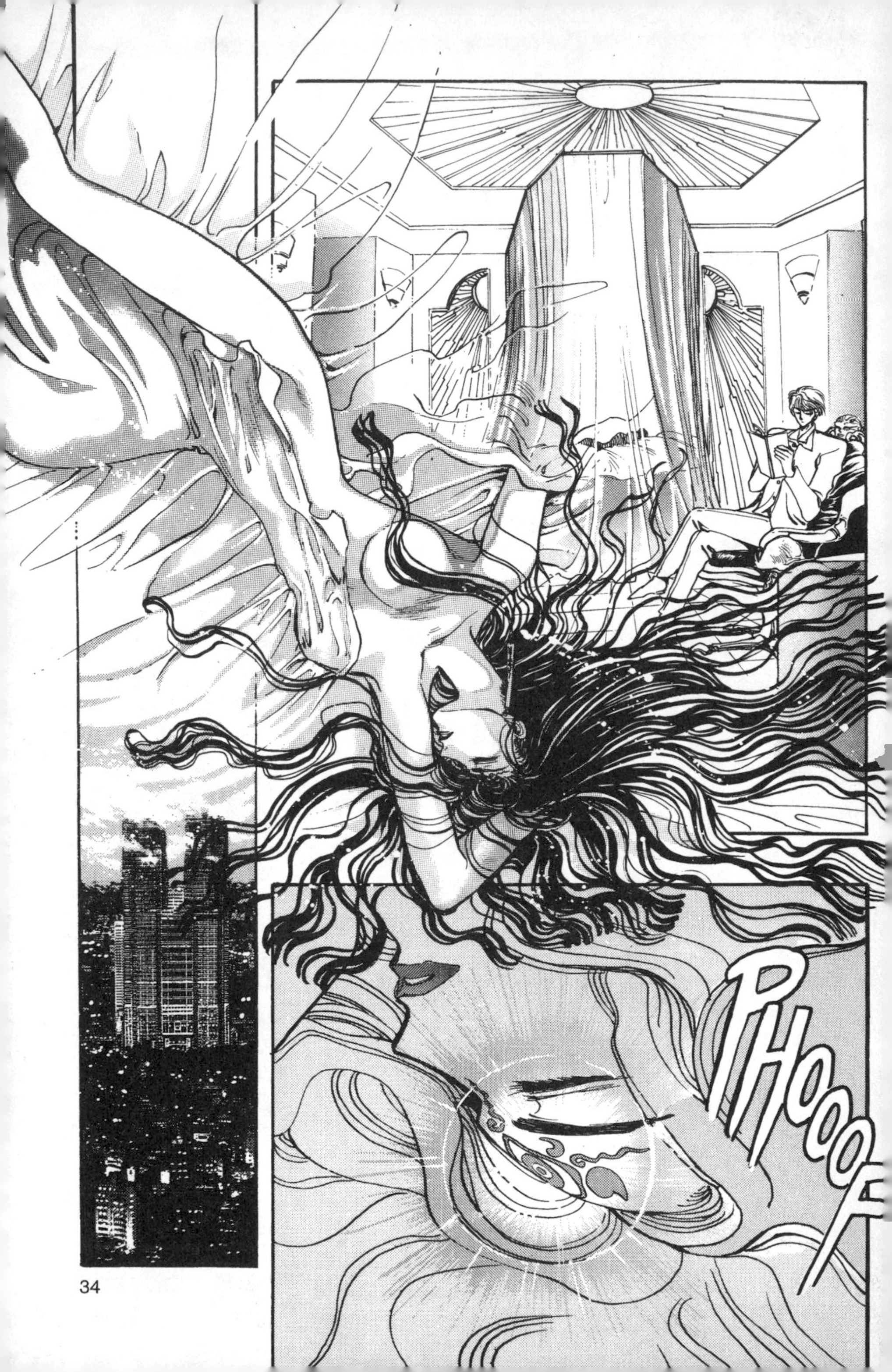
PHOOOF

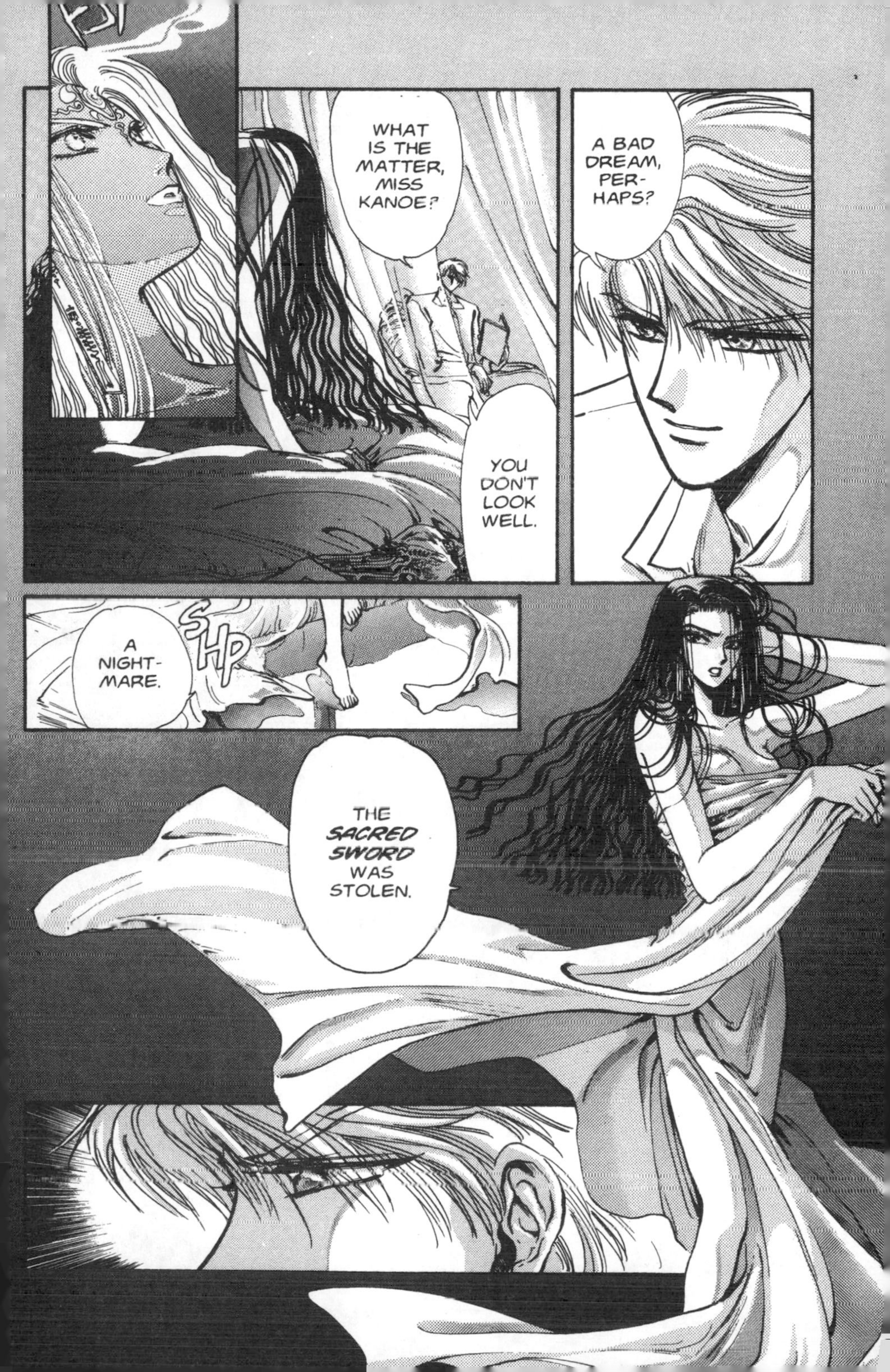
WHAT IS THE MATTER, MISS KANOE?
YOU DON'T LOOK WELL.
A BAD DREAM, PER-HAPS?
A NIGHT-MARE.
SHP
THE SACRED SWORD WAS STOLEN.

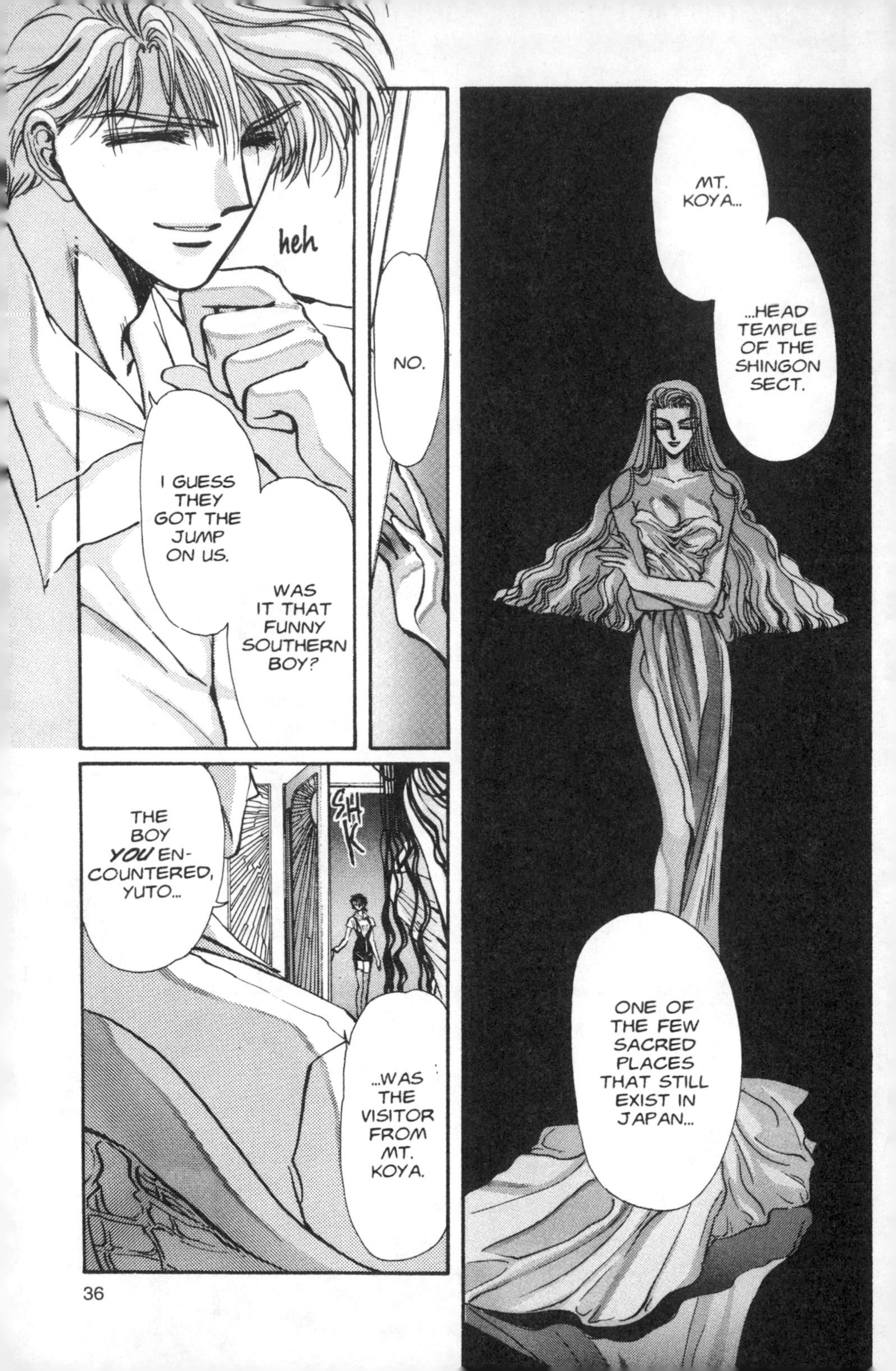
heh
I GUESS THEY GOT THE JUMP ON US.
WAS IT THAT FUNNY SOUTHERN BOY?
NO.
THE BOY *YOU* EN-COUNTERED, YUTO...
SHK
...WAS THE VISITOR FROM MT. KOYA.
MT. KOYA...
...HEAD TEMPLE OF THE SHINGON SECT.
ONE OF THE FEW SACRED PLACES THAT STILL EXIST IN JAPAN...

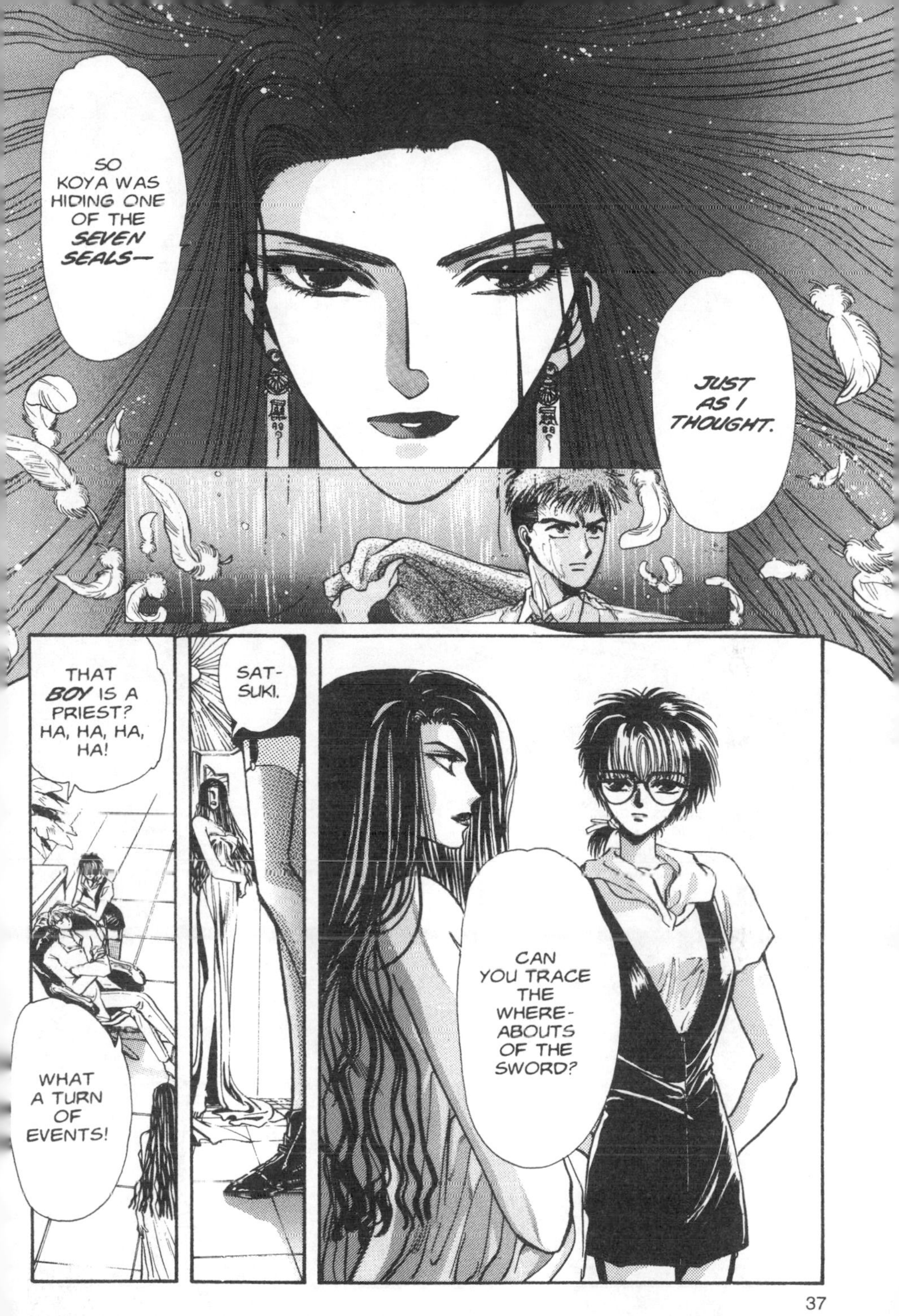
SO KOYA WAS HIDING ONE OF THE SEVEN SEALS—
JUST AS I THOUGHT.
THAT BOY IS A PRIEST? HA, HA, HA, HA!
WHAT A TURN OF EVENTS!
SAT-SUKI.
CAN YOU TRACE THE WHERE-ABOUTS OF THE SWORD?

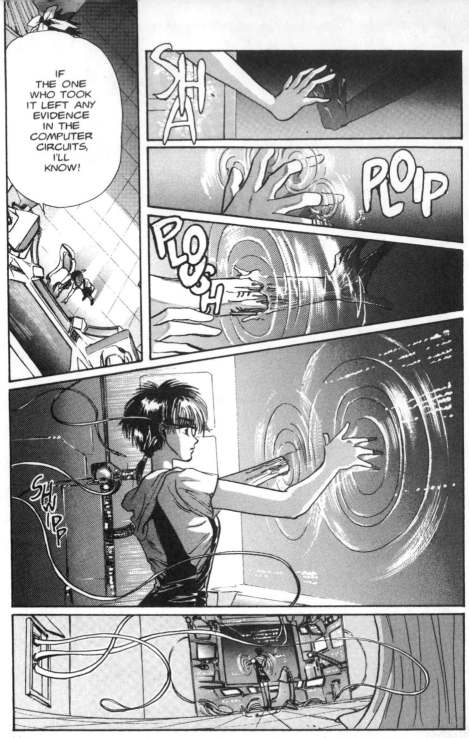

IF THE ONE WHO TOOK IT LEFT ANY EVIDENCE IN THE COMPUTER CIRCUITS, I'LL KNOW!

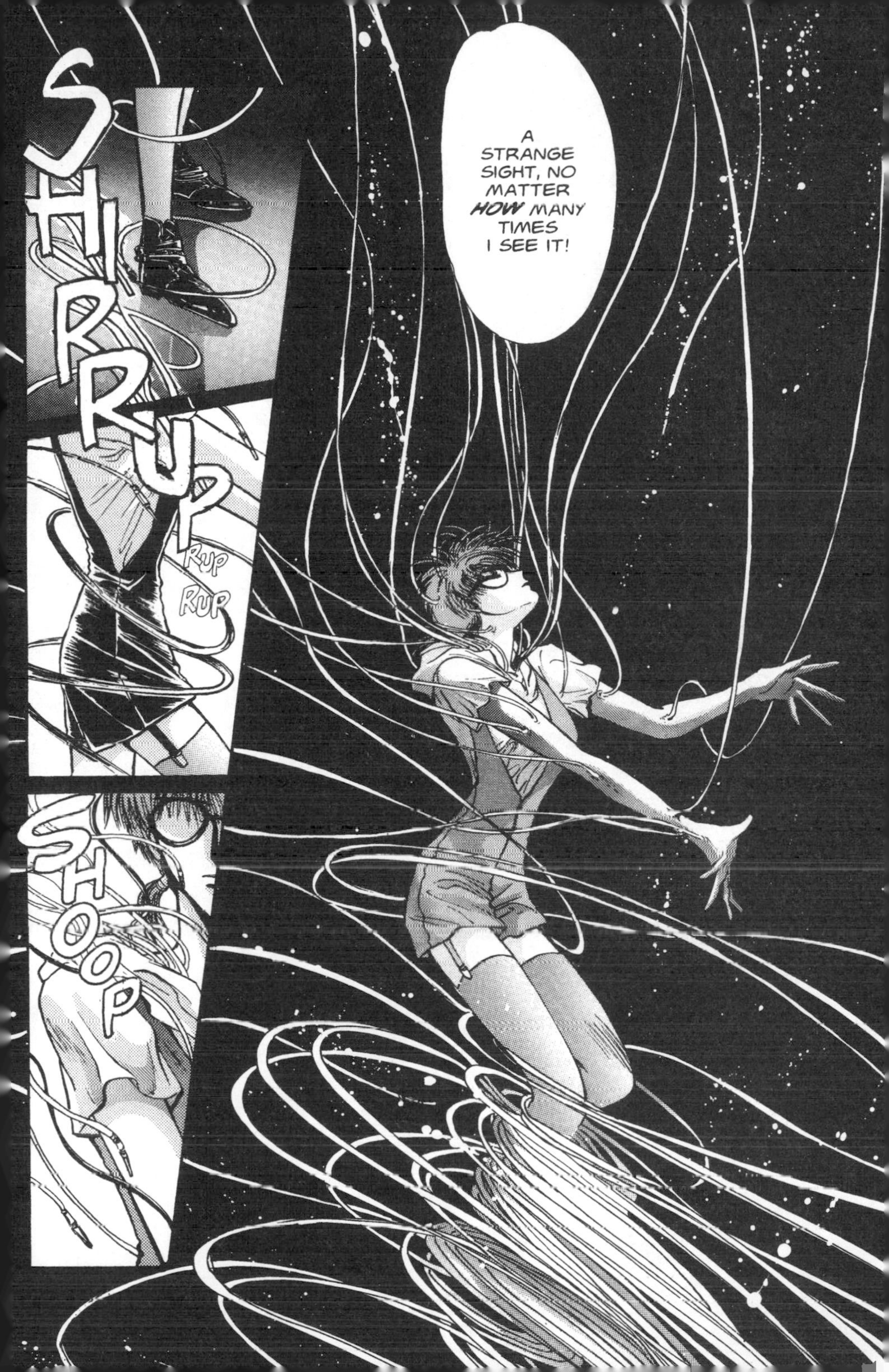
SHRRUP
RUP
RUP
SHOOP
A STRANGE SIGHT, NO MATTER *HOW* MANY TIMES I SEE IT!

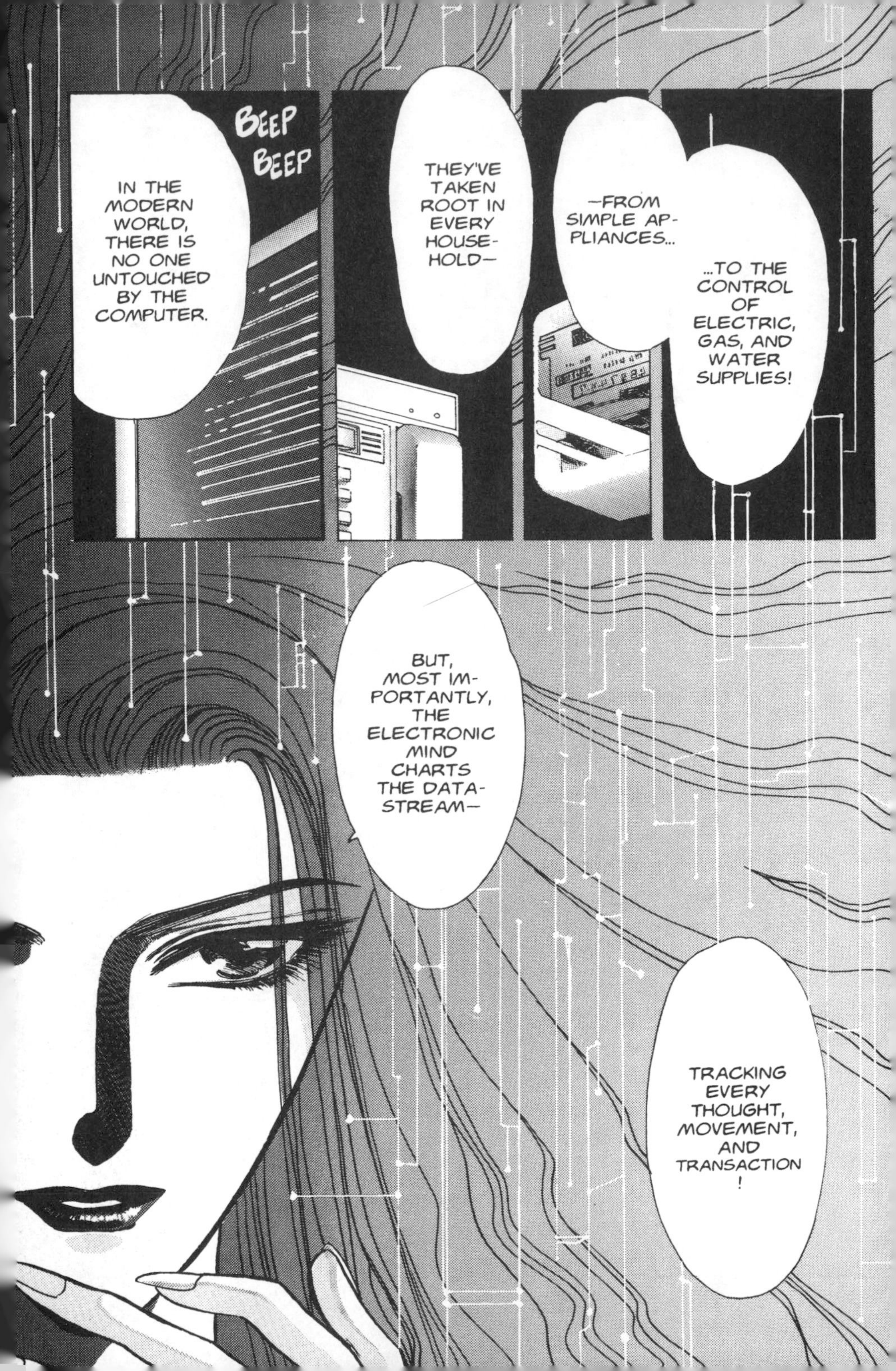
IN THE MODERN WORLD, THERE IS NO ONE UNTOUCHED BY THE COMPUTER.
BEEP BEEP
THEY'VE TAKEN ROOT IN EVERY HOUSE-HOLD—
—FROM SIMPLE AP-PLIANCES...
...TO THE CONTROL OF ELECTRIC, GAS, AND WATER SUPPLIES!
BUT, MOST IM-PORTANTLY, THE ELECTRONIC MIND CHARTS THE DATA-STREAM—
TRACKING EVERY THOUGHT, MOVEMENT, AND TRANSACTION!

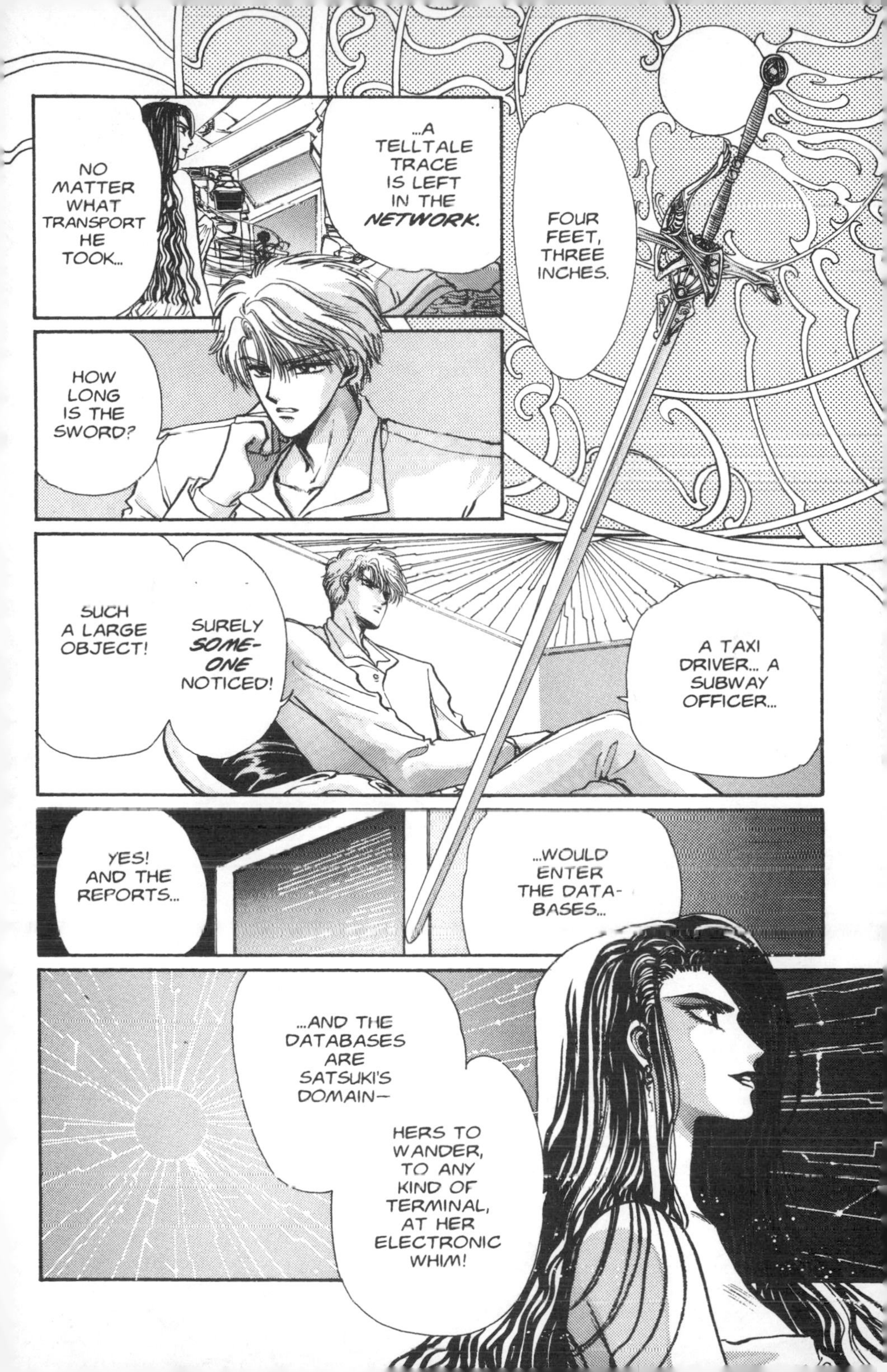
NO MATTER WHAT TRANSPORT HE TOOK...
...A TELLTALE TRACE IS LEFT IN THE ***NETWORK.***
FOUR FEET, THREE INCHES.
HOW LONG IS THE SWORD?
SUCH A LARGE OBJECT!
SURELY ***SOME-ONE*** NOTICED!
A TAXI DRIVER... A SUBWAY OFFICER...
YES! AND THE REPORTS...
...WOULD ENTER THE DATA-BASES...
...AND THE DATABASES ARE SATSUKI'S DOMAIN—
HERS TO WANDER, TO ANY KIND OF TERMINAL, AT HER ELECTRONIC WHIM!

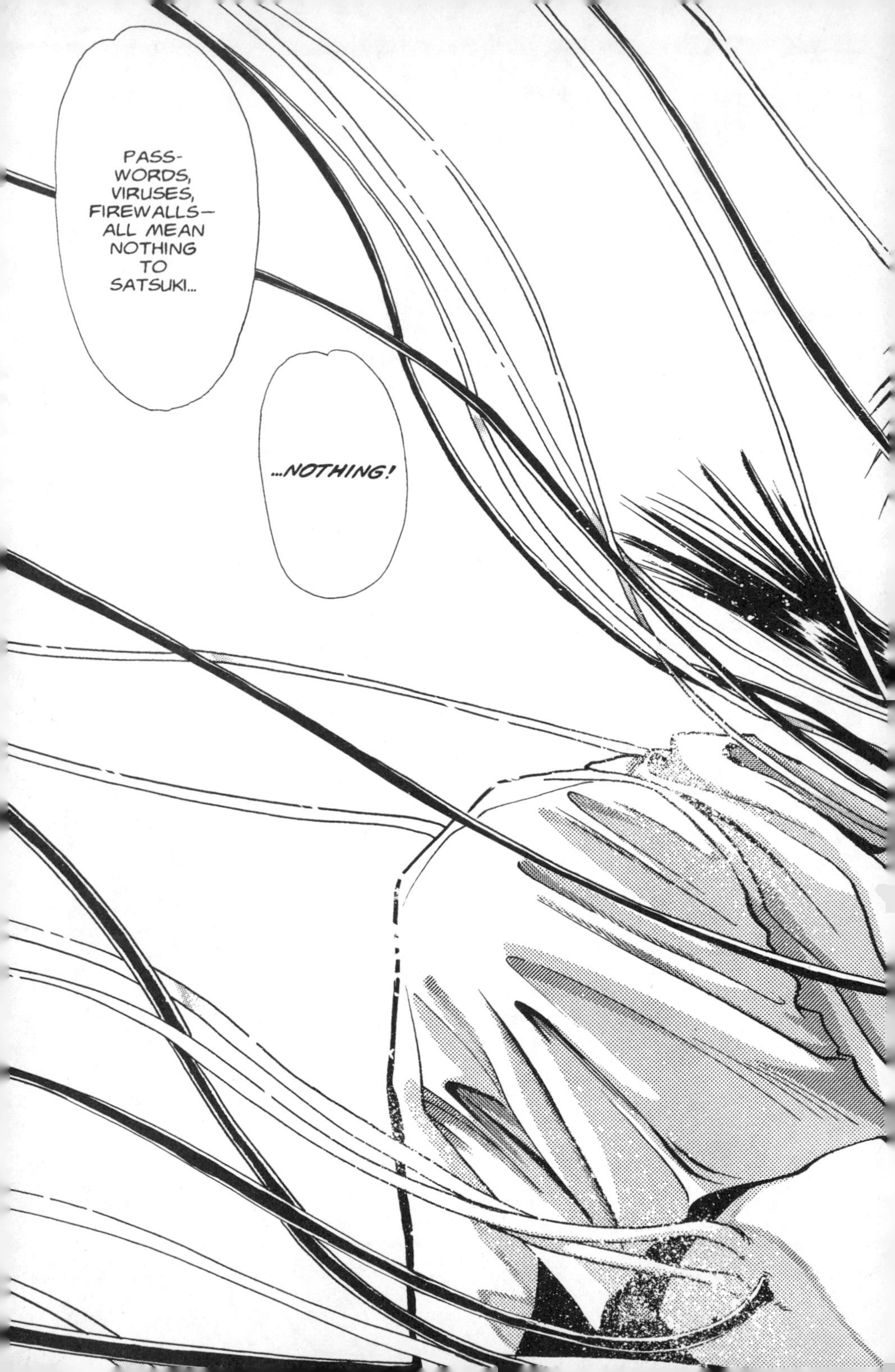
PASS-WORDS, VIRUSES, FIREWALLS—ALL MEAN NOTHING TO SATSUKI...
...NOTHING!

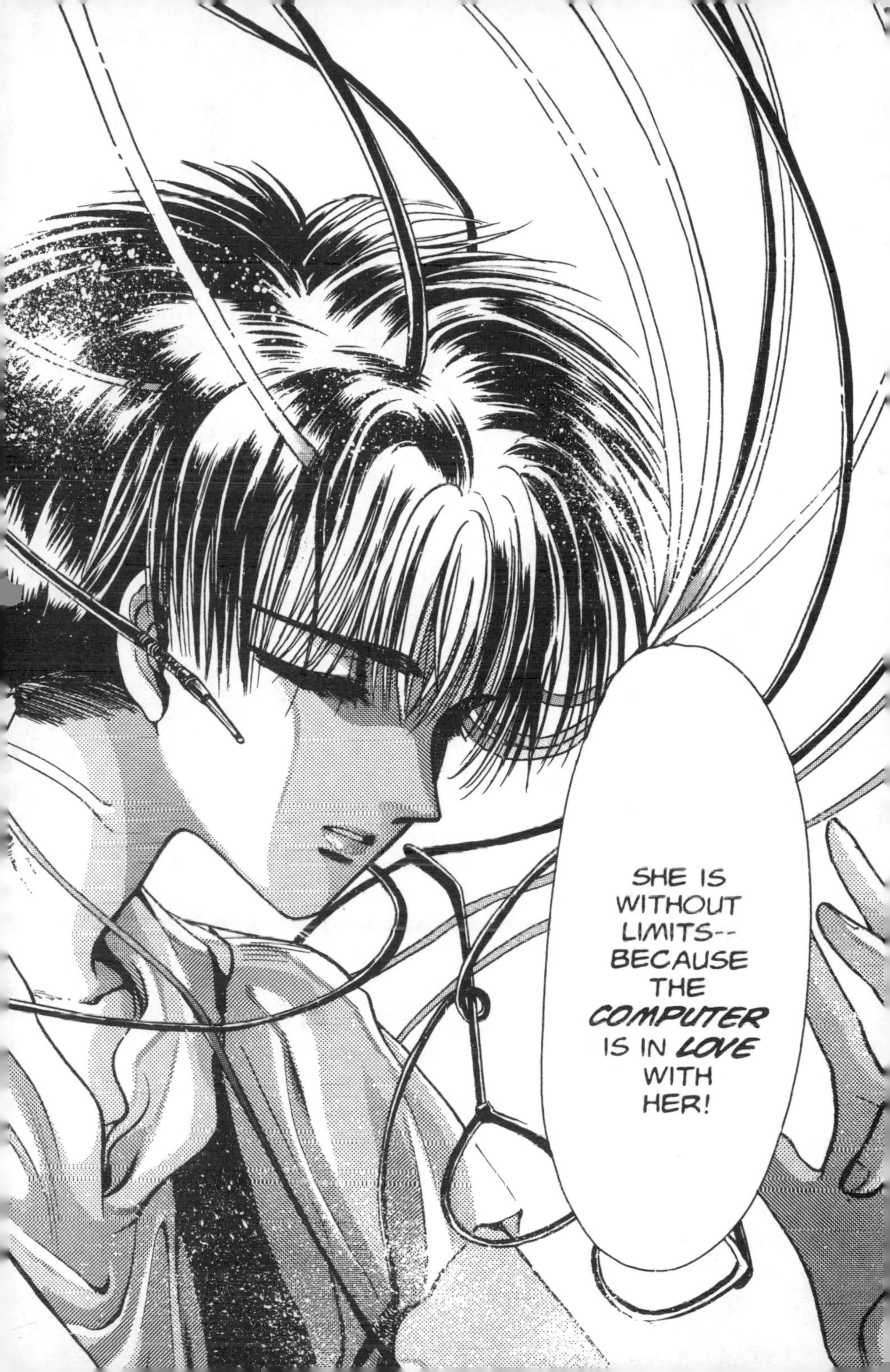
SHE IS WITHOUT LIMITS-- BECAUSE THE COMPUTER IS IN LOVE WITH HER!

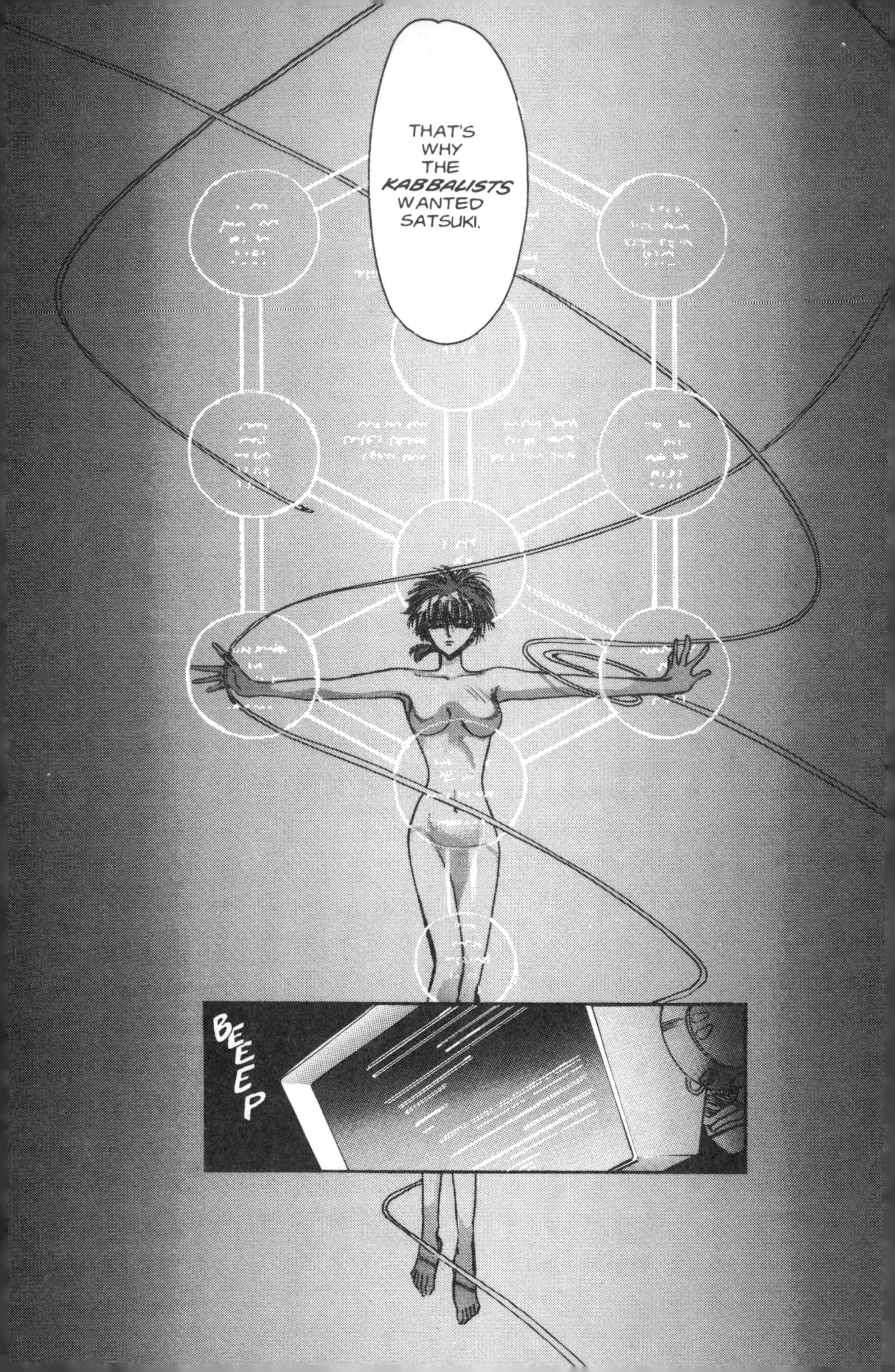
THAT'S WHY THE *KABBALISTS* WANTED SATSUKI.
BEEEP

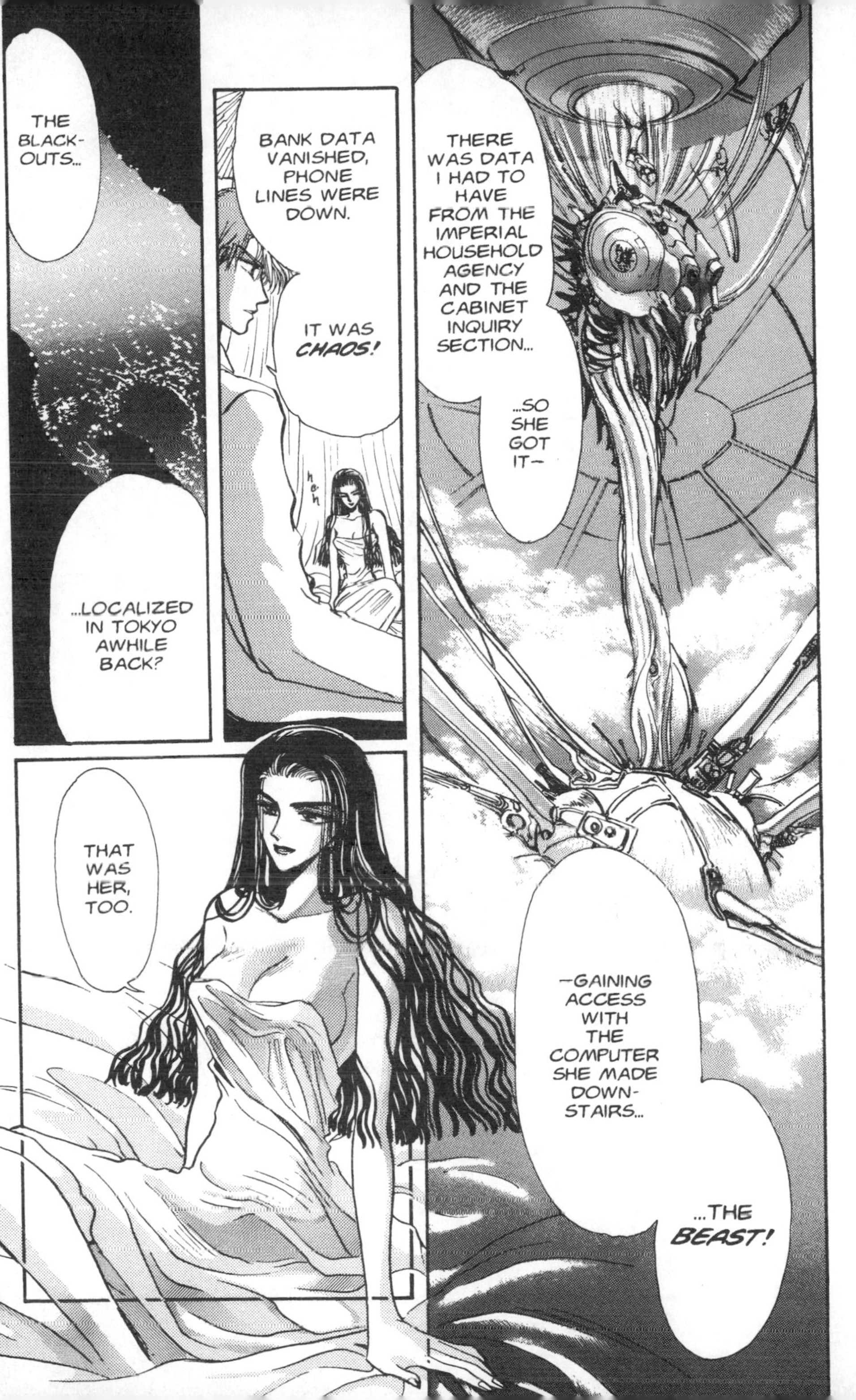
THE BLACK-OUTS...
...LOCALIZED IN TOKYO AWHILE BACK?
BANK DATA VANISHED, PHONE LINES WERE DOWN.
IT WAS *CHAOS!*
THAT WAS HER, TOO.
THERE WAS DATA I HAD TO HAVE FROM THE IMPERIAL HOUSEHOLD AGENCY AND THE CABINET INQUIRY SECTION...
...SO SHE GOT IT—
—GAINING ACCESS WITH THE COMPUTER SHE MADE DOWN-STAIRS...
...THE *BEAST!*

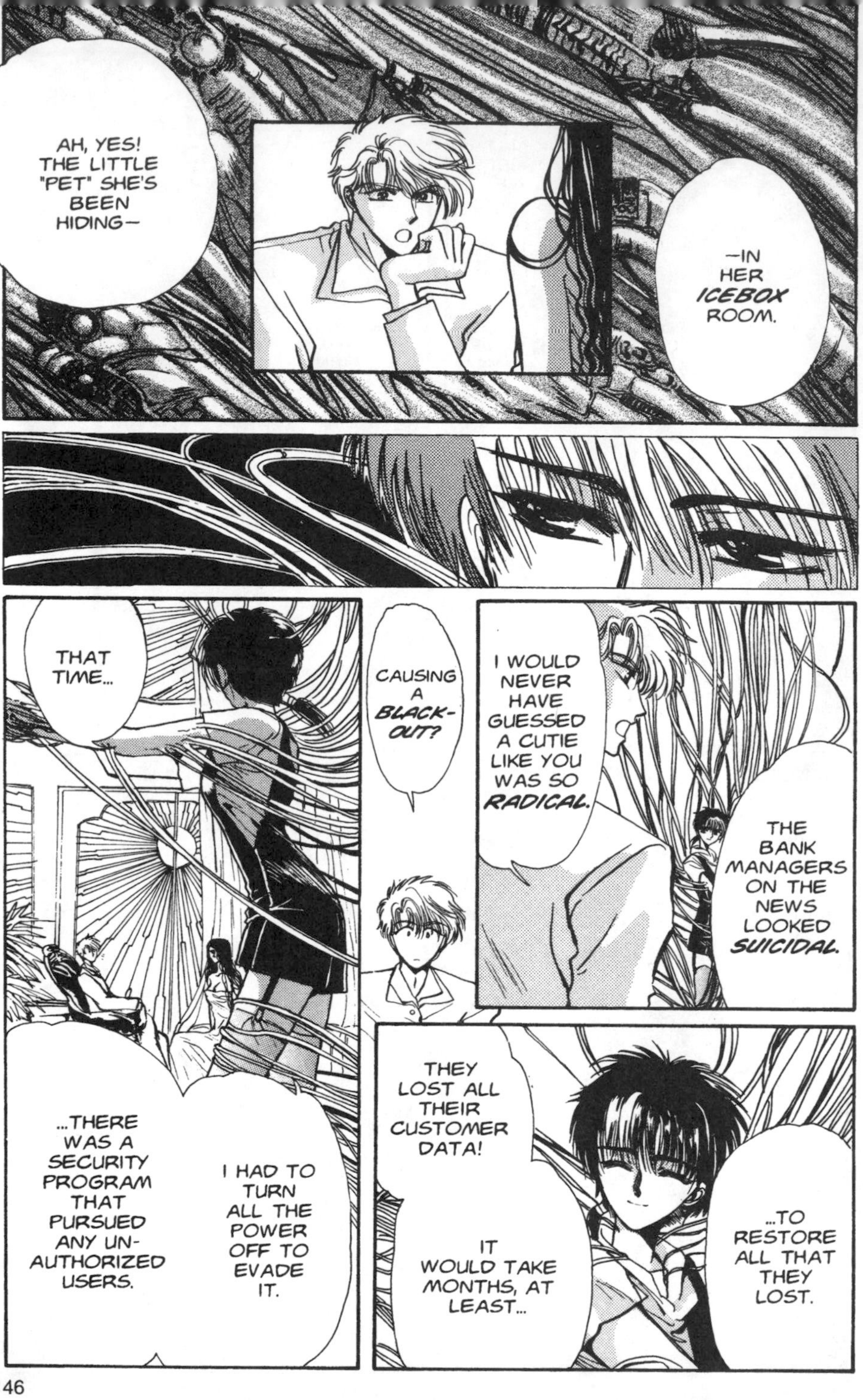
AH, YES! THE LITTLE "PET" SHE'S BEEN HIDING—
—IN HER ICEBOX ROOM.
THAT TIME...
CAUSING A BLACK-OUT?
I WOULD NEVER HAVE GUESSED A CUTIE LIKE YOU WAS SO RADICAL.
THE BANK MANAGERS ON THE NEWS LOOKED SUICIDAL.
...THERE WAS A SECURITY PROGRAM THAT PURSUED ANY UN-AUTHORIZED USERS.
I HAD TO TURN ALL THE POWER OFF TO EVADE IT.
THEY LOST ALL THEIR CUSTOMER DATA!
IT WOULD TAKE MONTHS, AT LEAST...
...TO RESTORE ALL THAT THEY LOST.

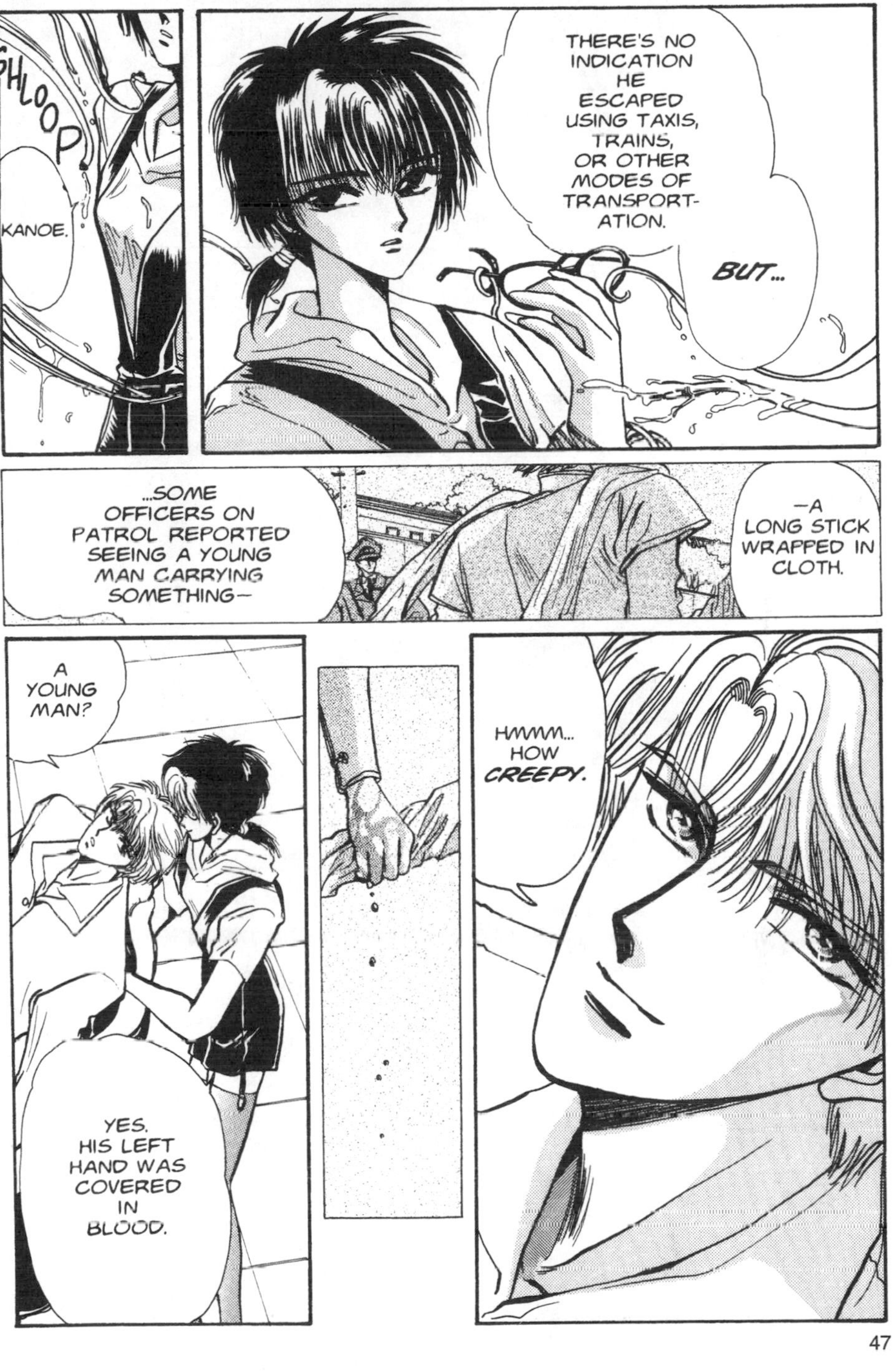
SHLOOP
KANOE.
THERE'S NO INDICATION HE ESCAPED USING TAXIS, TRAINS, OR OTHER MODES OF TRANSPORT-ATION.
BUT...
...SOME OFFICERS ON PATROL REPORTED SEEING A YOUNG MAN CARRYING SOMETHING—
—A LONG STICK WRAPPED IN CLOTH.
A YOUNG MAN?
YES. HIS LEFT HAND WAS COVERED IN BLOOD.
HMMM... HOW CREEPY.

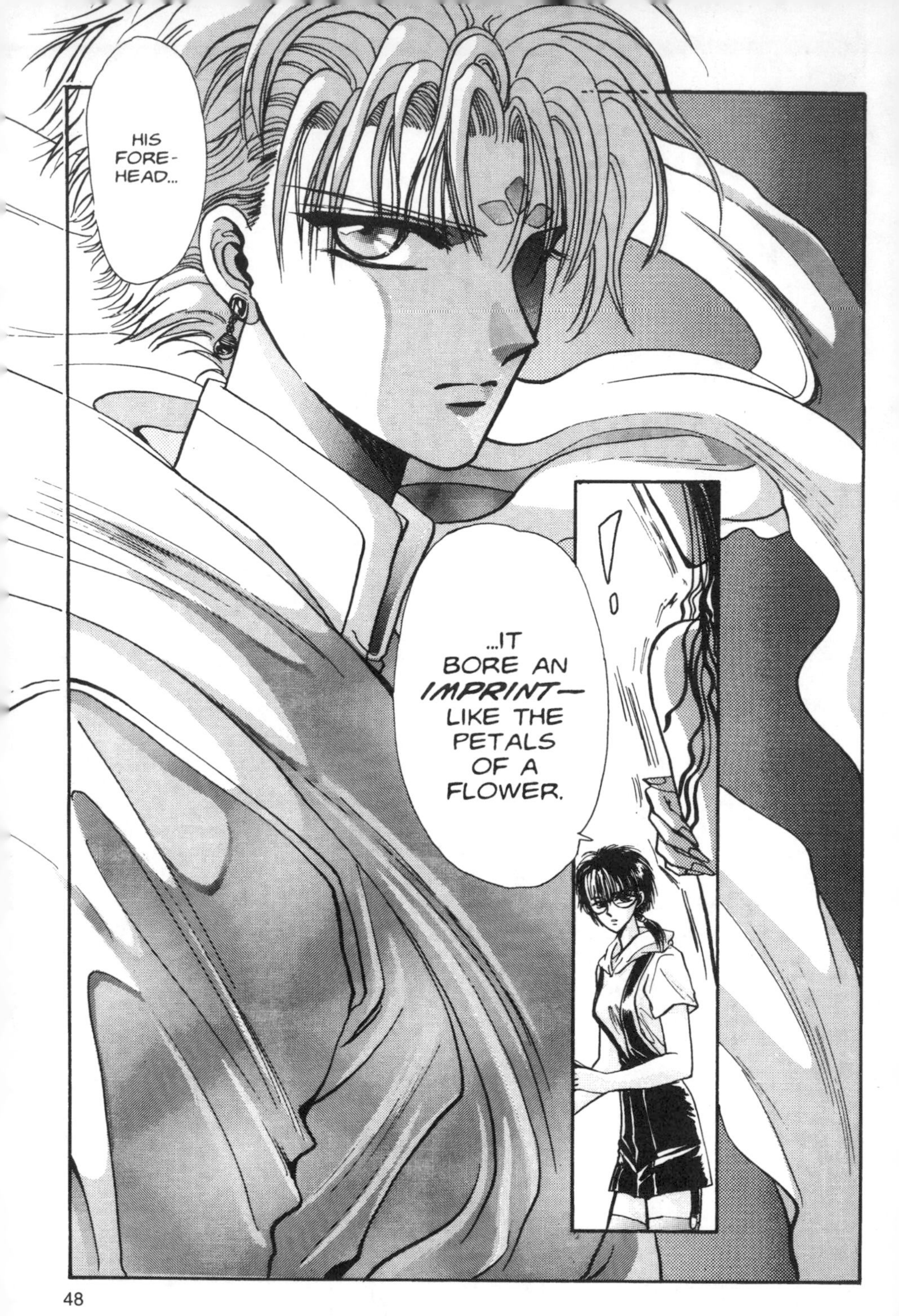
HIS FORE-HEAD...
...IT BORE AN *IMPRINT*—LIKE THE PETALS OF A FLOWER.
!

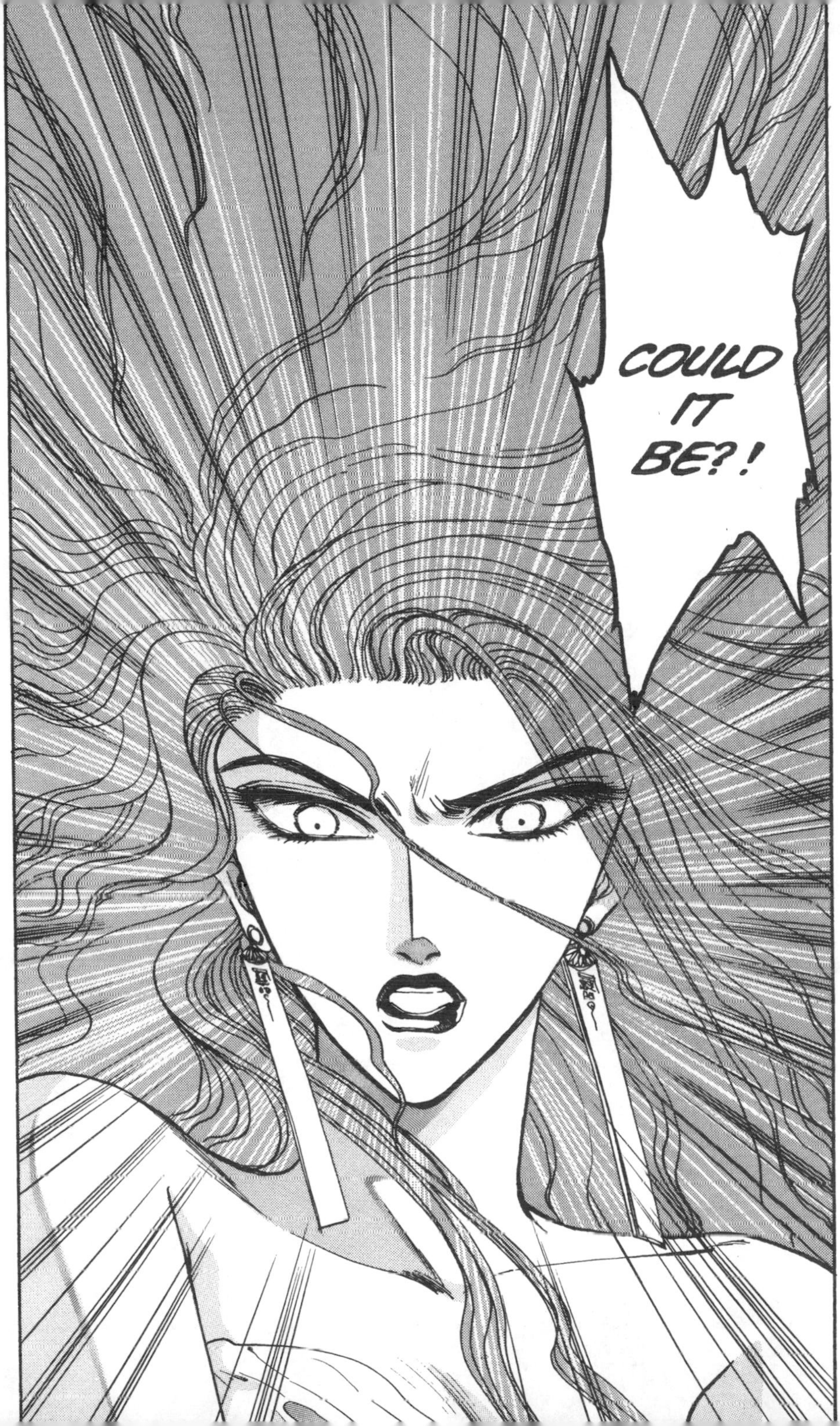
COULD IT BE?!

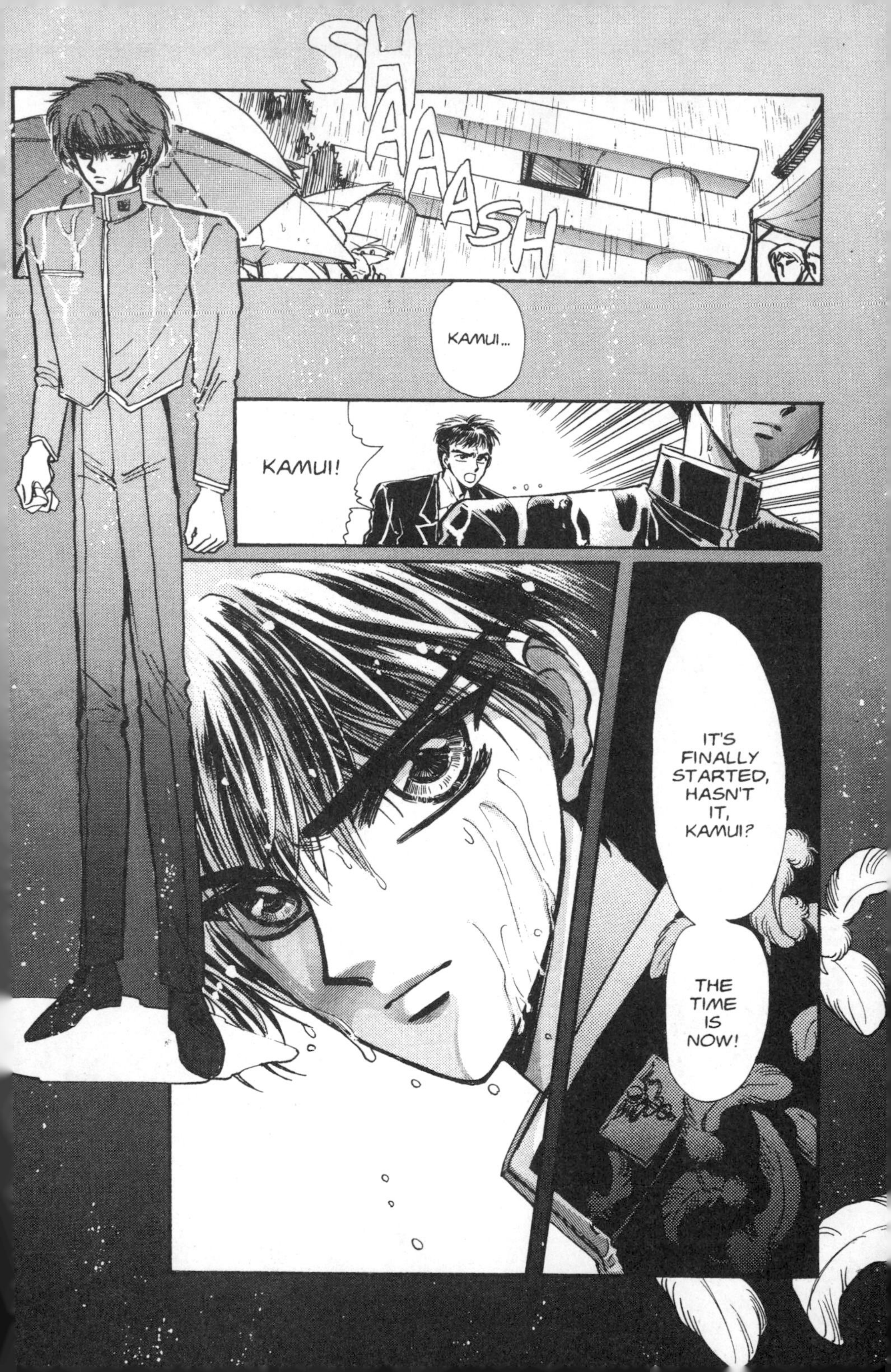
SHAAAASH
KAMUI...
KAMUI!
IT'S FINALLY STARTED, HASN'T IT, KAMUI?
THE TIME IS NOW!

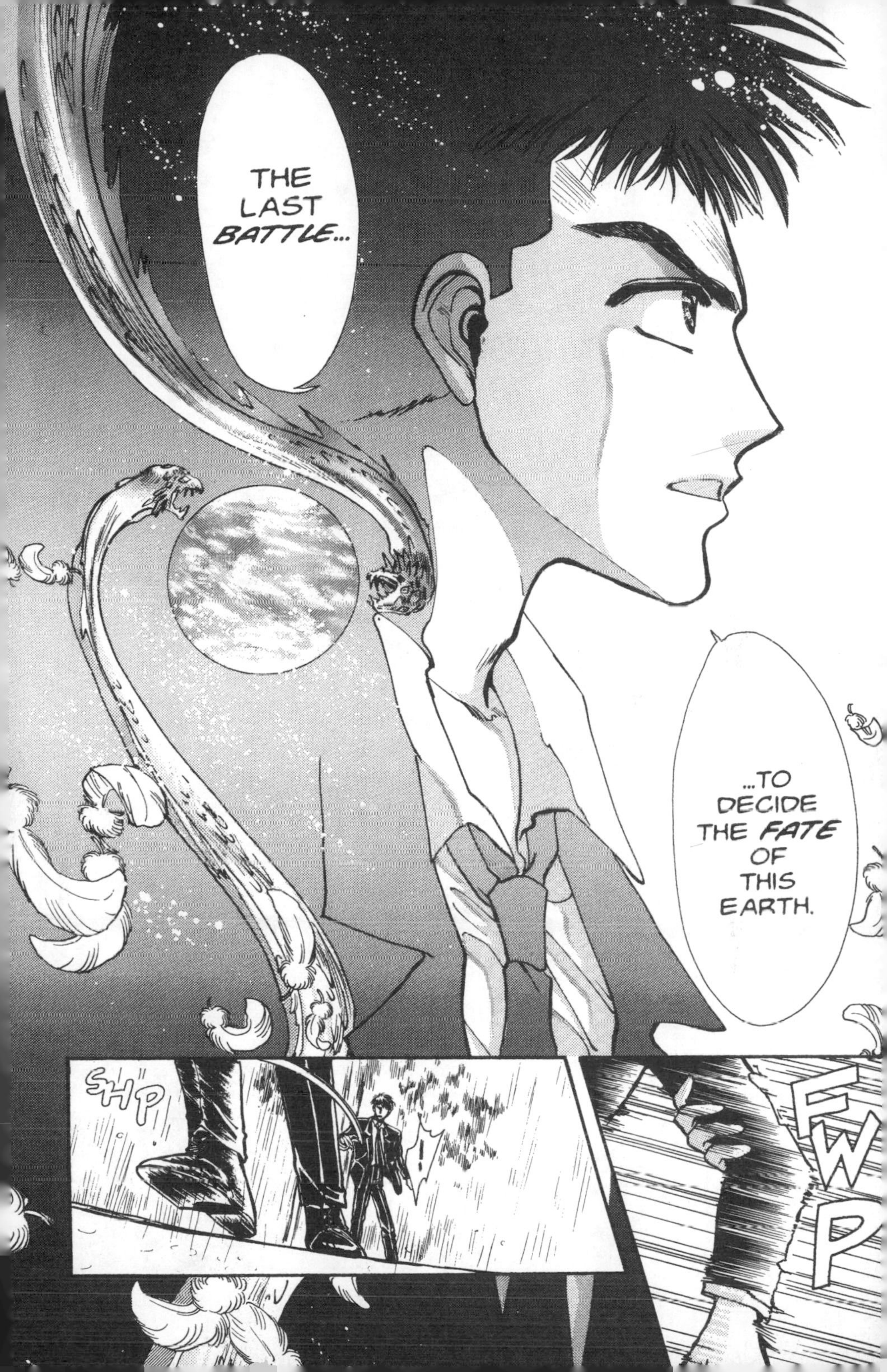
THE LAST BATTLE...
...TO DECIDE THE FATE OF THIS EARTH.
SHP
!
FWP

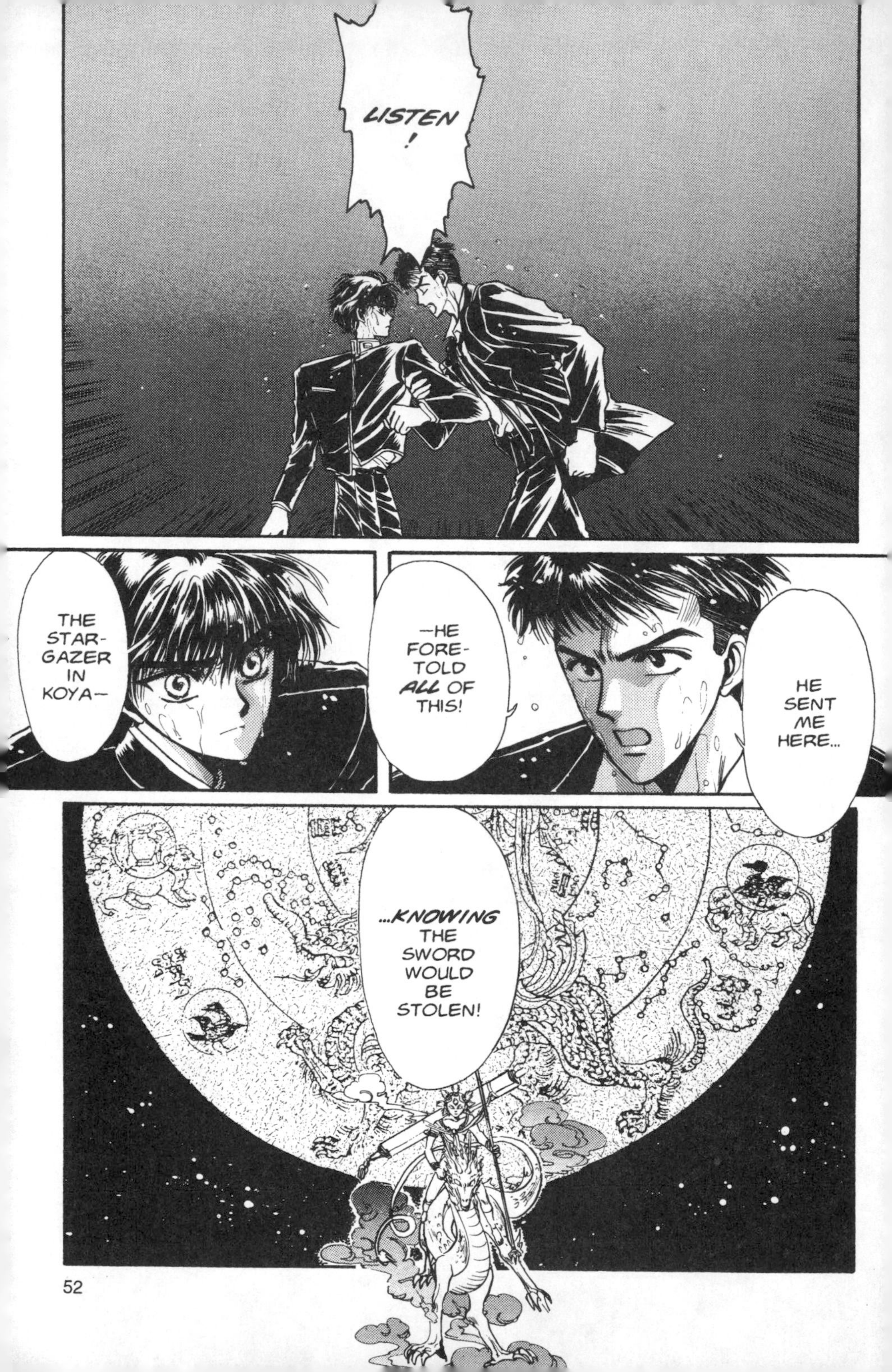
LISTEN!
THE STAR-GAZER IN KOYA--
--HE FORETOLD ALL OF THIS!
HE SENT ME HERE...
...KNOWING THE SWORD WOULD BE STOLEN!

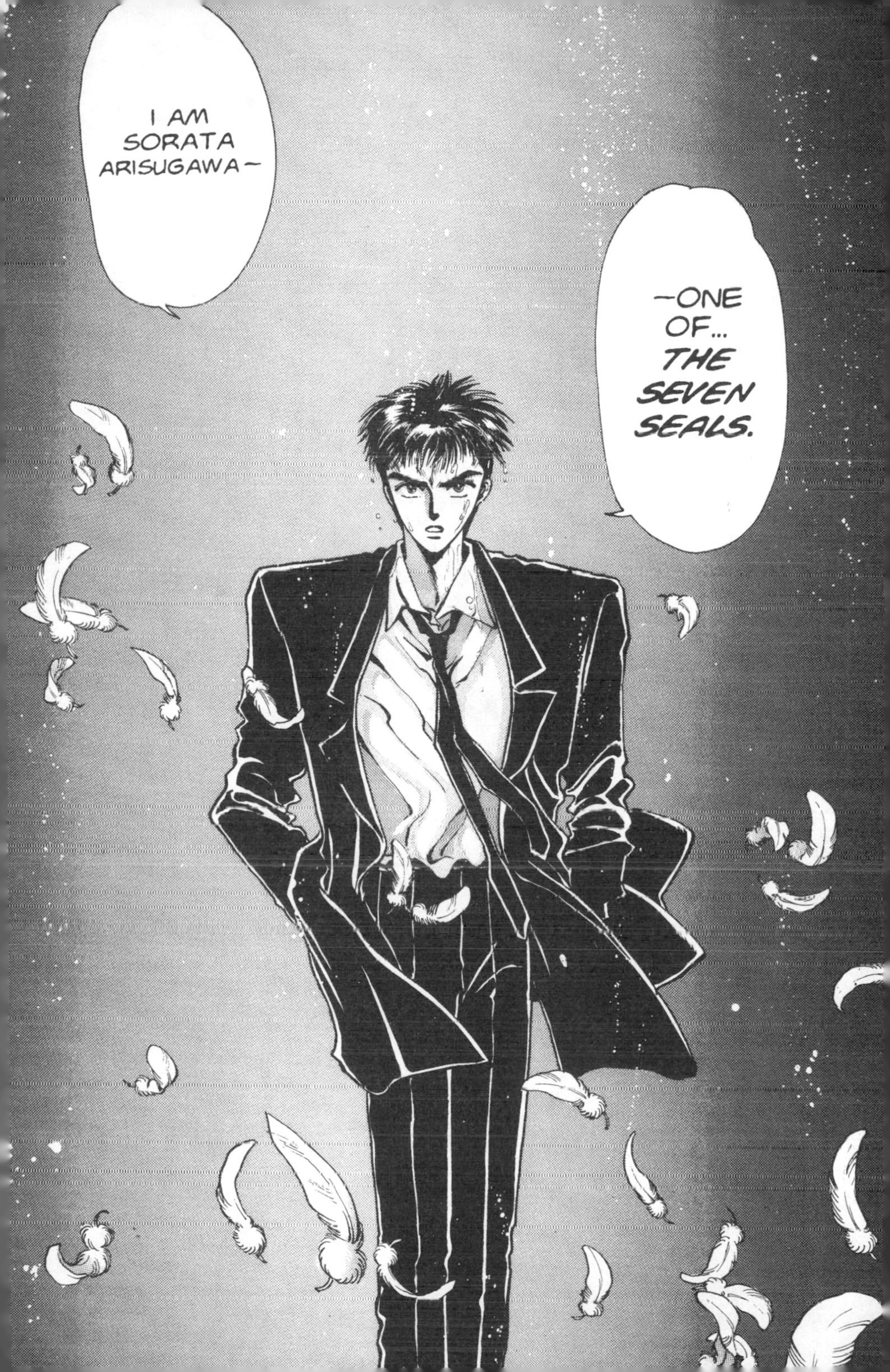
I AM SORATA ARISUGAWA—
—ONE OF... THE SEVEN SEALS.

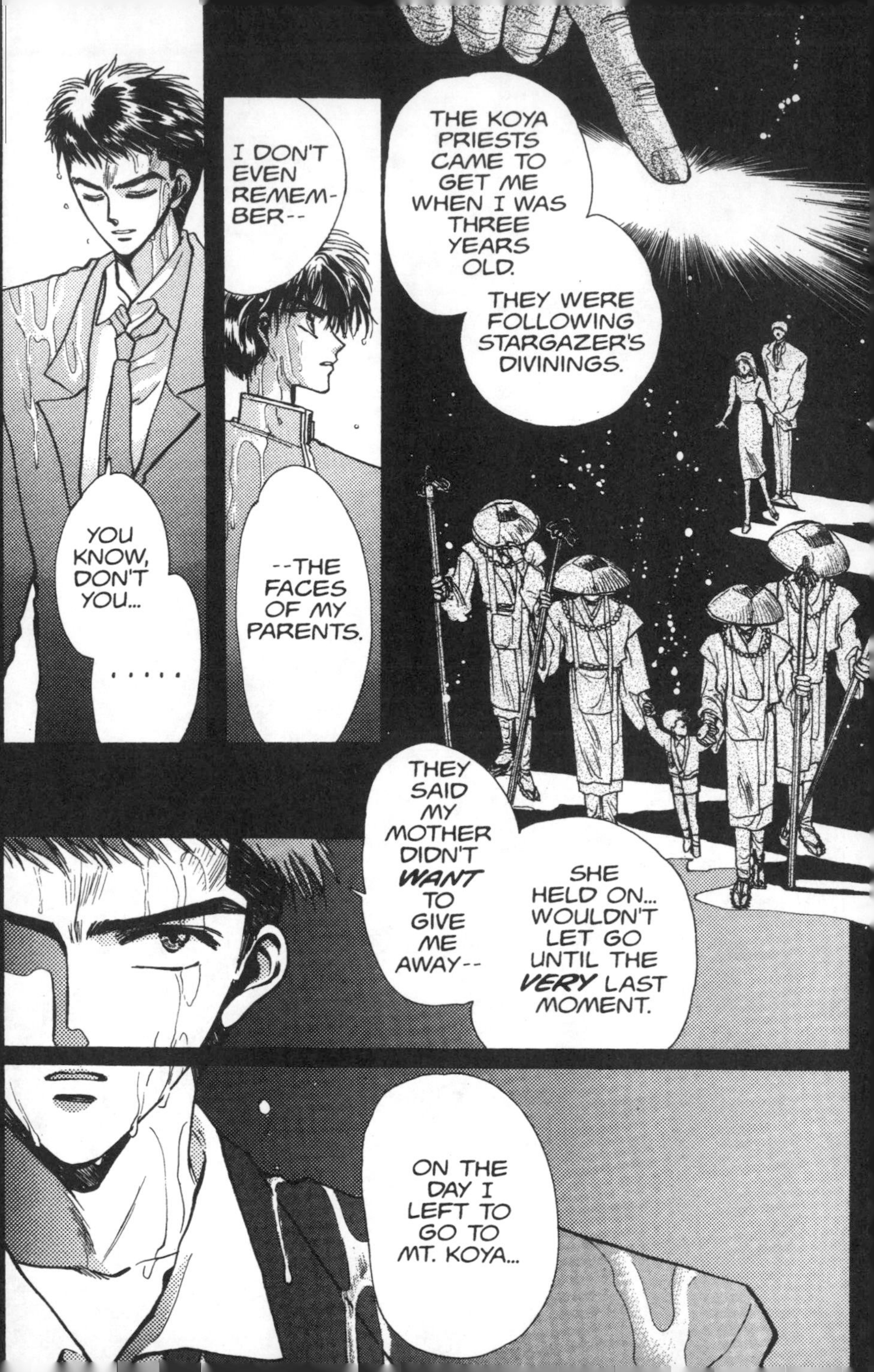
YOU KNOW, DON'T YOU...
.....
I DON'T EVEN REMEMBER--
--THE FACES OF MY PARENTS.
THE KOYA PRIESTS CAME TO GET ME WHEN I WAS THREE YEARS OLD.
THEY WERE FOLLOWING STARGAZER'S DIVININGS.
THEY SAID MY MOTHER DIDN'T *WANT* TO GIVE ME AWAY--
SHE HELD ON... WOULDN'T LET GO UNTIL THE *VERY* LAST MOMENT.
ON THE DAY I LEFT TO GO TO MT. KOYA...

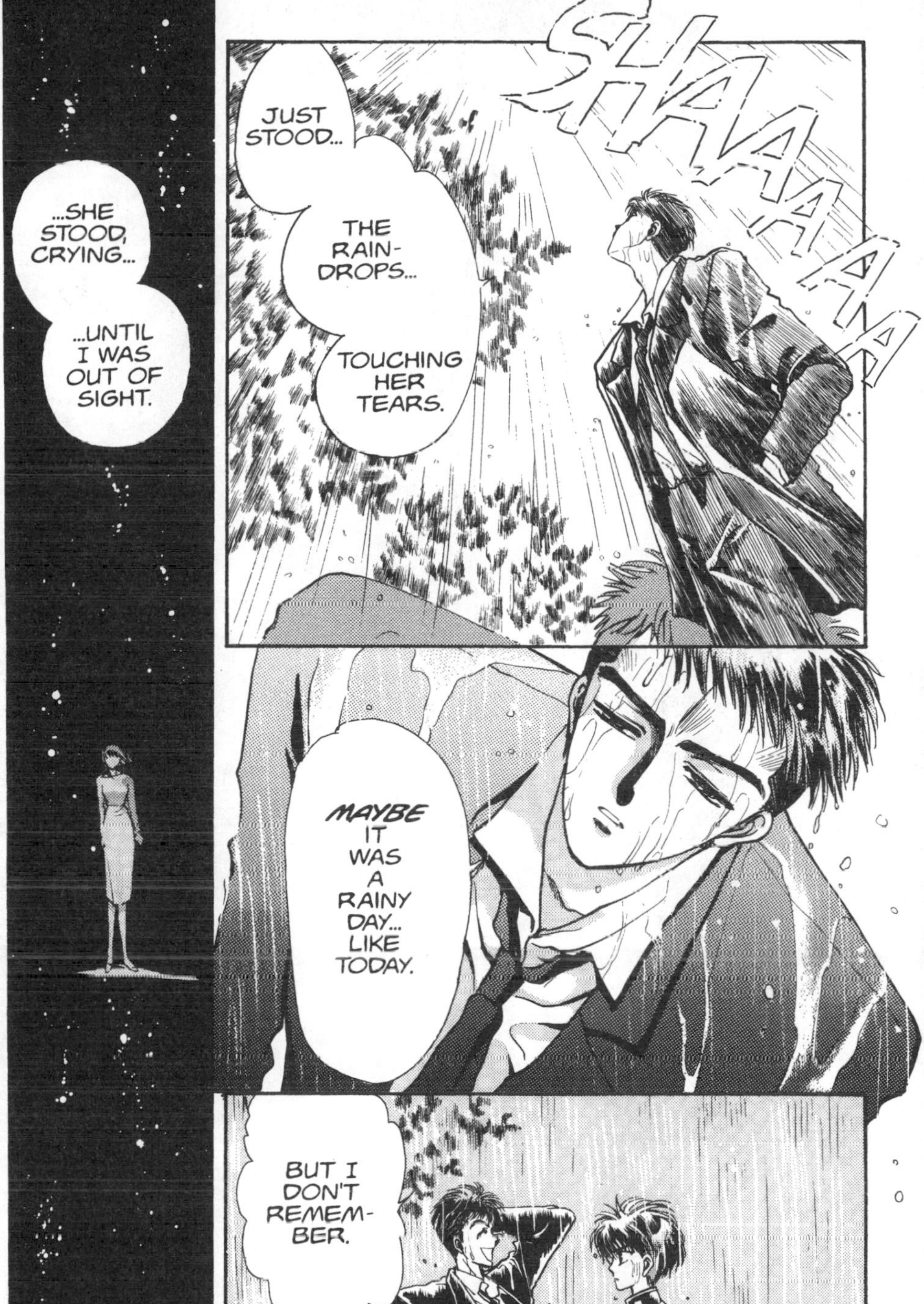
...SHE STOOD, CRYING...
...UNTIL I WAS OUT OF SIGHT.
JUST STOOD...
THE RAIN-DROPS...
TOUCHING HER TEARS.
SHAAAAAA
MAYBE IT WAS A RAINY DAY... LIKE TODAY.
BUT I DON'T REMEM-BER.

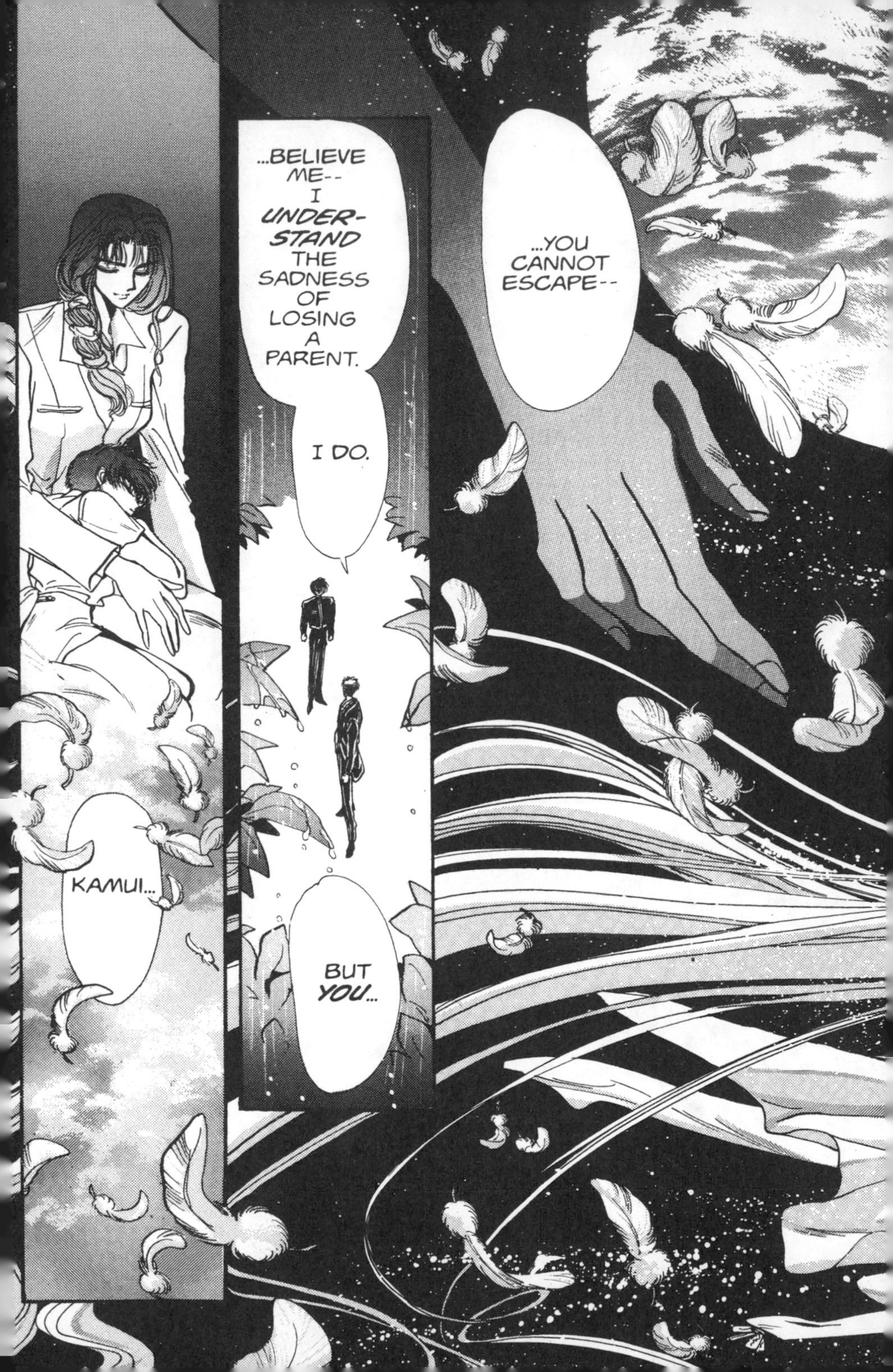
KAMUI...
...BELIEVE ME-- I *UNDERSTAND* THE SADNESS OF LOSING A PARENT.
I DO.
BUT *YOU*...
...YOU CANNOT ESCAPE--

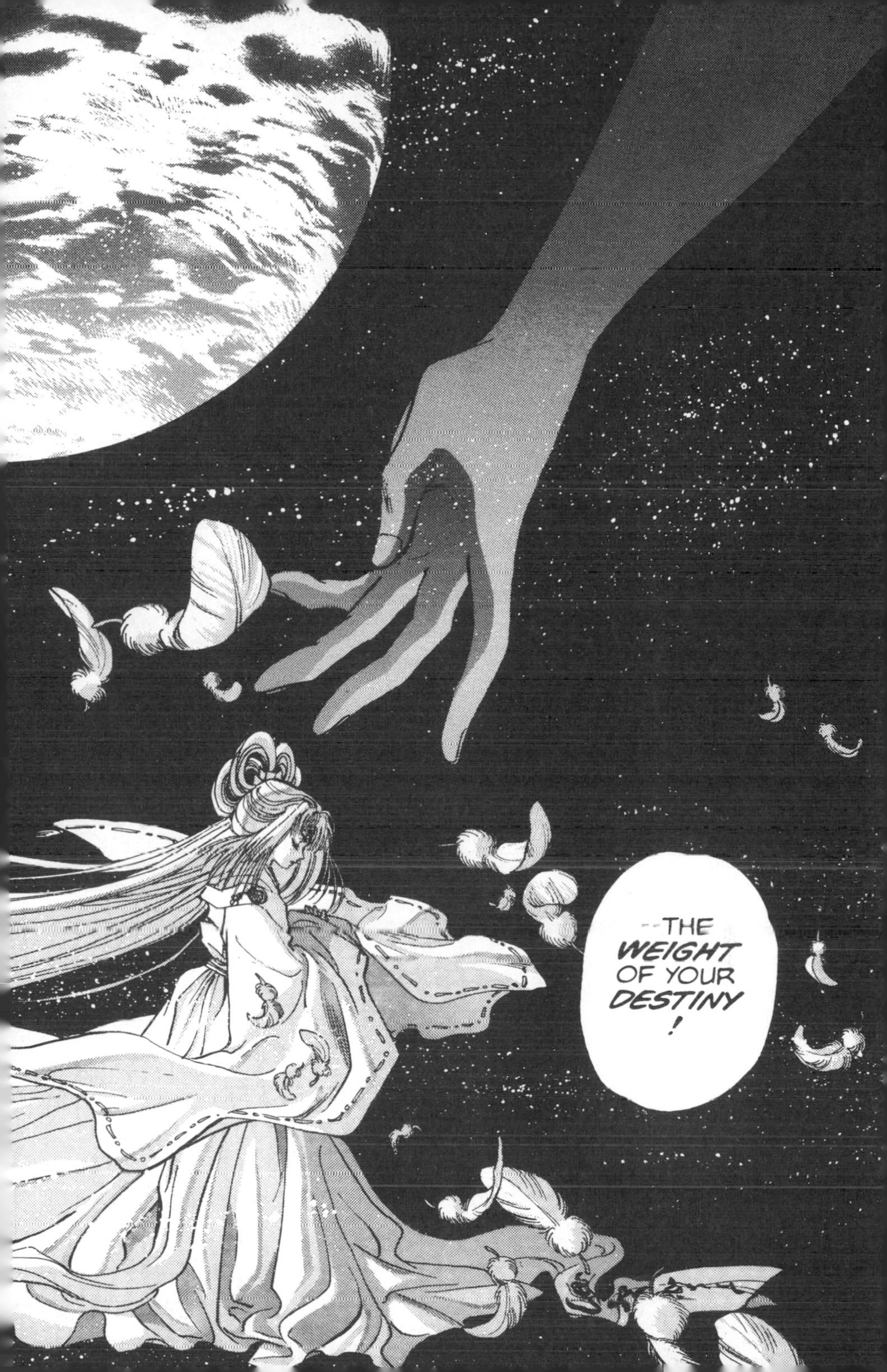
--THE WEIGHT OF YOUR DESTINY !

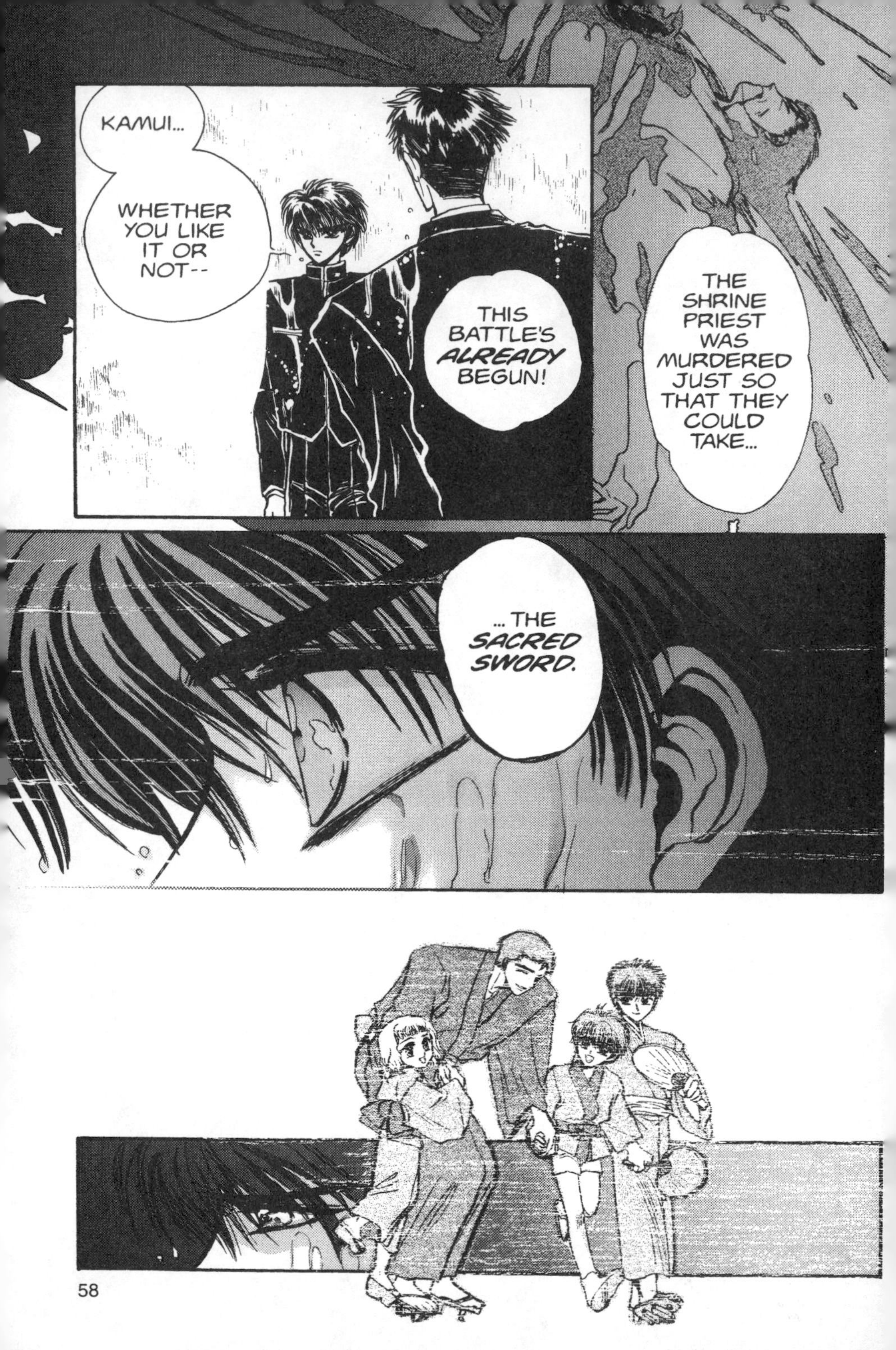
KAMUI...
WHETHER YOU LIKE IT OR NOT--
THIS BATTLE'S *ALREADY* BEGUN!
THE SHRINE PRIEST WAS MURDERED JUST SO THAT THEY COULD TAKE...
... THE *SACRED SWORD.*

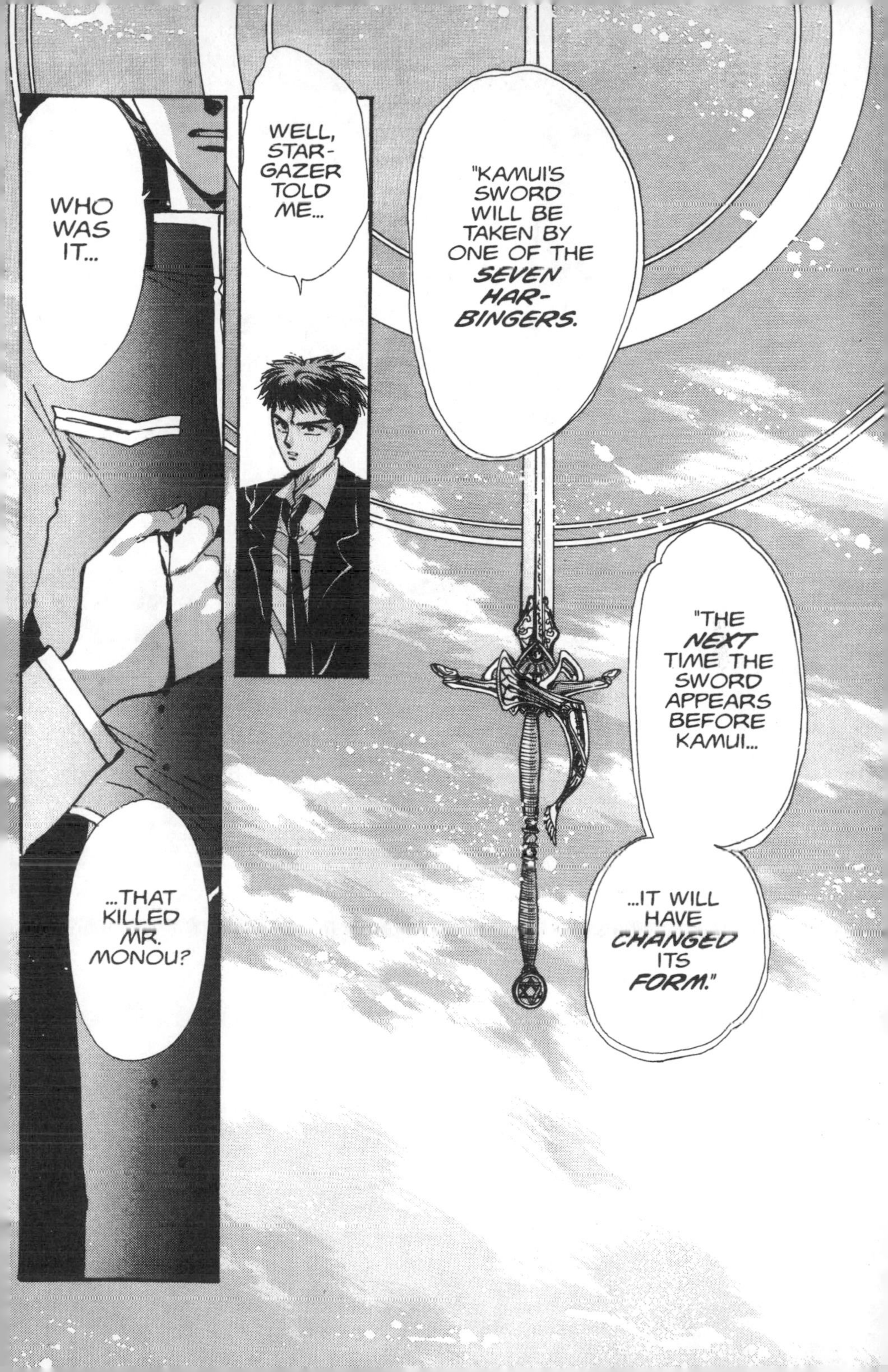
WHO WAS IT...
...THAT KILLED MR. MONOU?
WELL, STAR-GAZER TOLD ME...
"KAMUI'S SWORD WILL BE TAKEN BY ONE OF THE *SEVEN HAR-BINGERS.*
"THE *NEXT* TIME THE SWORD APPEARS BEFORE KAMUI...
...IT WILL HAVE *CHANGED* ITS *FORM.*"

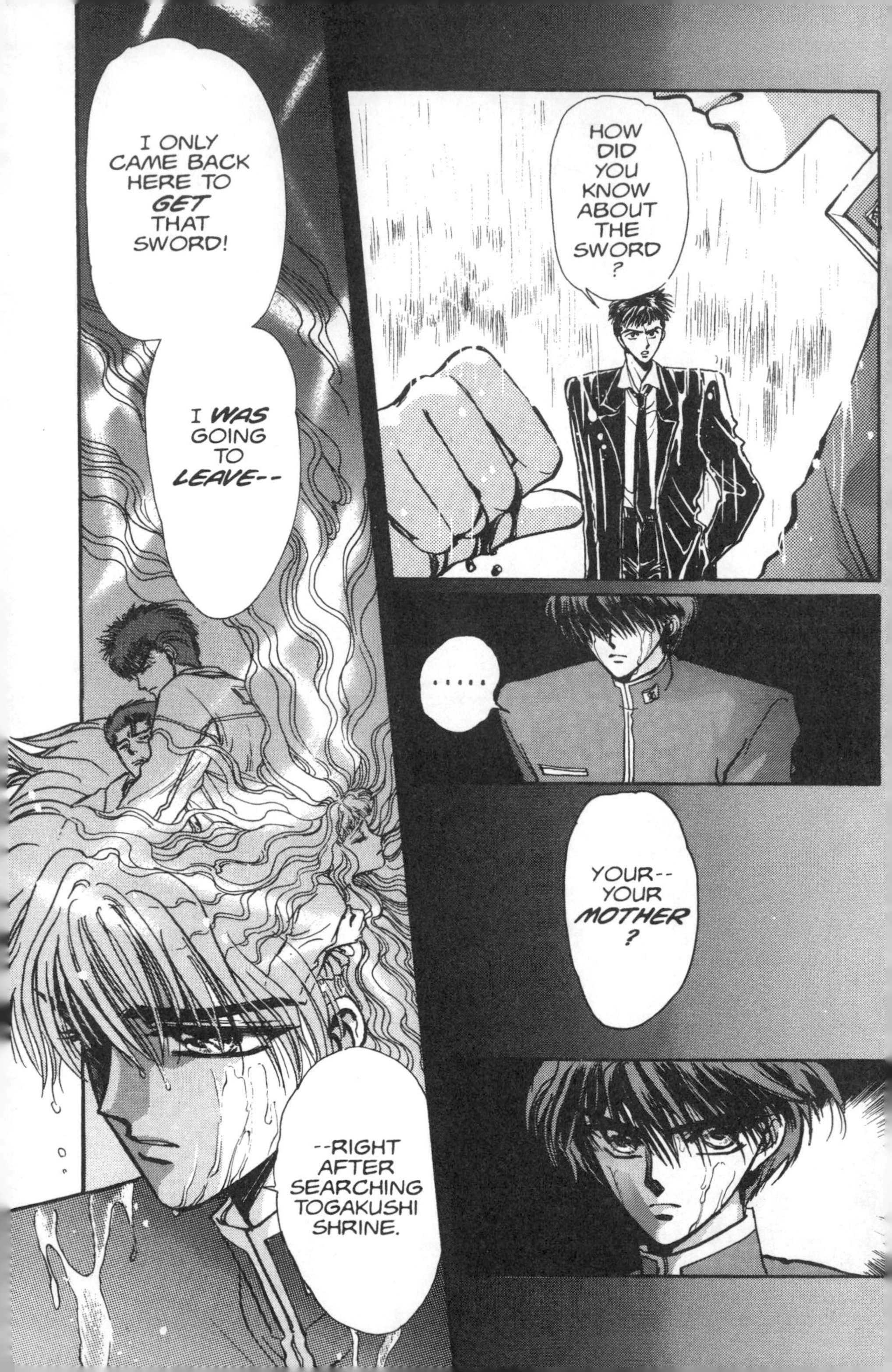
I ONLY CAME BACK HERE TO GET THAT SWORD!
I WAS GOING TO LEAVE--
--RIGHT AFTER SEARCHING TOGAKUSHI SHRINE.
HOW DID YOU KNOW ABOUT THE SWORD ?
.....
YOUR-- YOUR MOTHER ?

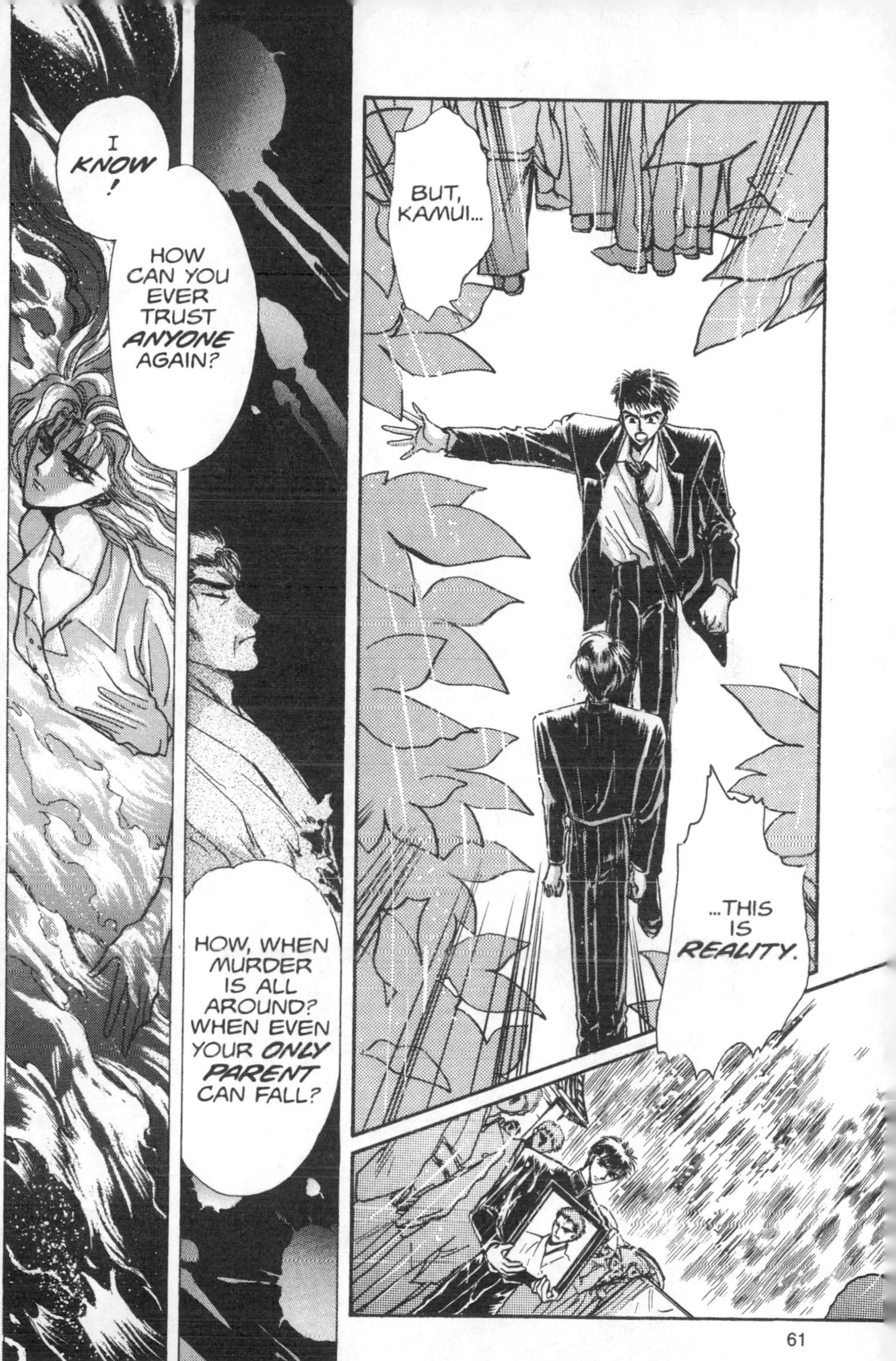
I KNOW!
HOW CAN YOU EVER TRUST ANYONE AGAIN?
HOW, WHEN MURDER IS ALL AROUND? WHEN EVEN YOUR ONLY PARENT CAN FALL?
BUT, KAMUI...
...THIS IS REALITY.

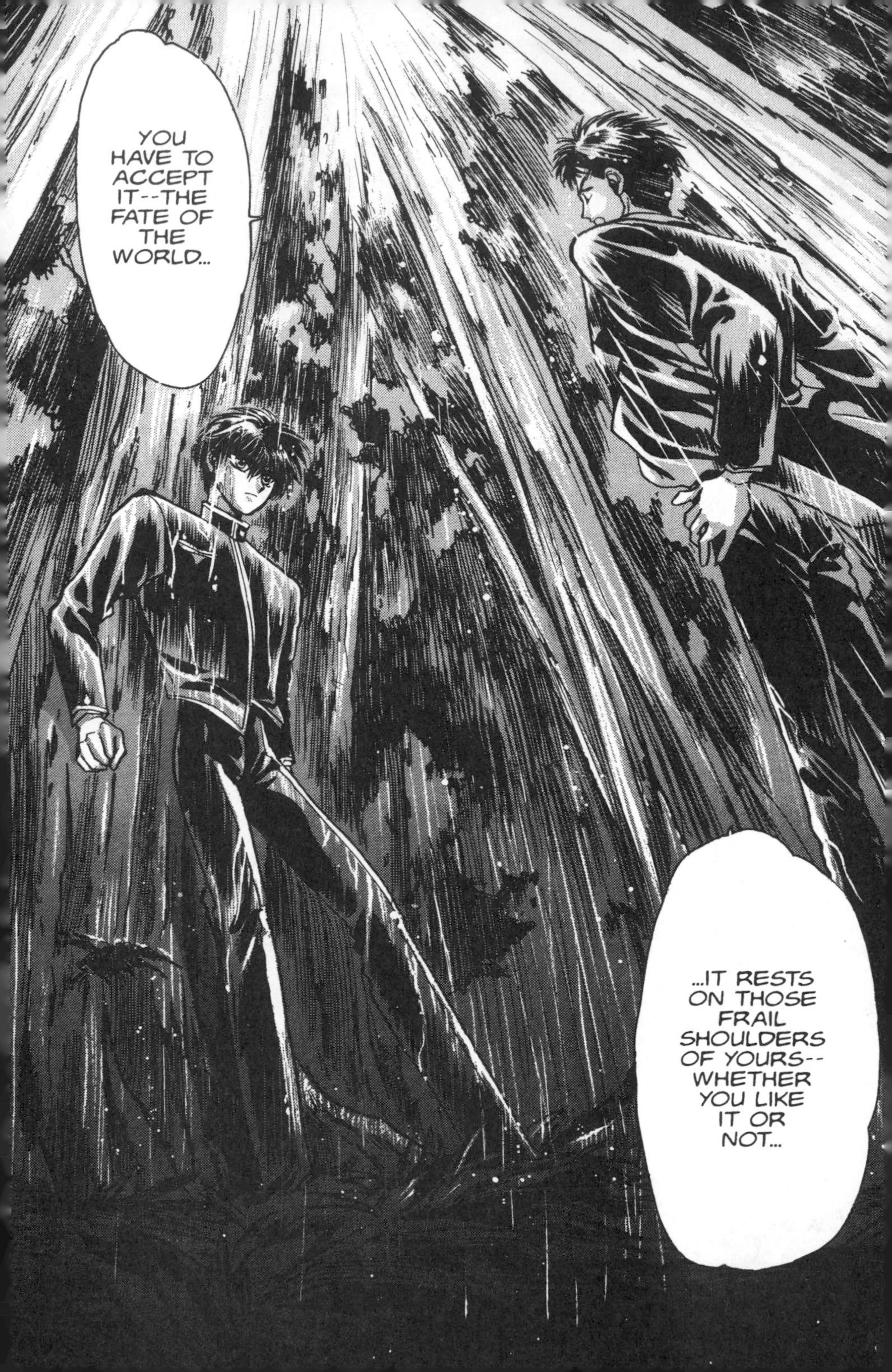
YOU HAVE TO ACCEPT IT--THE FATE OF THE WORLD...
...IT RESTS ON THOSE FRAIL SHOULDERS OF YOURS--WHETHER YOU LIKE IT OR NOT...

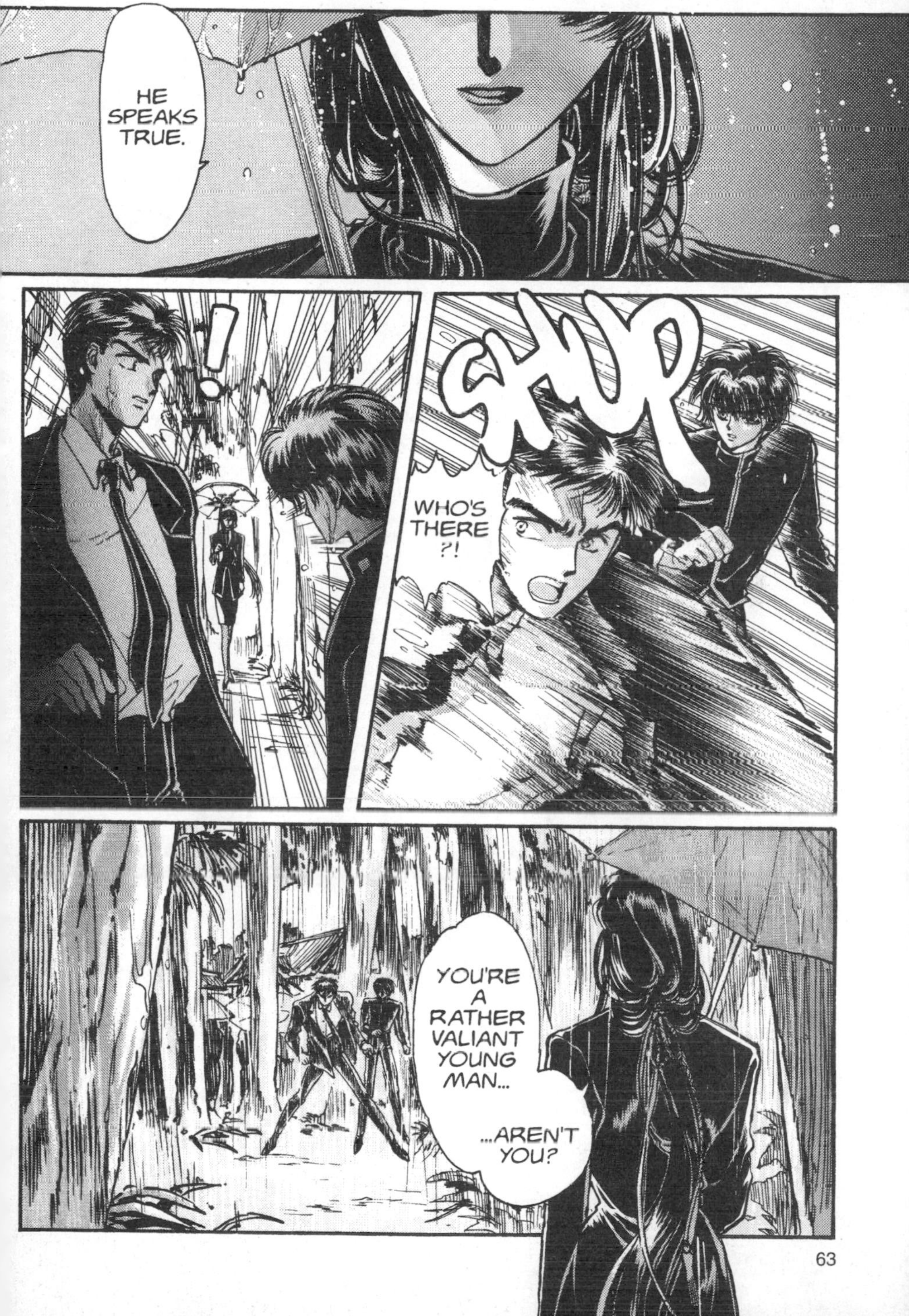
HE SPEAKS TRUE.
!
SHUP
WHO'S THERE ?!
YOU'RE A RATHER VALIANT YOUNG MAN...
...AREN'T YOU?

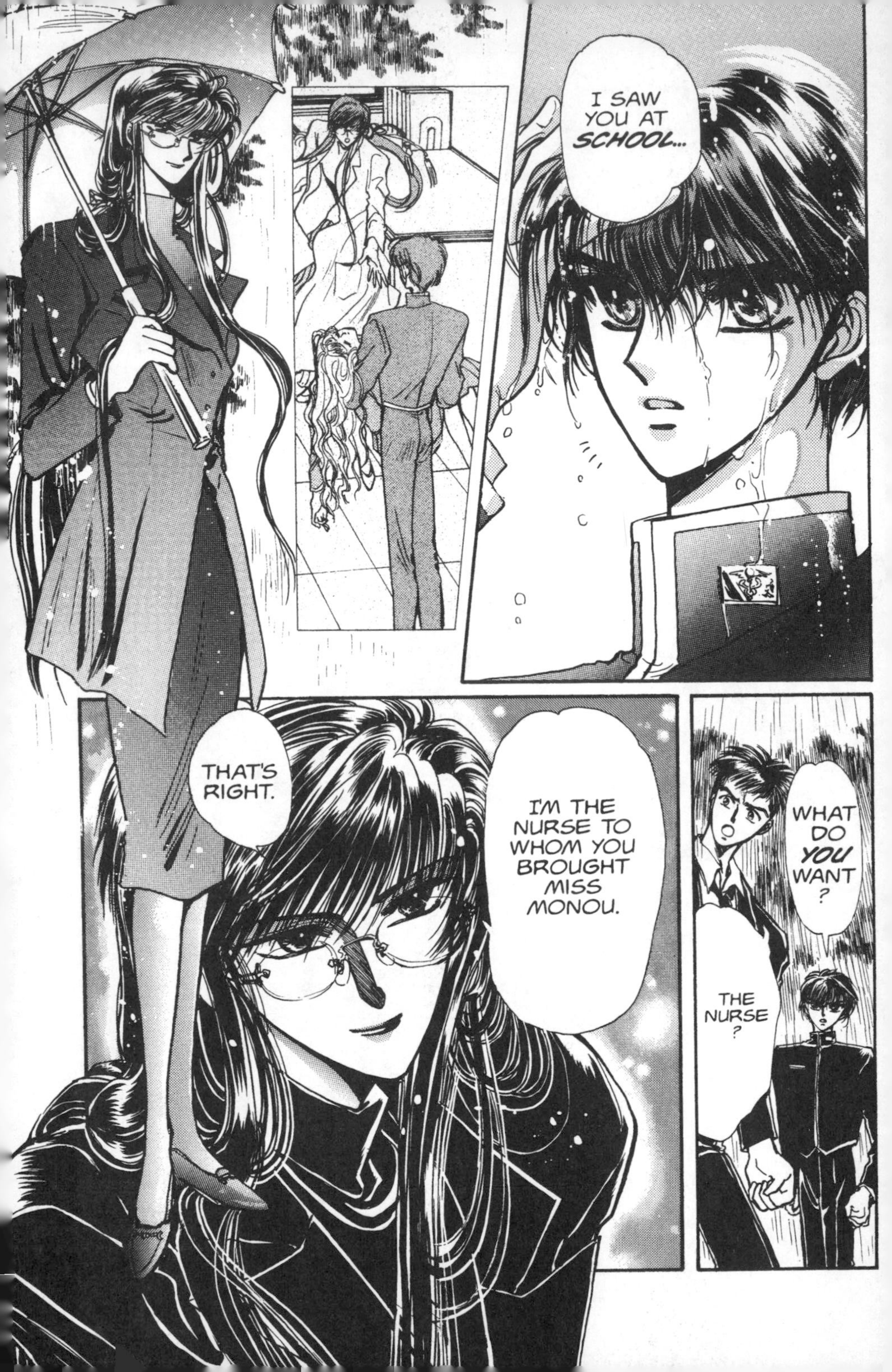
I SAW YOU AT *SCHOOL*...
THAT'S RIGHT.
I'M THE NURSE TO WHOM YOU BROUGHT MISS MONOU.
WHAT DO *YOU* WANT?
THE NURSE?

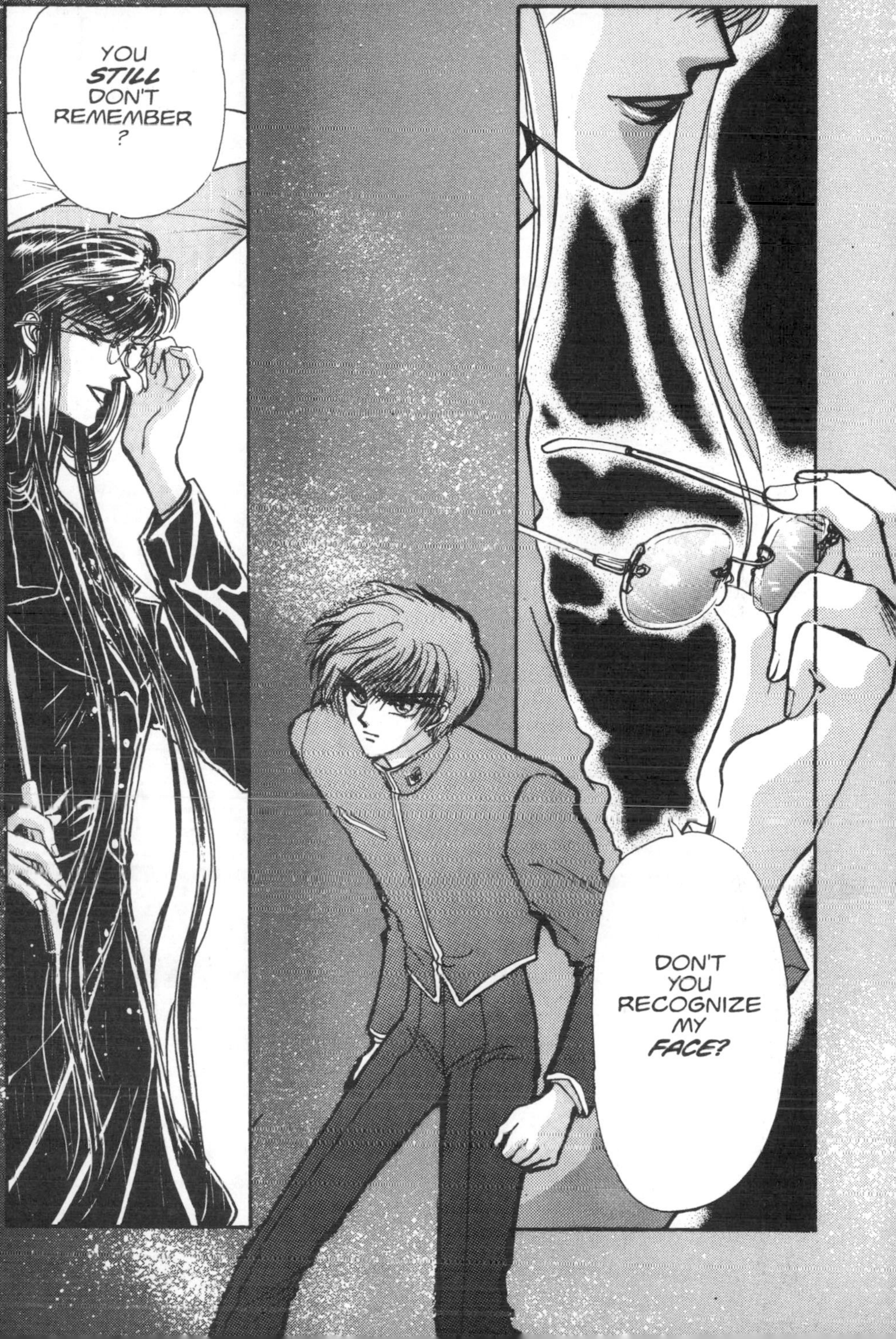
YOU STILL DON'T REMEMBER?
DON'T YOU RECOGNIZE MY FACE?

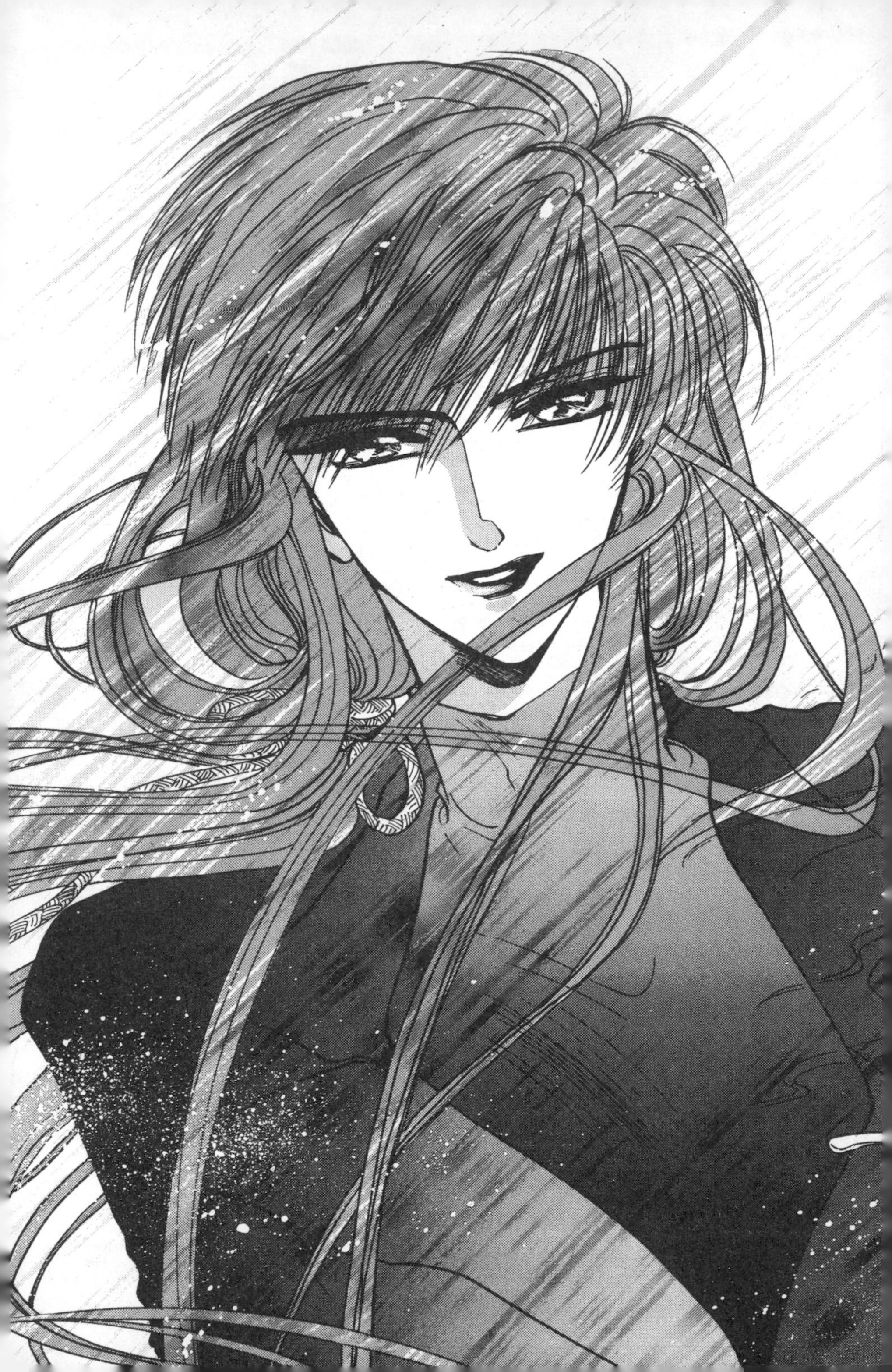

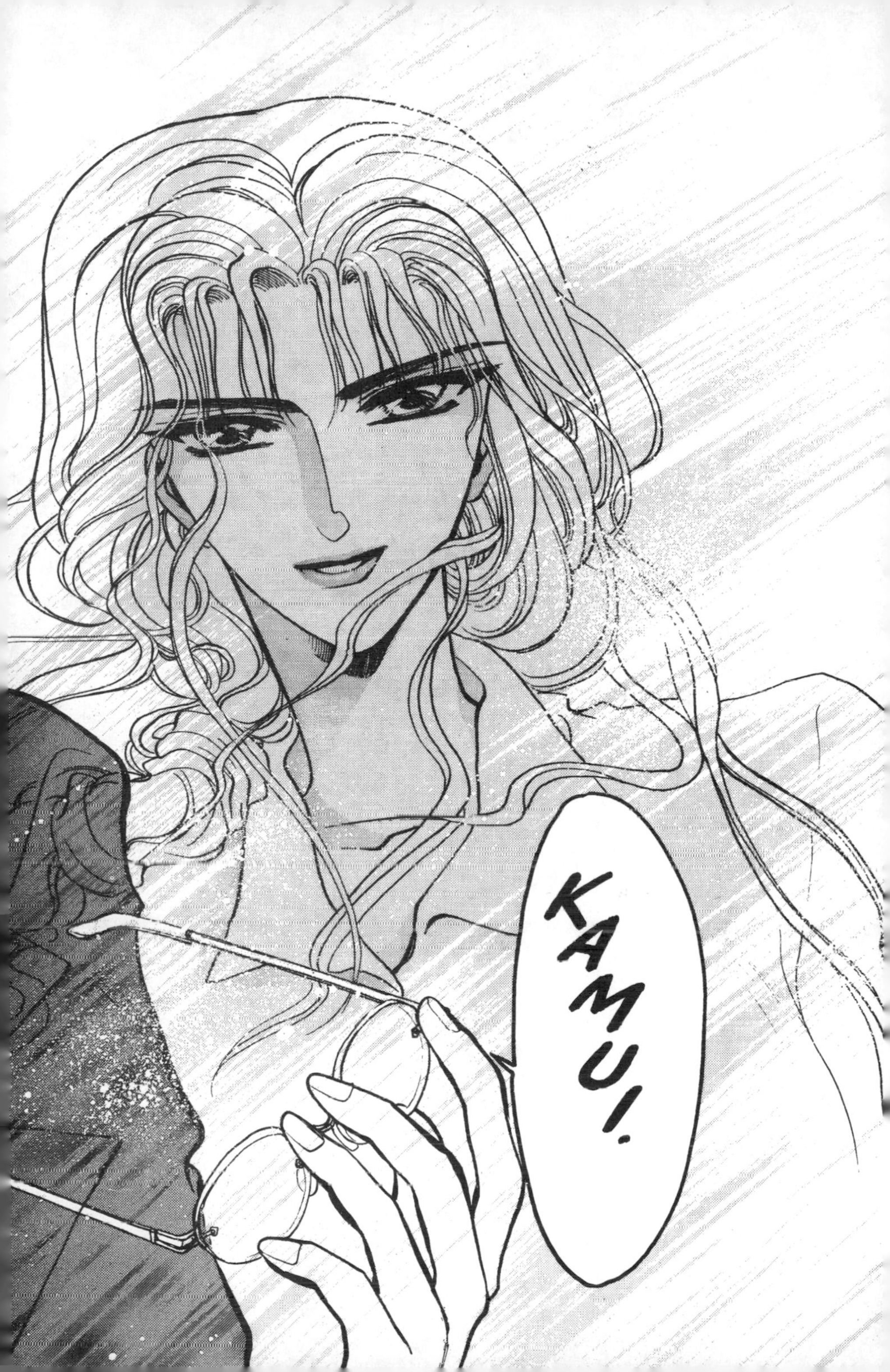
KAMUI.

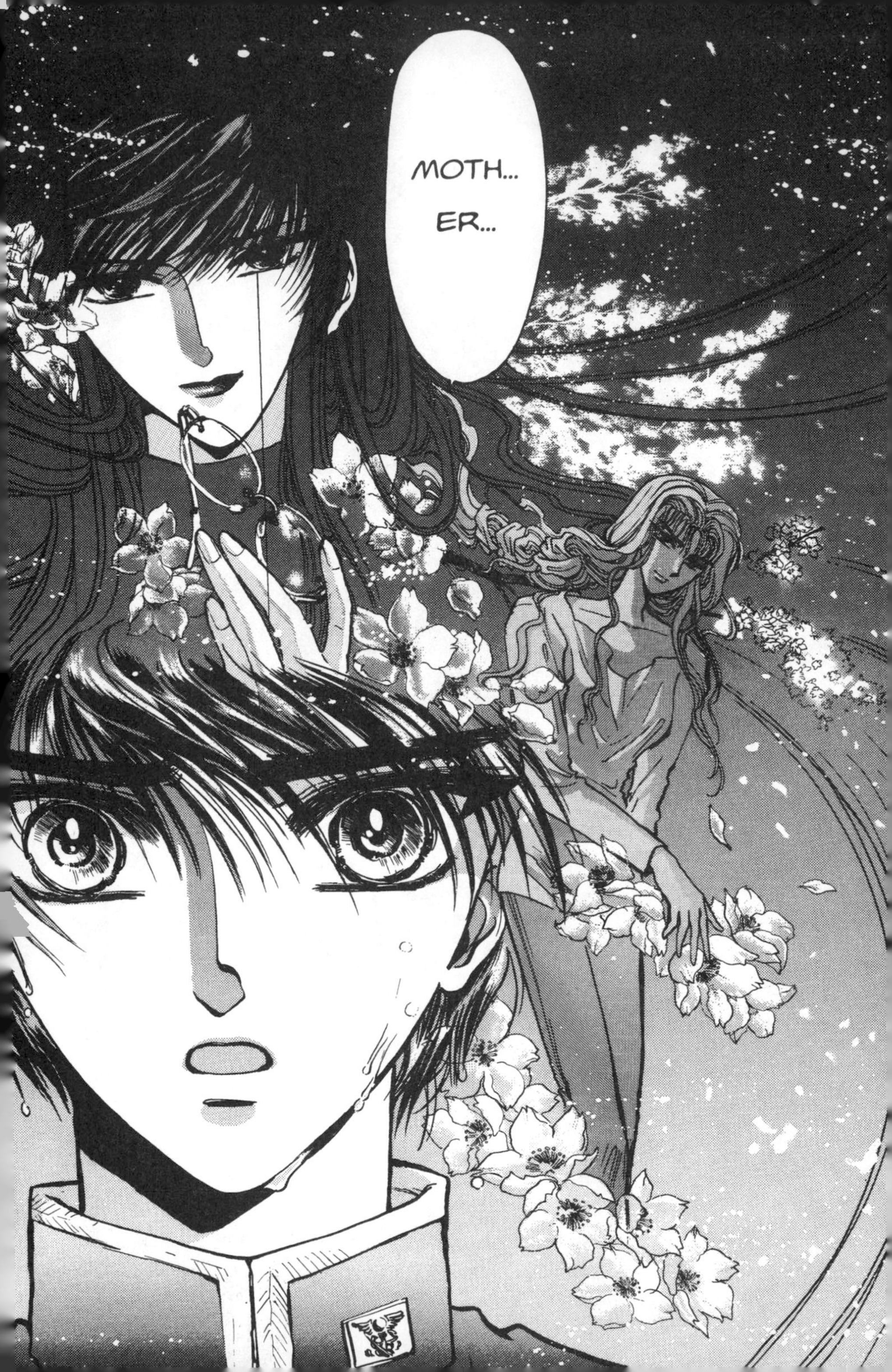
MOTH... ER...

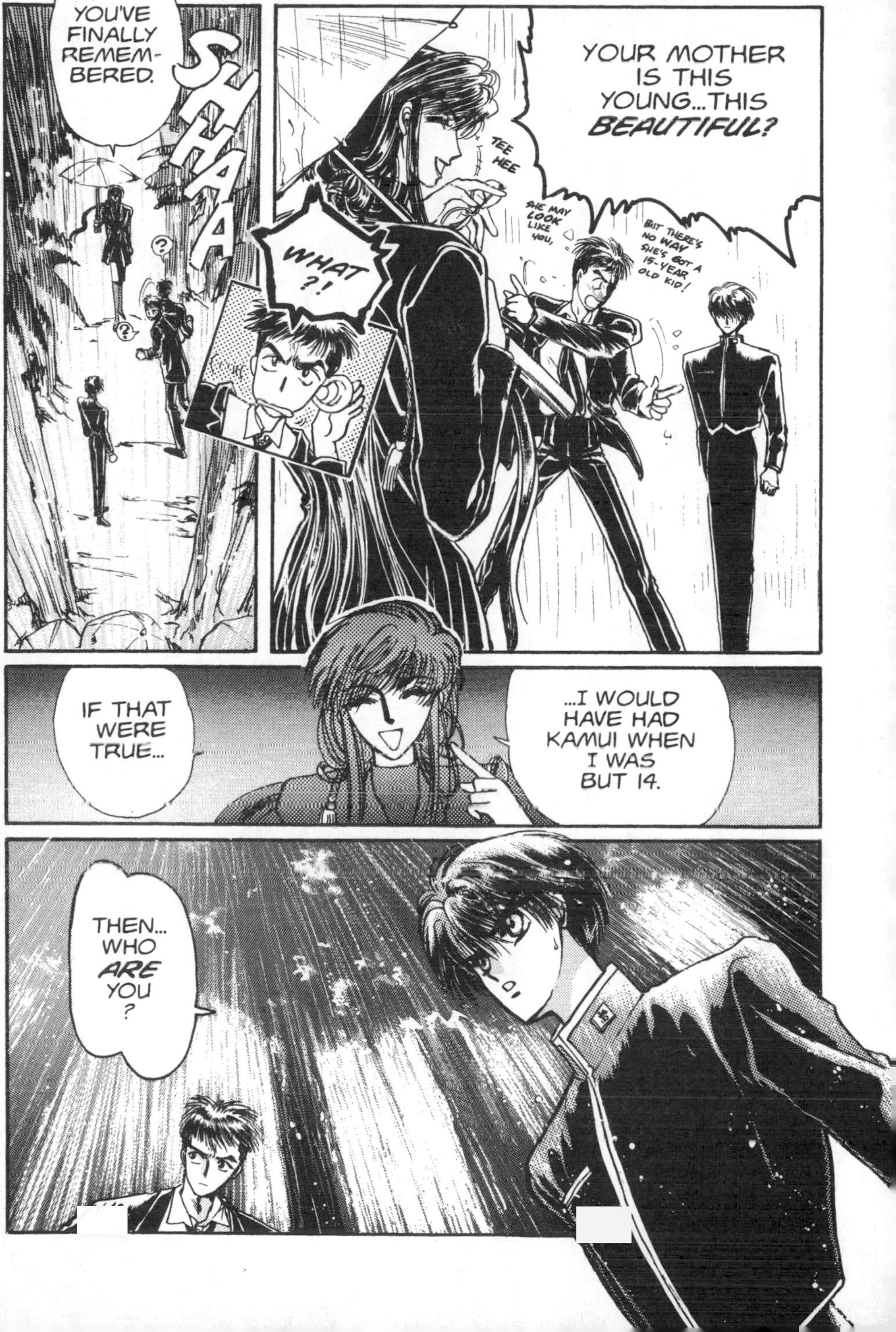
YOU'VE FINALLY REMEMBERED.
SHAHA
YOUR MOTHER IS THIS YOUNG...THIS *BEAUTIFUL?*
TEE HEE
WHAT ?!
SHE MAY LOOK LIKE YOU,
BUT THERE'S NO WAY SHE'S GOT A 15-YEAR OLD KID!
IF THAT WERE TRUE...
...I WOULD HAVE HAD KAMUI WHEN I WAS BUT 14.
THEN... WHO *ARE* YOU ?

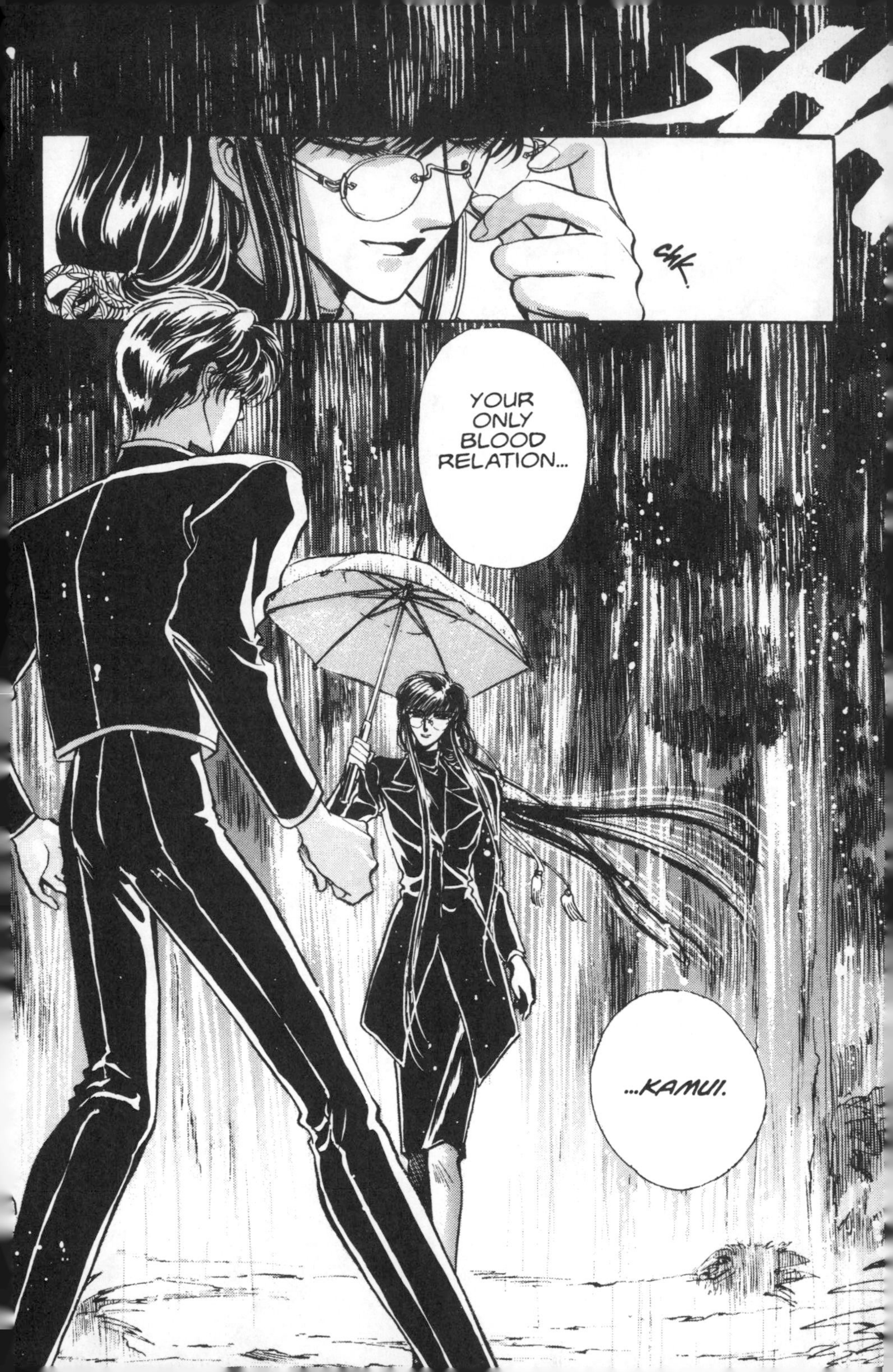
SHA
CHK.
YOUR ONLY BLOOD RELATION...
...KAMUI.

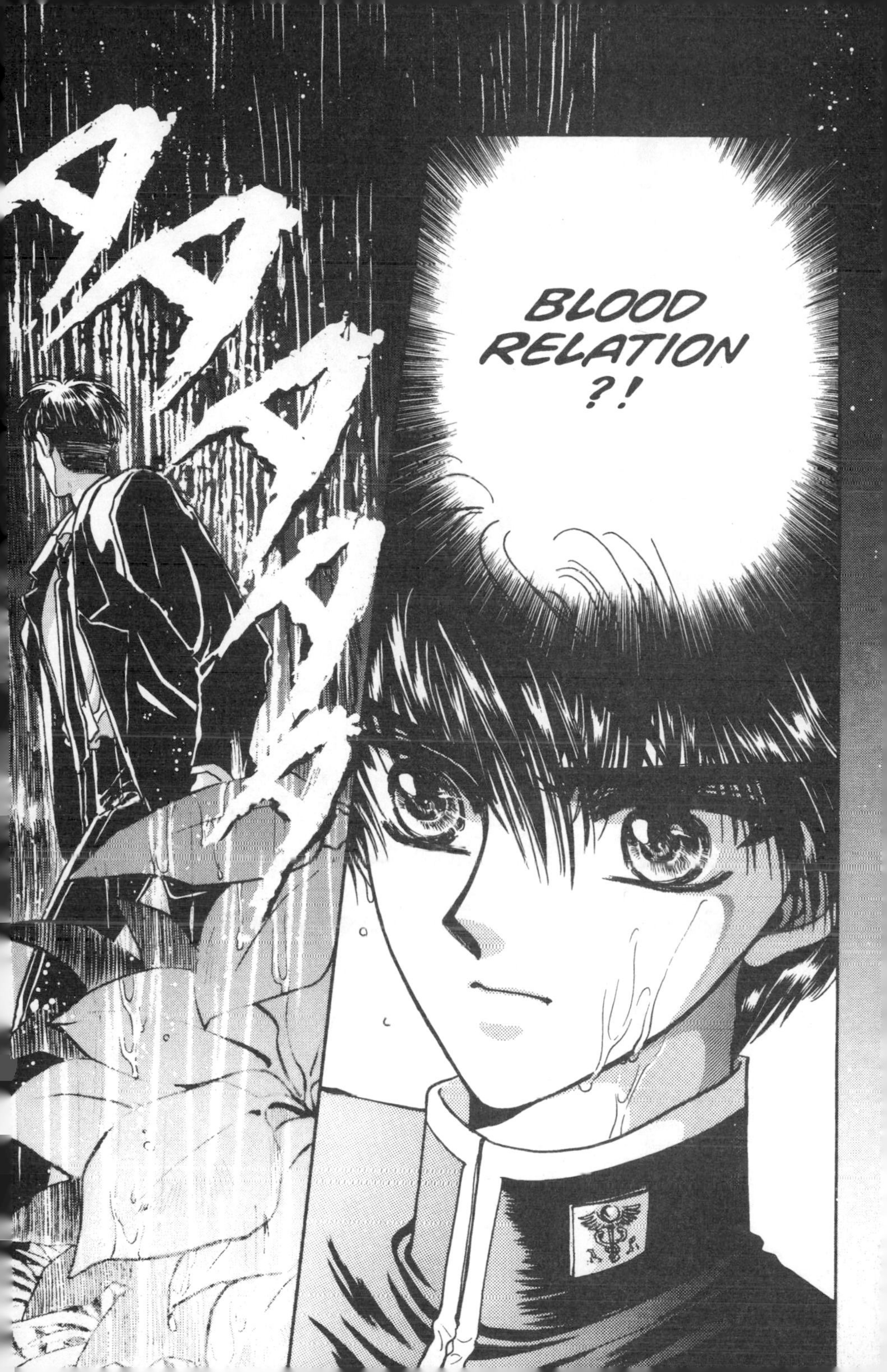
BLOOD RELATION ?!

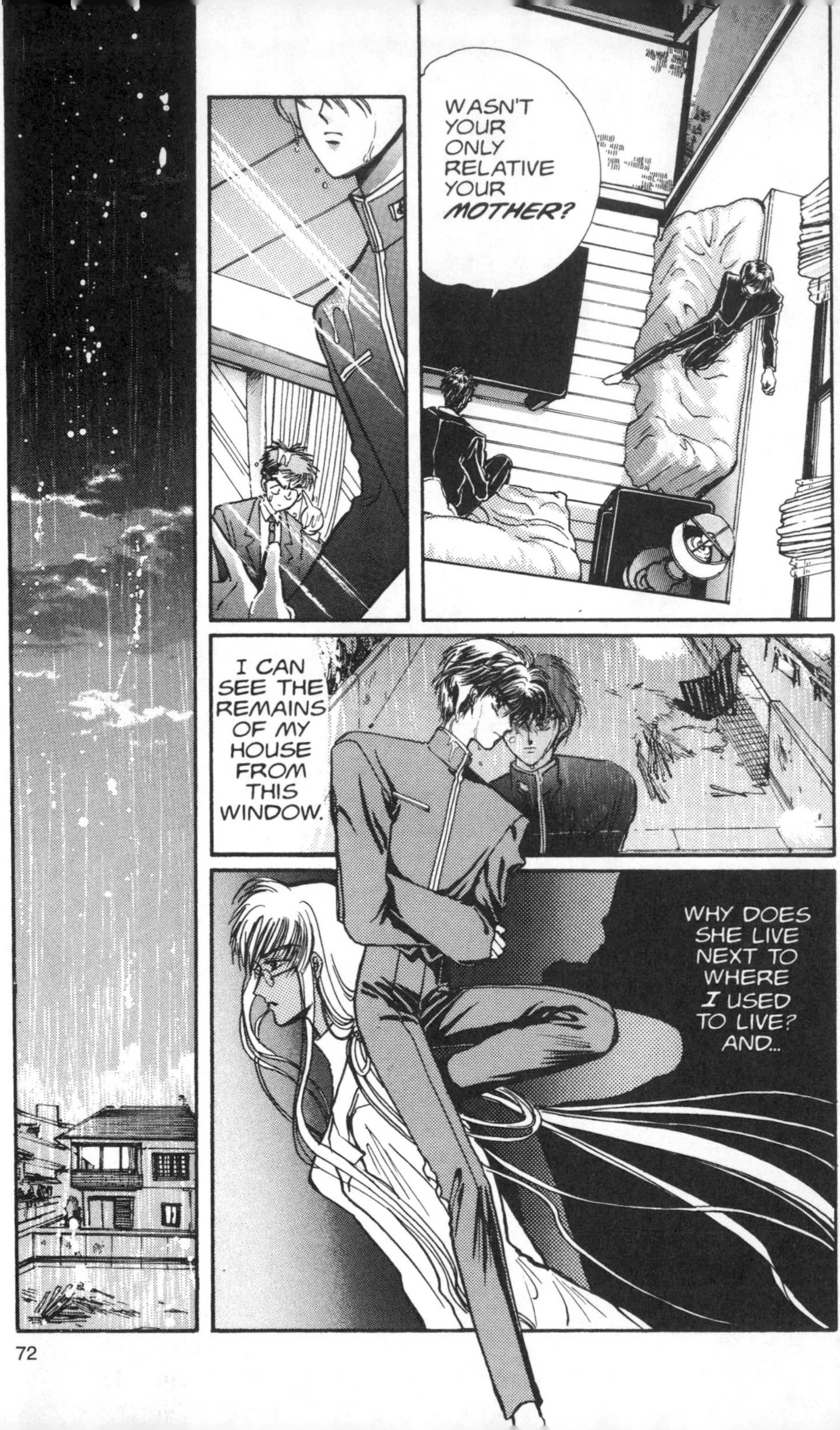
WASN'T YOUR ONLY RELATIVE YOUR *MOTHER?*
I CAN SEE THE REMAINS OF MY HOUSE FROM THIS WINDOW.
WHY DOES SHE LIVE NEXT TO WHERE *I* USED TO LIVE? AND...

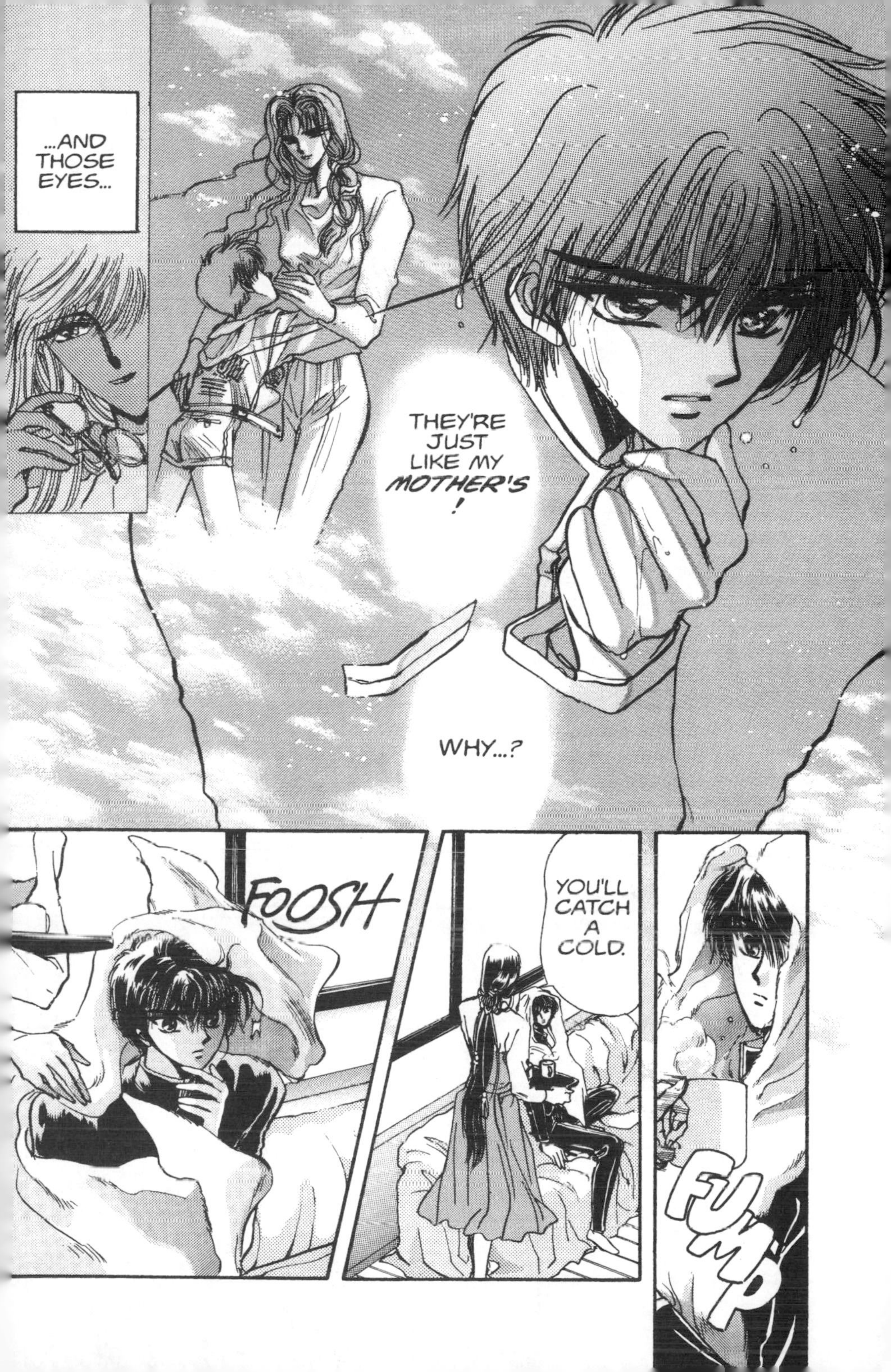
...AND THOSE EYES...
THEY'RE JUST LIKE MY *MOTHER'S* !
WHY...?
FOOSH
YOU'LL CATCH A COLD.
FUMP

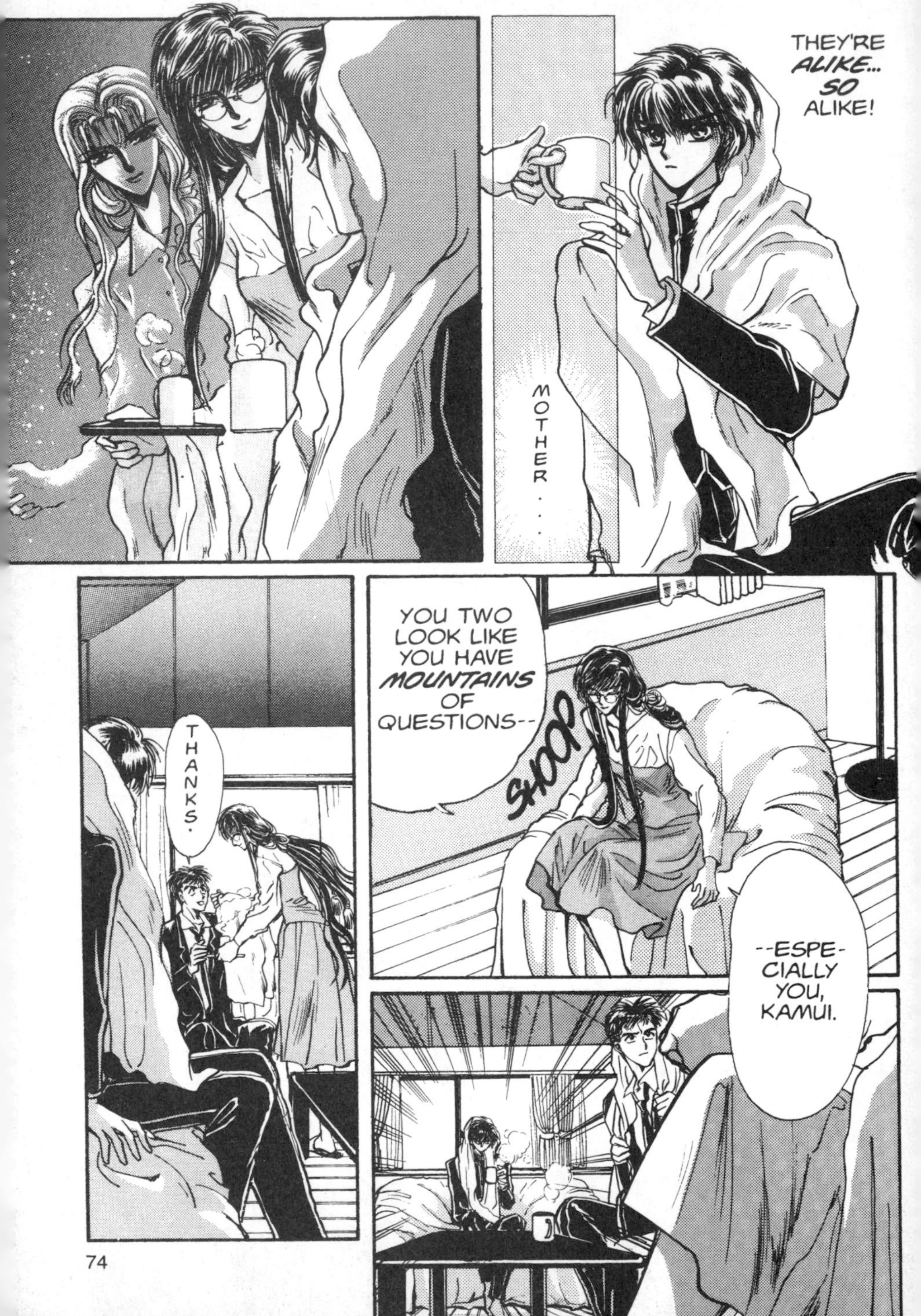
THEY'RE ALIKE... SO ALIKE!
MOTHER...
THANKS.
YOU TWO LOOK LIKE YOU HAVE MOUNTAINS OF QUESTIONS--
SHOOP
--ESPE-CIALLY YOU, KAMUI.

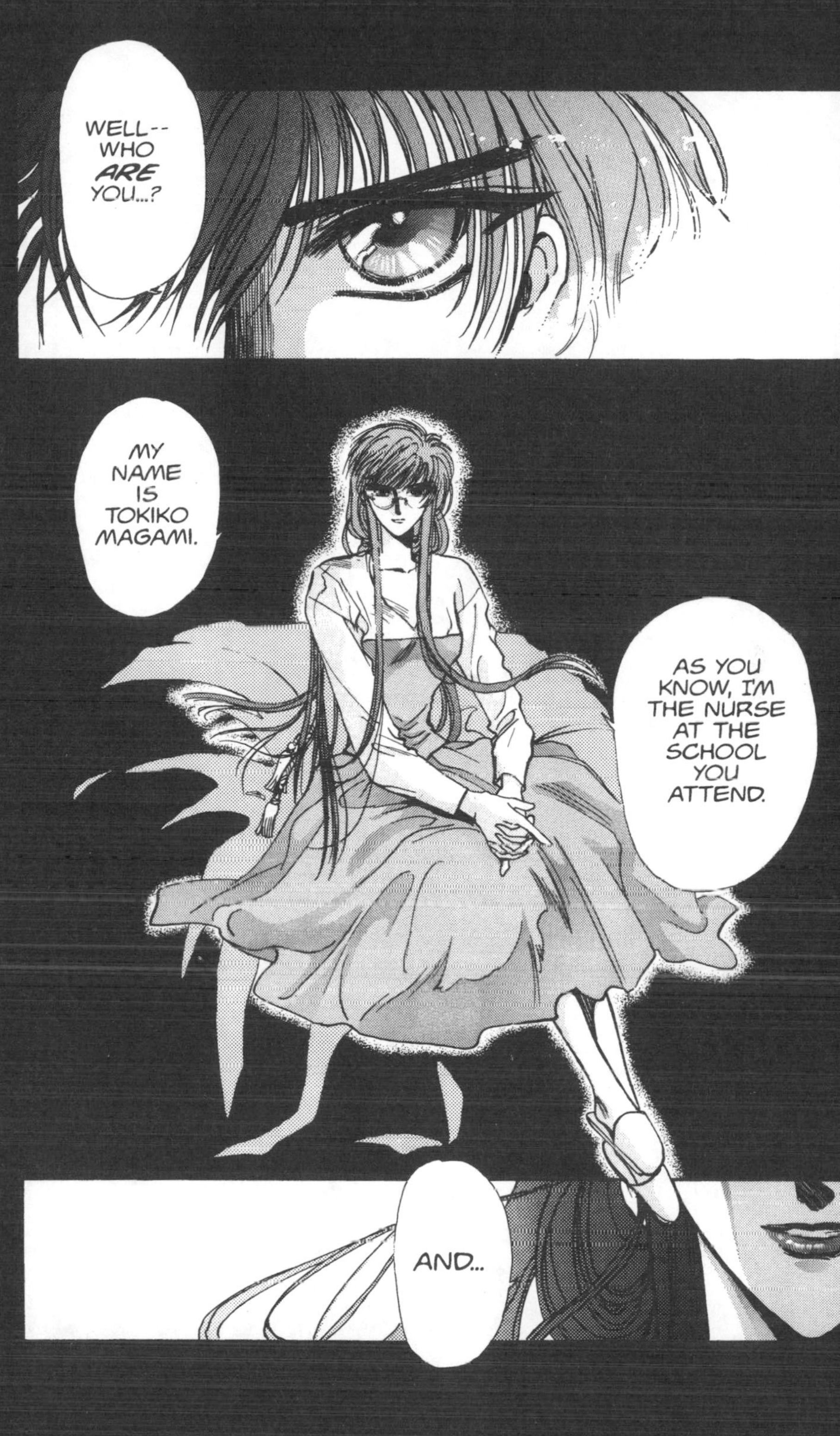
WELL-- WHO ***ARE*** YOU...?
MY NAME IS TOKIKO MAGAMI.
AS YOU KNOW, I'M THE NURSE AT THE SCHOOL YOU ATTEND.
AND...

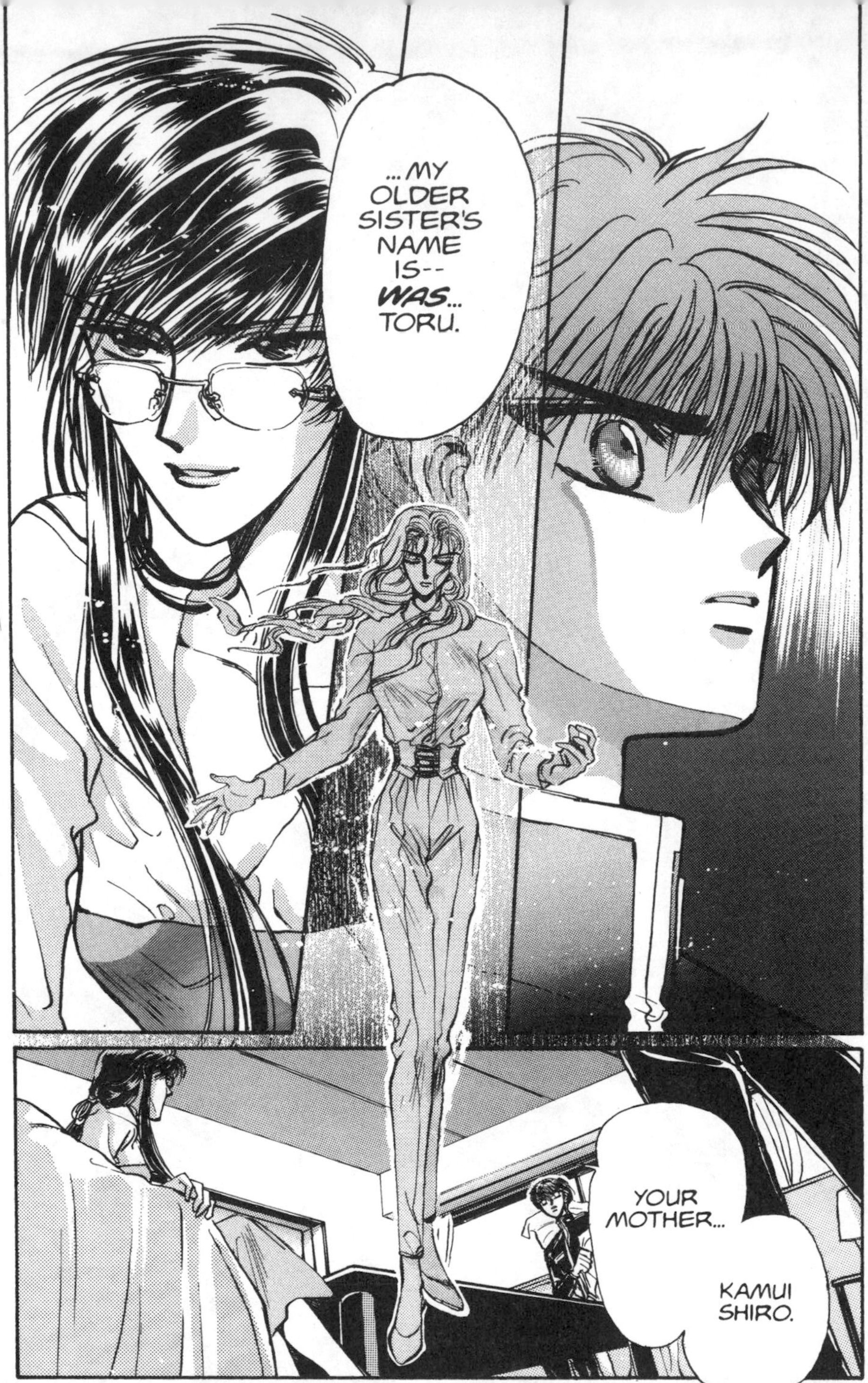
...MY OLDER SISTER'S NAME IS-- WAS... TORU.
YOUR MOTHER...
KAMUI SHIRO.

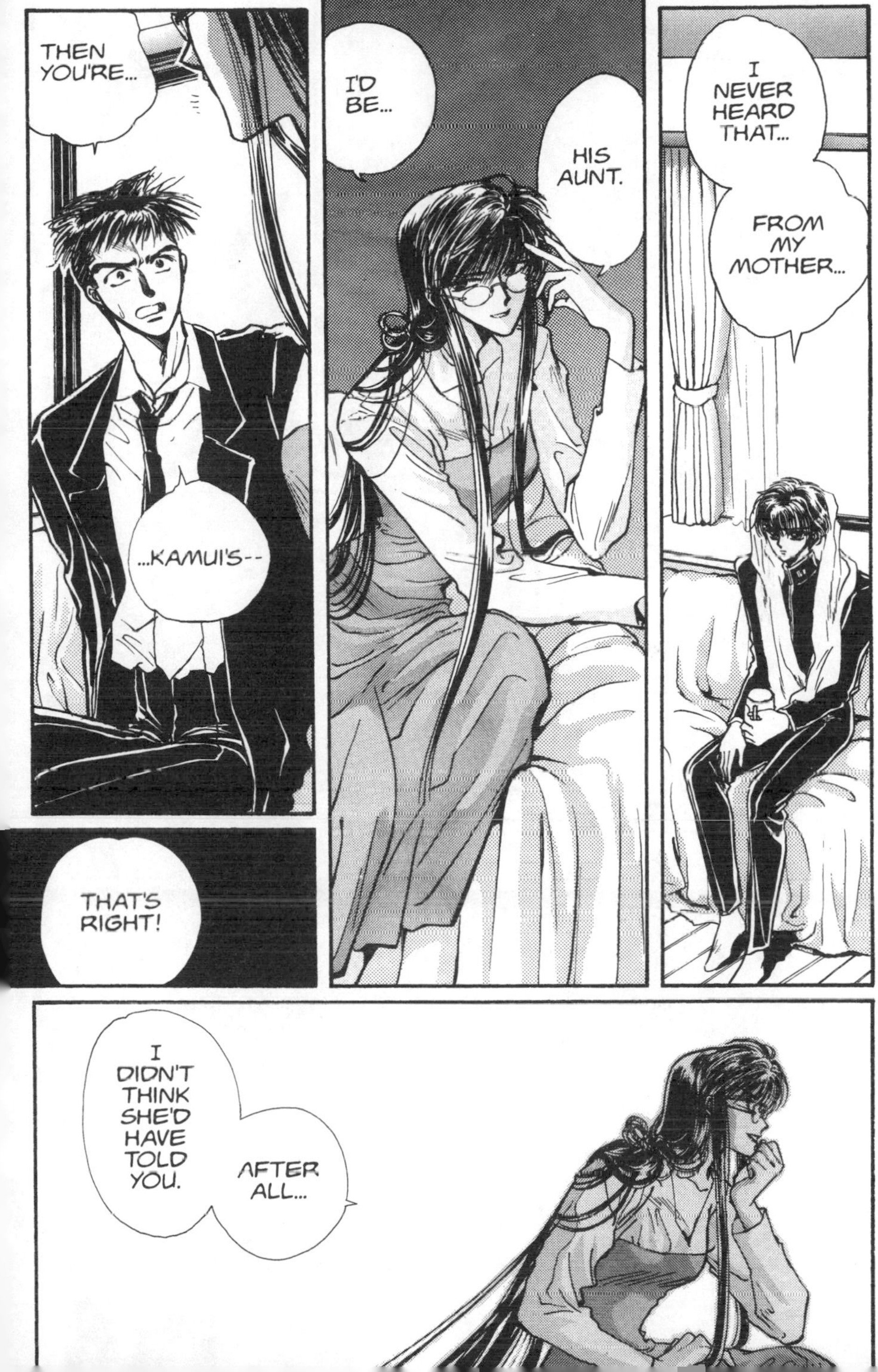
THEN YOU'RE...
...KAMUI'S--
THAT'S RIGHT!
I'D BE...
HIS AUNT.
I NEVER HEARD THAT...
FROM MY MOTHER...
I DIDN'T THINK SHE'D HAVE TOLD YOU.
AFTER ALL...

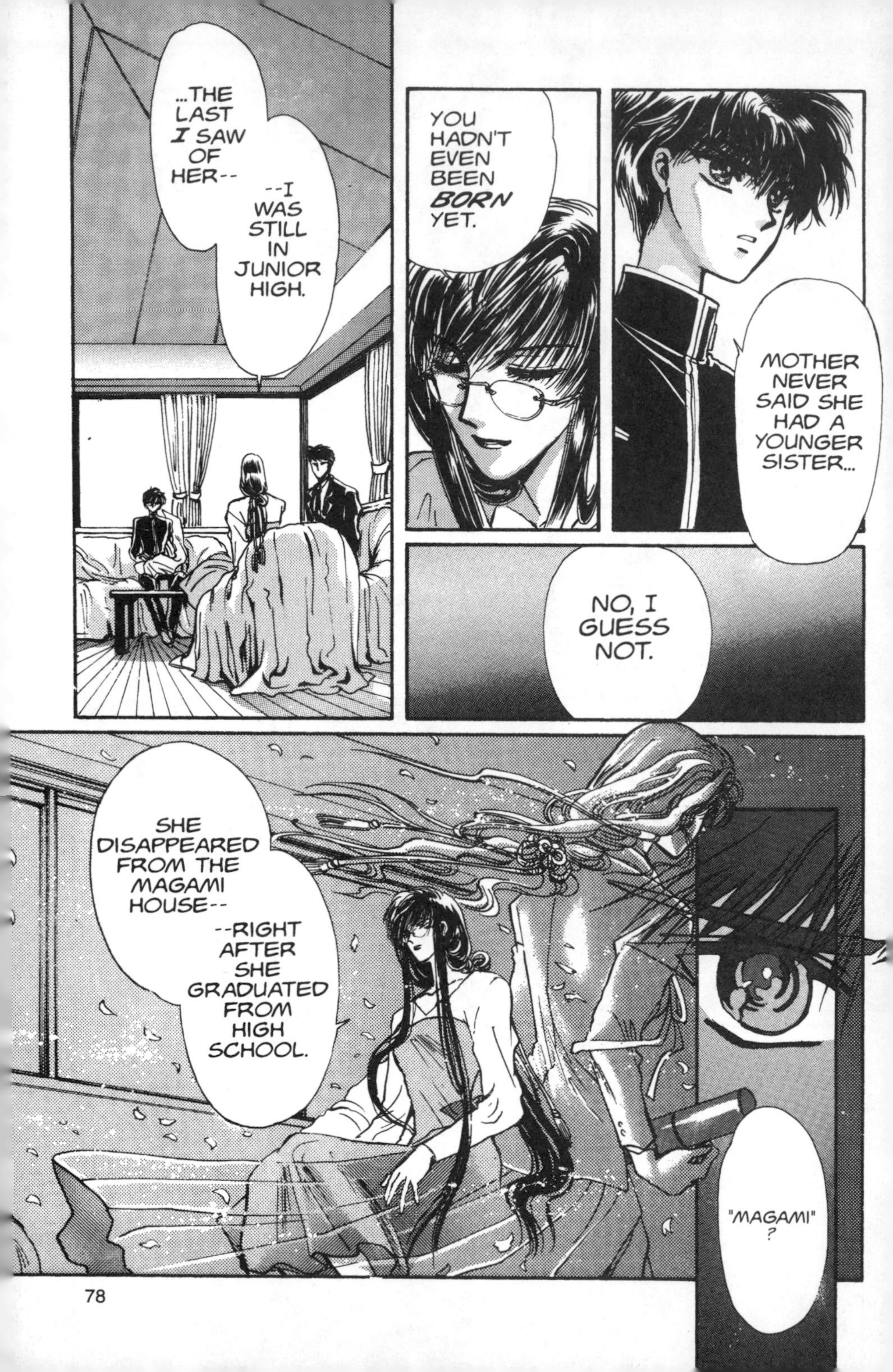
...THE LAST I SAW OF HER--
--I WAS STILL IN JUNIOR HIGH.
YOU HADN'T EVEN BEEN BORN YET.
MOTHER NEVER SAID SHE HAD A YOUNGER SISTER...
NO, I GUESS NOT.
SHE DISAPPEARED FROM THE MAGAMI HOUSE--
--RIGHT AFTER SHE GRADUATED FROM HIGH SCHOOL.
"MAGAMI"?

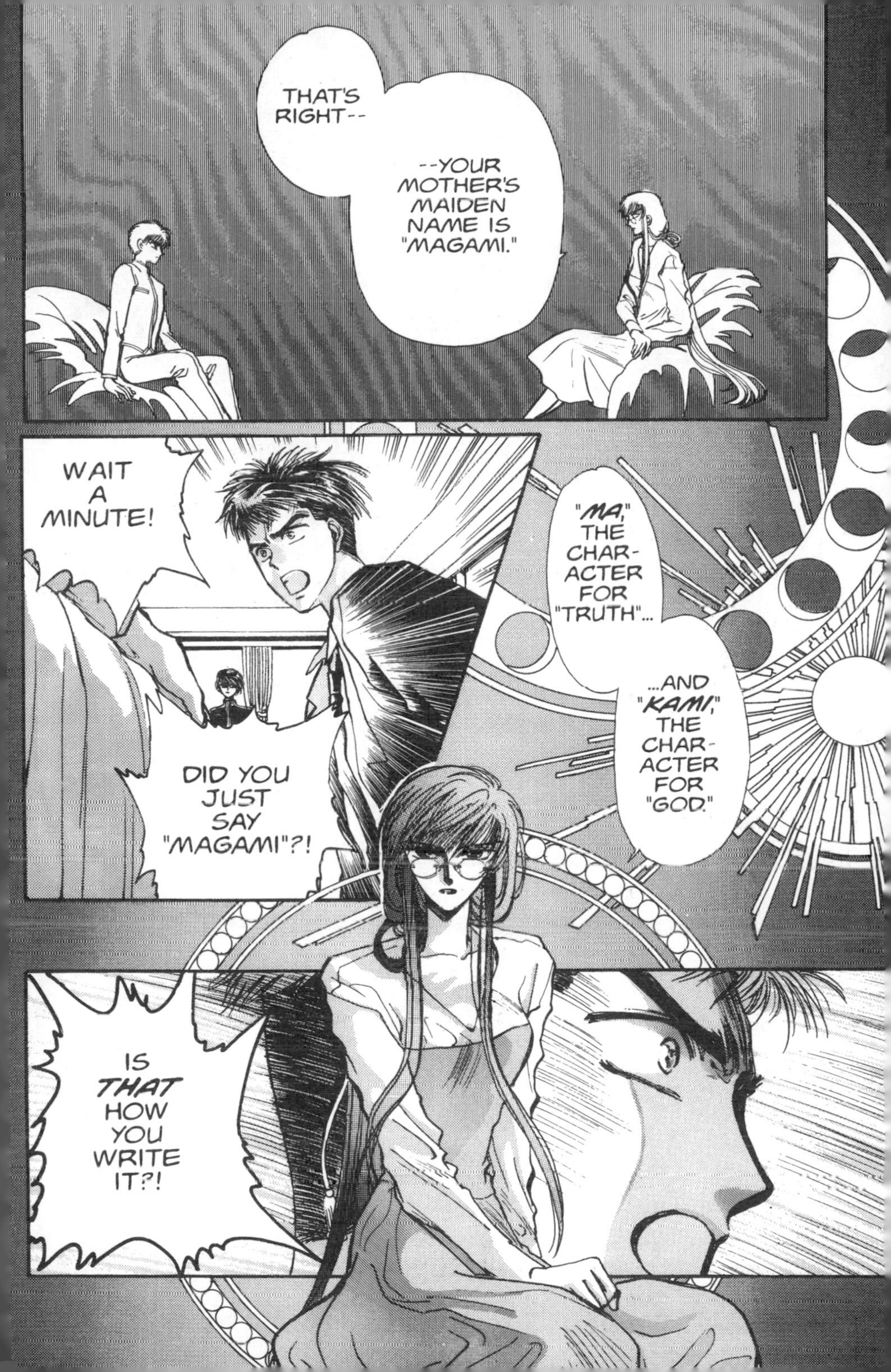
THAT'S RIGHT--
--YOUR MOTHER'S MAIDEN NAME IS "MAGAMI."
WAIT A MINUTE!
DID YOU JUST SAY "MAGAMI"?!
"MA," THE CHAR-ACTER FOR "TRUTH"...
...AND "KAMI," THE CHAR-ACTER FOR "GOD."
IS THAT HOW YOU WRITE IT?!

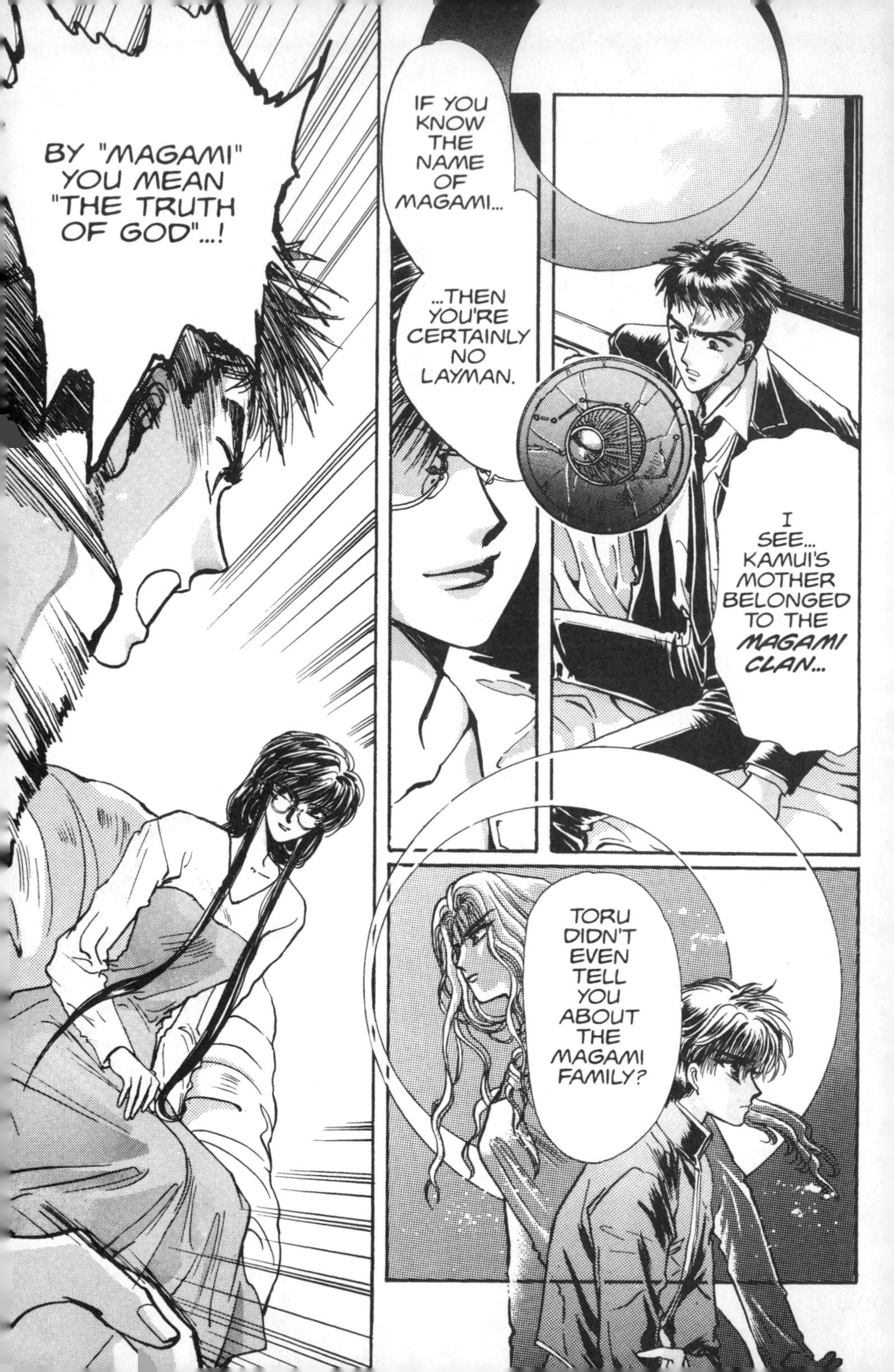
BY "MAGAMI" YOU MEAN "THE TRUTH OF GOD"...!
IF YOU KNOW THE NAME OF MAGAMI...
...THEN YOU'RE CERTAINLY NO LAYMAN.
I SEE... KAMUI'S MOTHER BELONGED TO THE *MAGAMI CLAN*...
TORU DIDN'T EVEN TELL YOU ABOUT THE MAGAMI FAMILY?

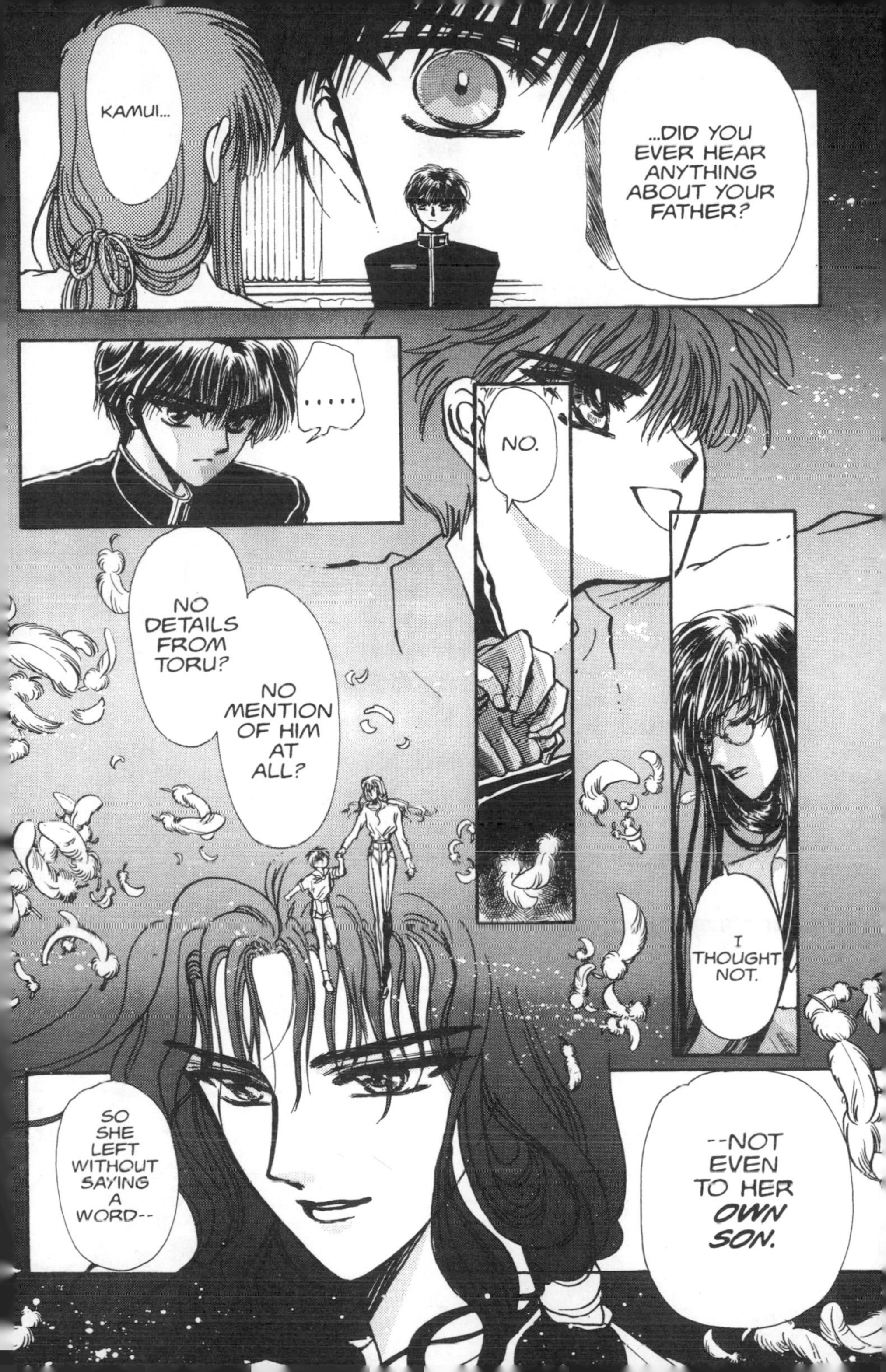
KAMUI...
...DID YOU EVER HEAR ANYTHING ABOUT YOUR FATHER?
......
NO.
NO DETAILS FROM TORU?
NO MENTION OF HIM AT ALL?
I THOUGHT NOT.
SO SHE LEFT WITHOUT SAYING A WORD--
--NOT EVEN TO HER *OWN SON.*

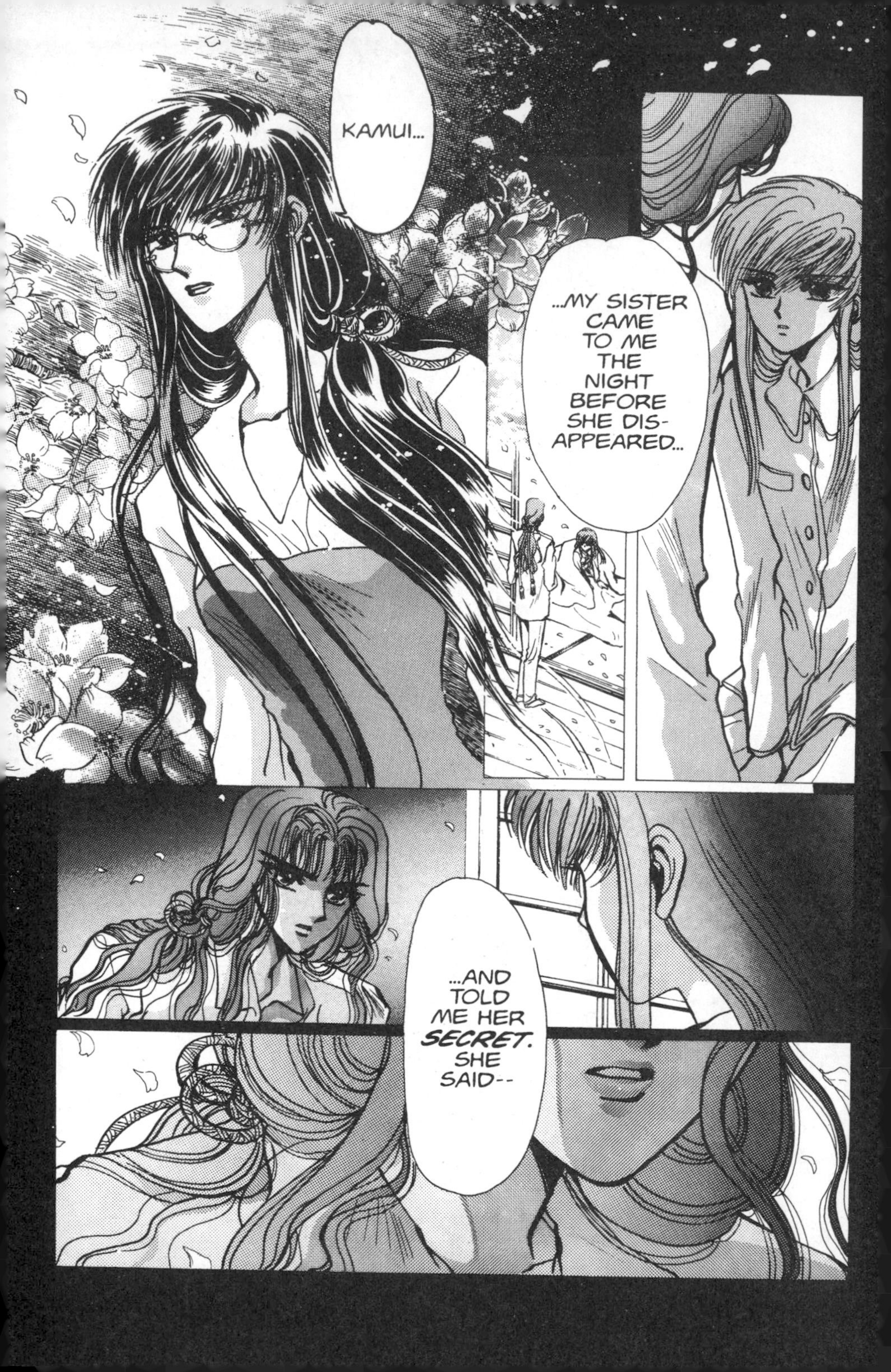
KAMUI...
...MY SISTER CAME TO ME THE NIGHT BEFORE SHE DIS-APPEARED...
...AND TOLD ME HER ***SECRET.*** SHE SAID--

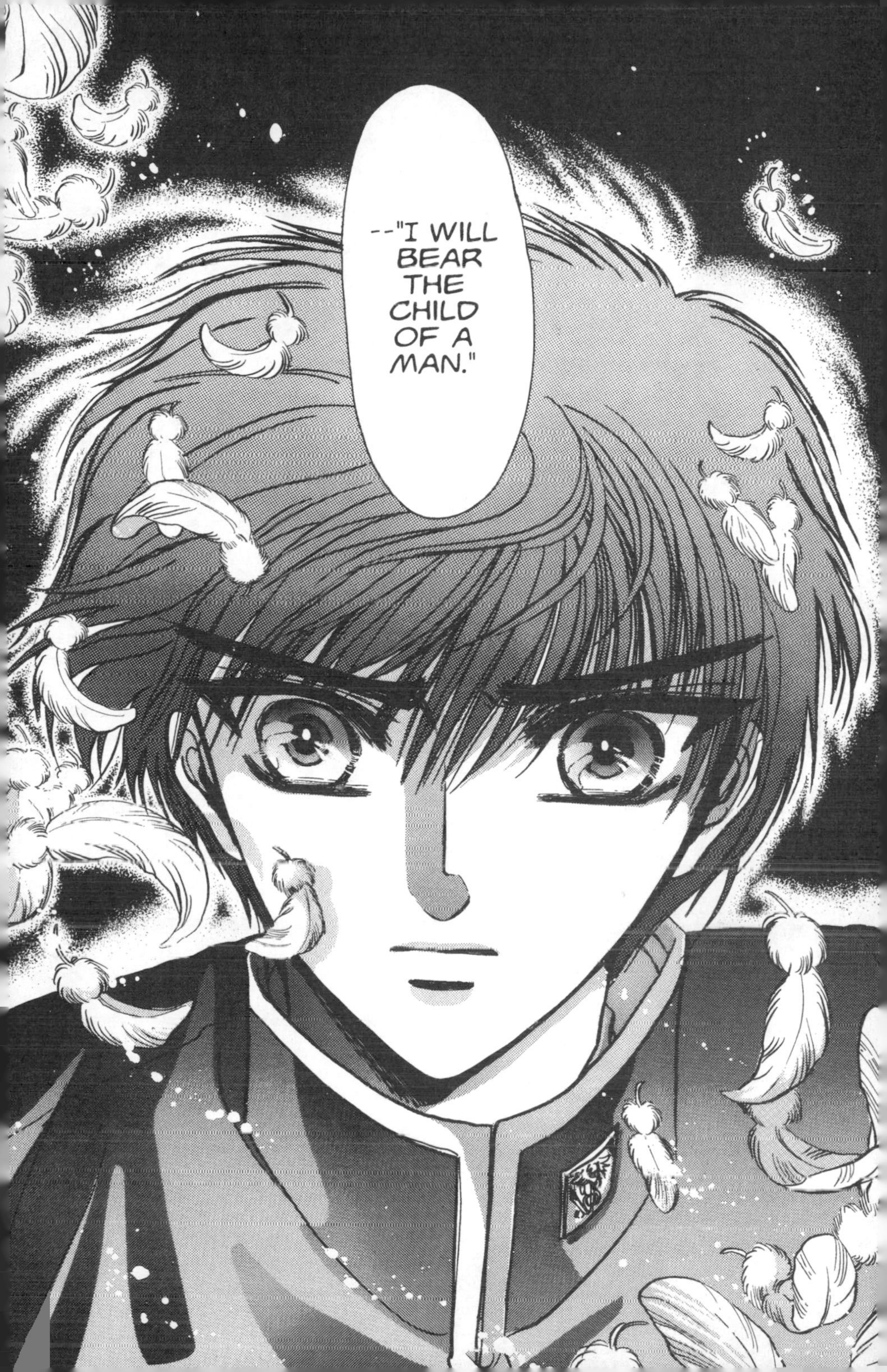
--"I WILL BEAR THE CHILD OF A MAN."

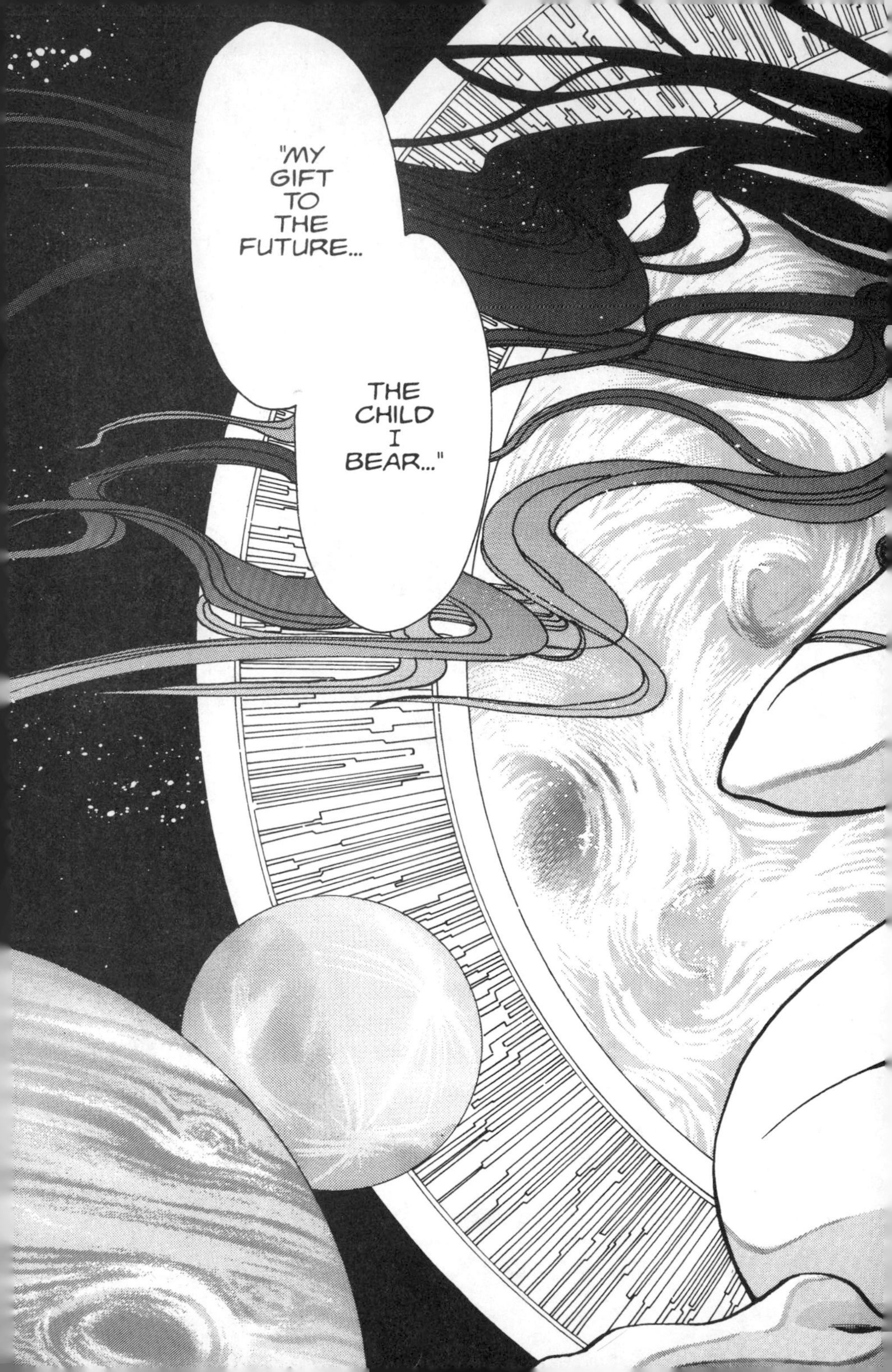
"MY GIFT TO THE FUTURE...
THE CHILD I BEAR..."

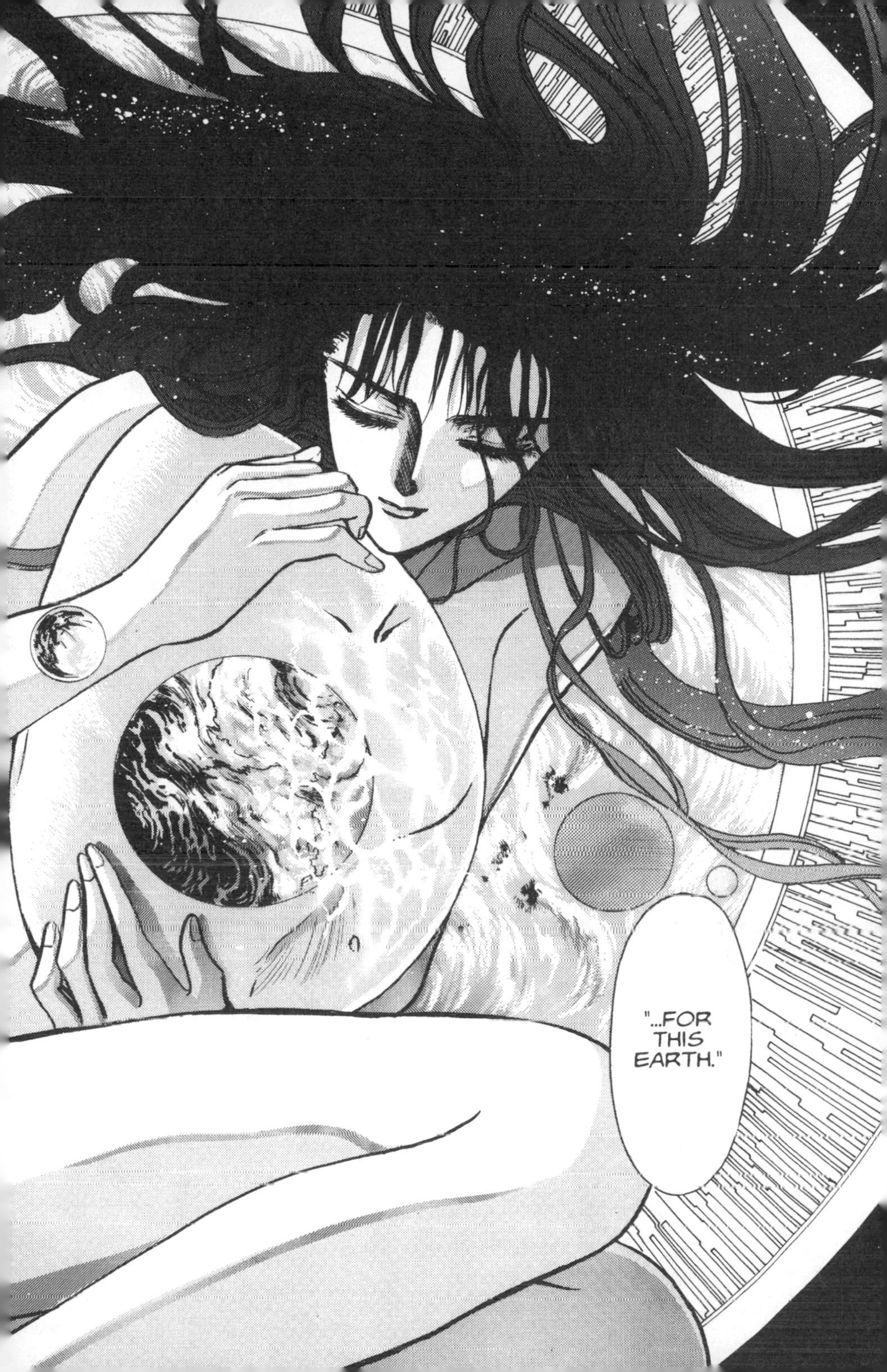
"...FOR THIS EARTH."

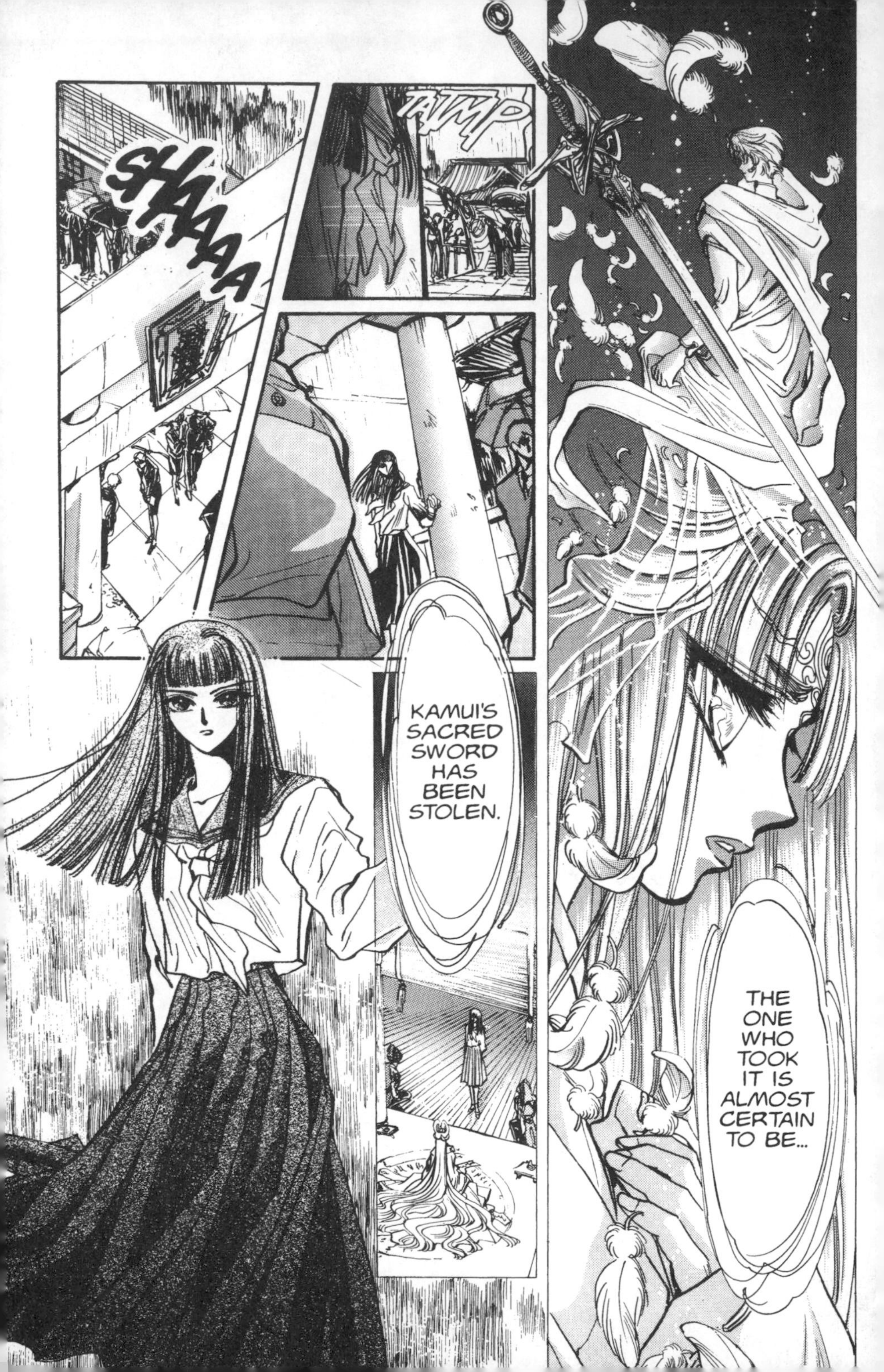
SHAAAA
TMP
KAMUI'S SACRED SWORD HAS BEEN STOLEN.
THE ONE WHO TOOK IT IS ALMOST CERTAIN TO BE...

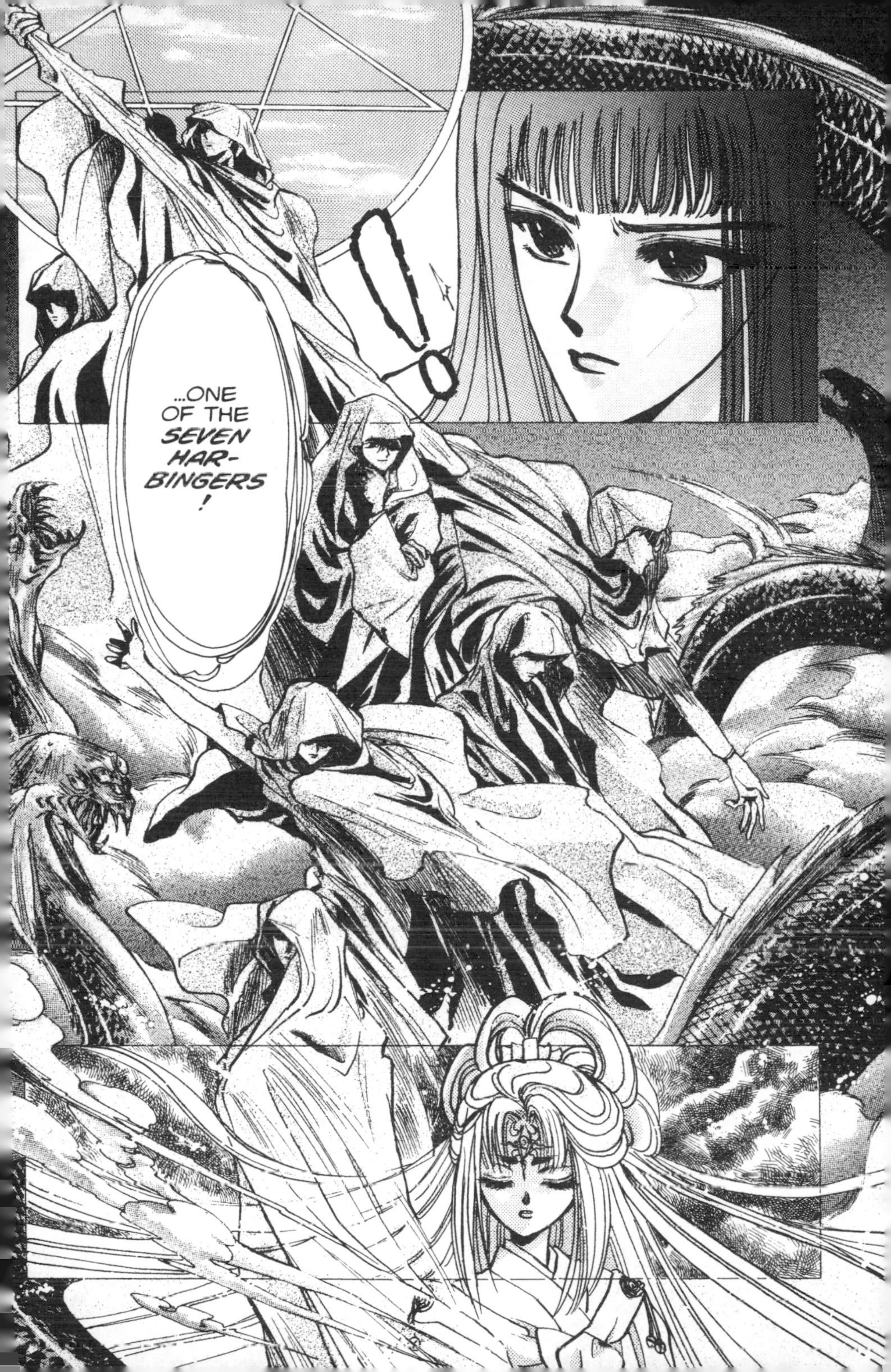
...ONE OF THE SEVEN HAR-BINGERS!

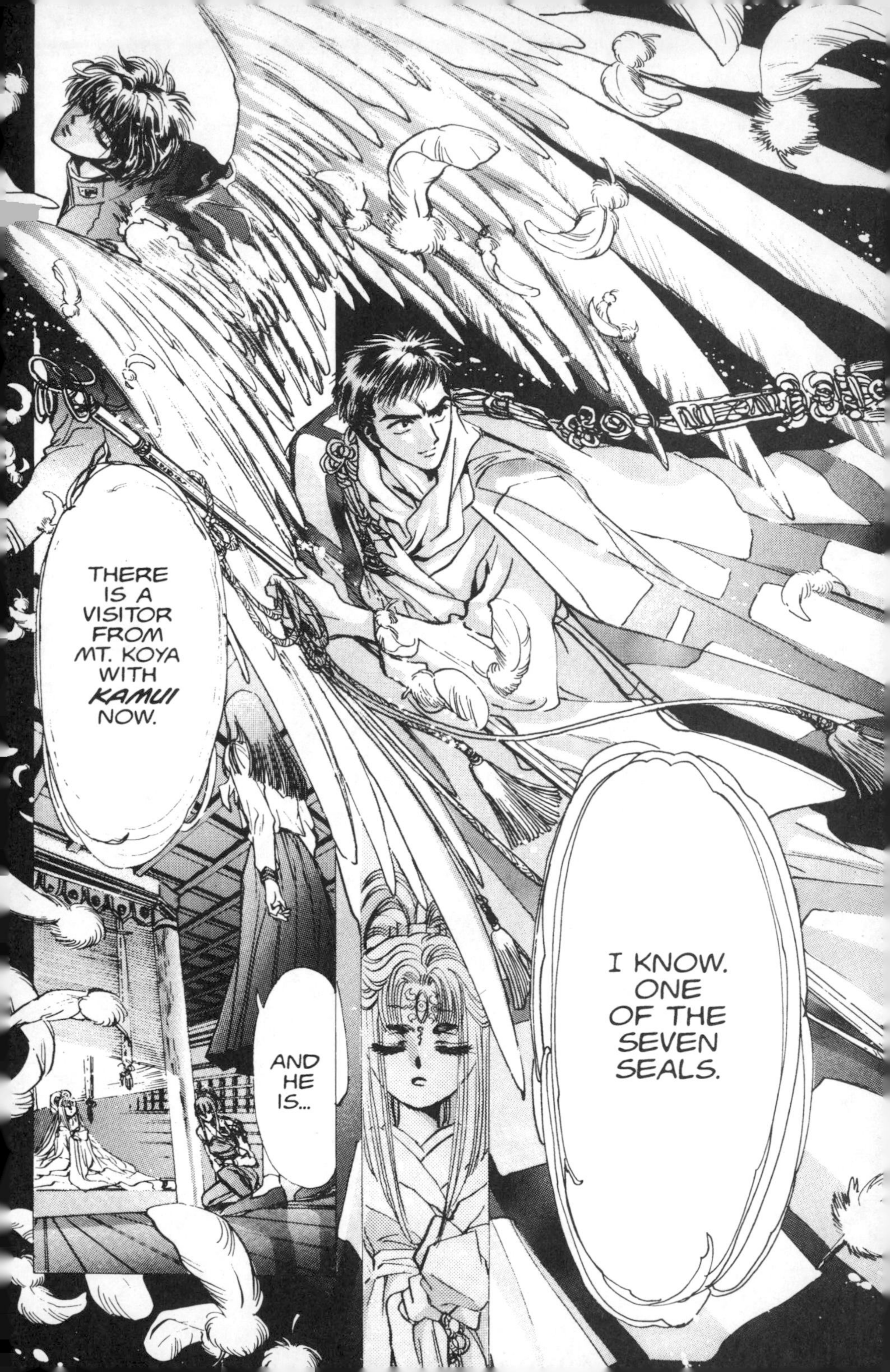
THERE IS A VISITOR FROM MT. KOYA WITH *KAMUI* NOW.
AND HE IS...
I KNOW. ONE OF THE SEVEN SEALS.

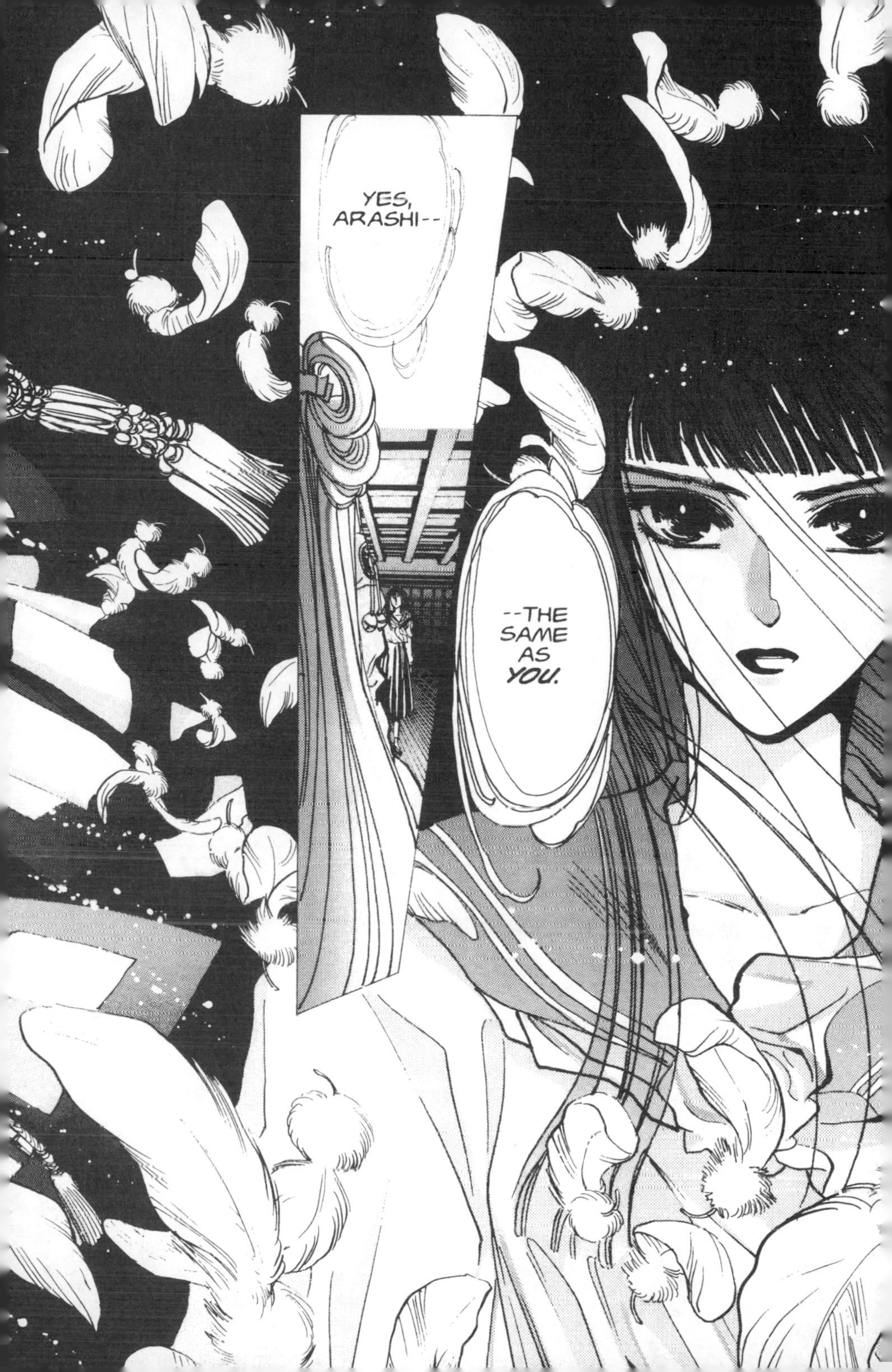
YES, ARASHI--
--THE SAME AS *YOU*.

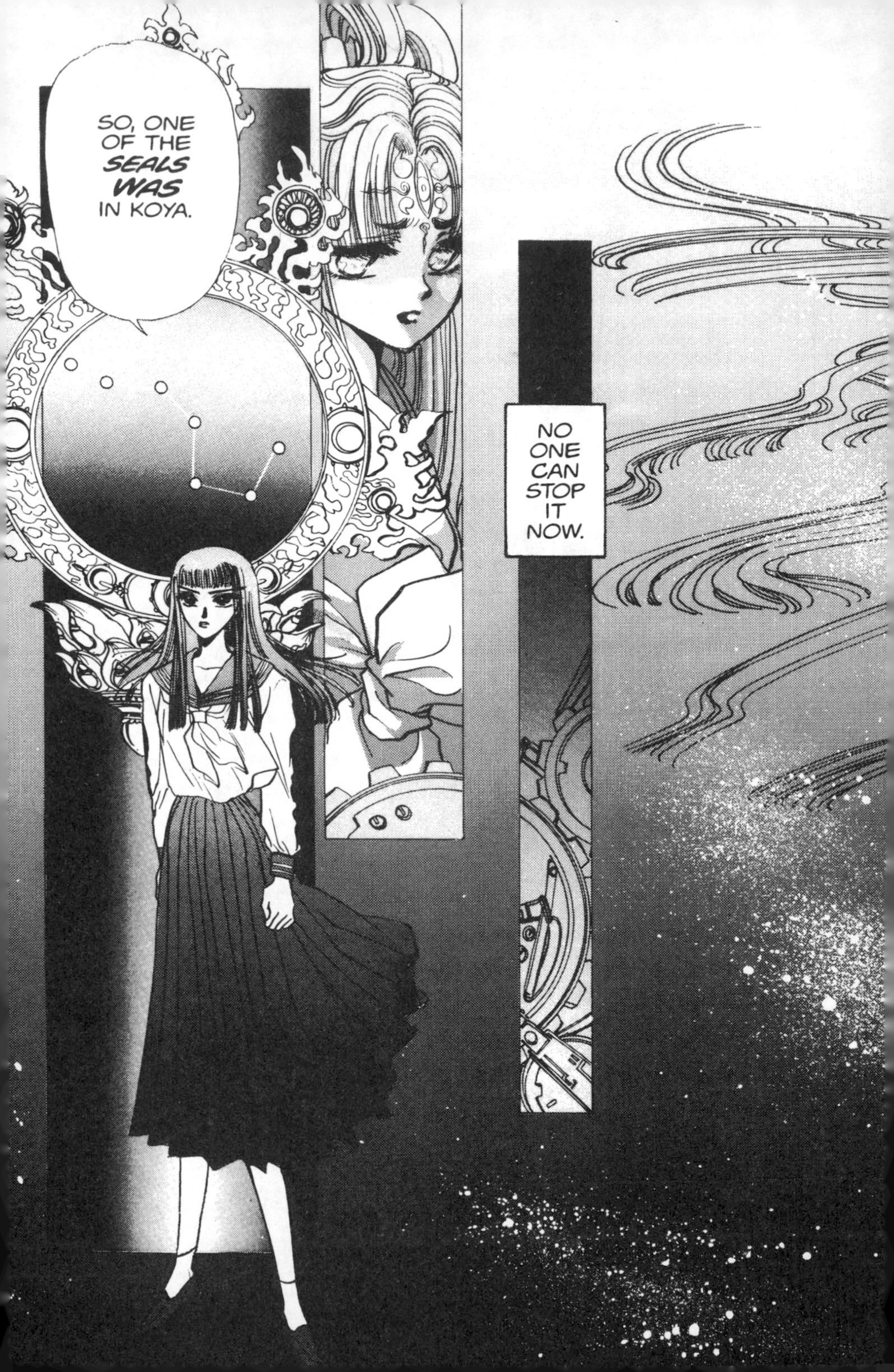
SO, ONE OF THE *SEALS WAS* IN KOYA.
NO ONE CAN STOP IT NOW.

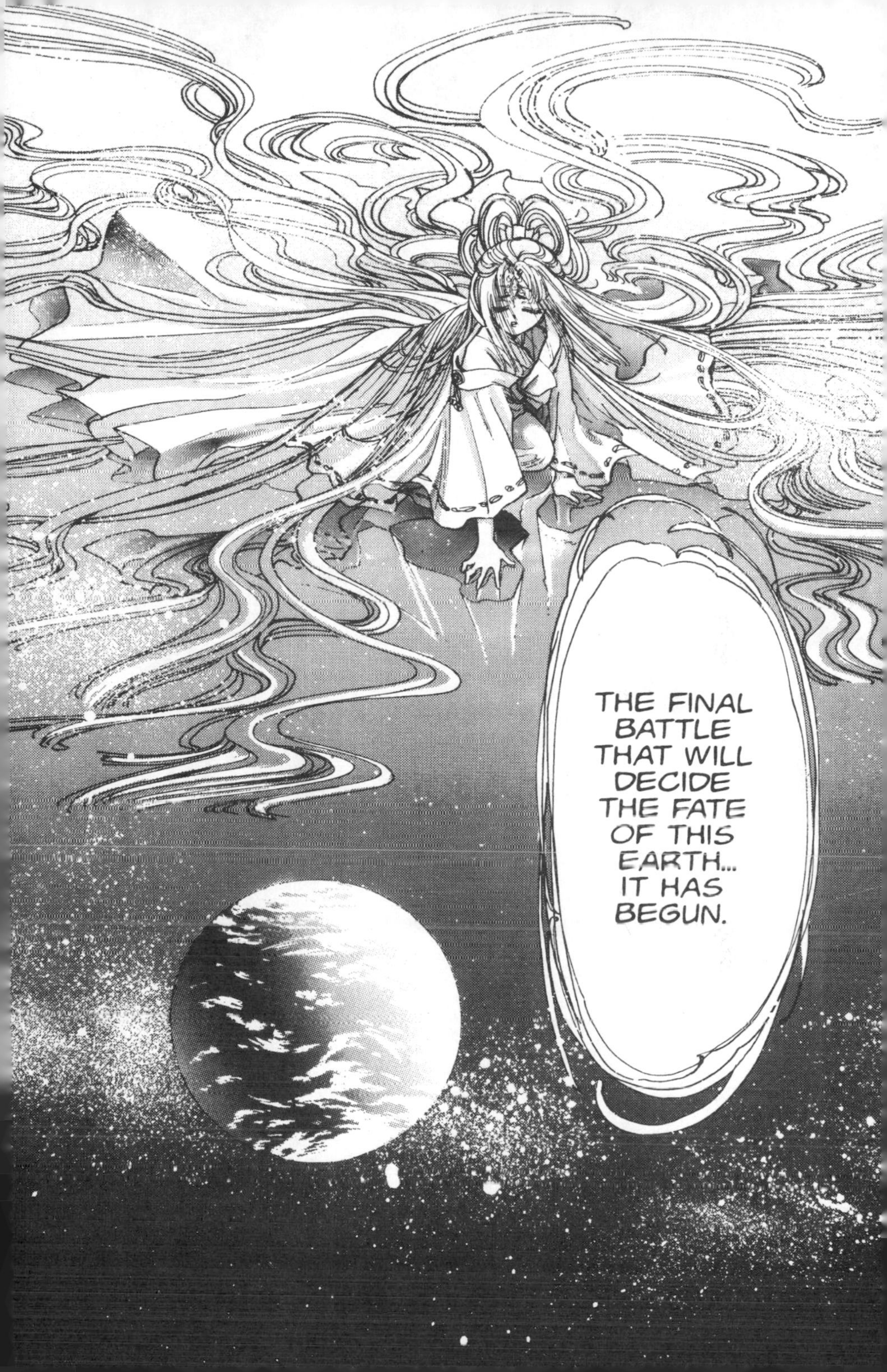
THE FINAL BATTLE THAT WILL DECIDE THE FATE OF THIS EARTH... IT HAS BEGUN.

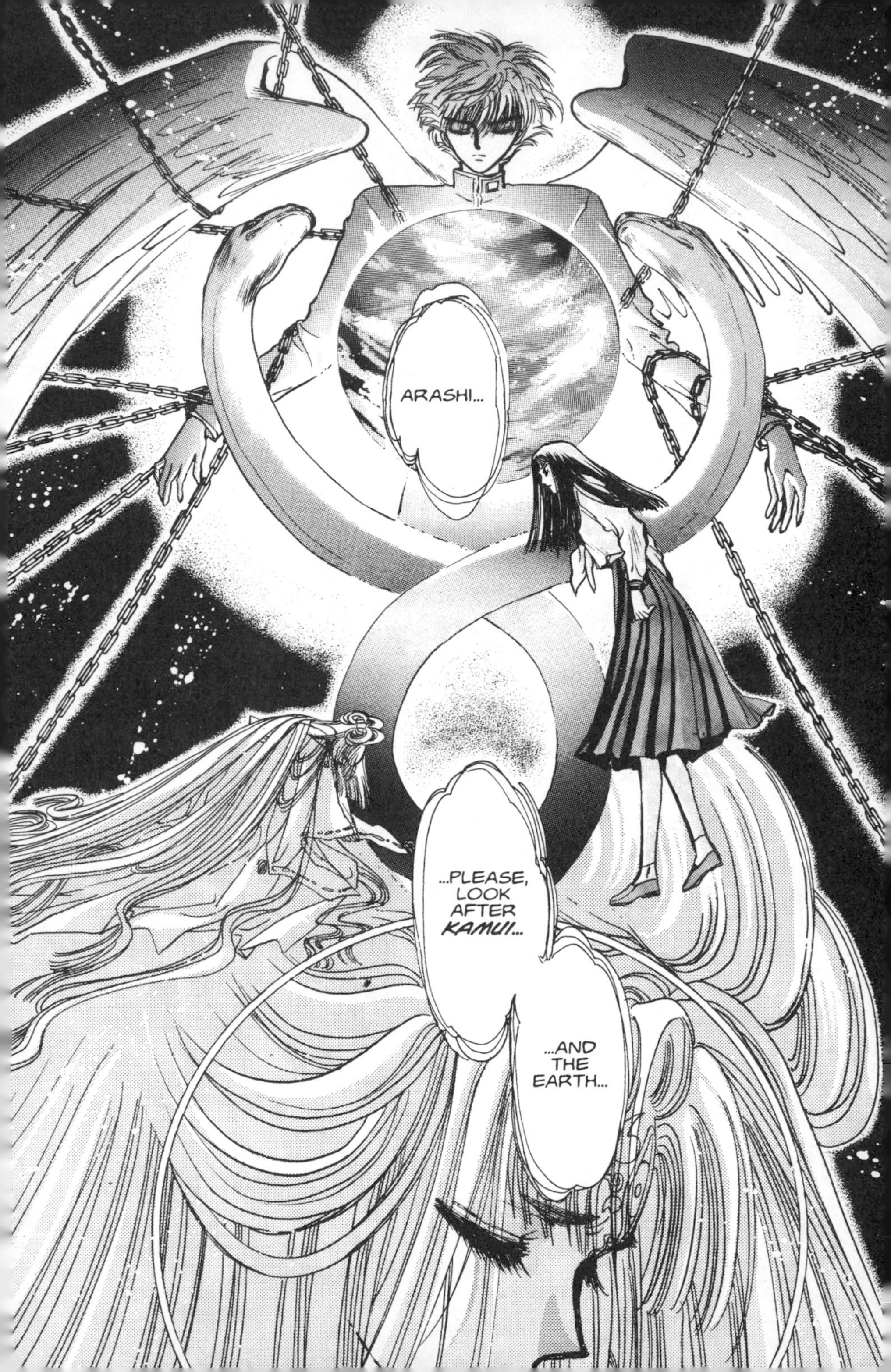
ARASHI...
...PLEASE, LOOK AFTER *KAMUI*...
...AND THE EARTH...

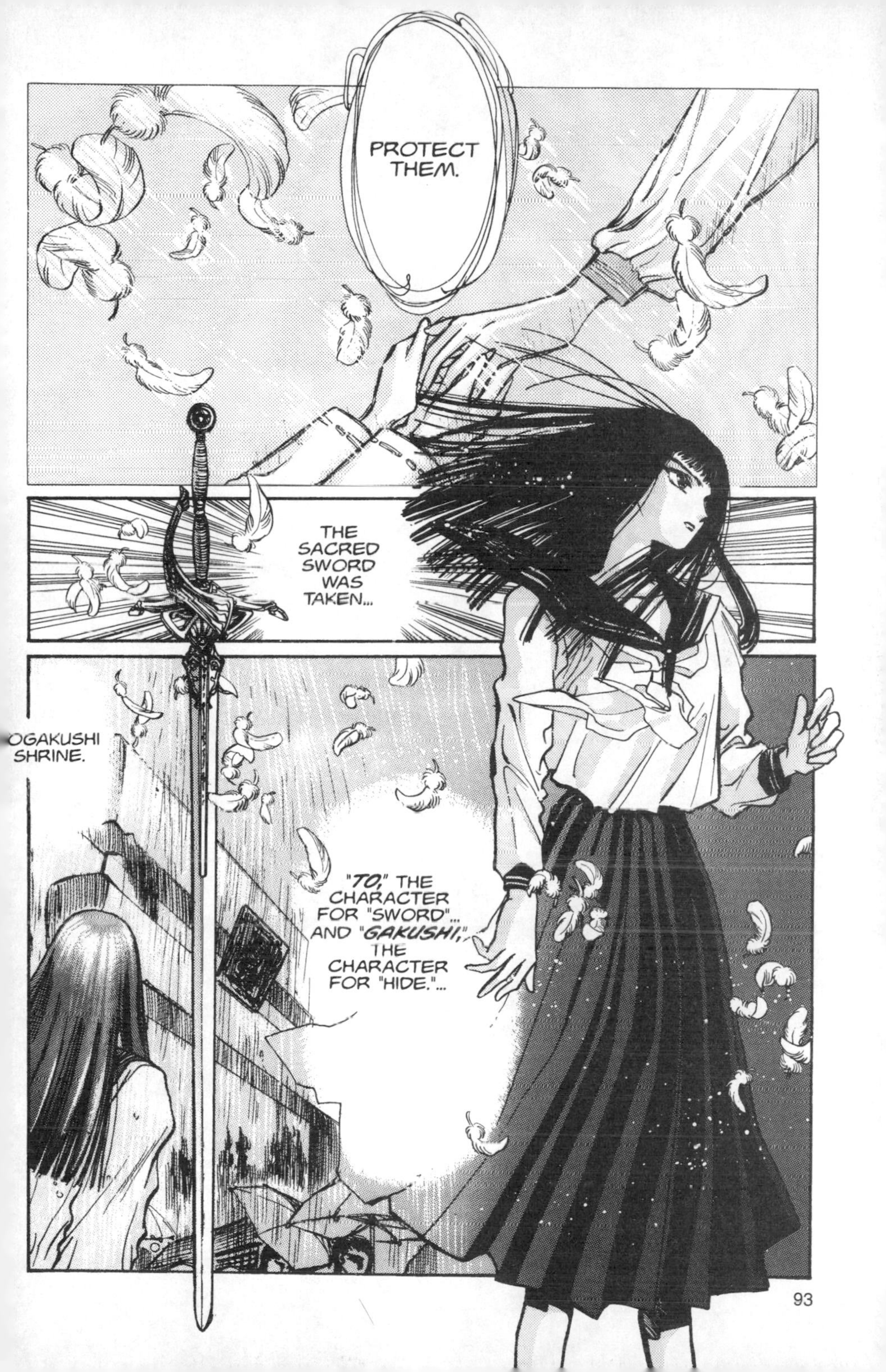
PROTECT THEM.
THE SACRED SWORD WAS TAKEN...
OGAKUSHI SHRINE.
"TO," THE CHARACTER FOR "SWORD"... AND "GAKUSHI," THE CHARACTER FOR "HIDE."...

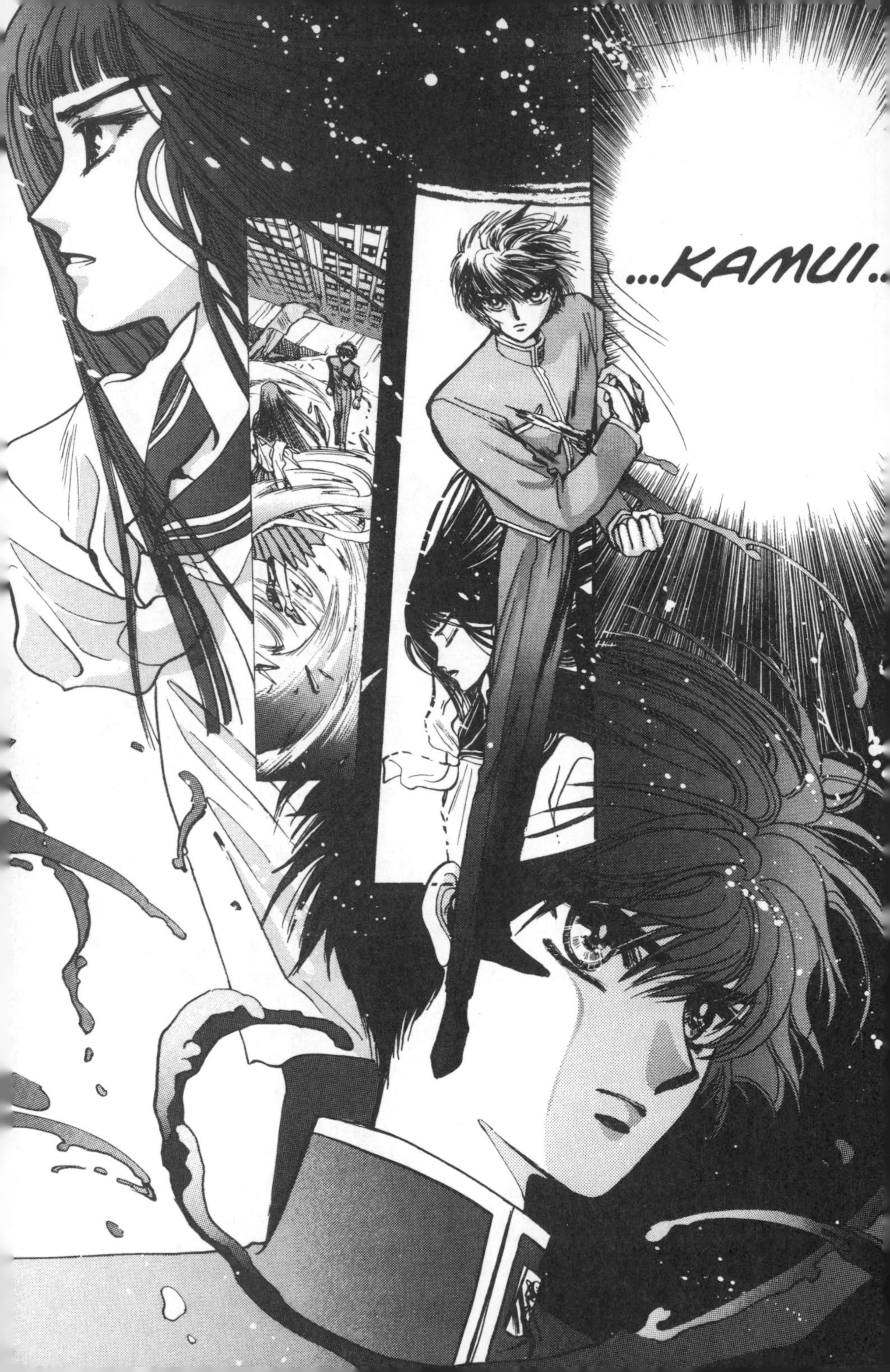
...KAMUI...

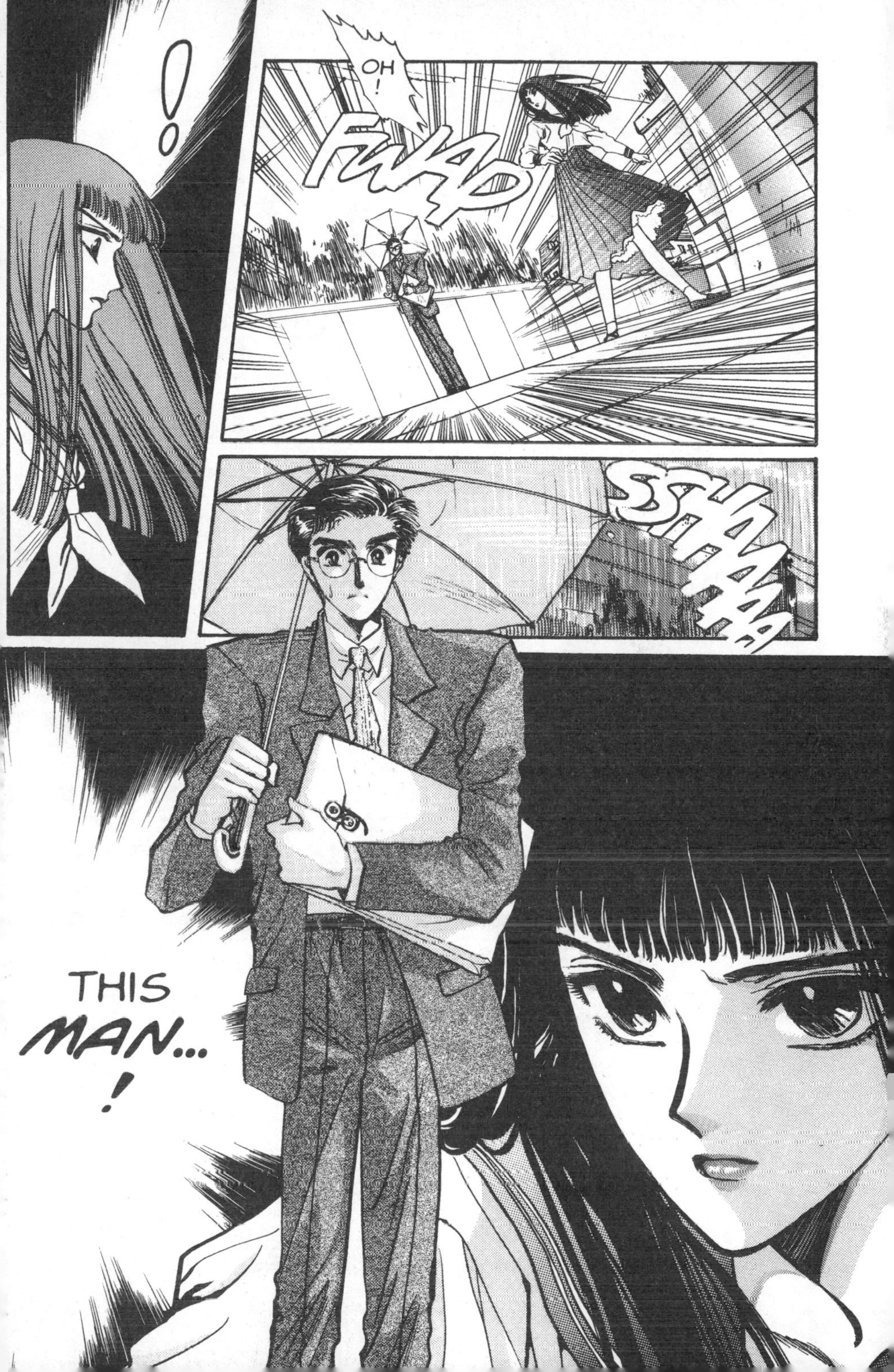
OH !
FWAP
!
SSHAAA
THIS MAN... !

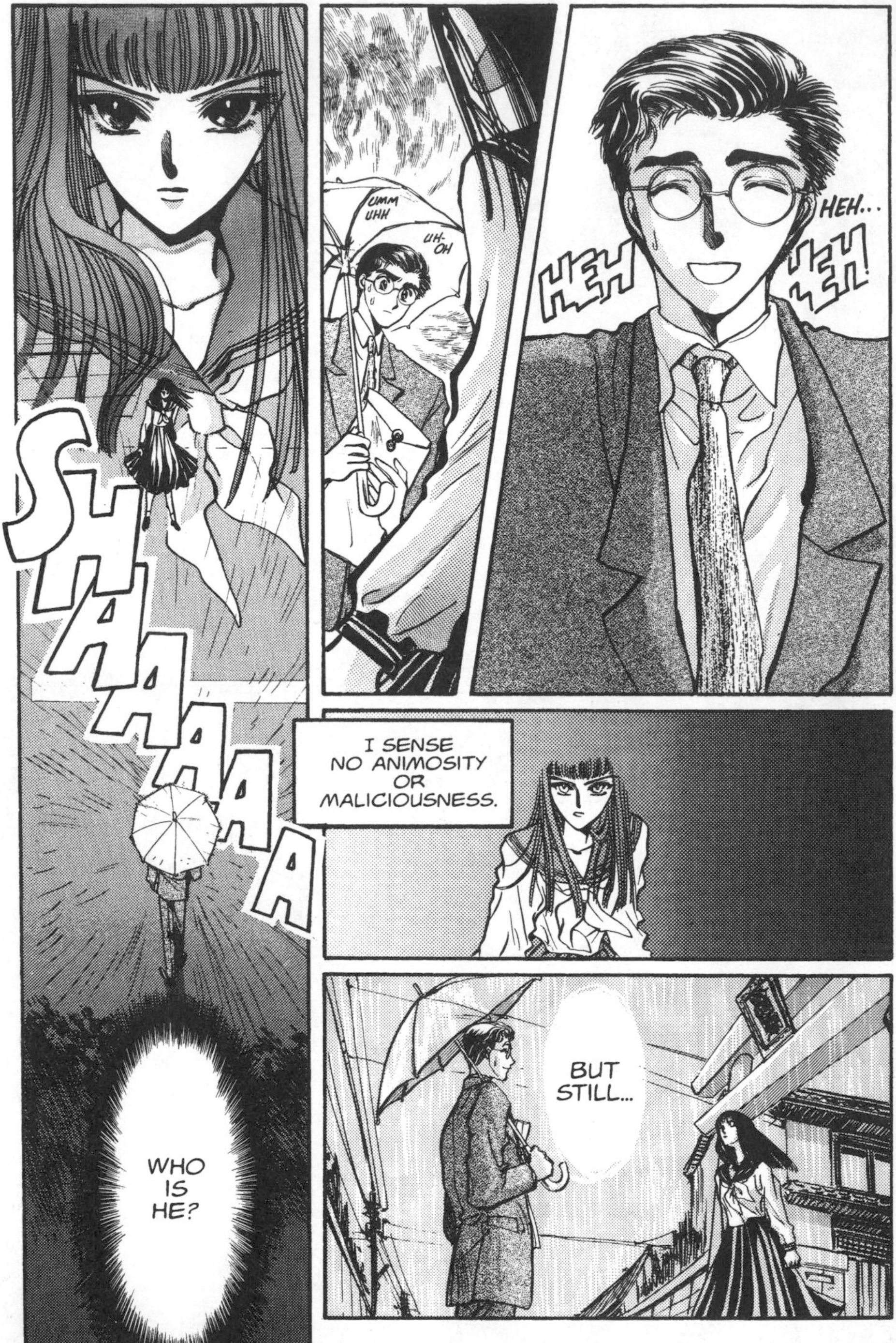
SHAAAAAAA
WHO IS HE?
UMM UHH
UH-OH
HEH...
HEH
HEH!
I SENSE NO ANIMOSITY OR MALICIOUSNESS.
BUT STILL...

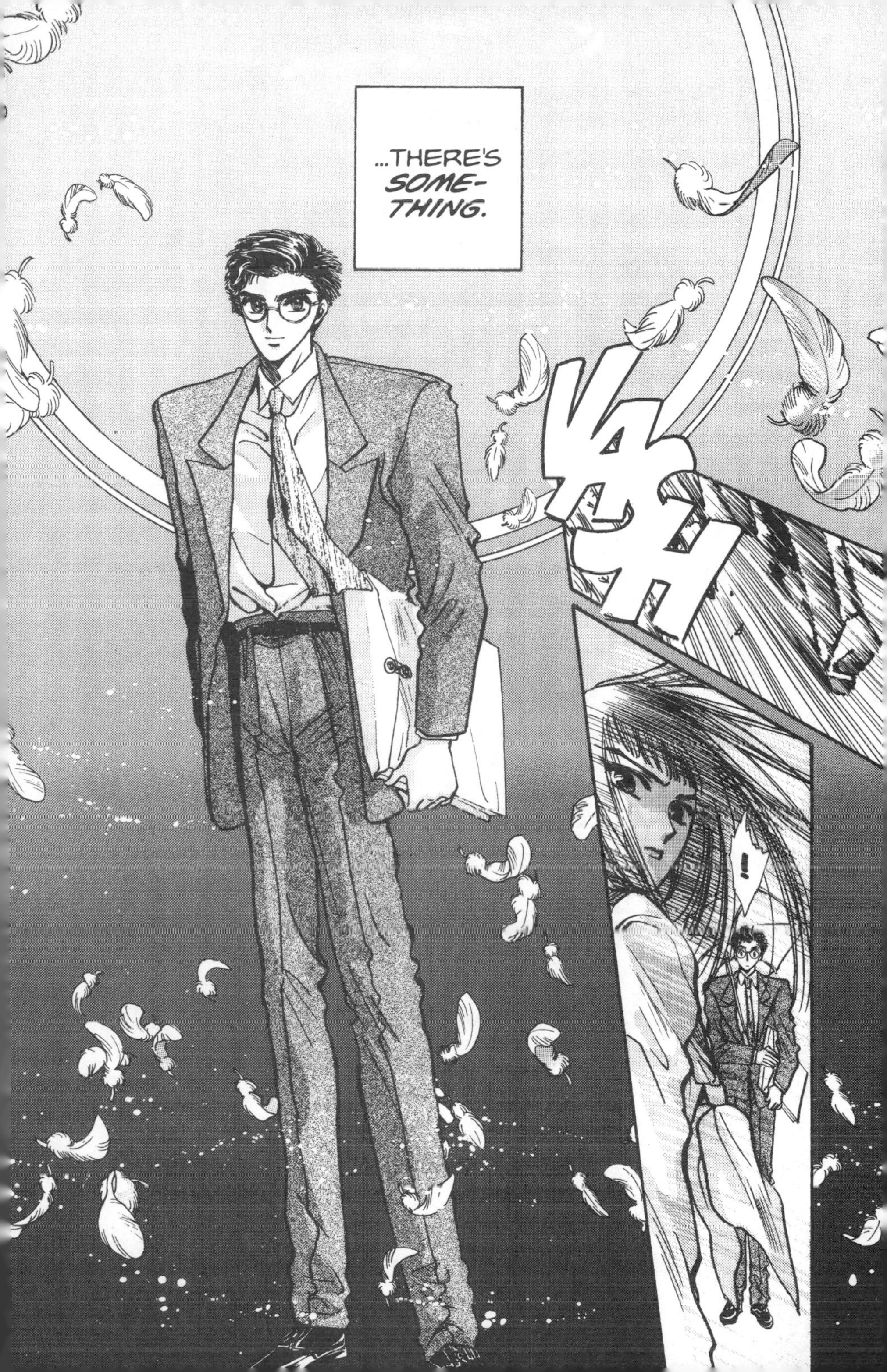
...THERE'S SOME-THING.
!

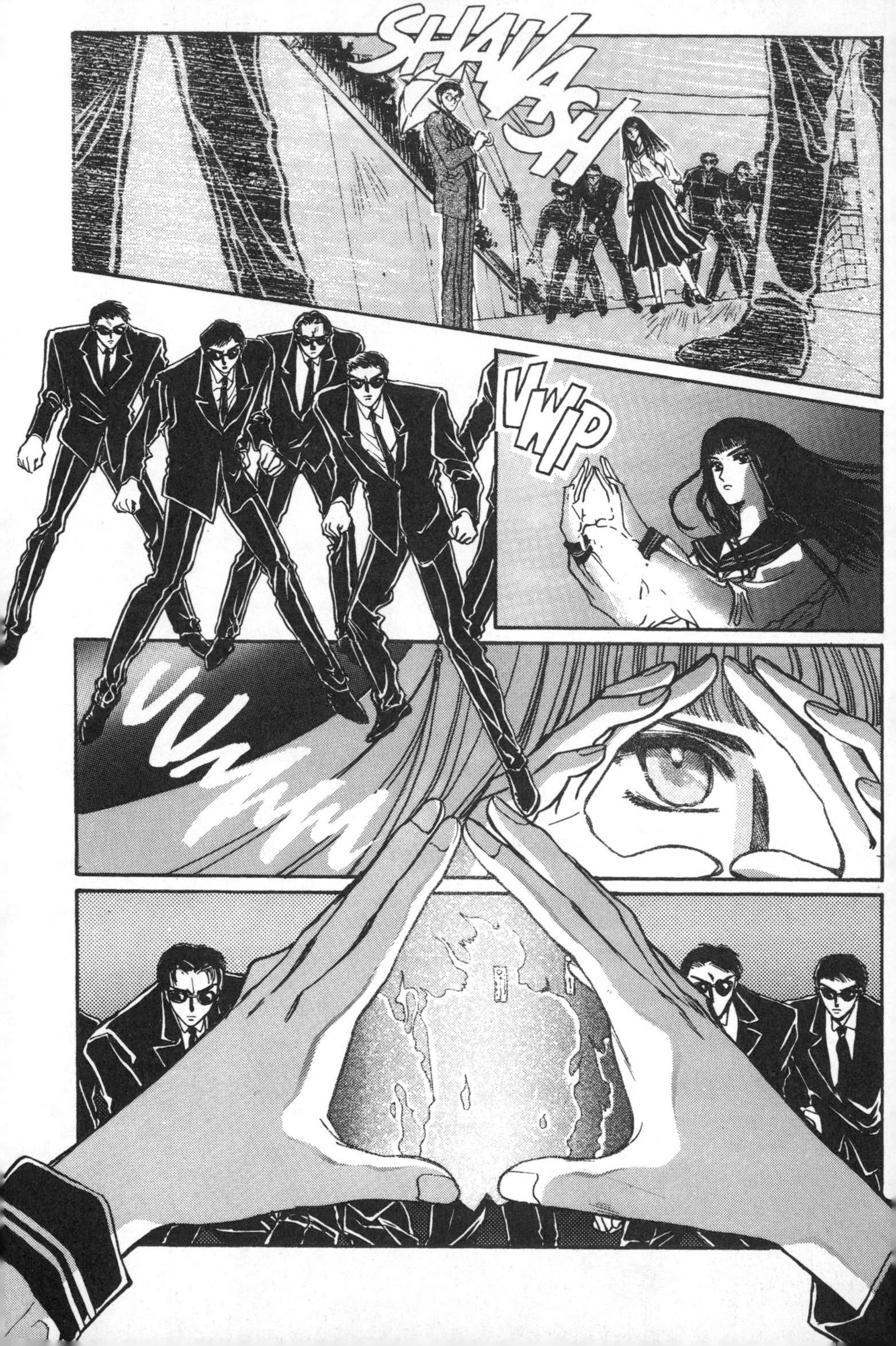
SHAVASH
VWIP
VVMMM

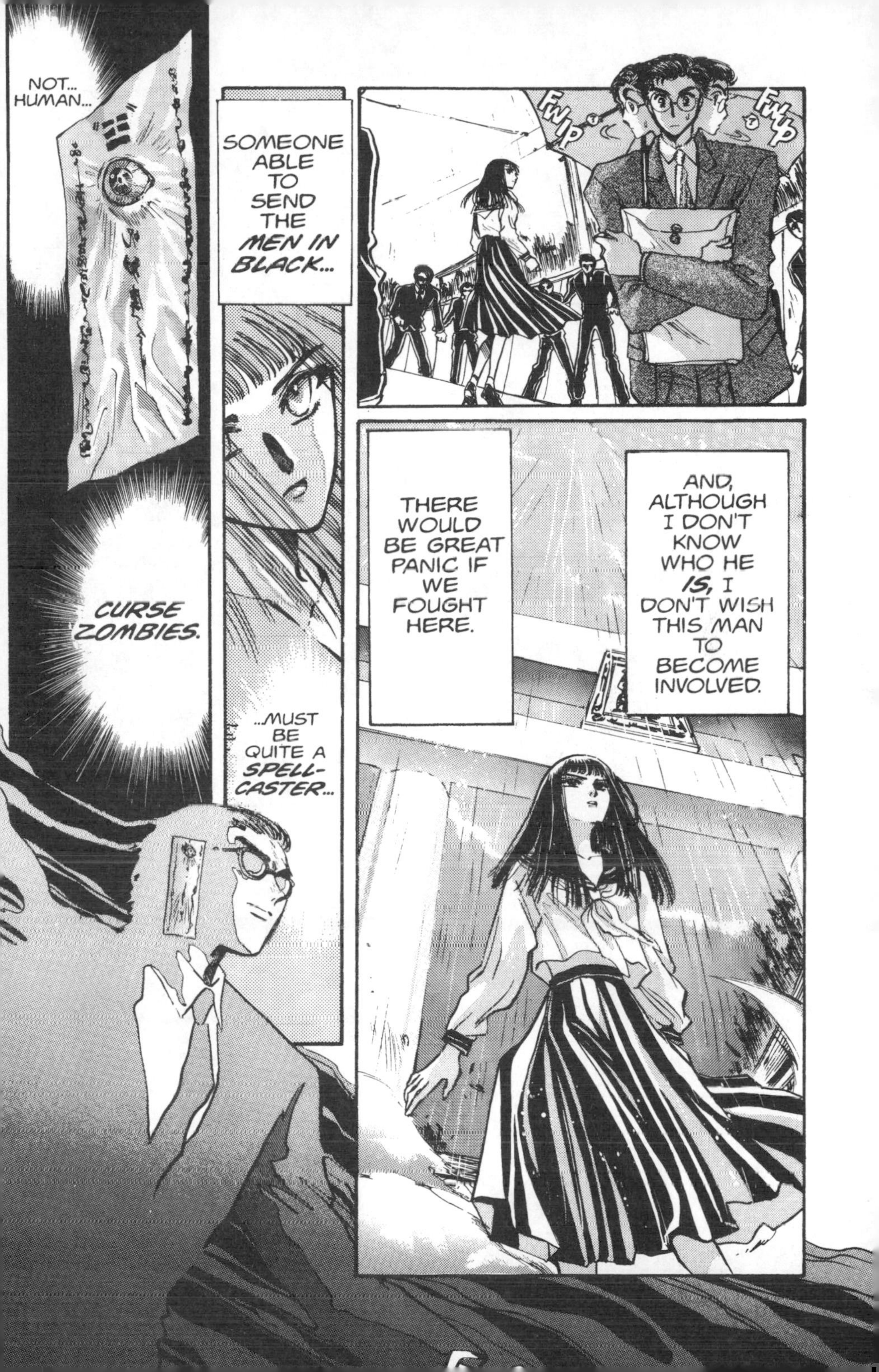
NOT... HUMAN...
CURSE ZOMBIES.
SOMEONE ABLE TO SEND THE MEN IN BLACK...
...MUST BE QUITE A SPELL-CASTER...
FWIP
FWIP
THERE WOULD BE GREAT PANIC IF WE FOUGHT HERE.
AND, ALTHOUGH I DON'T KNOW WHO HE IS, I DON'T WISH THIS MAN TO BECOME INVOLVED.

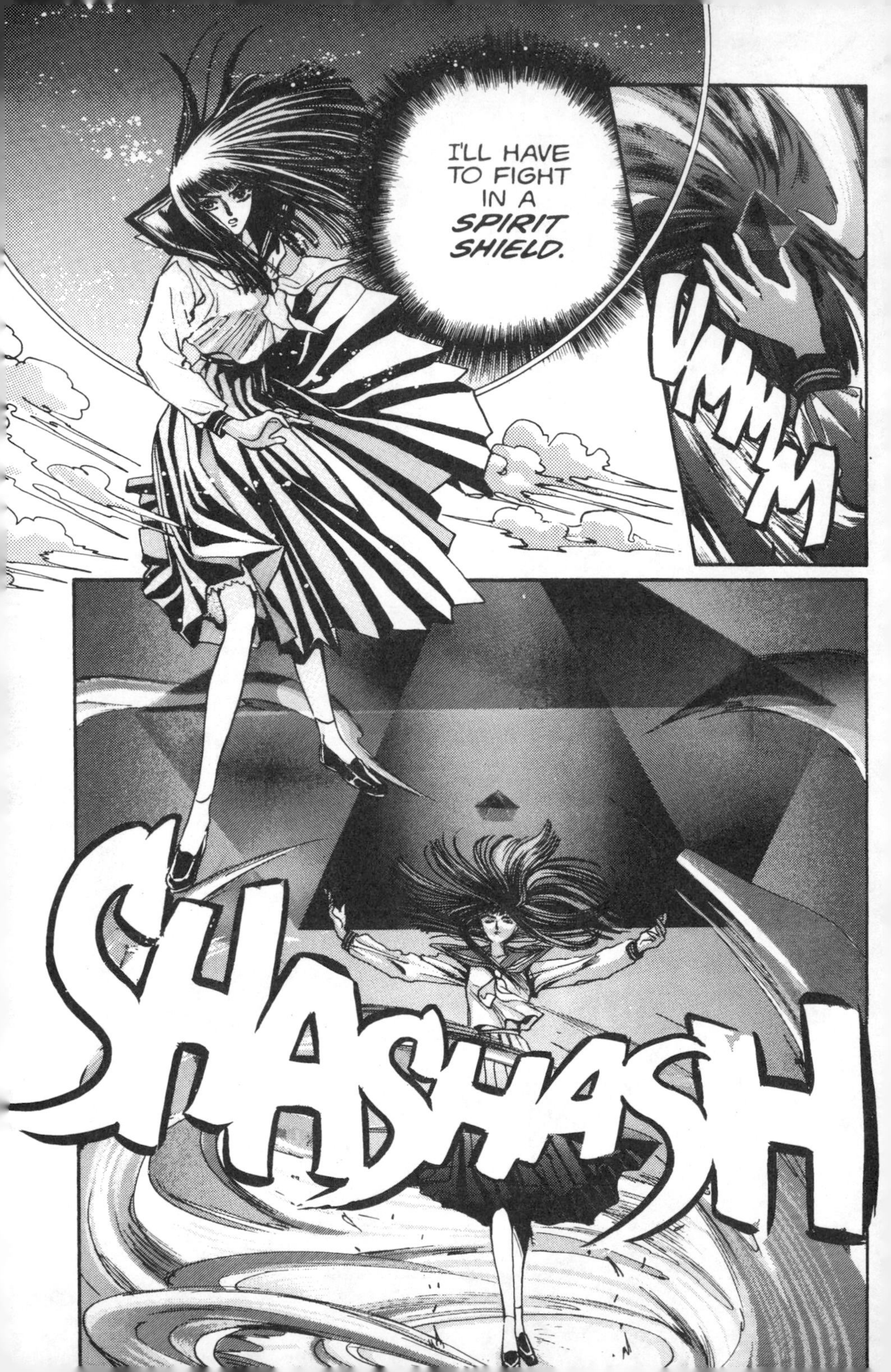
I'LL HAVE TO FIGHT IN A *SPIRIT SHIELD.*
UMMM
SHASHASH

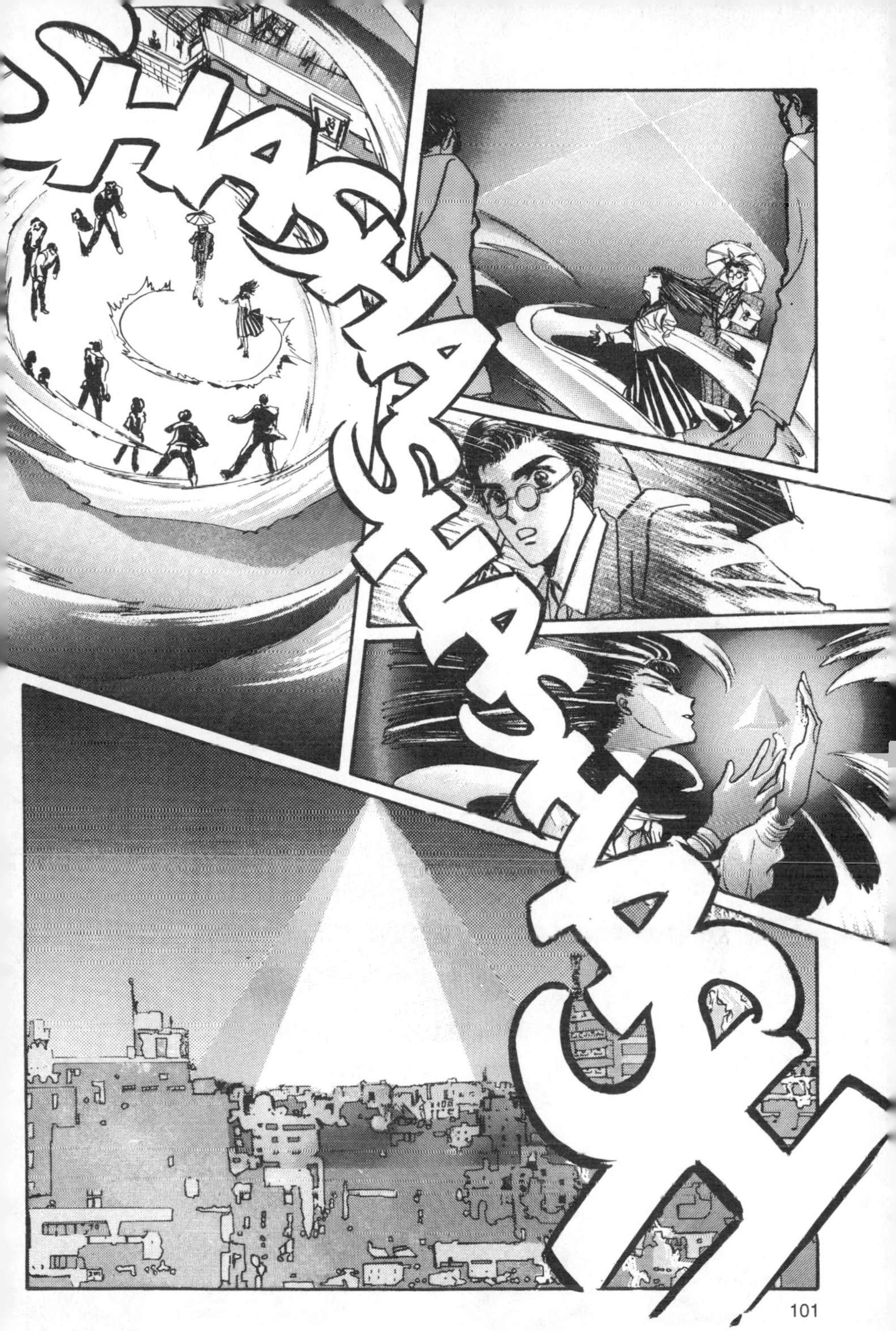

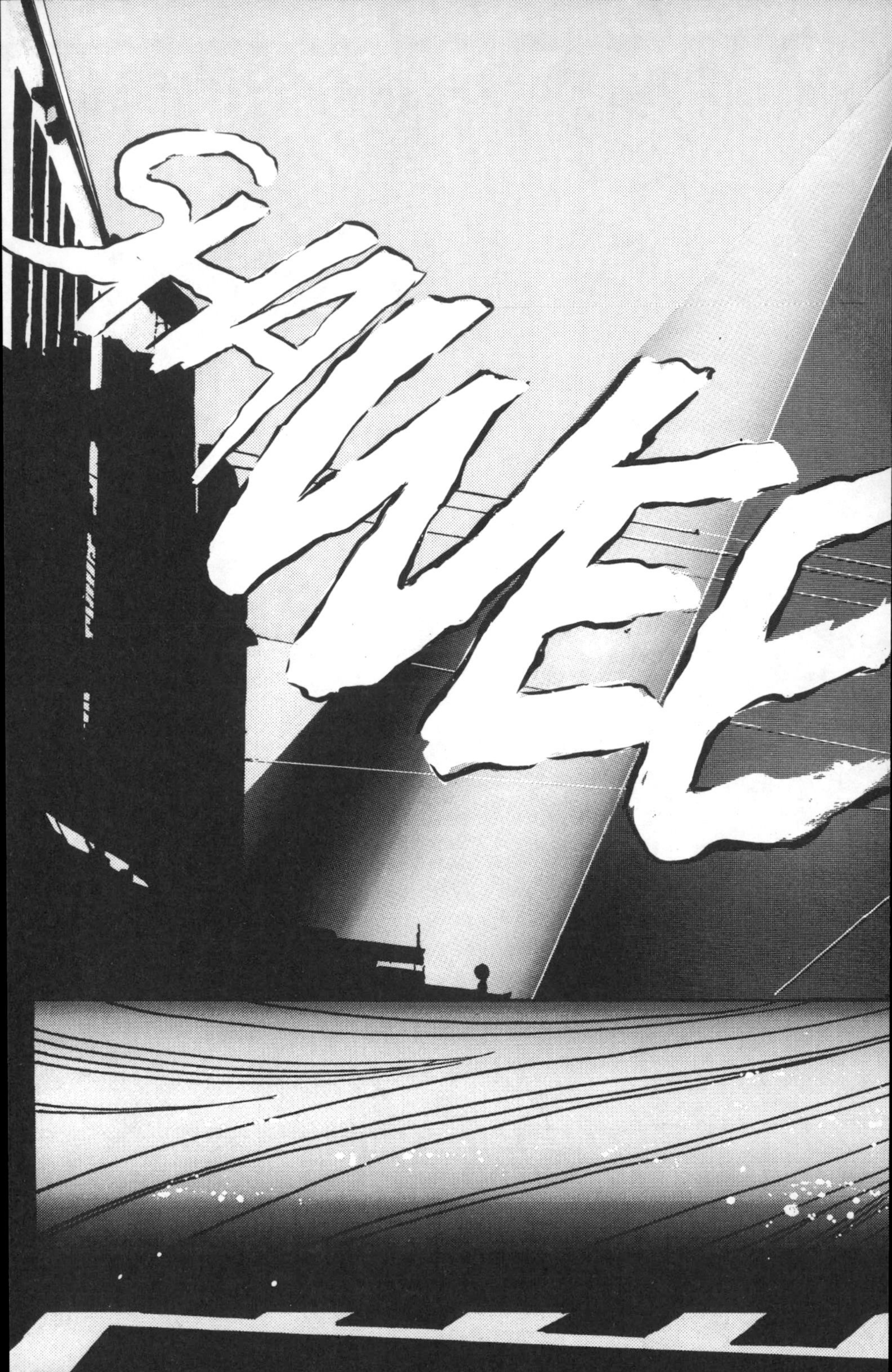
SHWEE

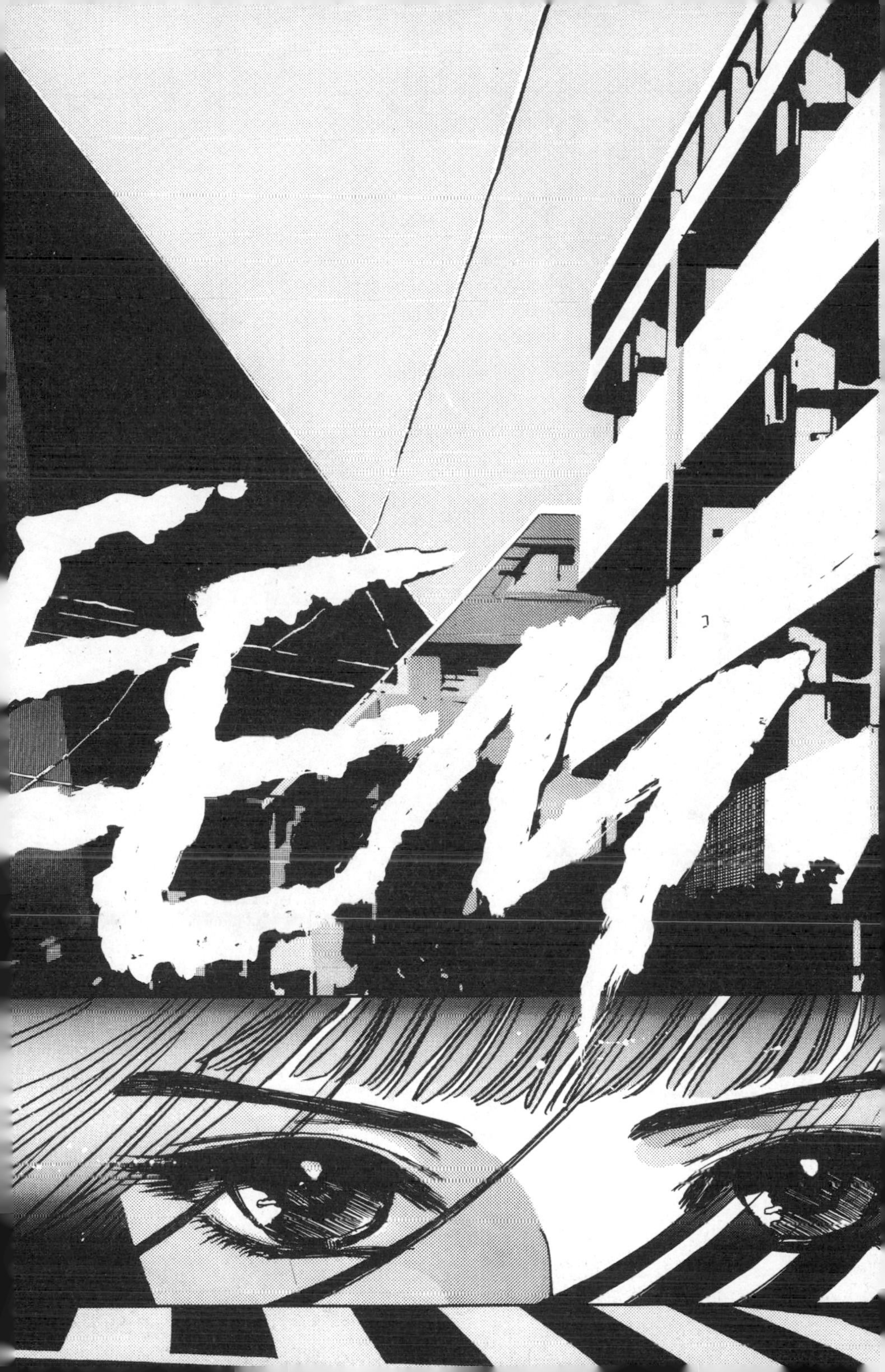

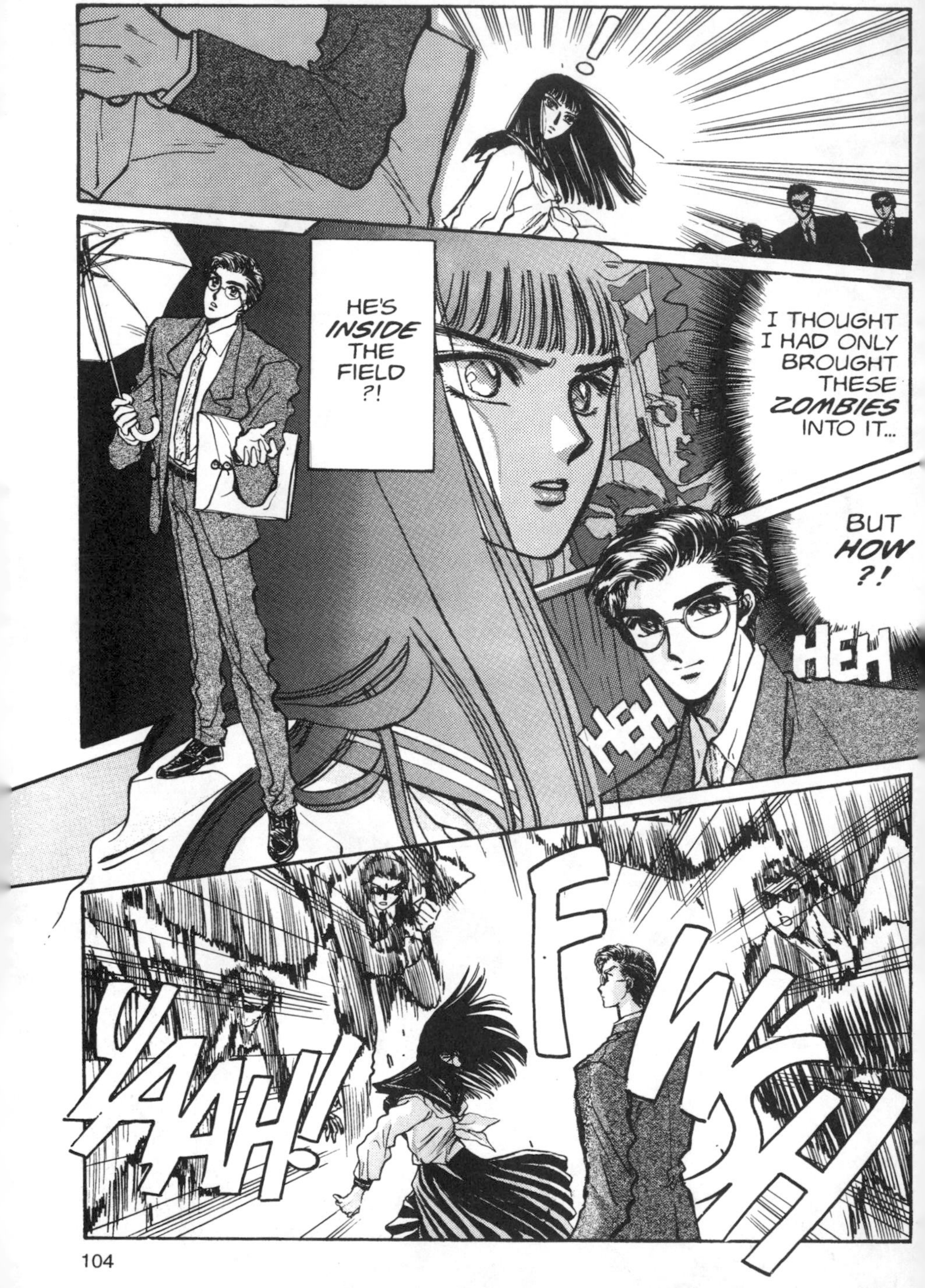
!
HE'S *INSIDE* THE FIELD ?!
I THOUGHT I HAD ONLY BROUGHT THESE *ZOMBIES* INTO IT...
BUT *HOW* ?!
HEH
HEH
YAAH!
FWSH

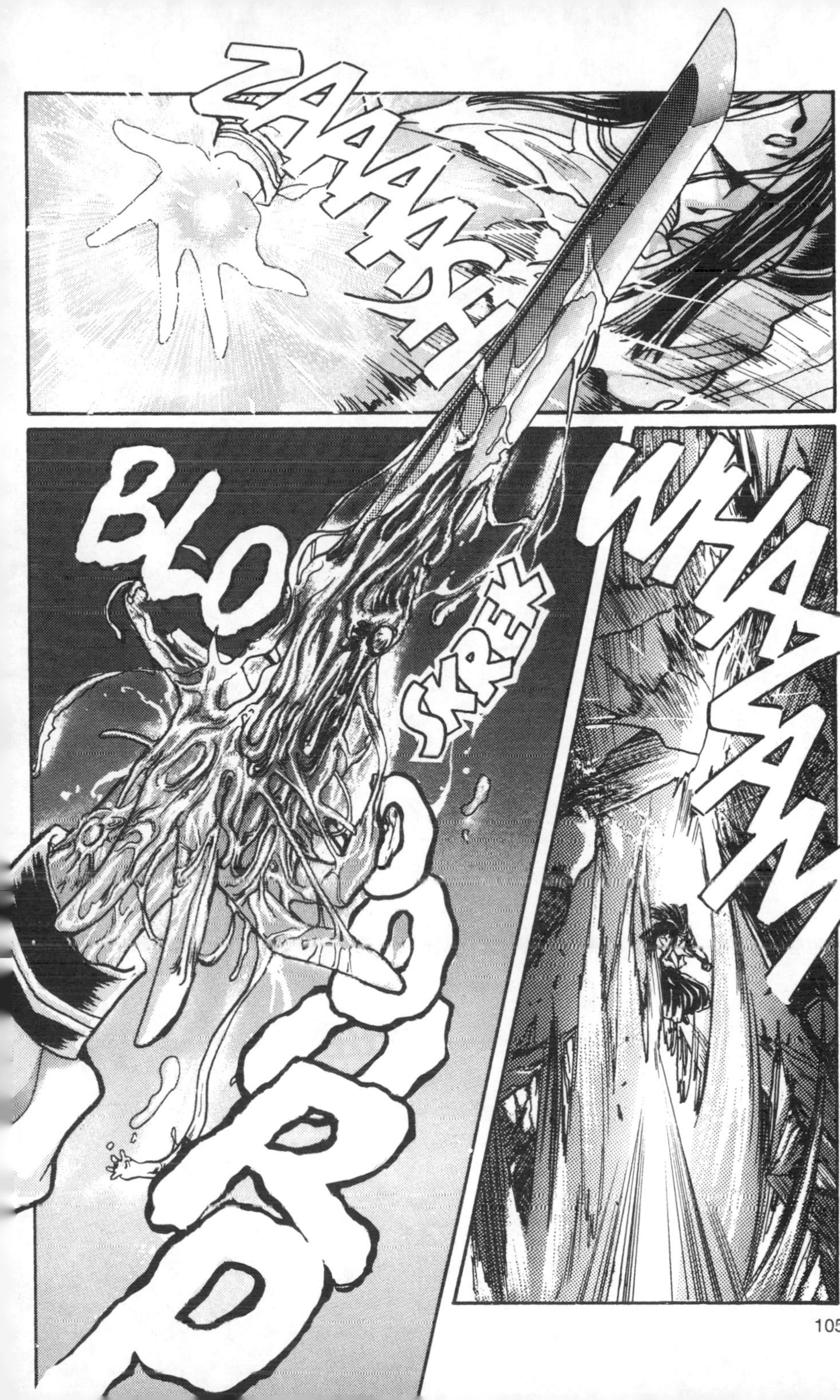
ZAAAASH!
BLO
SKREK

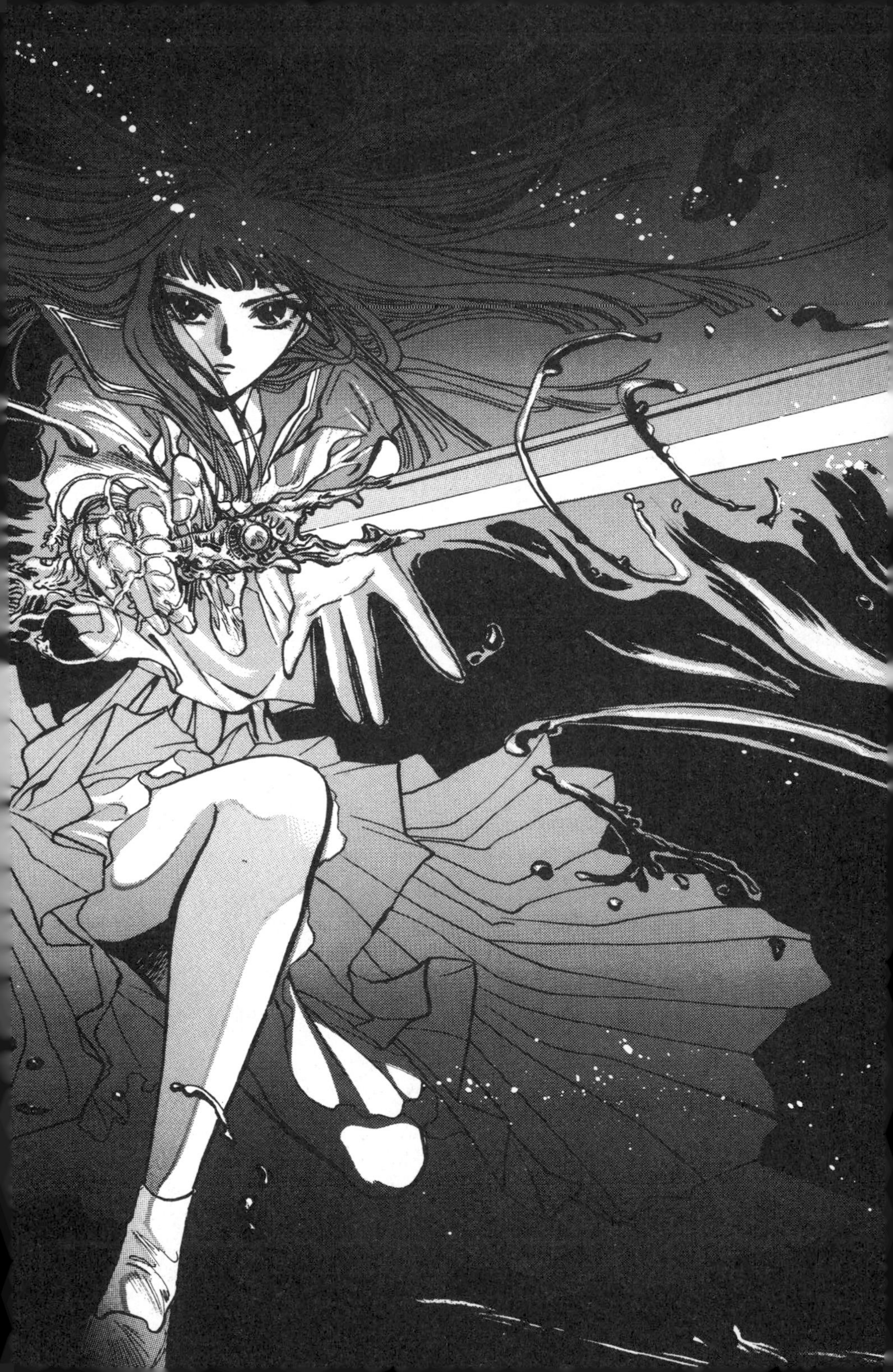

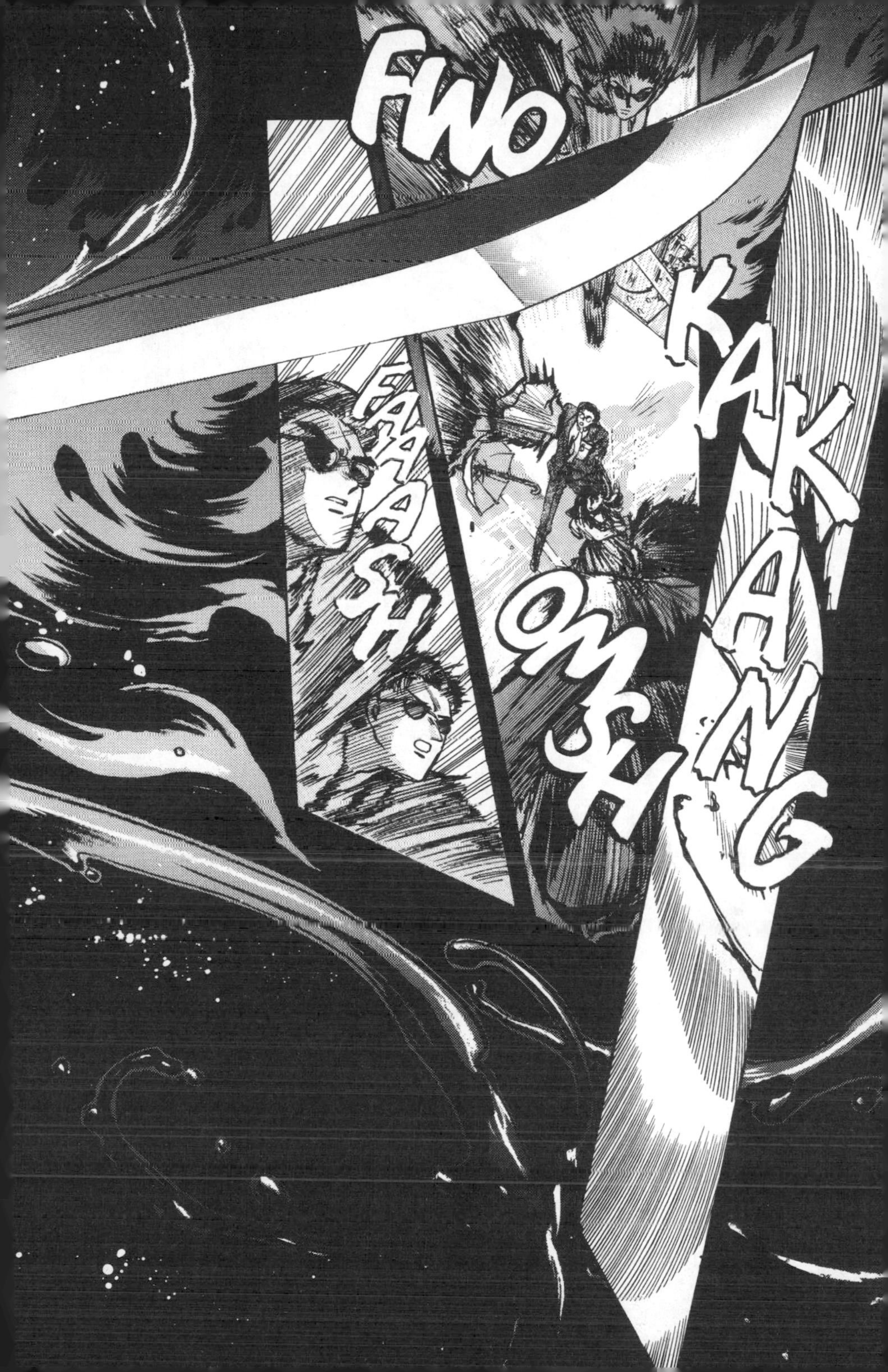
FWO
FAAAAASH
OMSH
KAKAKANG

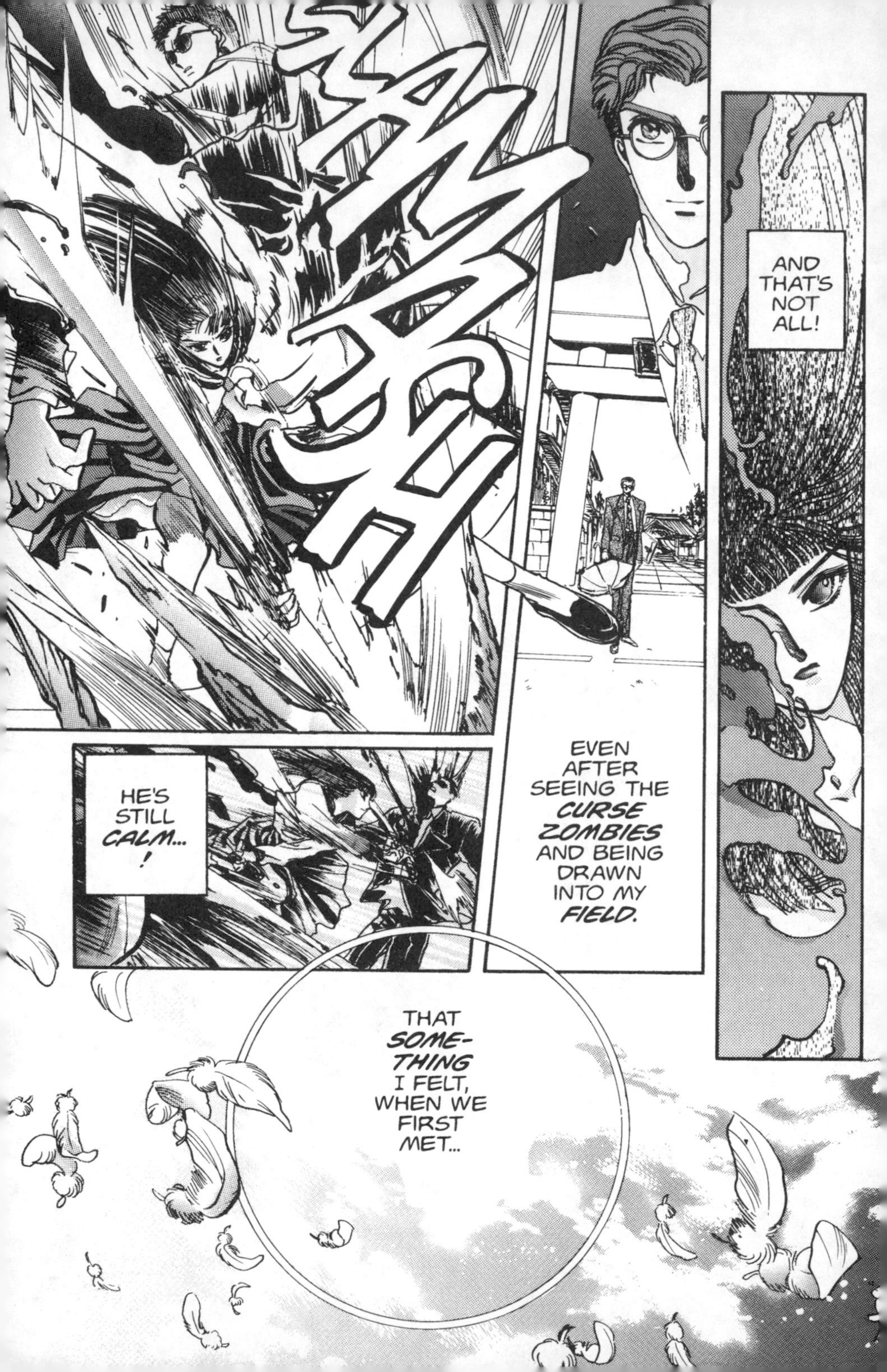
SWASH
HE'S STILL CALM...!
EVEN AFTER SEEING THE CURSE ZOMBIES AND BEING DRAWN INTO MY FIELD.
AND THAT'S NOT ALL!
THAT SOME-THING I FELT, WHEN WE FIRST MET...

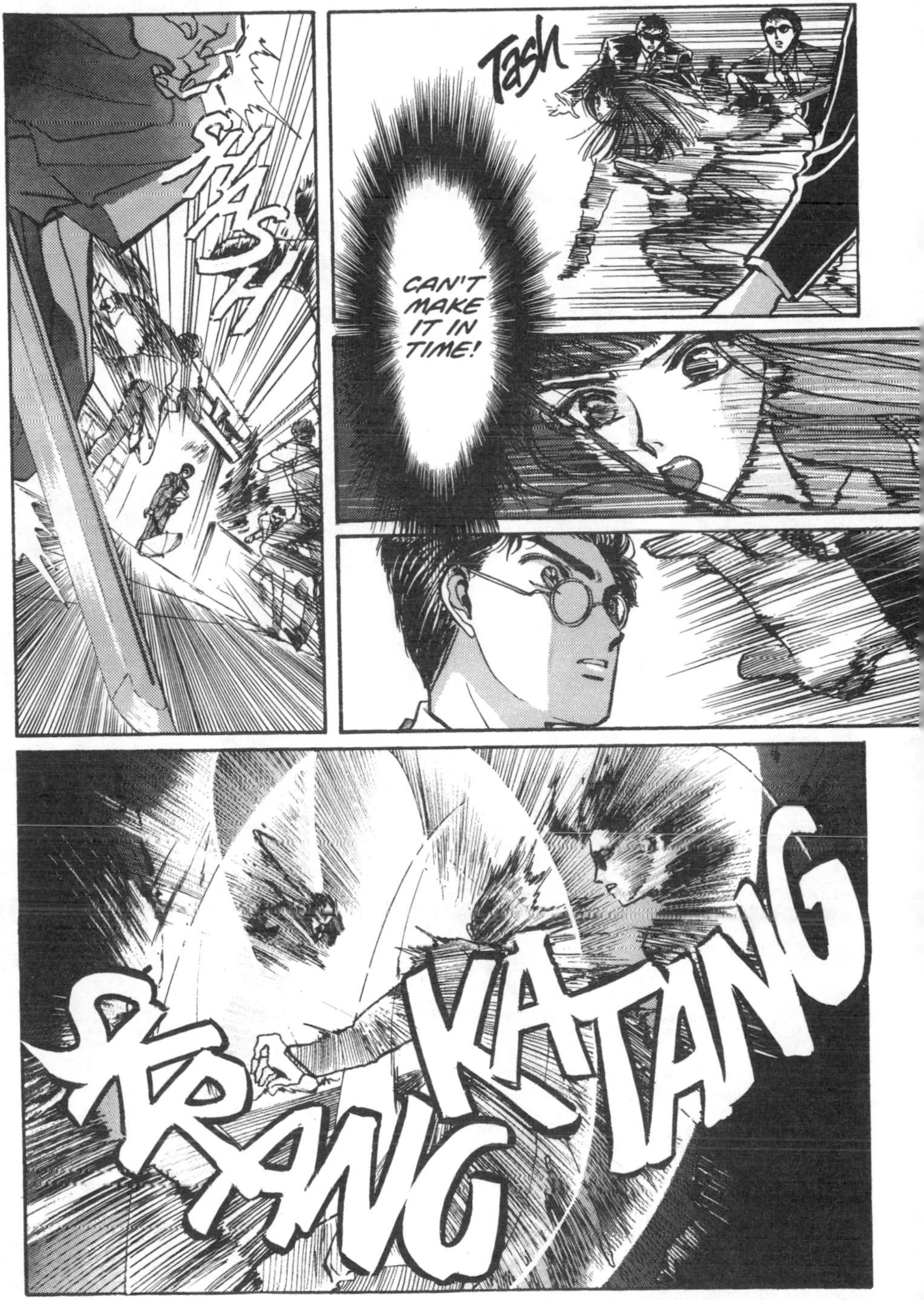
SHASH
TASH
CAN'T MAKE IT IN TIME!
SKRANG
KATANG

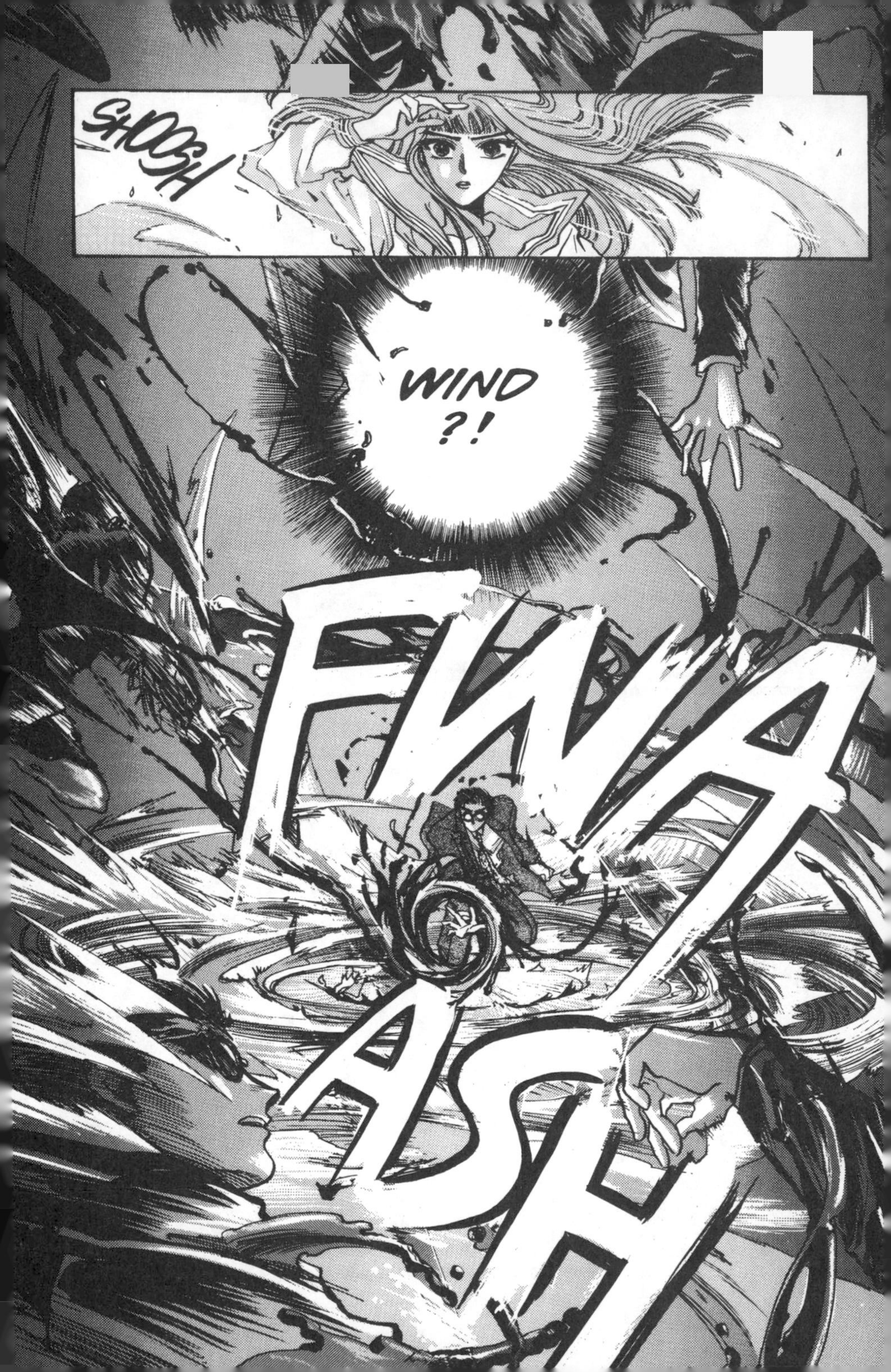
SHOOSH
WIND?!
FWAASH

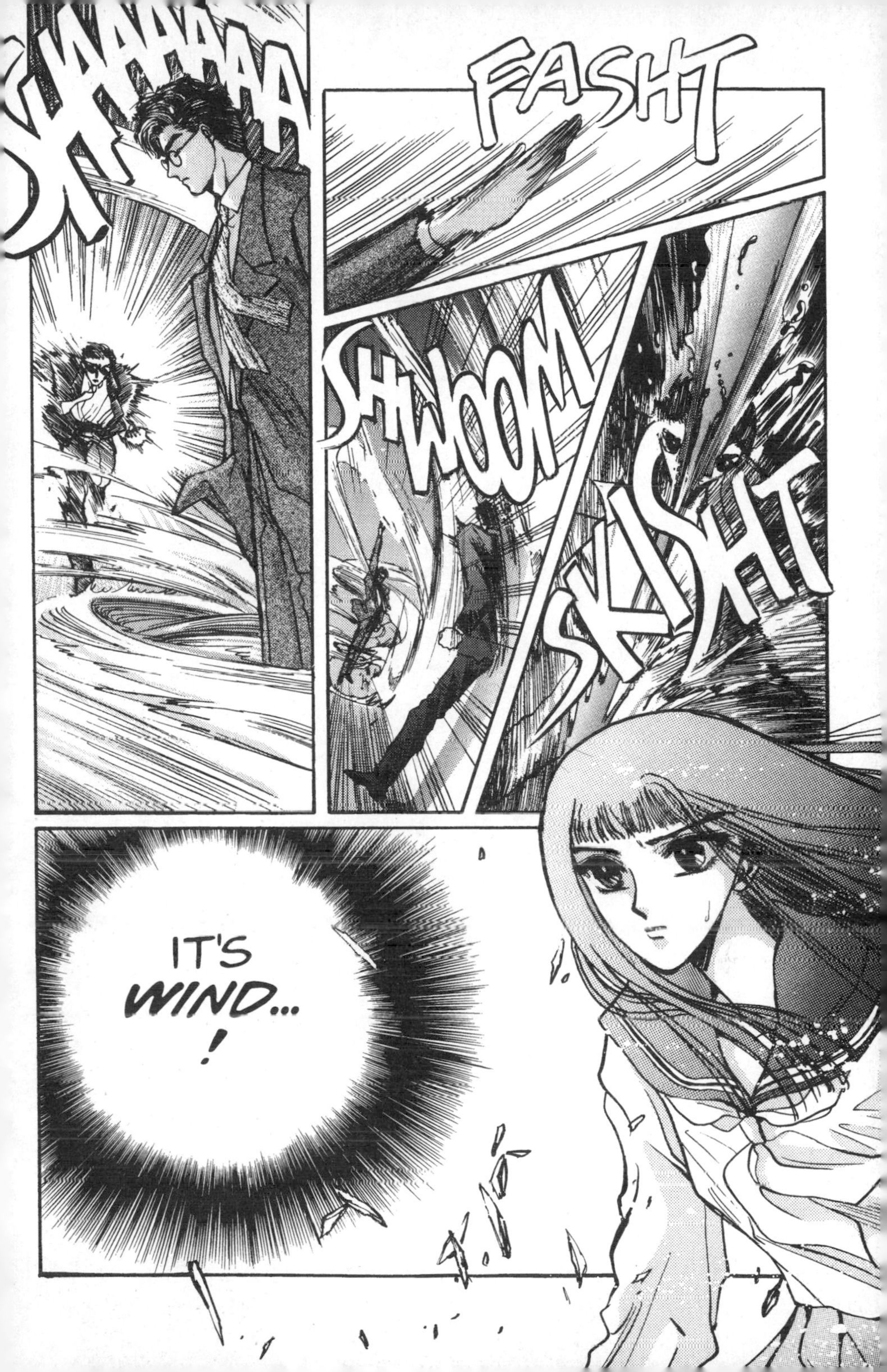
SHAAAAA
FASHT
SHWOOM
SKISHT
IT'S
WIND...
!

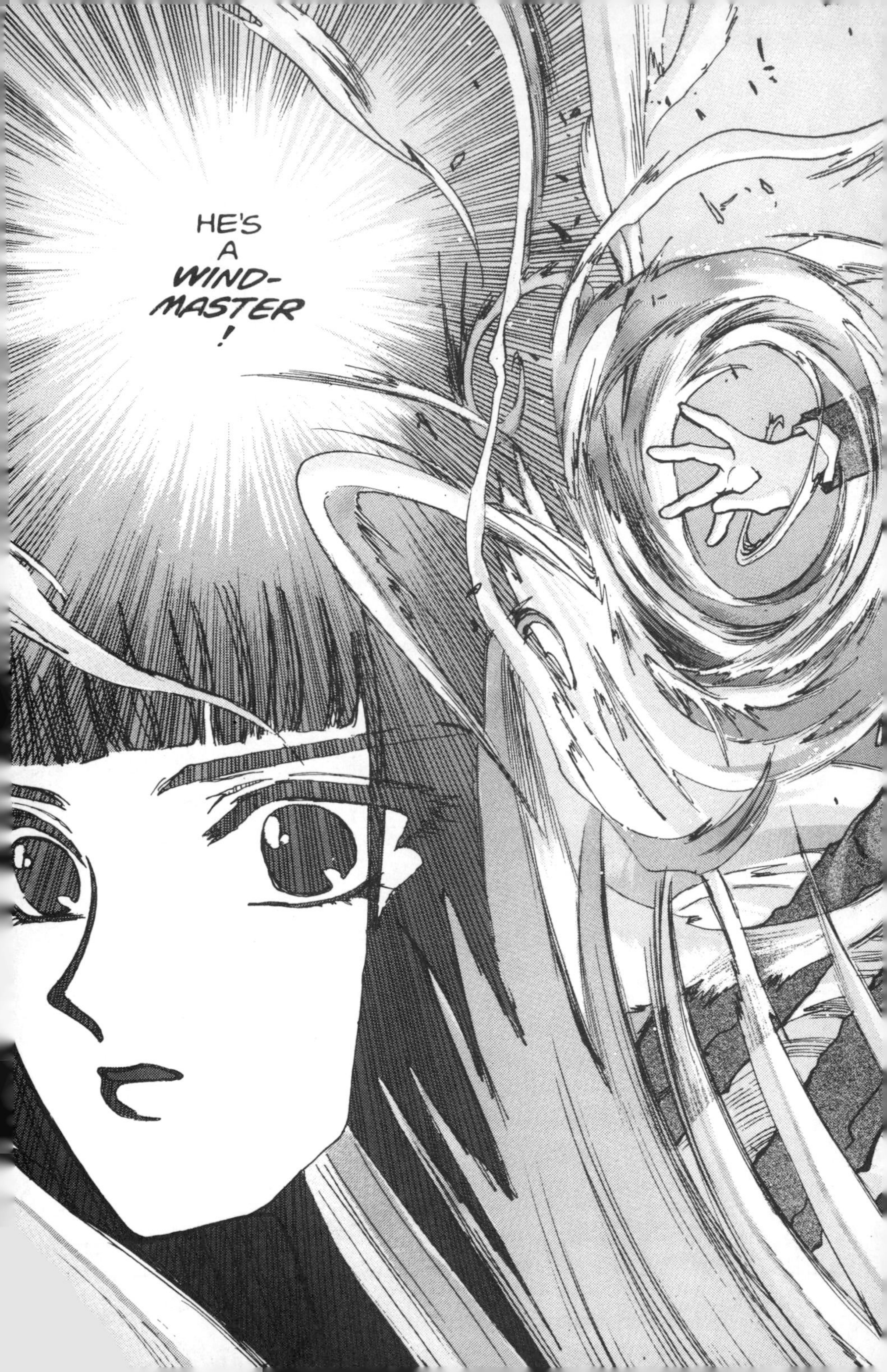
HE'S A WIND-MASTER!

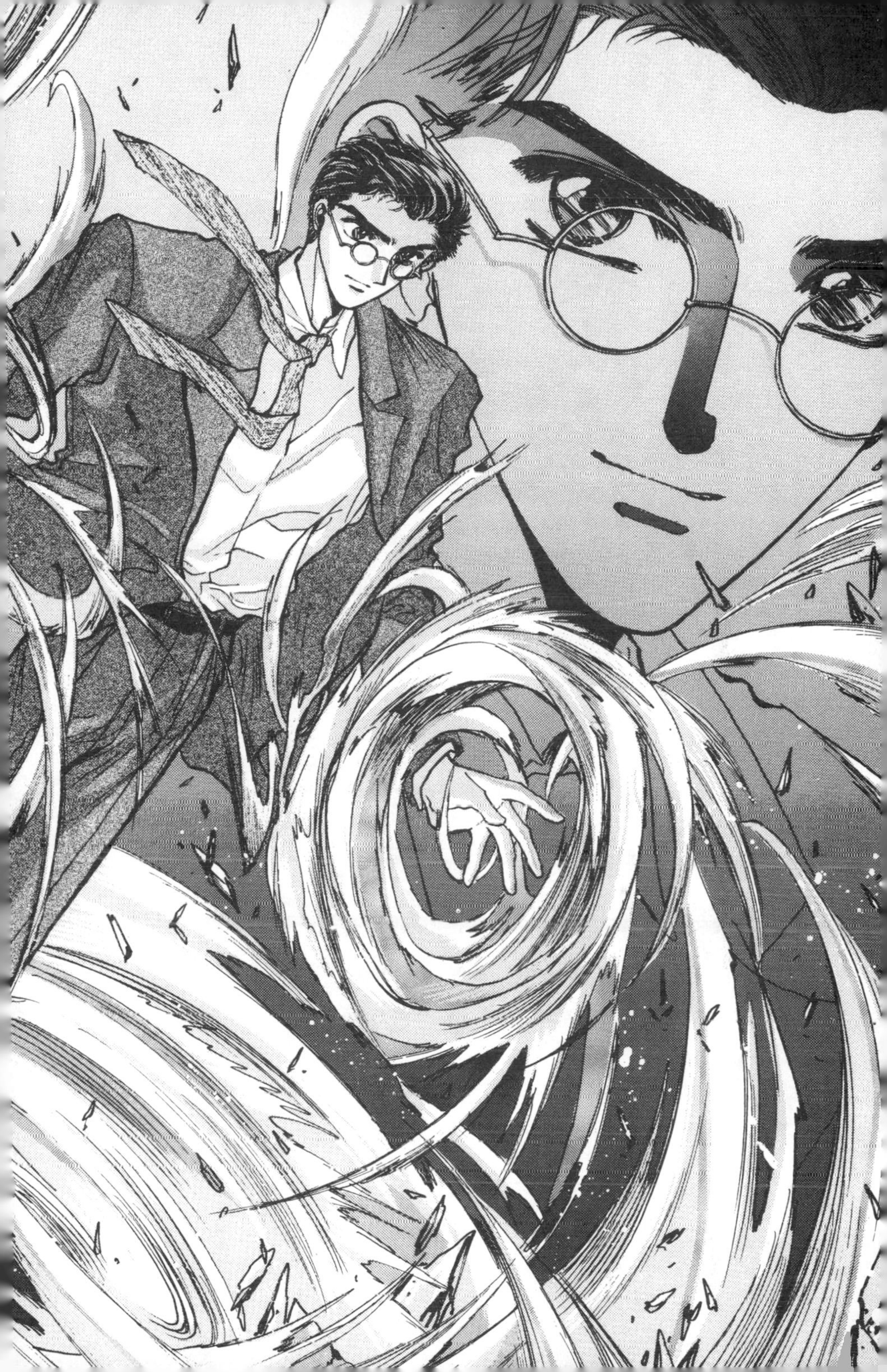

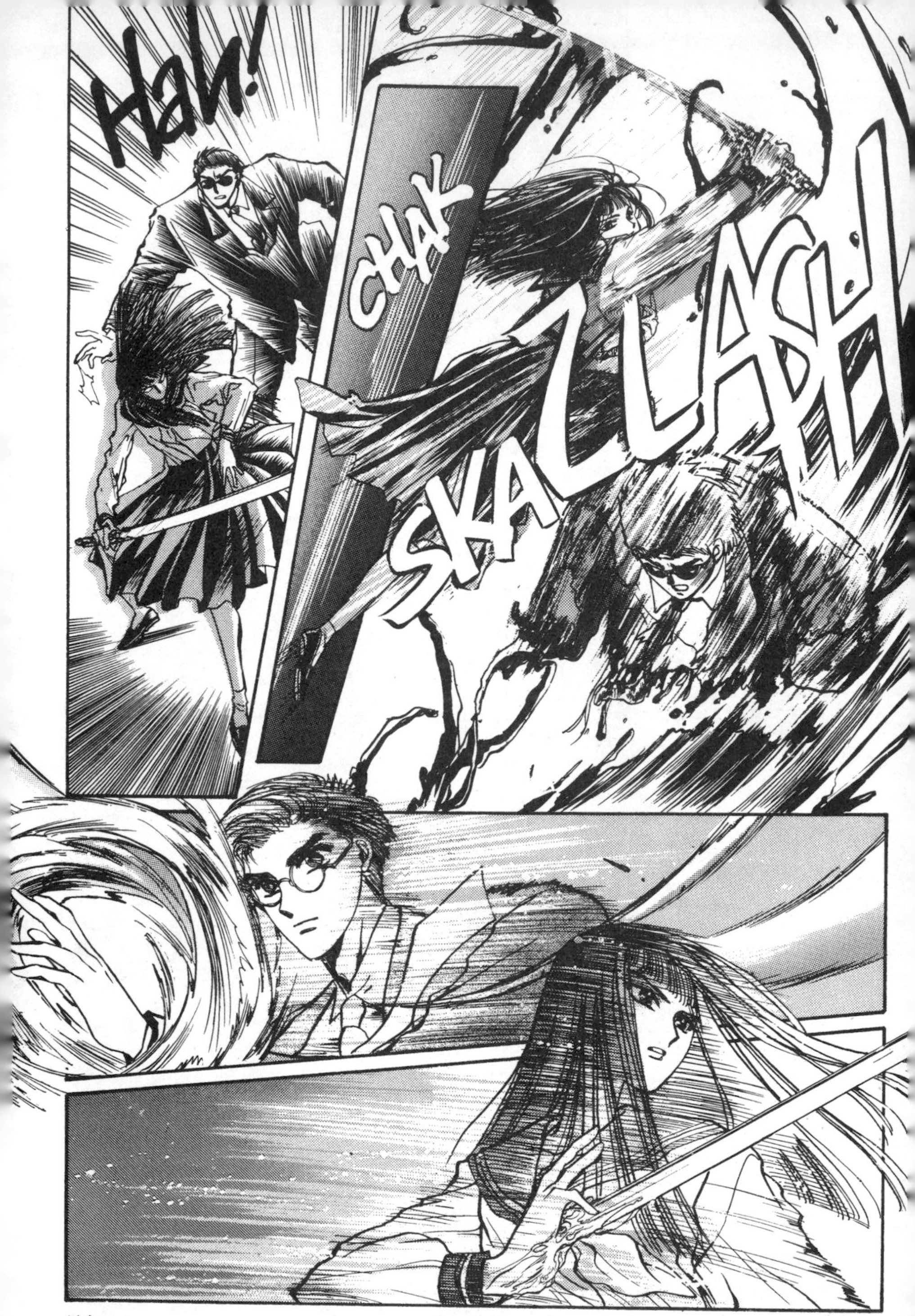
Hah!
CHAK
SKALLASH!

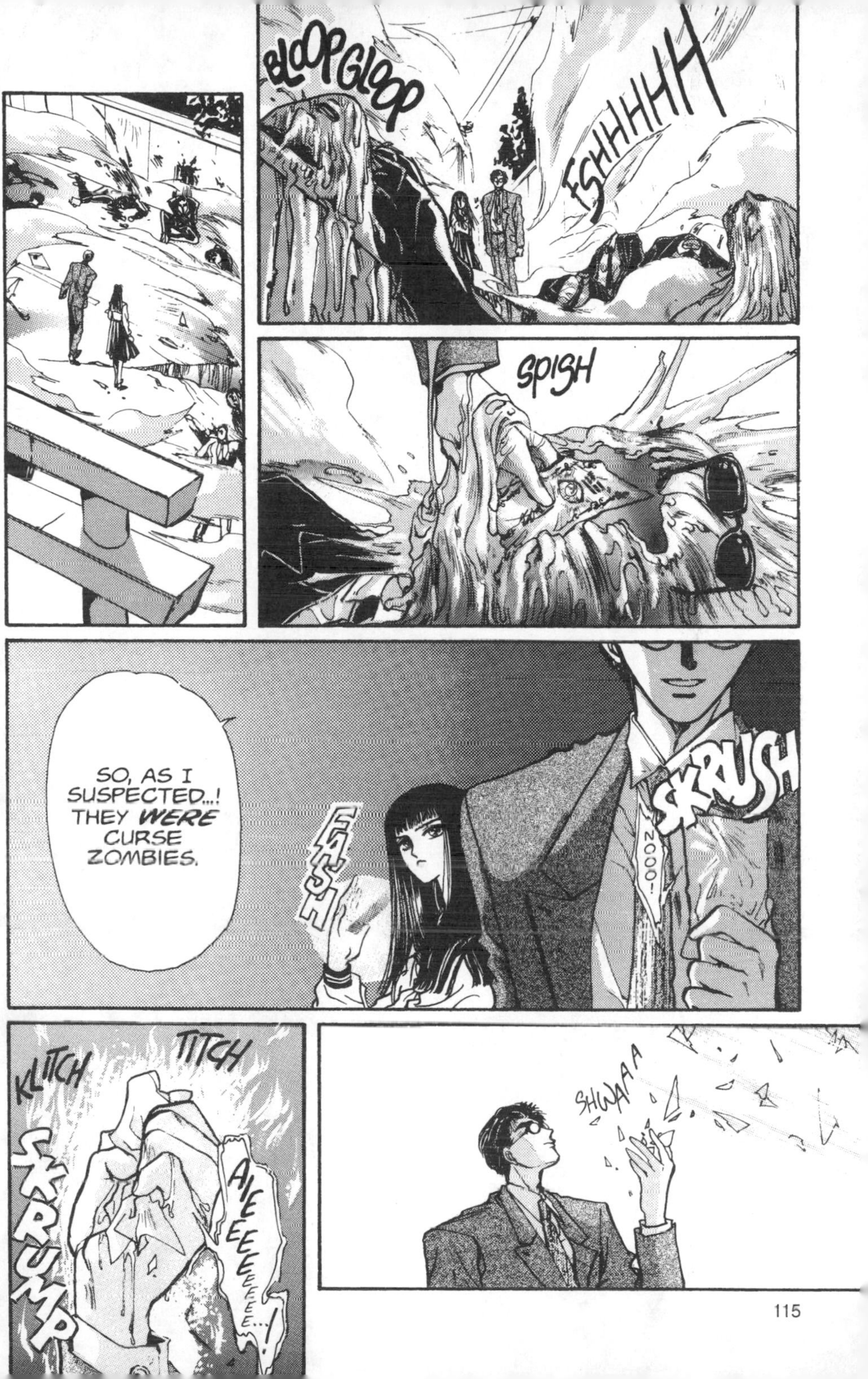
BLOOP GLOOP
FSHHHHH
SPISH
SO, AS I SUSPECTED...! THEY *WERE* CURSE ZOMBIES.
FASH
NOOO!
SKRUSH
KLITCH
TITCH
SKRUMP
AIEEEEEEEEE...!
SHWAAA

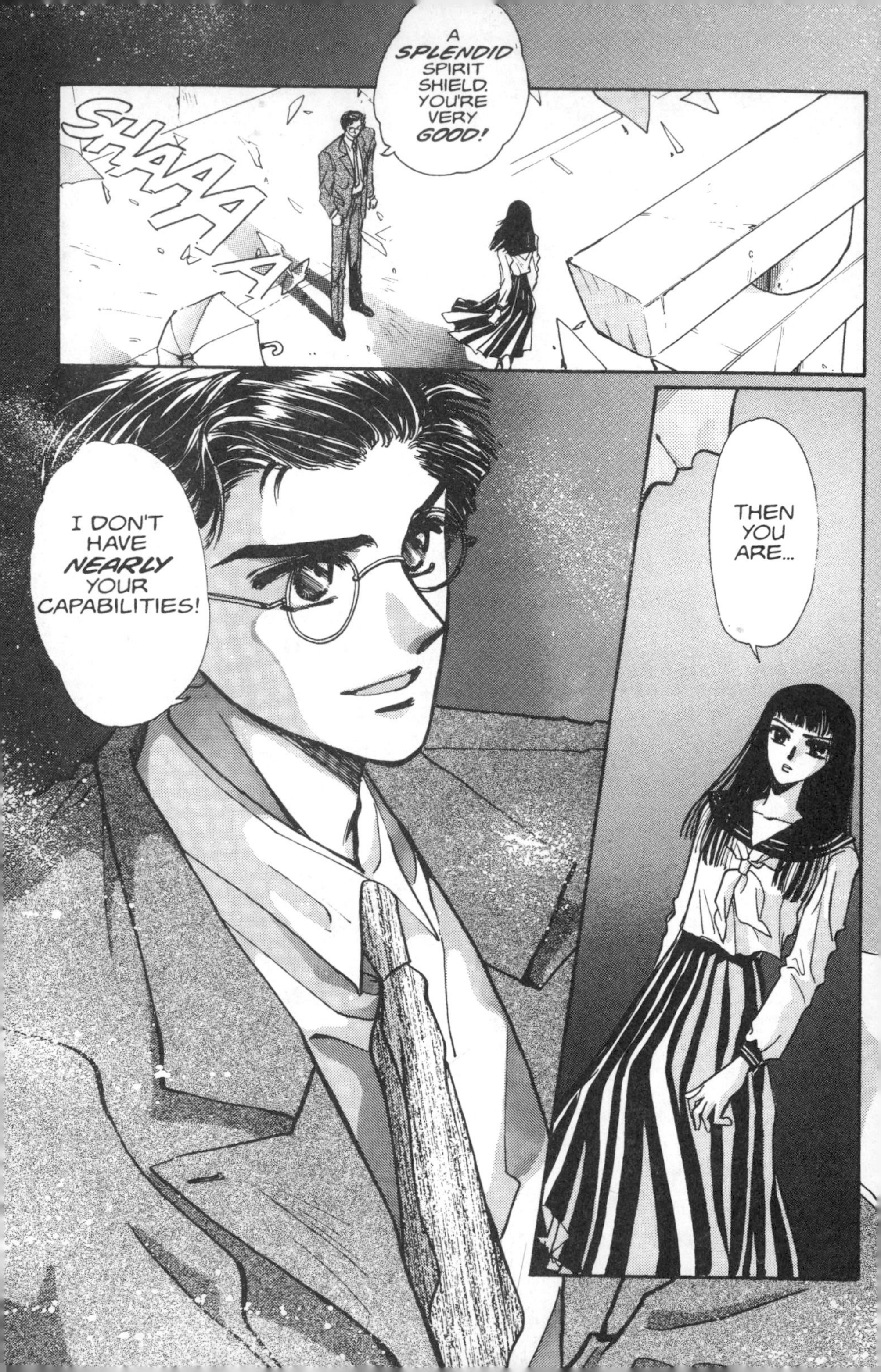
SHAAAA
A SPLENDID SPIRIT SHIELD. YOU'RE VERY GOOD!
I DON'T HAVE NEARLY YOUR CAPABILITIES!
THEN YOU ARE...

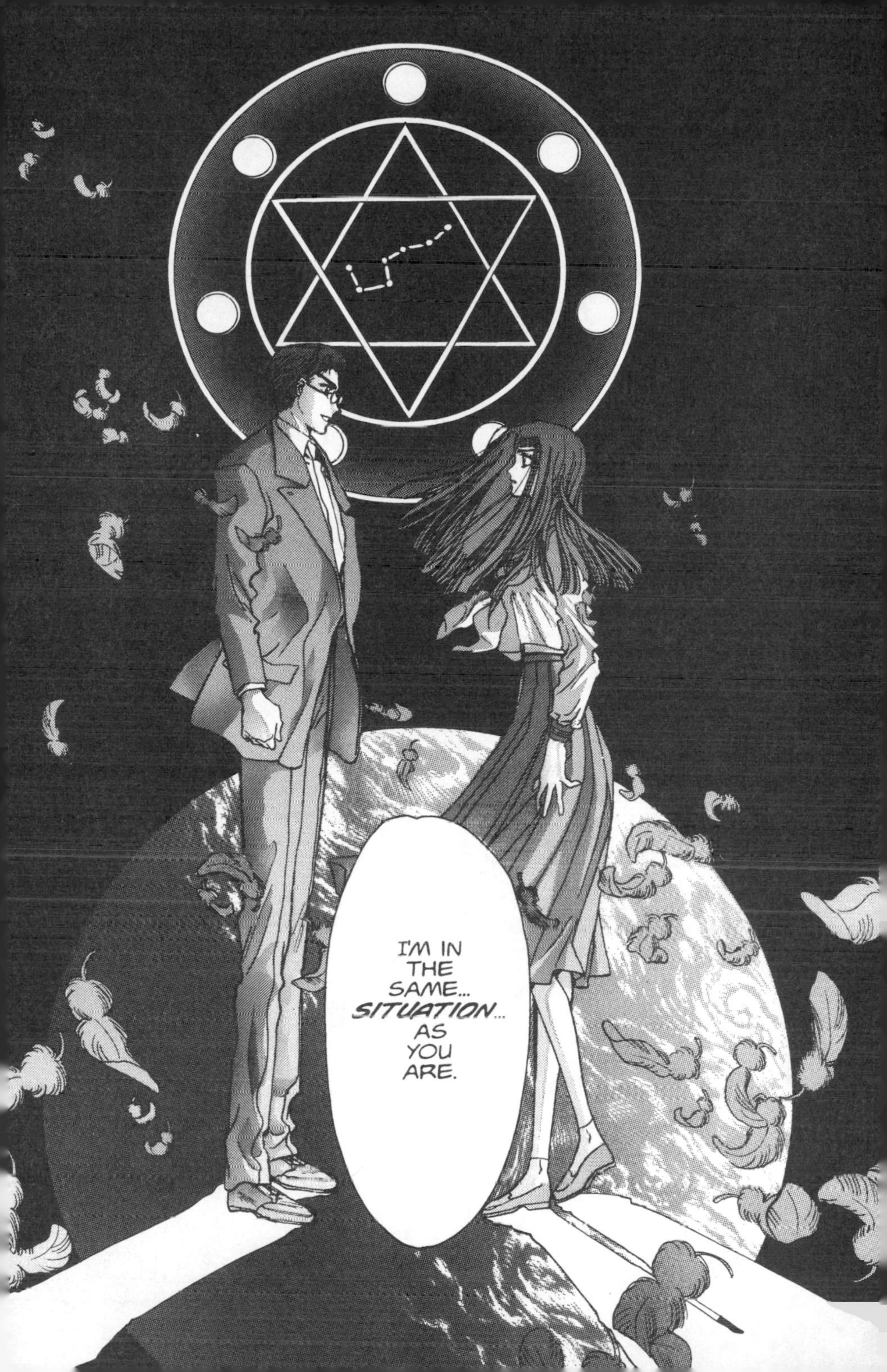
I'M IN THE SAME... SITUATION... AS YOU ARE.

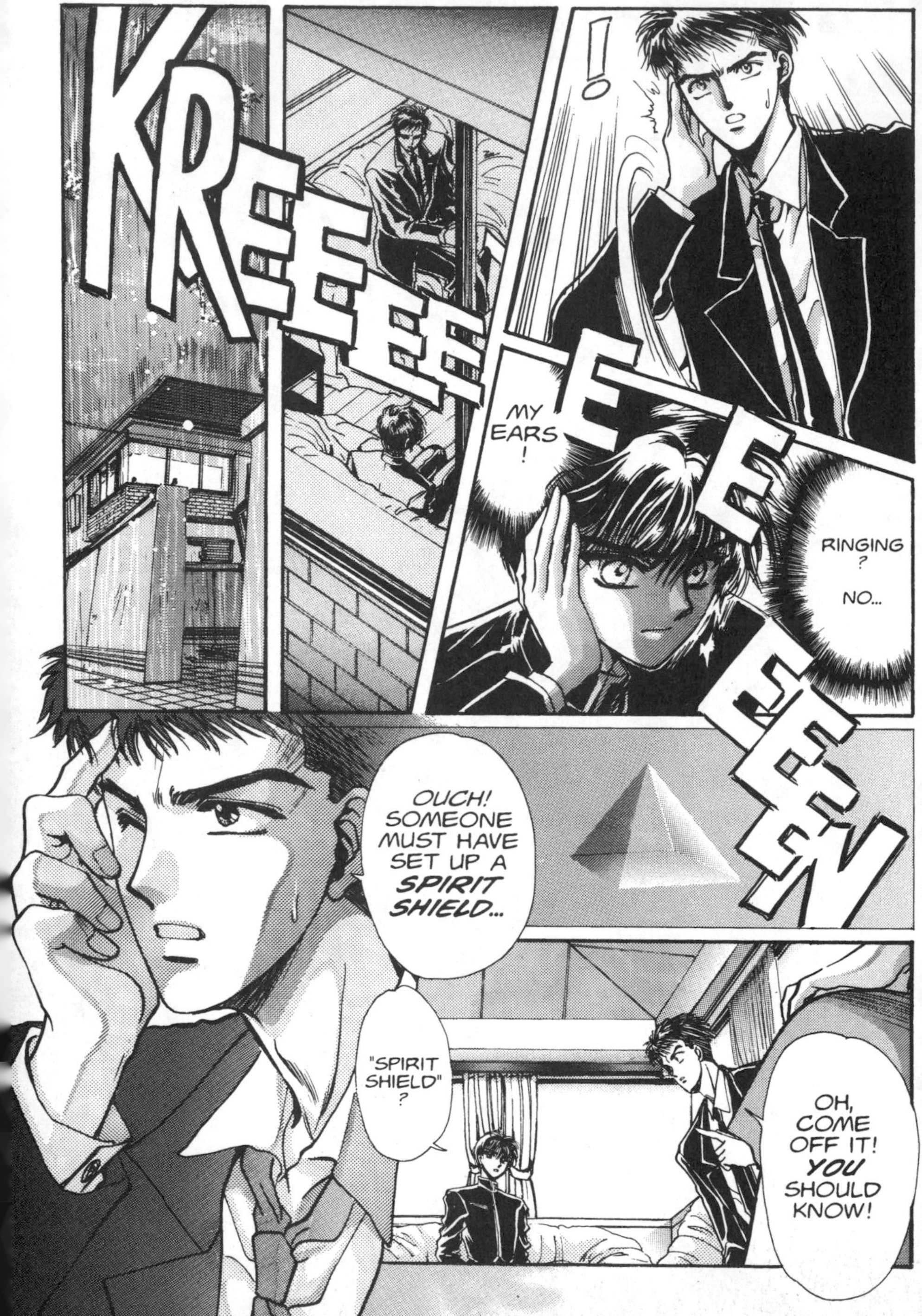
KREEEEEEEEEEEEN
!
MY EARS!
RINGING? NO...
OUCH! SOMEONE MUST HAVE SET UP A SPIRIT SHIELD...
"SPIRIT SHIELD"?
OH, COME OFF IT! YOU SHOULD KNOW!

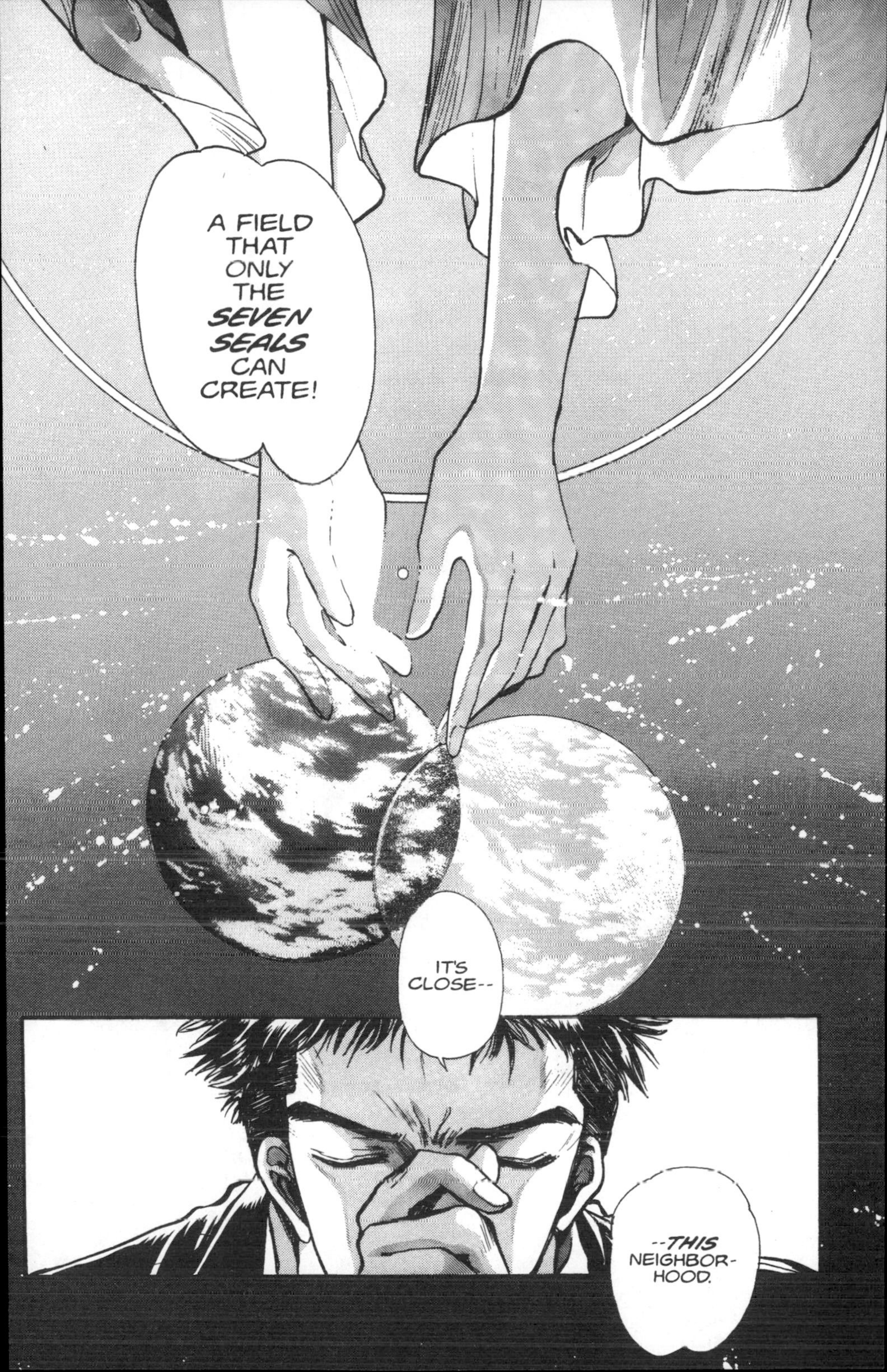
A FIELD THAT ONLY THE *SEVEN SEALS* CAN CREATE!
IT'S CLOSE--
--*THIS* NEIGHBORHOOD.

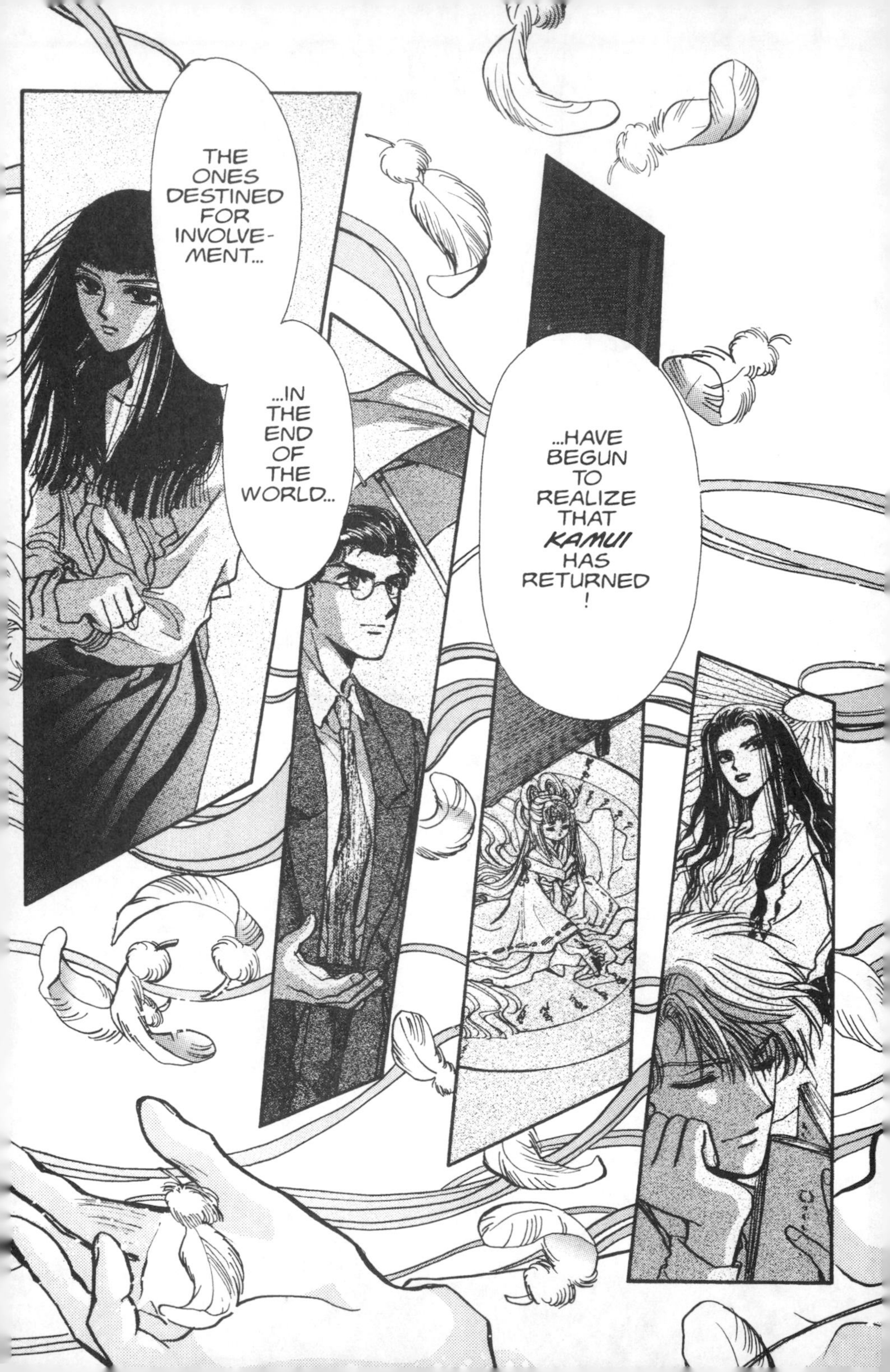
THE ONES DESTINED FOR INVOLVE-MENT...
...IN THE END OF THE WORLD...
...HAVE BEGUN TO REALIZE THAT KAMUI HAS RETURNED!
...

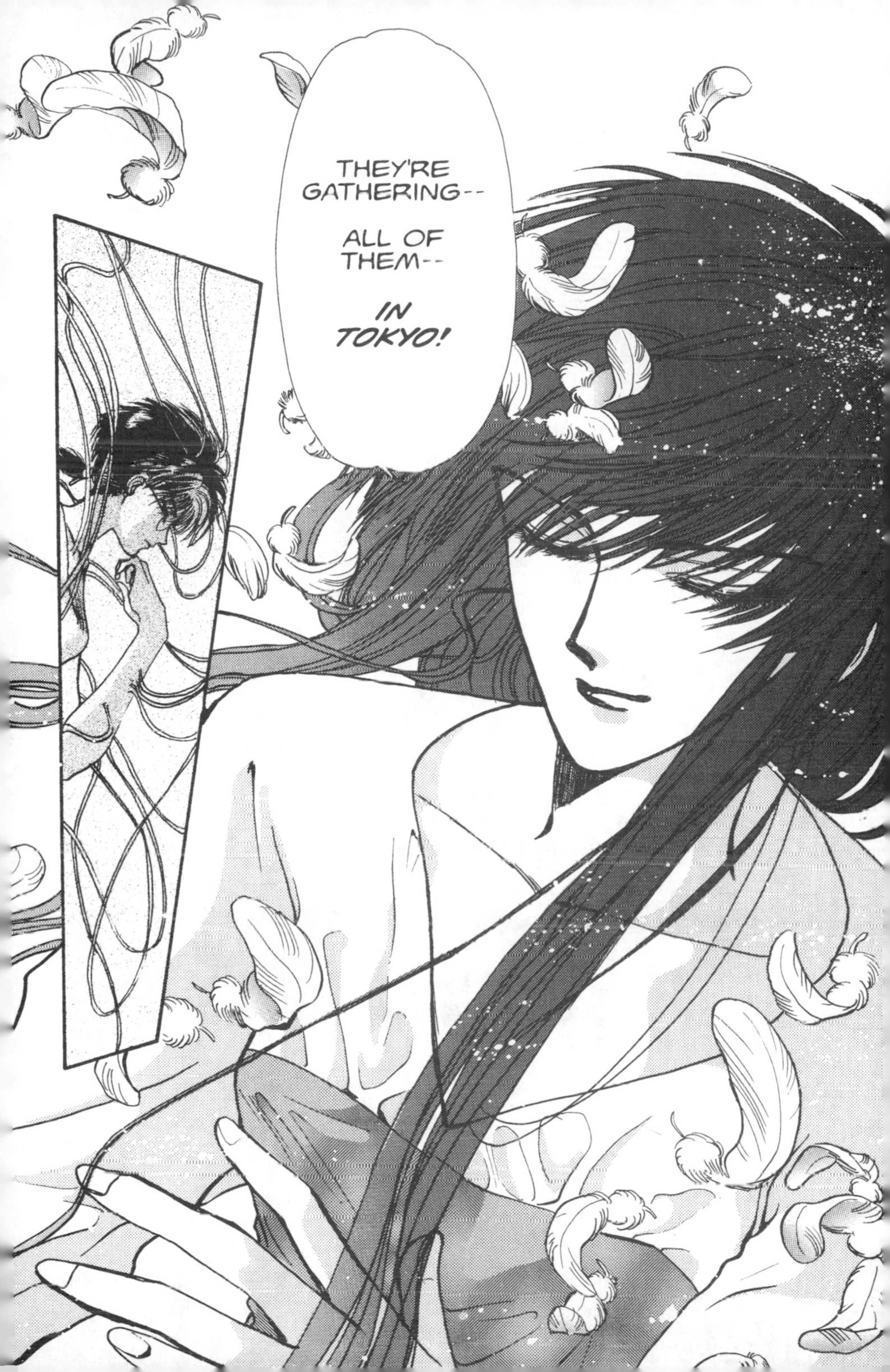

THEY'RE GATHERING--
ALL OF THEM--
IN TOKYO!

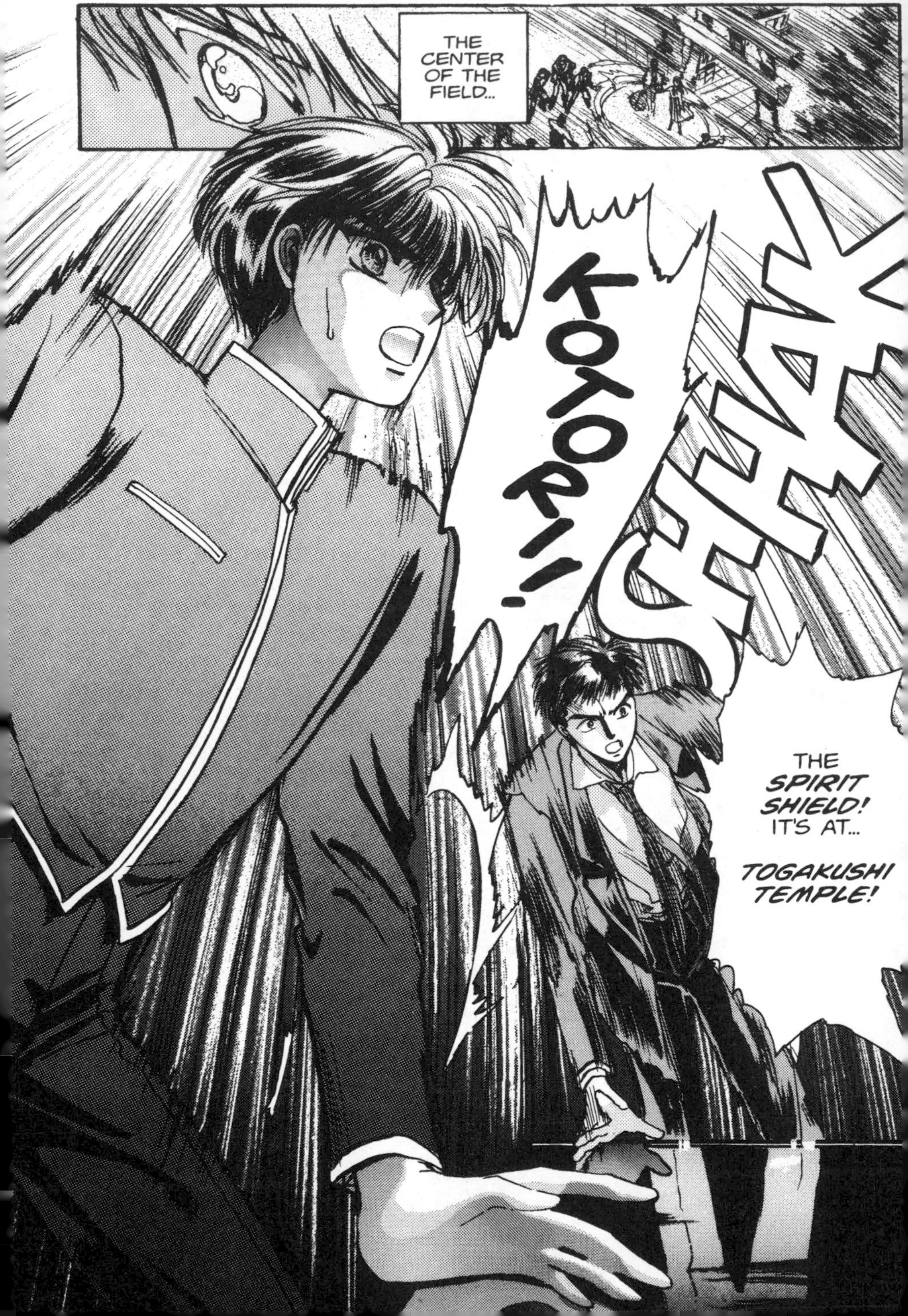
THE CENTER OF THE FIELD...
KOTORI!!
THE *SPIRIT SHIELD!* IT'S AT...
TOGAKUSHI TEMPLE!

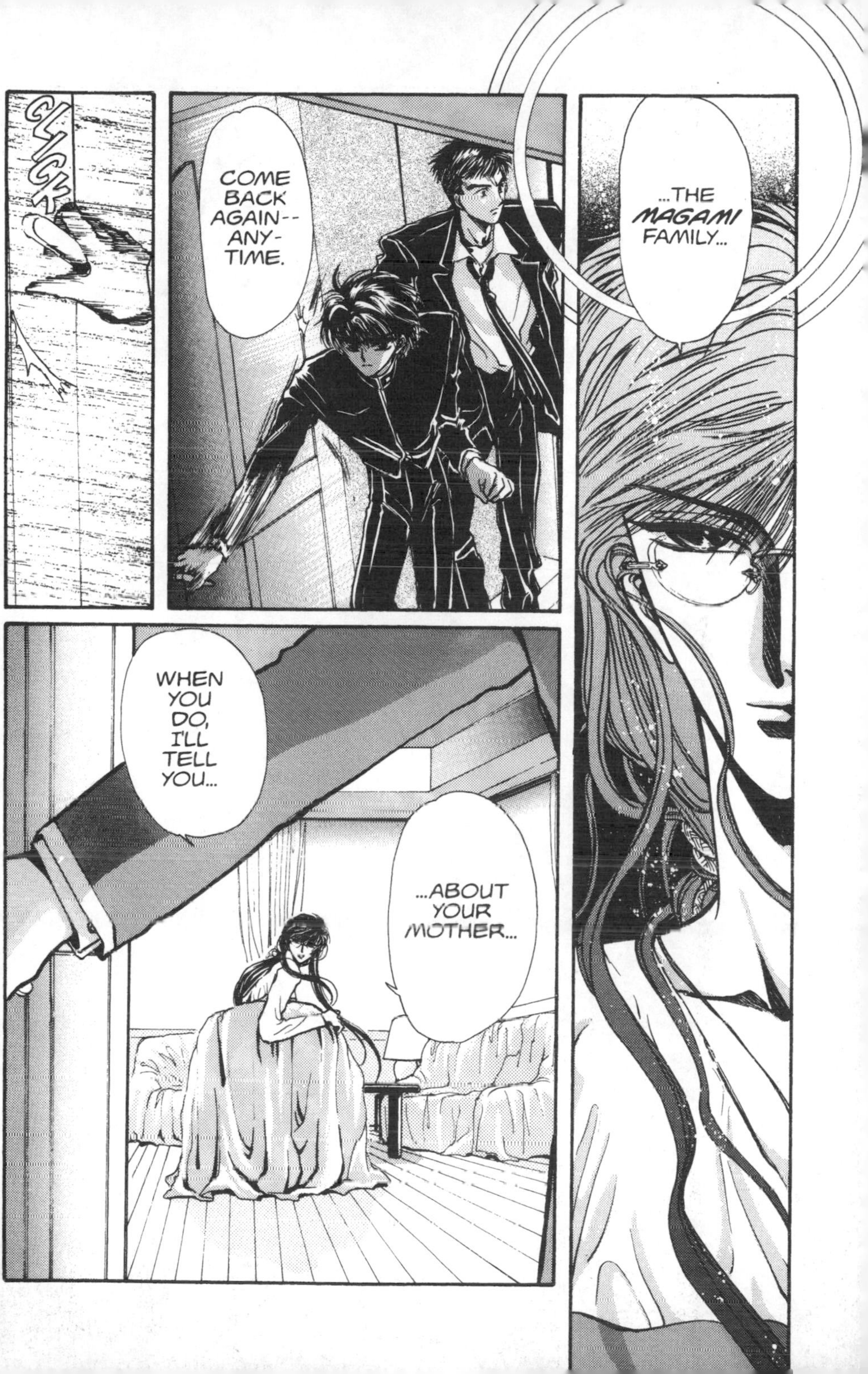
CLICK
COME BACK AGAIN-- ANY-TIME.
WHEN YOU DO, I'LL TELL YOU...
...ABOUT YOUR MOTHER...
...THE MAGAMI FAMILY...

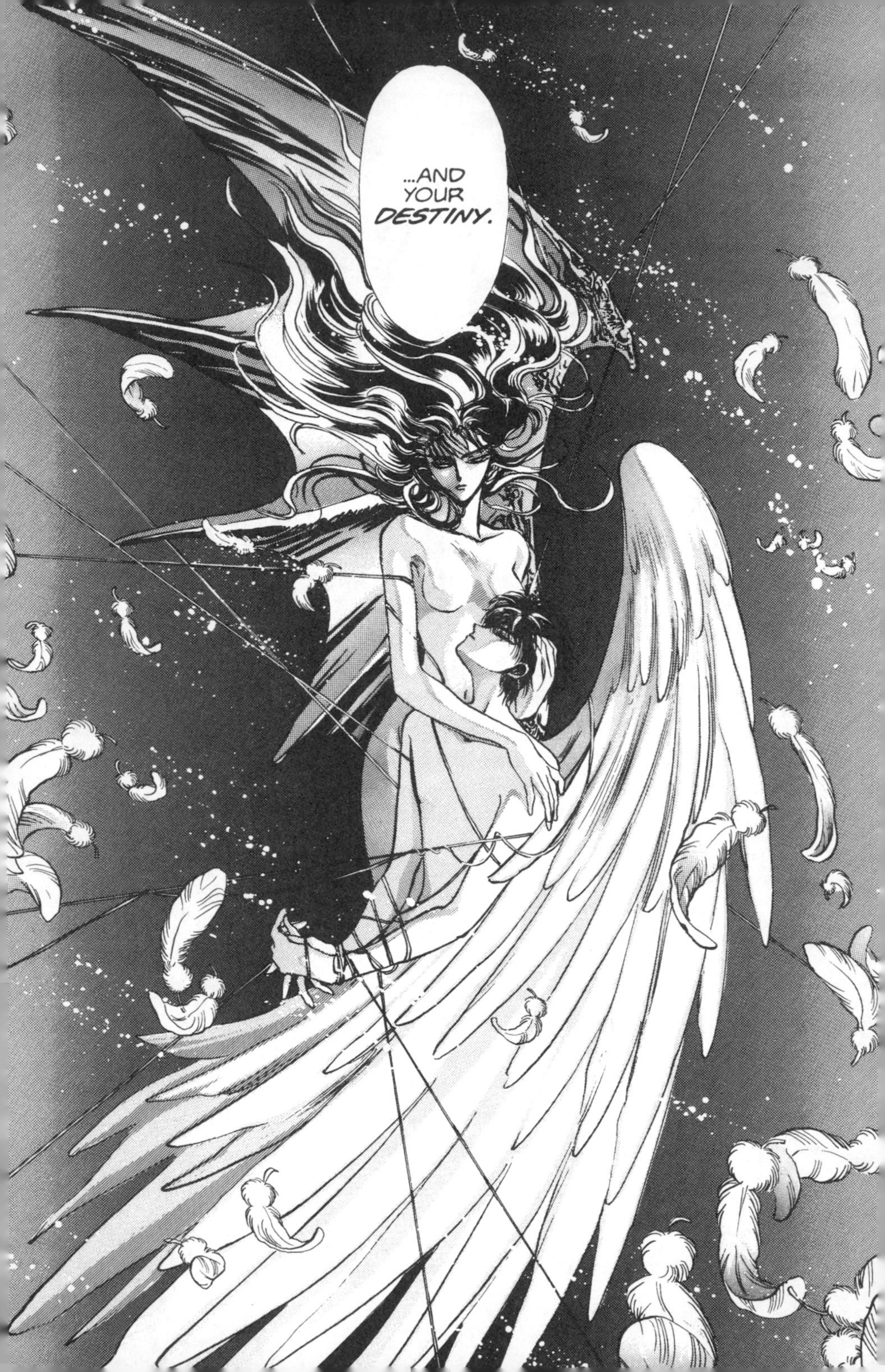
...AND YOUR DESTINY.

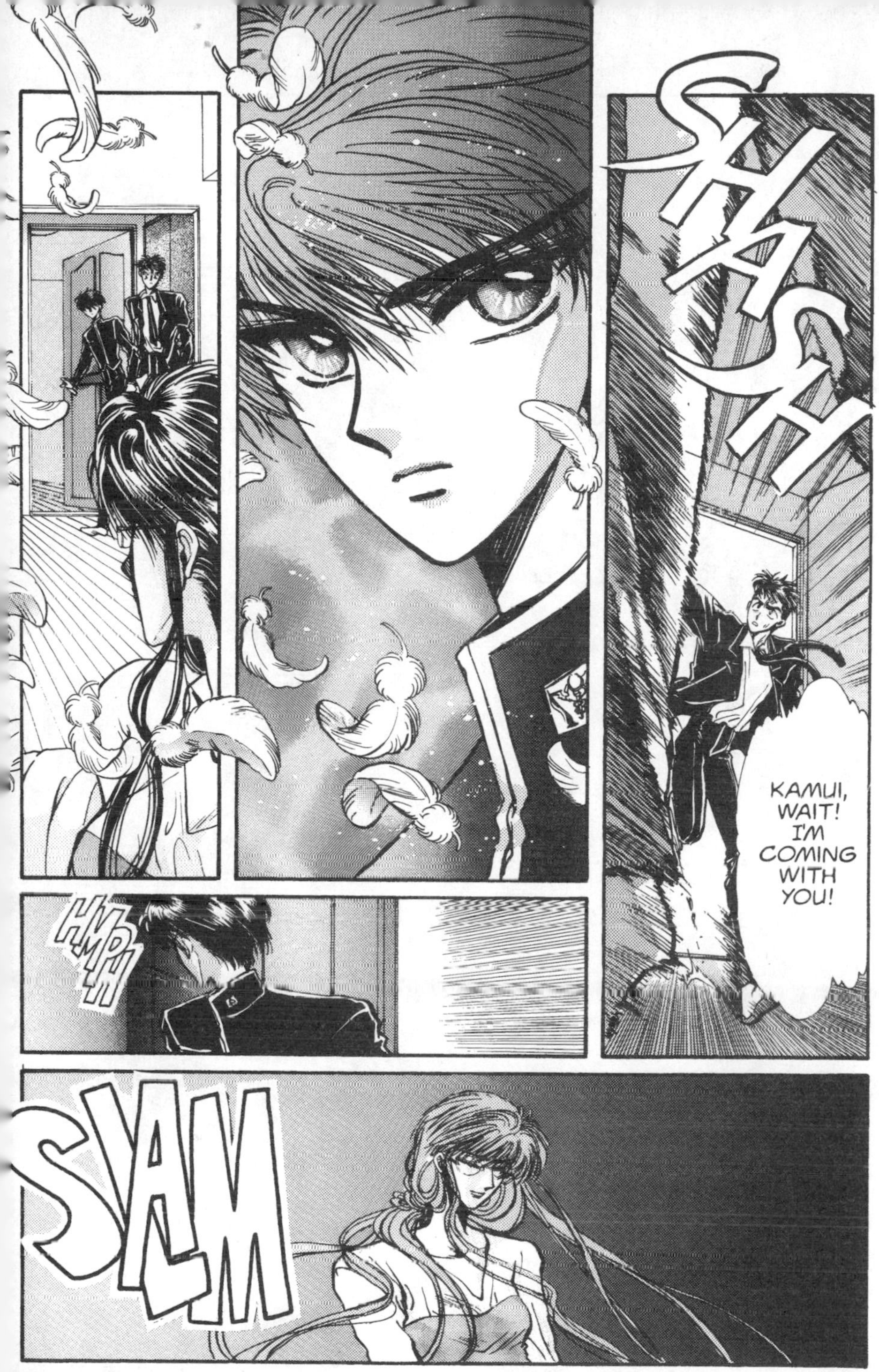
SHASH
KAMUI, WAIT! I'M COMING WITH YOU!
HMPH
SLAM

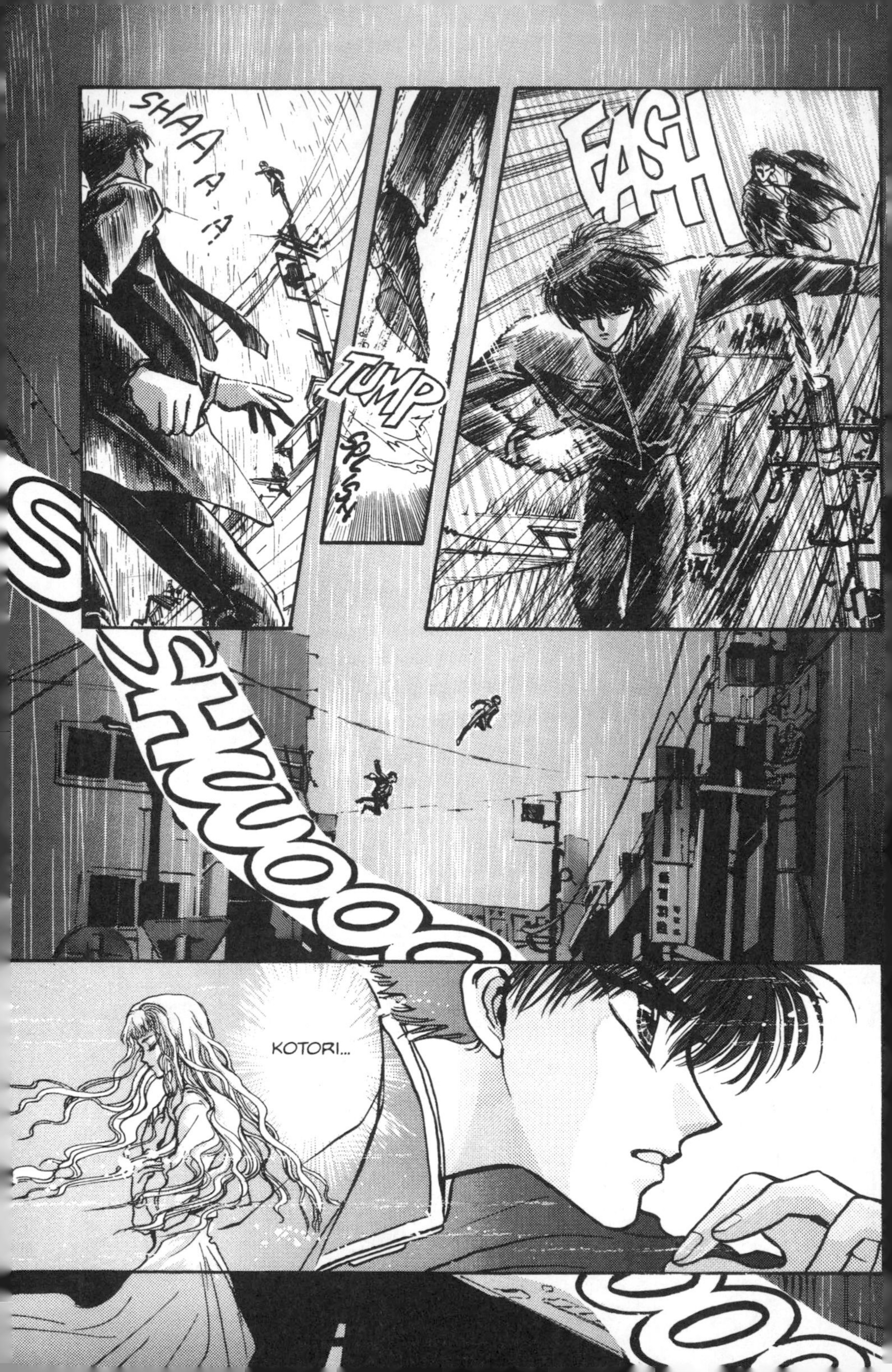
SHAAA A A
TUMP
SPLISH
FASH
SHUOOO
KOTORI...

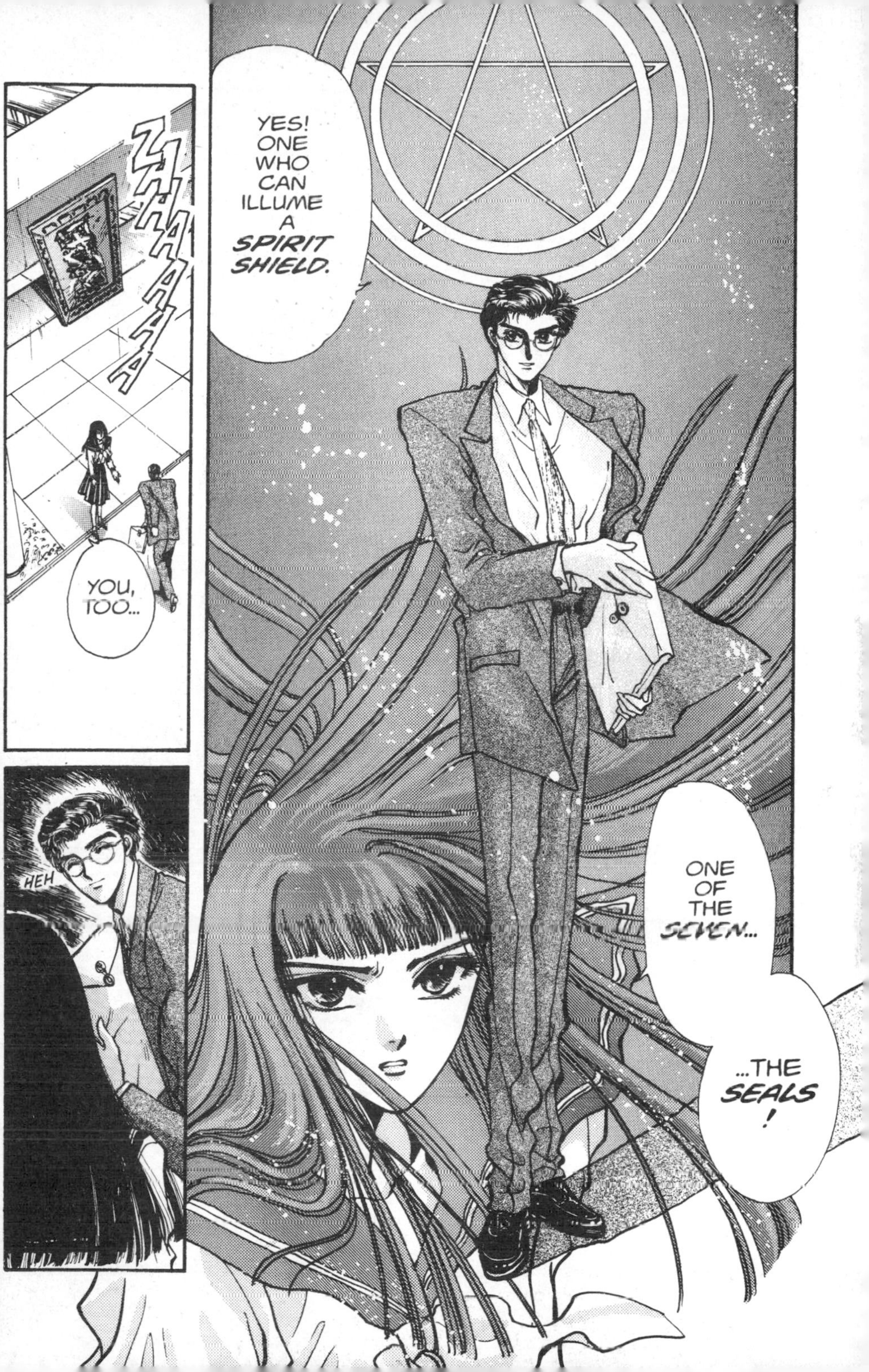
ZAHAAAA
YOU, TOO...
HEH
YES! ONE WHO CAN ILLUME A *SPIRIT SHIELD*.
ONE OF THE *SEVEN*...
...THE *SEALS*!

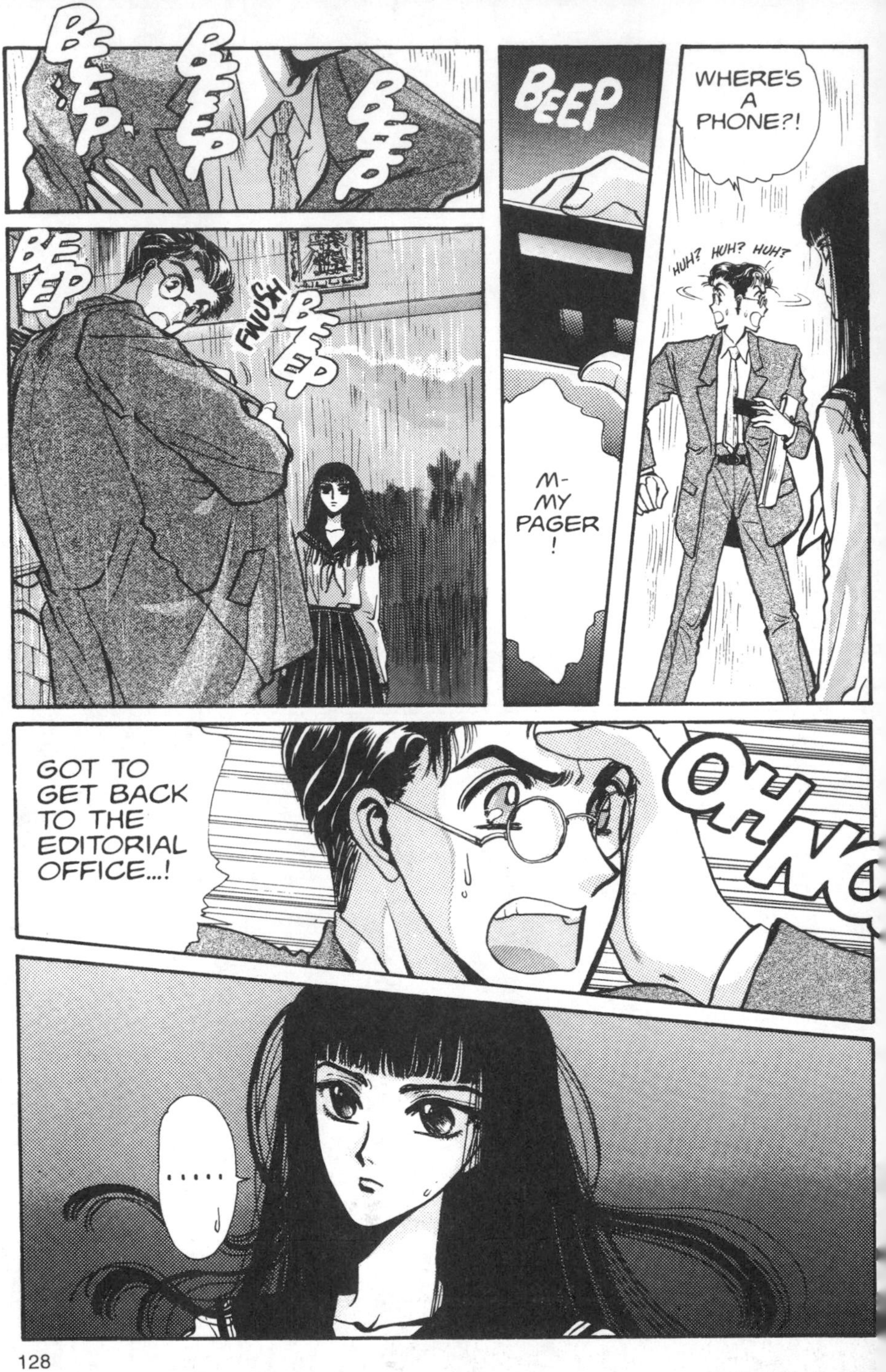
BEEP BEEP BEEP
BEEP
WHERE'S A PHONE?!
BEEP
FWUSH
BEEP
M-MY PAGER!
HUH? HUH? HUH?
GOT TO GET BACK TO THE EDITORIAL OFFICE...!
OH NO
......

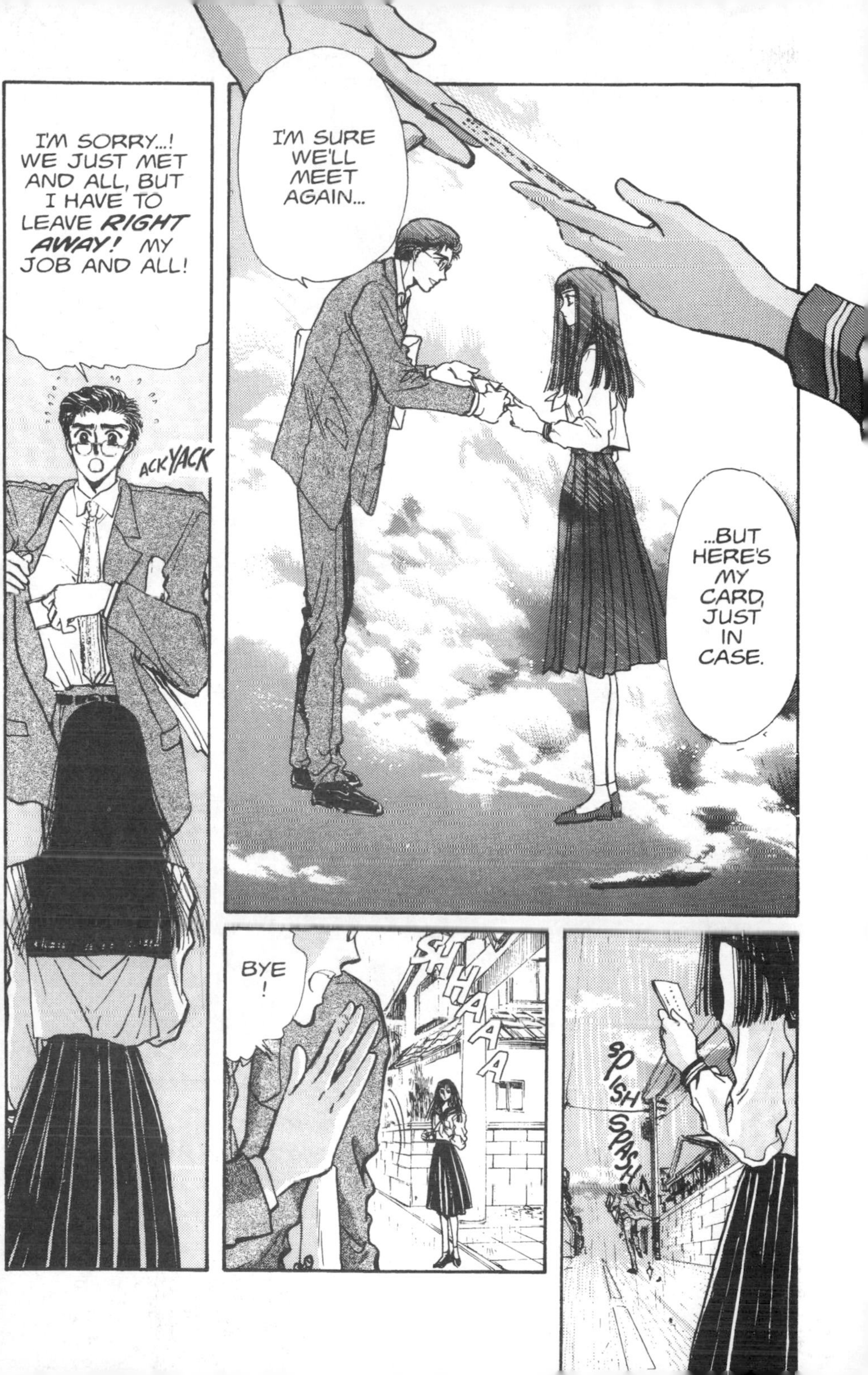
I'M SORRY...! WE JUST MET AND ALL, BUT I HAVE TO LEAVE ***RIGHT AWAY!*** MY JOB AND ALL!
ACKYACK
I'M SURE WE'LL MEET AGAIN...
...BUT HERE'S MY CARD, JUST IN CASE.
BYE!
SHHAAAA
SPISH SPASH

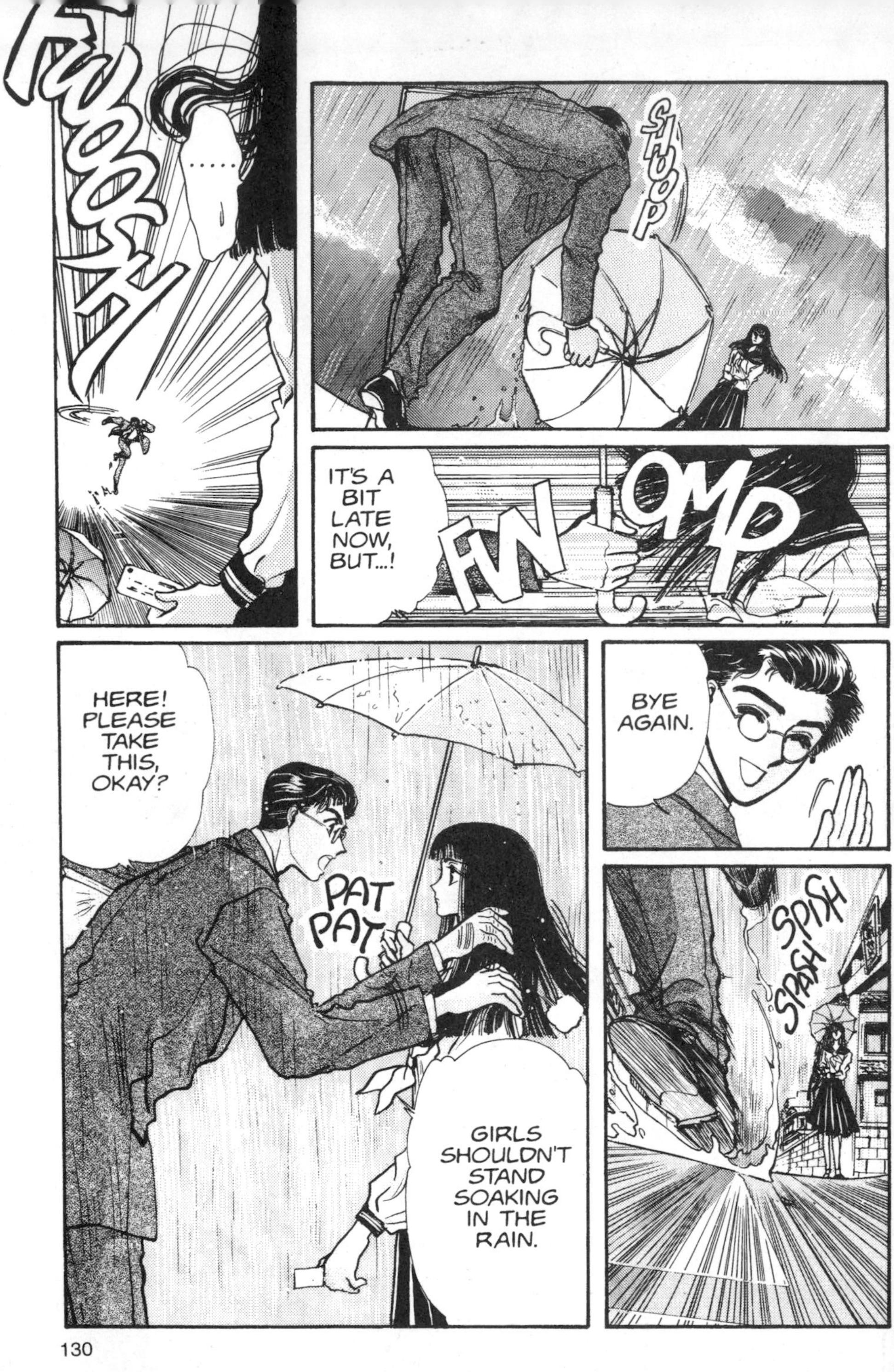
FWOOSH
......
SHOOP
IT'S A BIT LATE NOW, BUT...!
FWOMP
HERE! PLEASE TAKE THIS, OKAY?
PAT PAT
GIRLS SHOULDN'T STAND SOAKING IN THE RAIN.
BYE AGAIN.
SPISH SPASH

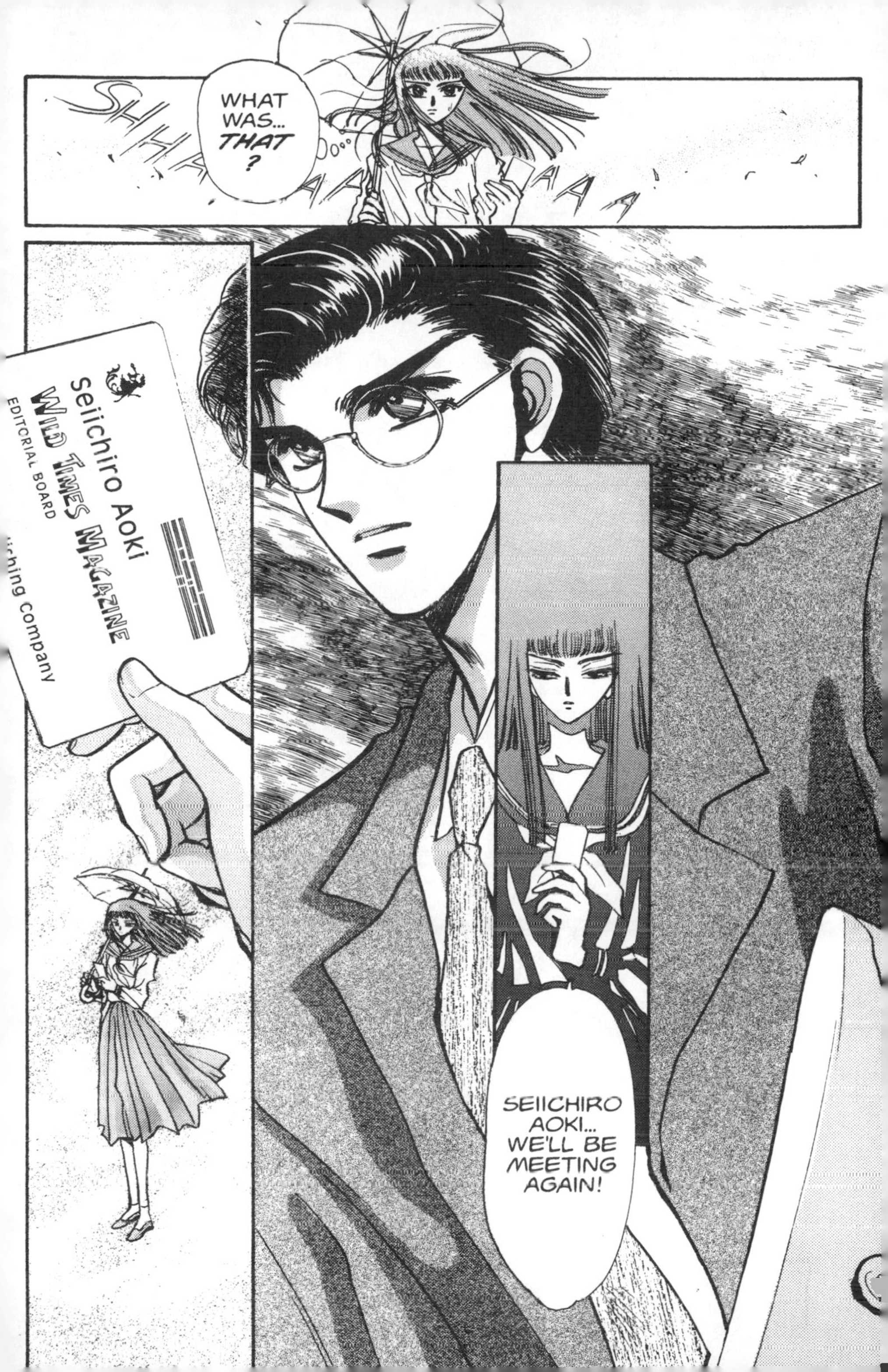
SHHAAAAAA
WHAT WAS... THAT?
Seiichiro Aoki
WILD TIMES MAGAZINE
EDITORIAL BOARD
Company
SEIICHIRO AOKI... WE'LL BE MEETING AGAIN!

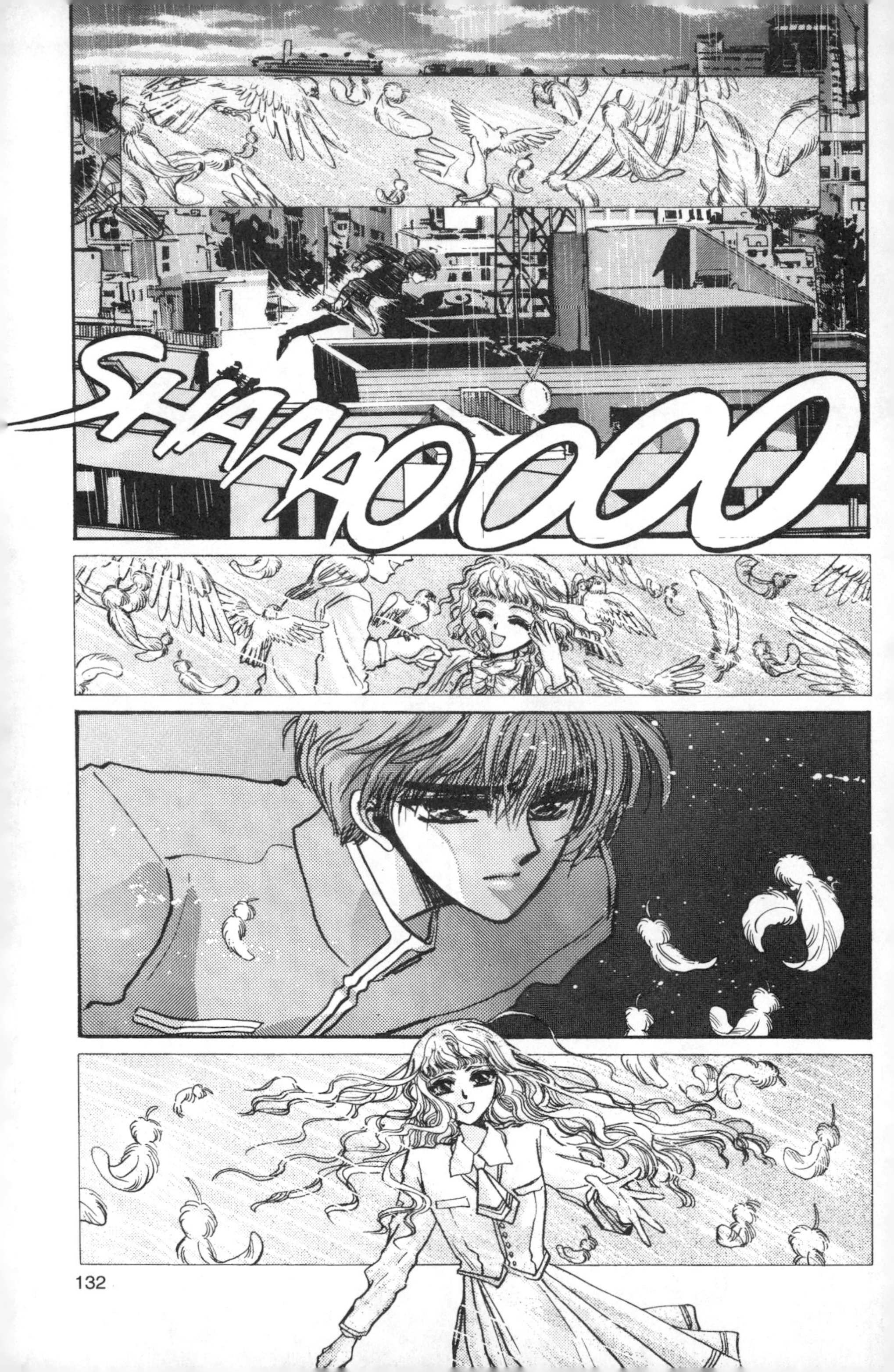
SHAAOOOOO

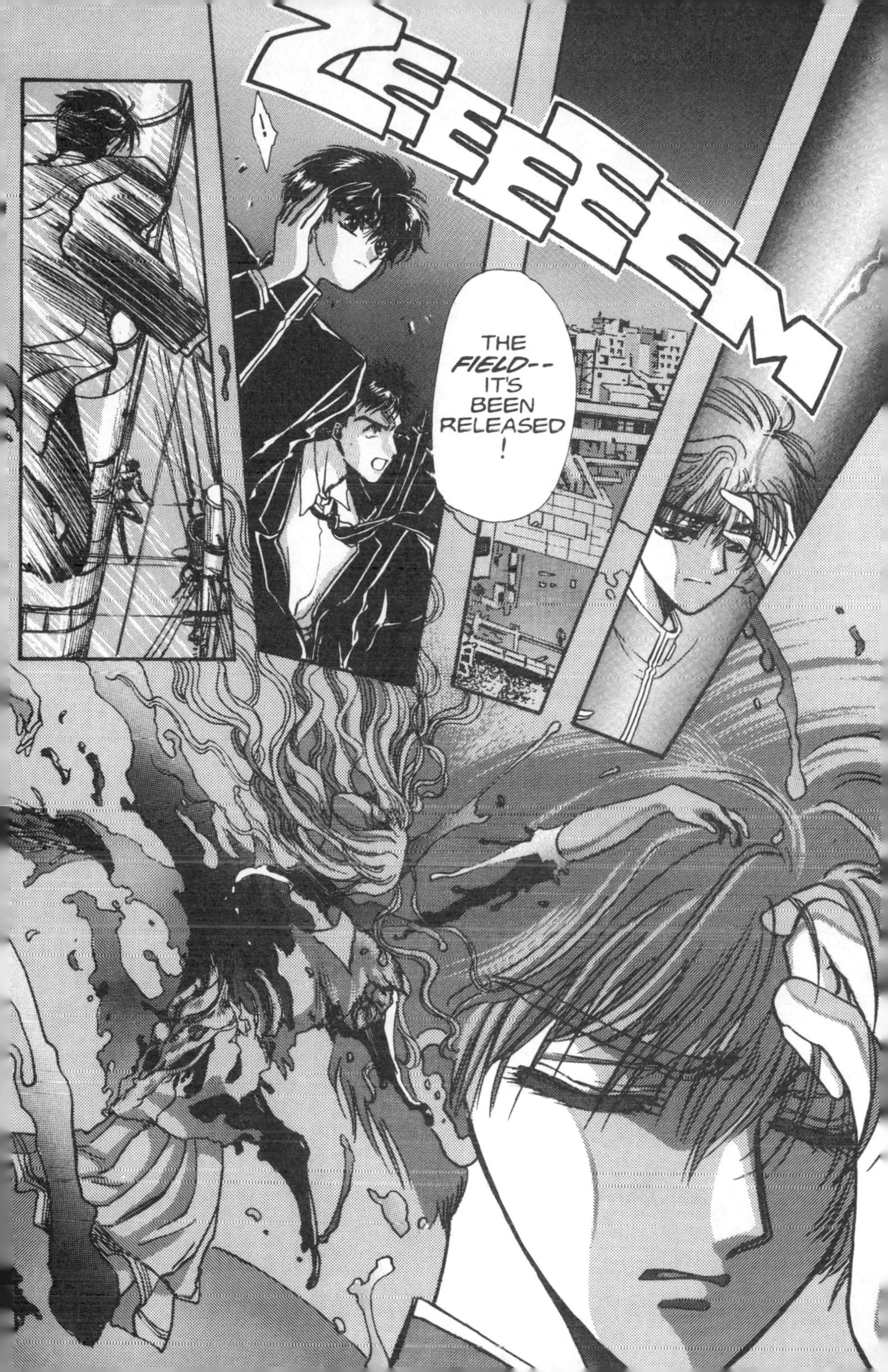
!
ZEEEEEM
THE *FIELD*--
IT'S BEEN RELEASED!

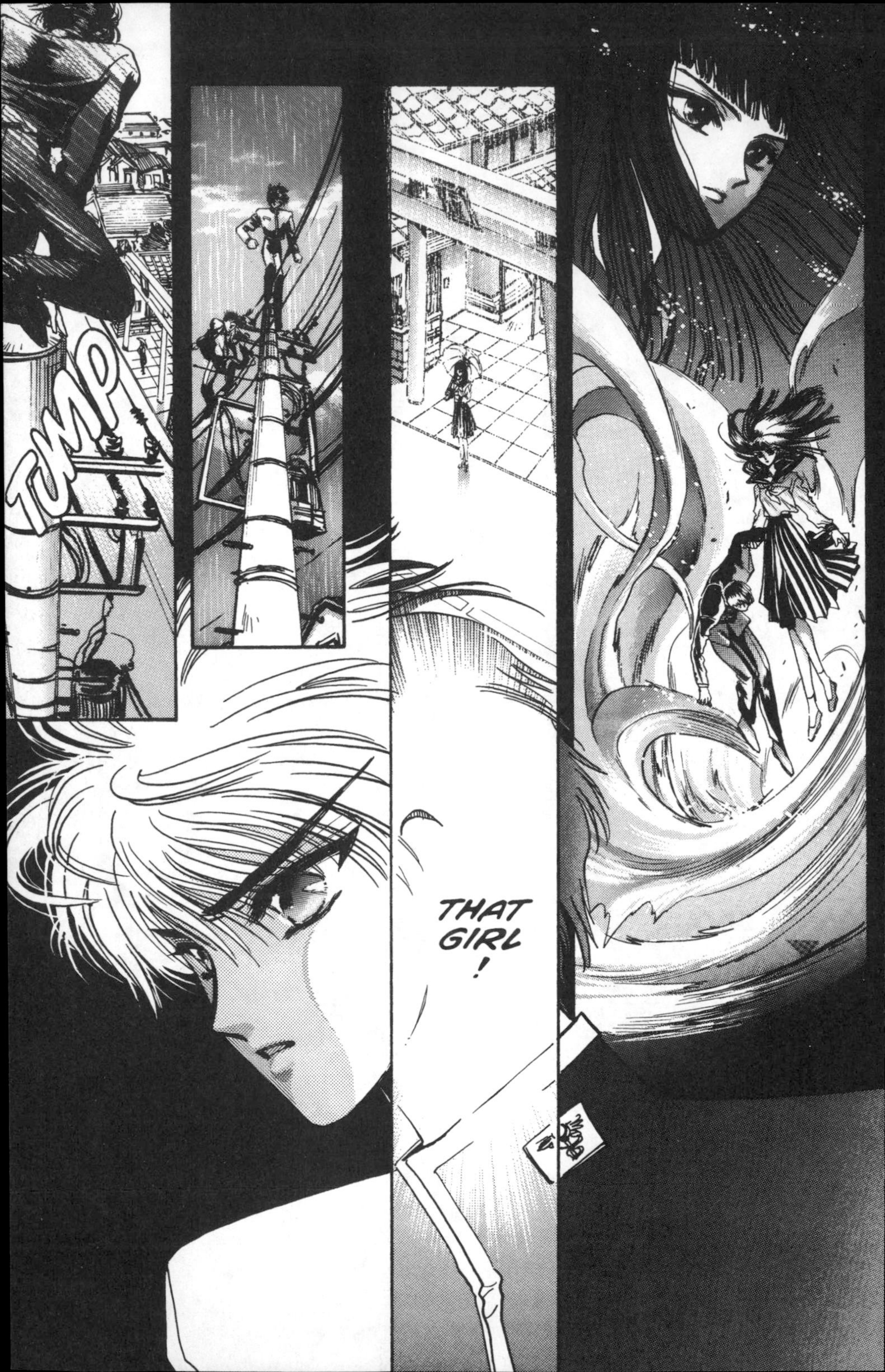
TUMP
THAT GIRL!

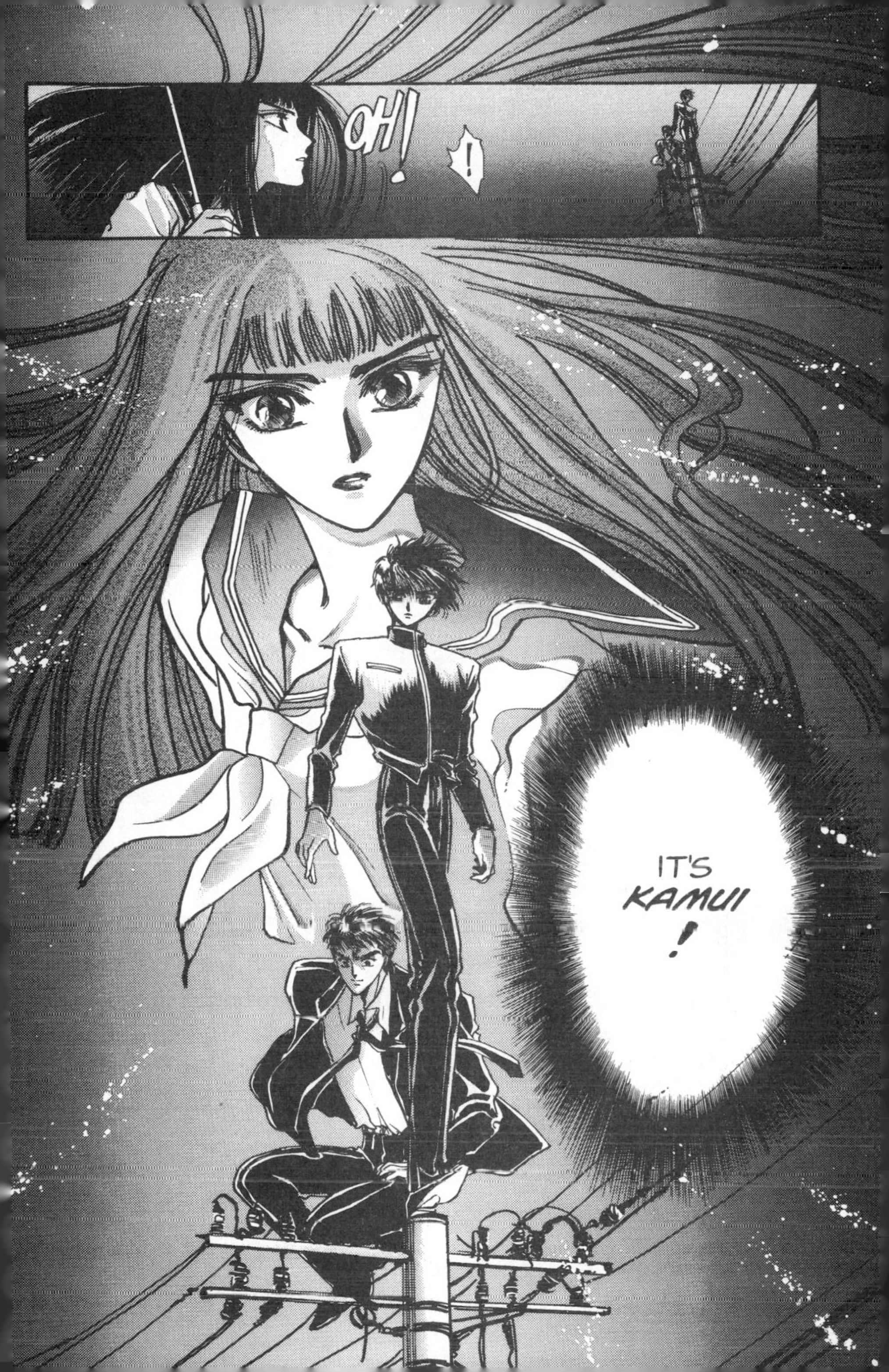
OH!
!
IT'S KAMUI!

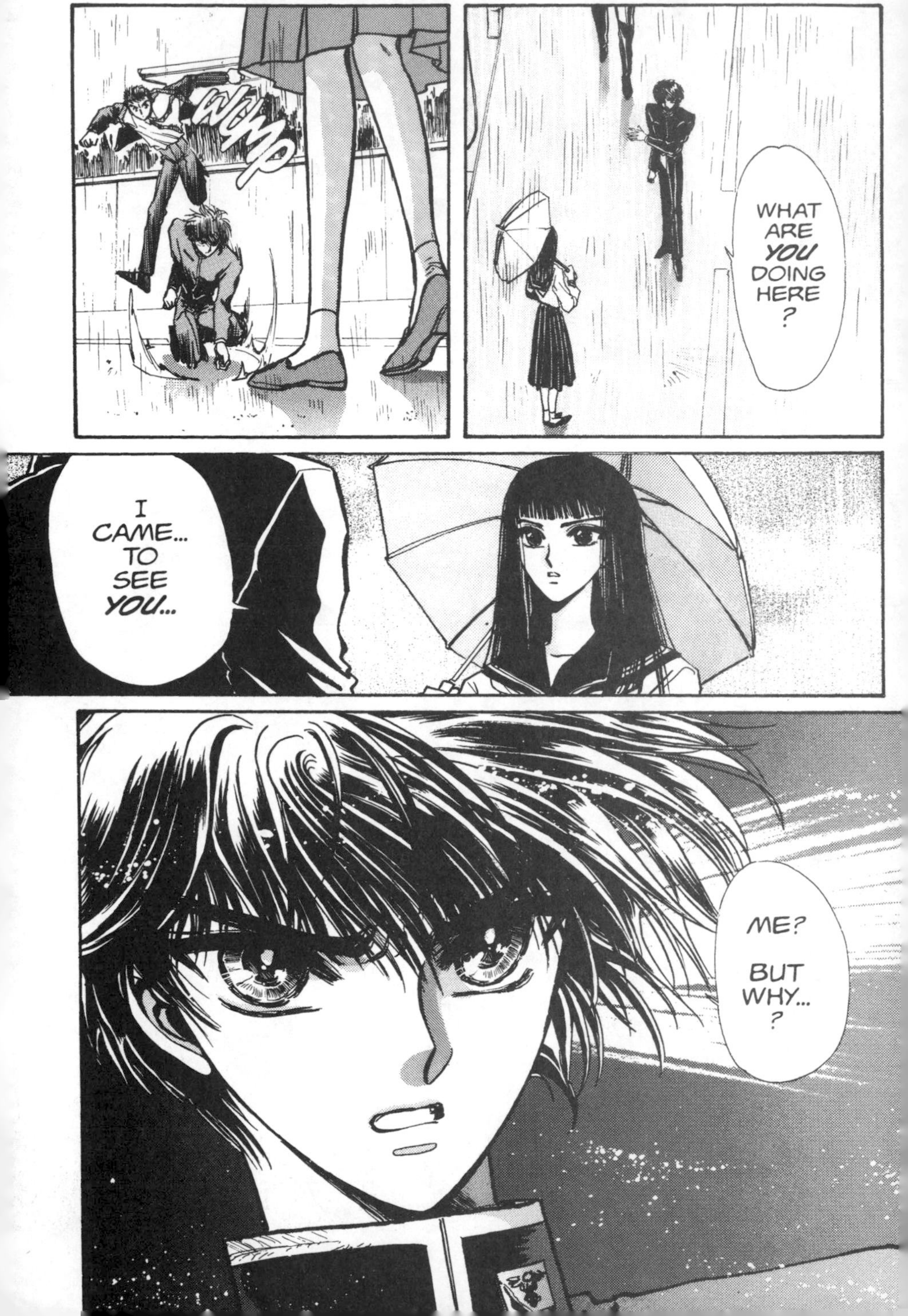
WUMP
WHAT ARE YOU DOING HERE?
I CAME... TO SEE YOU...
ME? BUT WHY...?

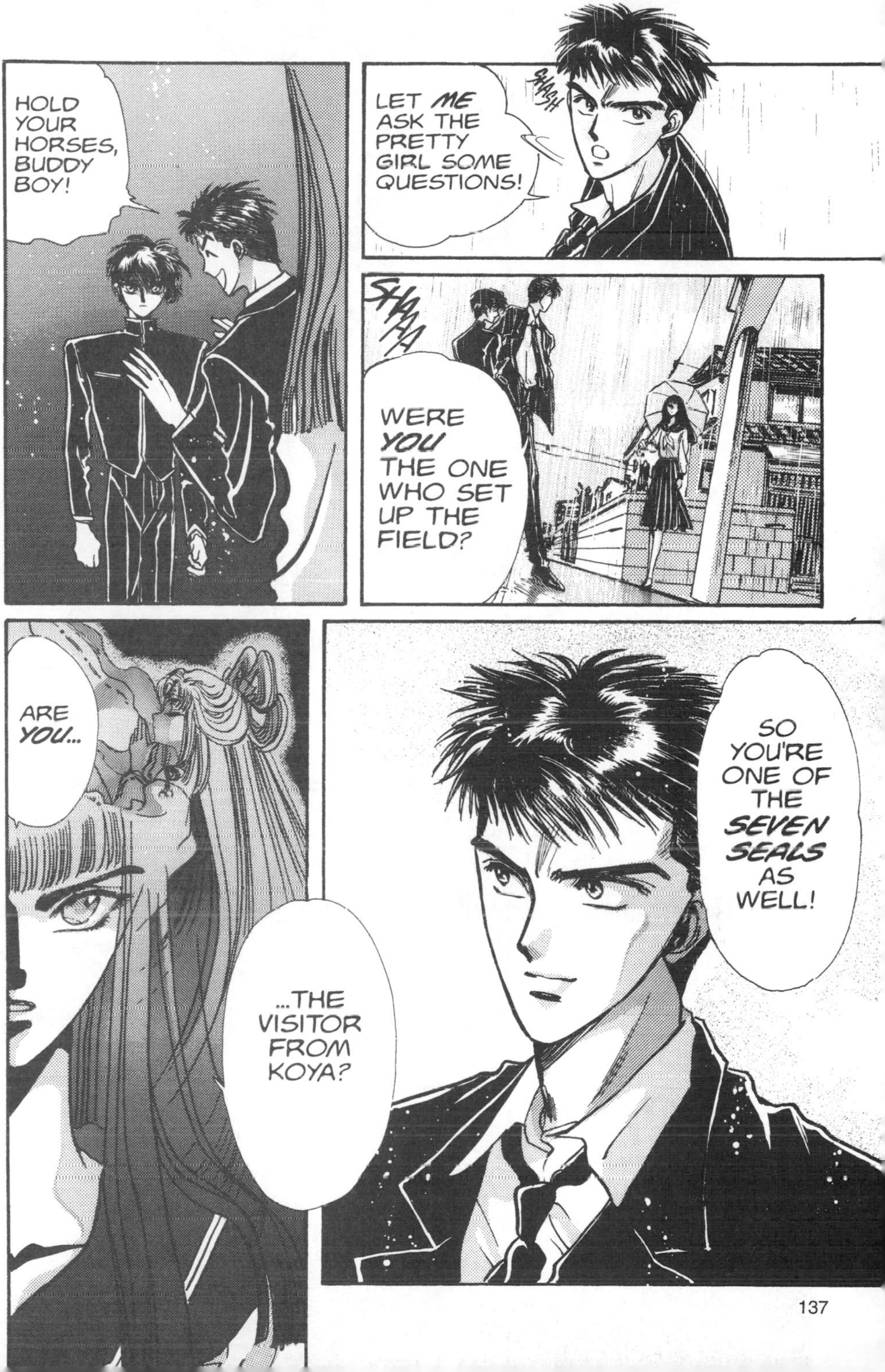
HOLD YOUR HORSES, BUDDY BOY!
SHASH
LET *ME* ASK THE PRETTY GIRL SOME QUESTIONS!
SHAAA
WERE *YOU* THE ONE WHO SET UP THE FIELD?
ARE *YOU*...
...THE VISITOR FROM KOYA?
SO YOU'RE ONE OF THE *SEVEN SEALS* AS WELL!

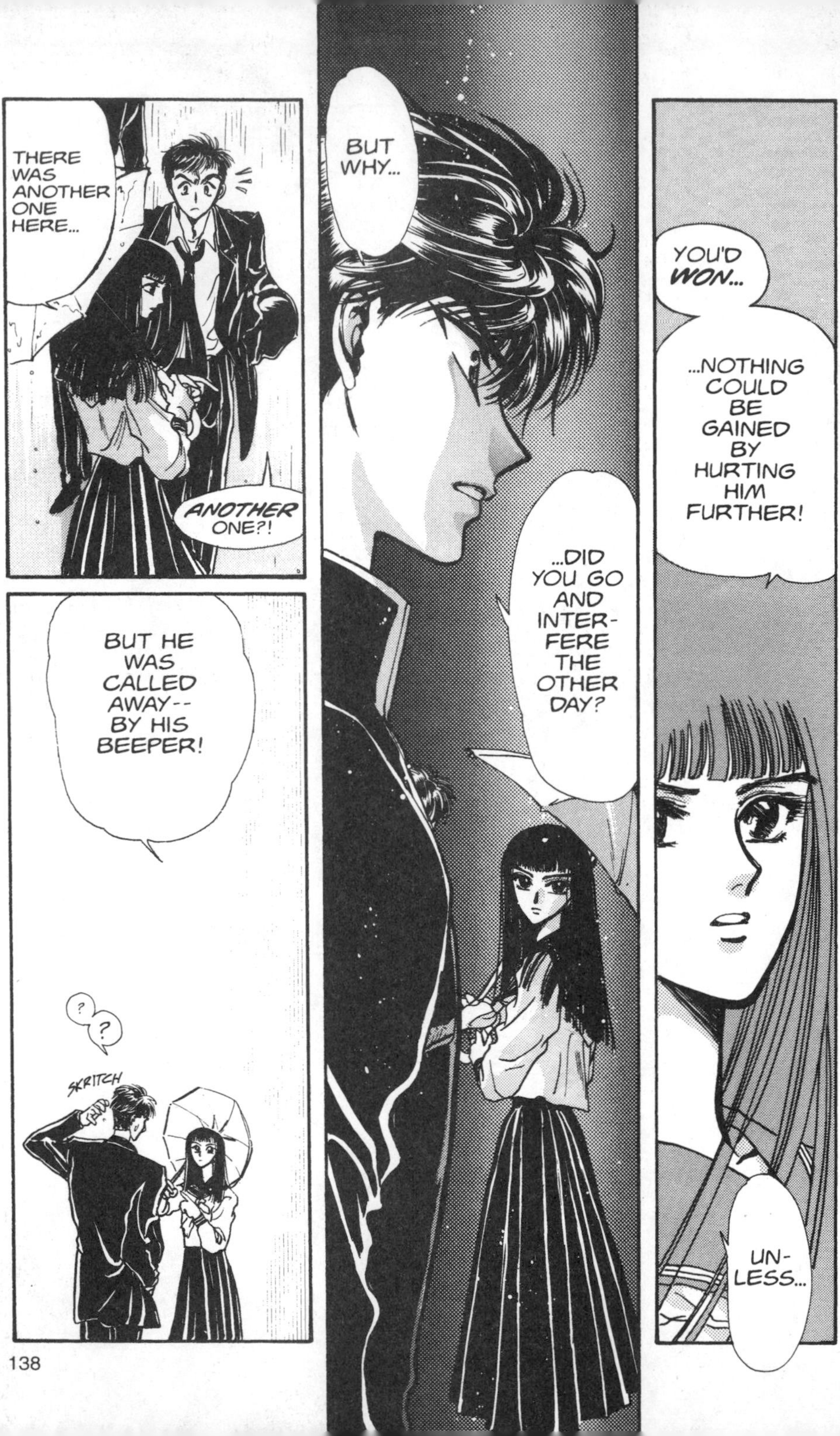
THERE WAS ANOTHER ONE HERE...
ANOTHER ONE?!
BUT HE WAS CALLED AWAY-- BY HIS BEEPER!
?
?
SKRITCH
BUT WHY...
...DID YOU GO AND INTER-FERE THE OTHER DAY?
YOU'D WON...
...NOTHING COULD BE GAINED BY HURTING HIM FURTHER!
UN-LESS...

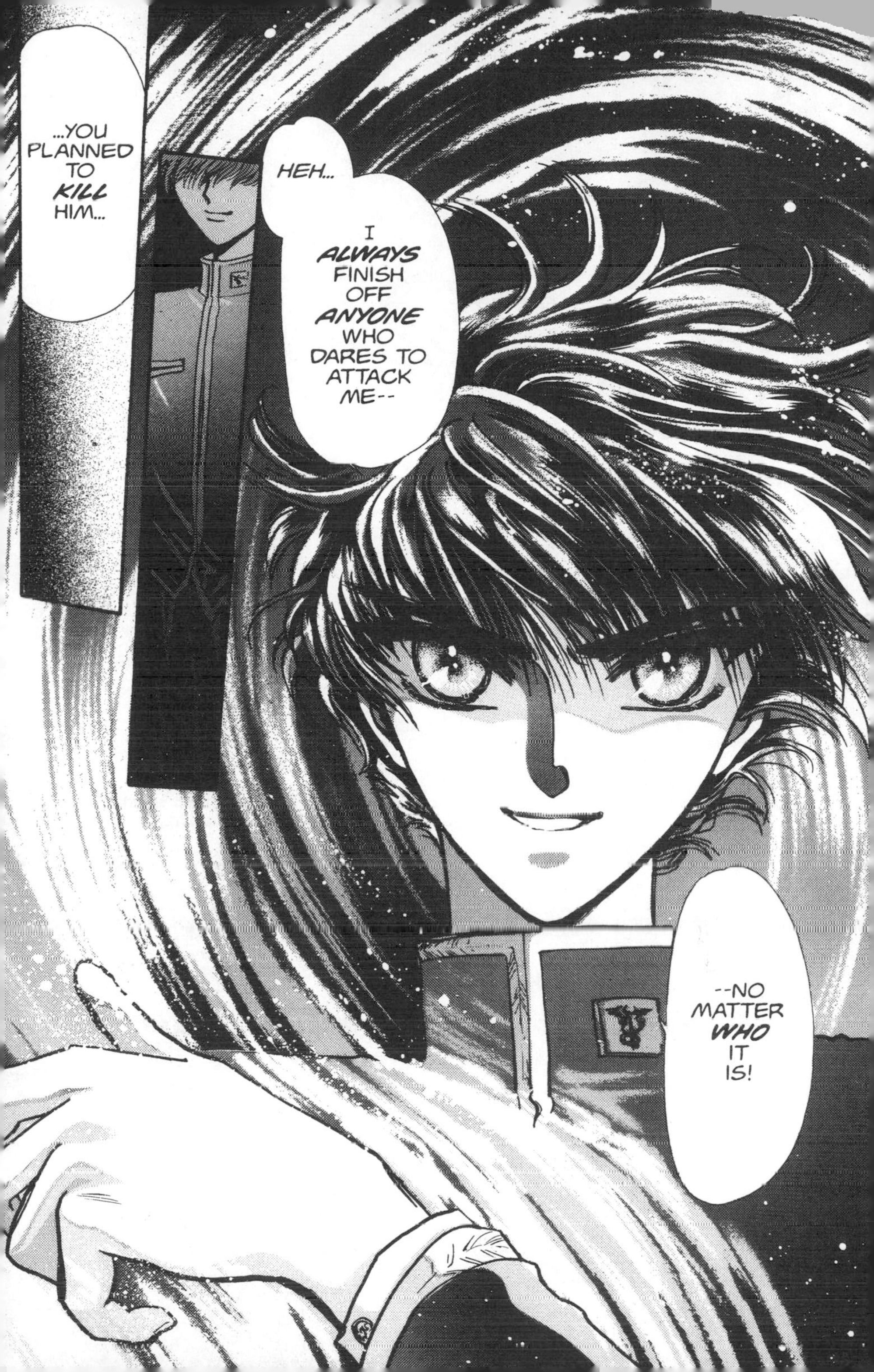
...YOU PLANNED TO KILL HIM...
HEH...
I ALWAYS FINISH OFF ANYONE WHO DARES TO ATTACK ME--
--NO MATTER WHO IT IS!

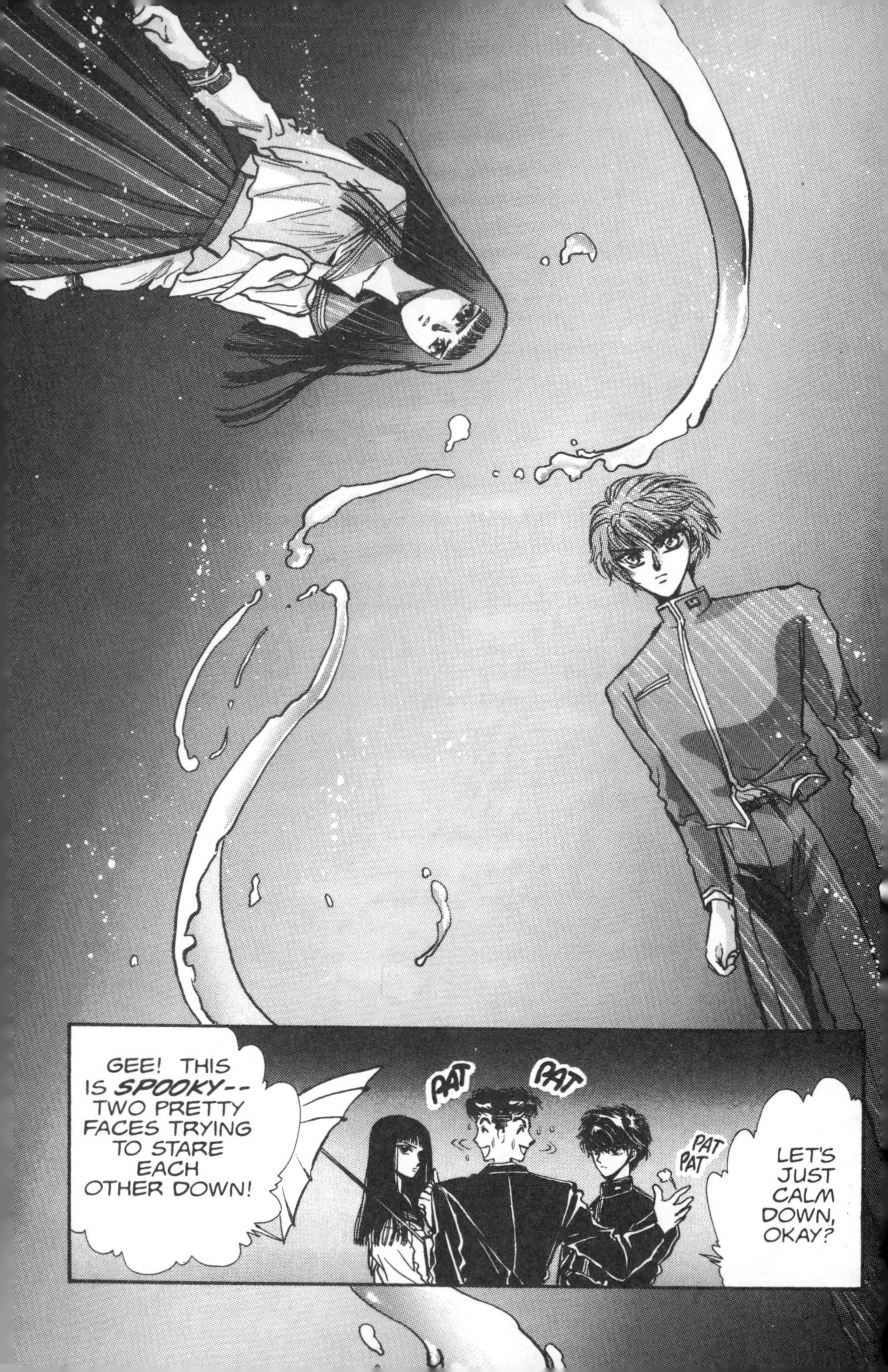

LET'S JUST CALM DOWN, OKAY?
PAT PAT
PAT
PAT
GEE! THIS IS SPOOKY-- TWO PRETTY FACES TRYING TO STARE EACH OTHER DOWN!

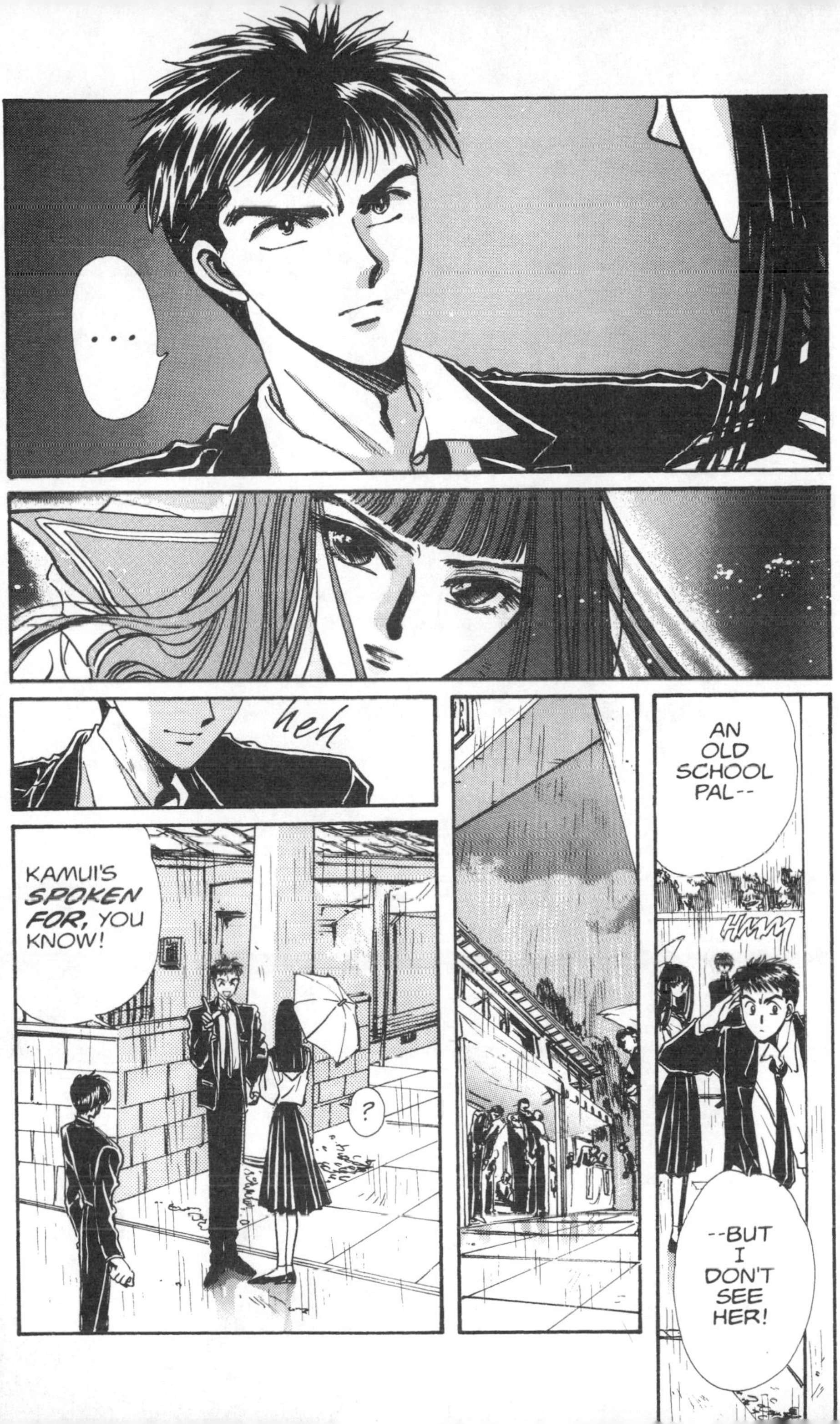
...
heh
KAMUI'S **SPOKEN FOR,** YOU KNOW!
?
AN OLD SCHOOL PAL--
HMM
--BUT I DON'T SEE HER!

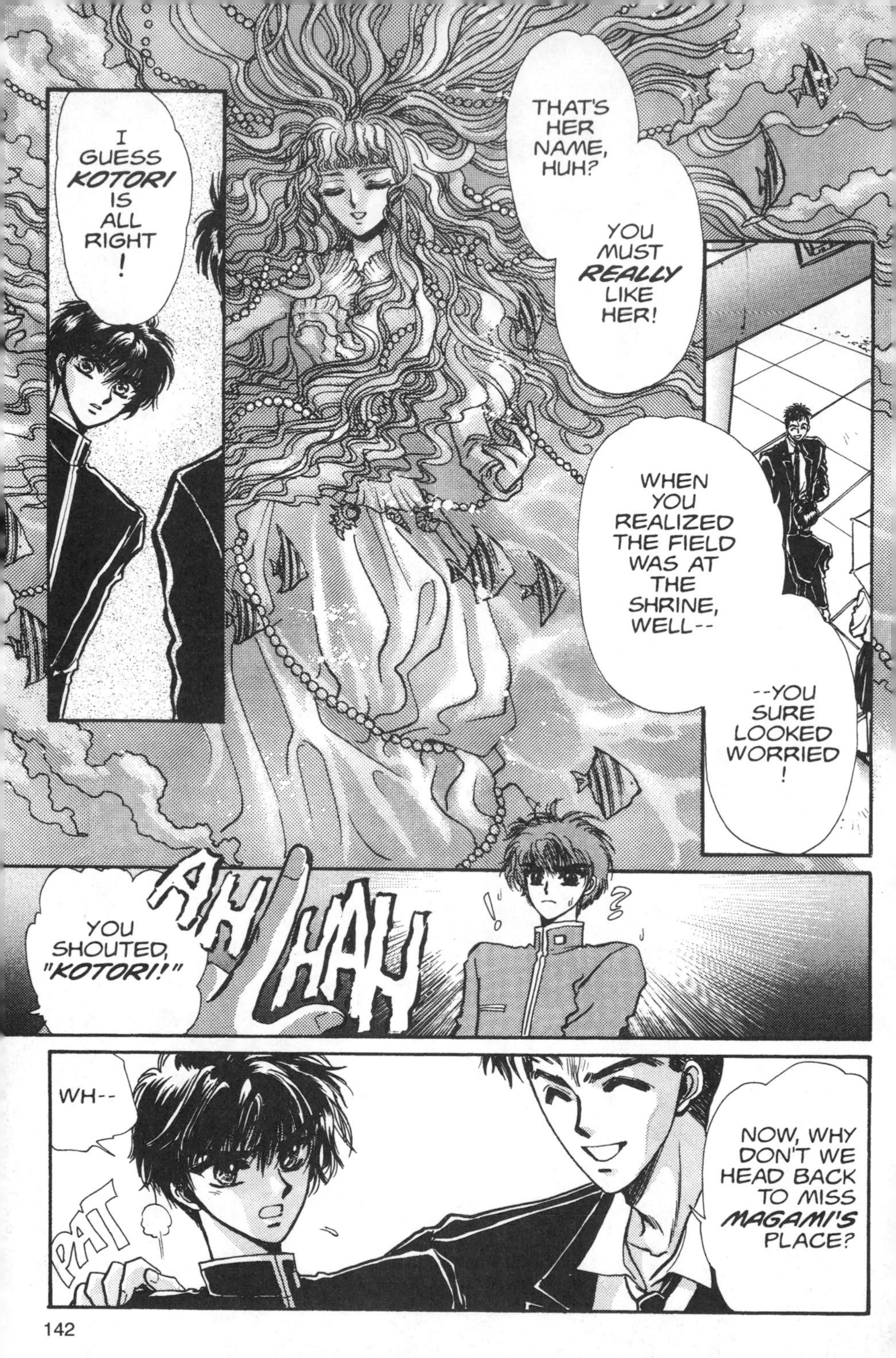
I GUESS KOTORI IS ALL RIGHT!
THAT'S HER NAME, HUH?
YOU MUST REALLY LIKE HER!
WHEN YOU REALIZED THE FIELD WAS AT THE SHRINE, WELL--
--YOU SURE LOOKED WORRIED!
YOU SHOUTED, "KOTORI!"
AH HAH HAH
WH--
PAT
NOW, WHY DON'T WE HEAD BACK TO MISS MAGAMI'S PLACE?

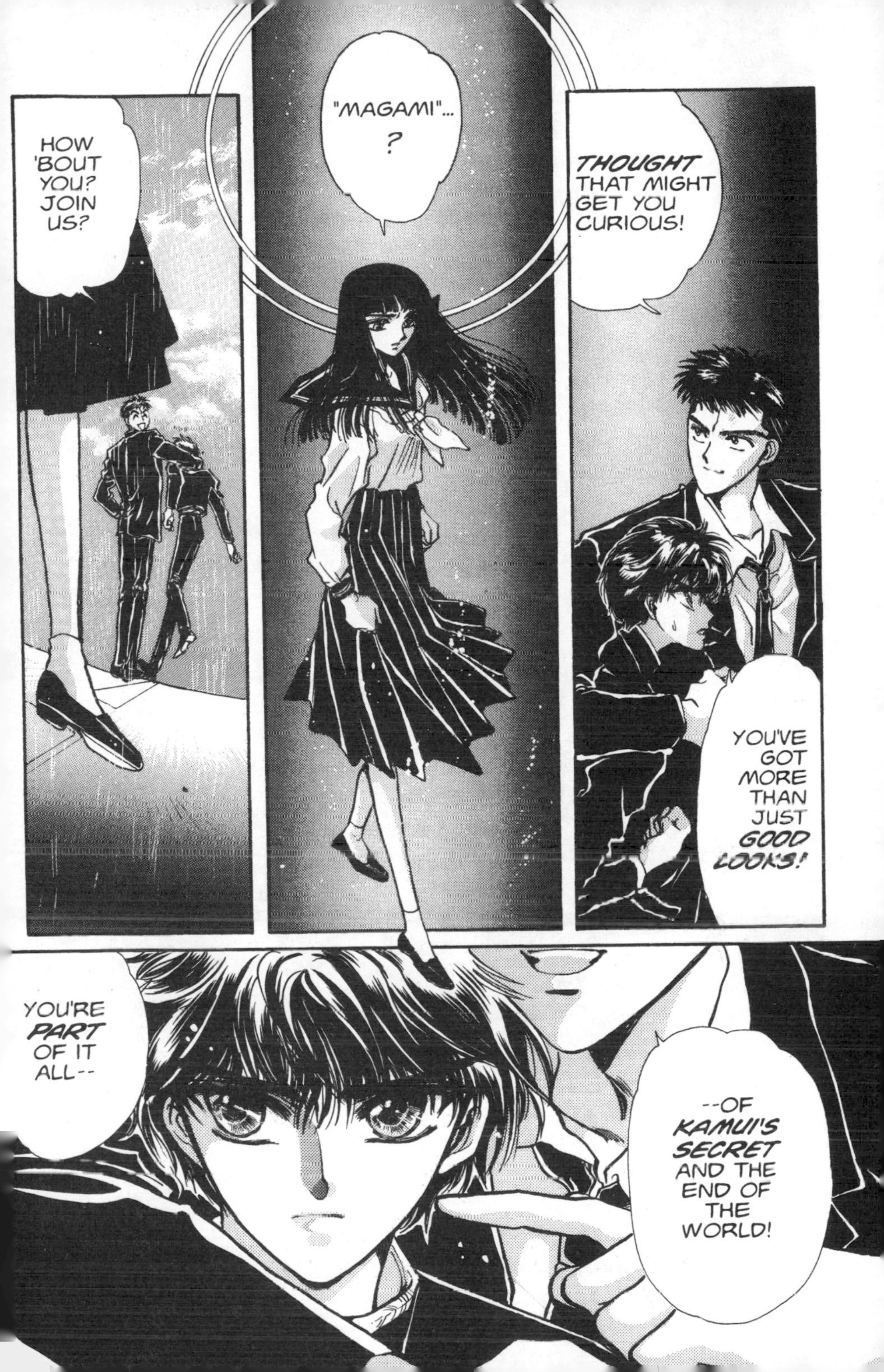
HOW 'BOUT YOU? JOIN US?
"MAGAMI"... ?
THOUGHT THAT MIGHT GET YOU CURIOUS!
YOU'VE GOT MORE THAN JUST GOOD LOOKS!
YOU'RE PART OF IT ALL--
--OF KAMUI'S SECRET AND THE END OF THE WORLD!

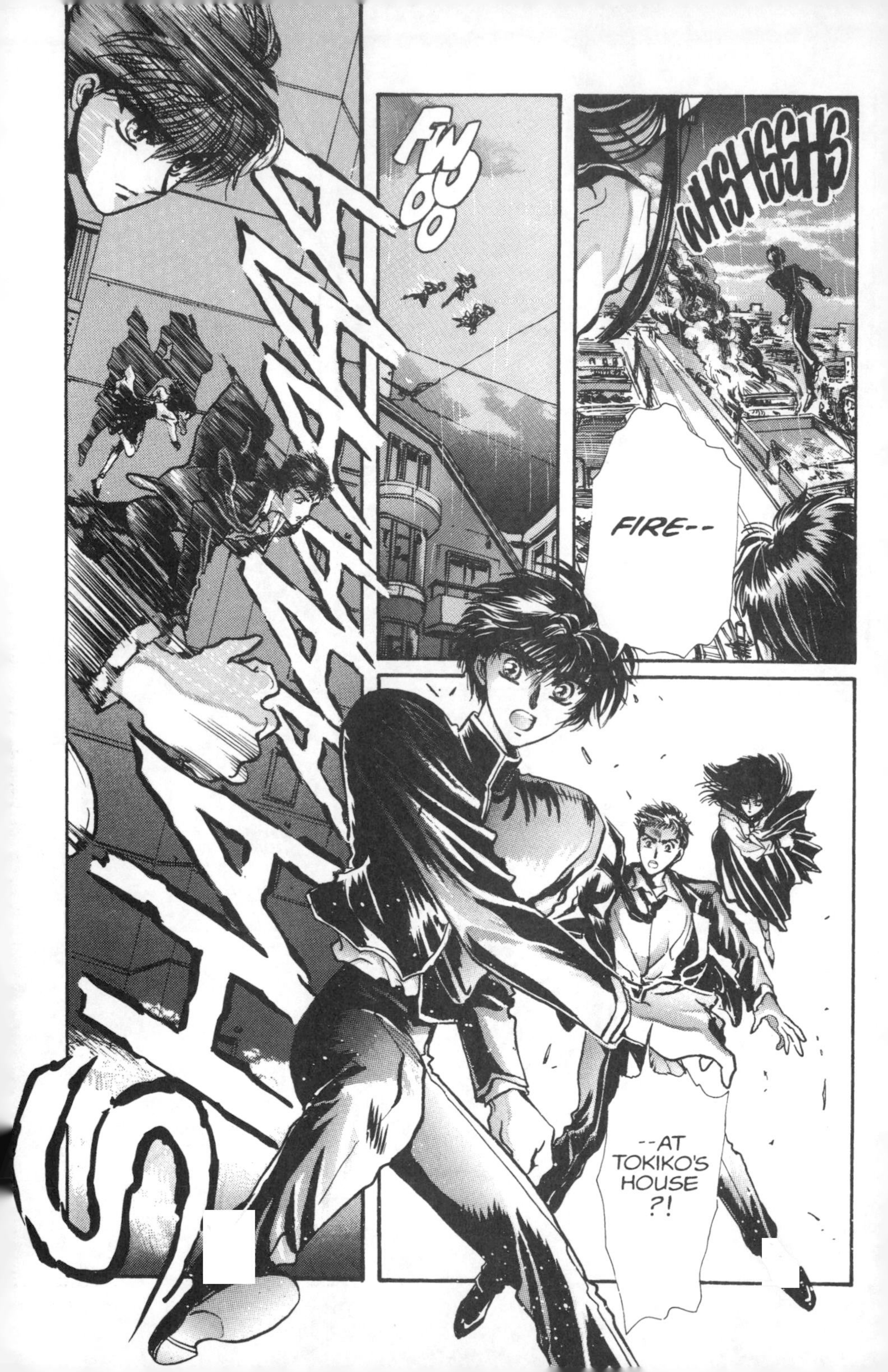
WHSHSSHS
FIRE--
--AT TOKIKO'S HOUSE ?!

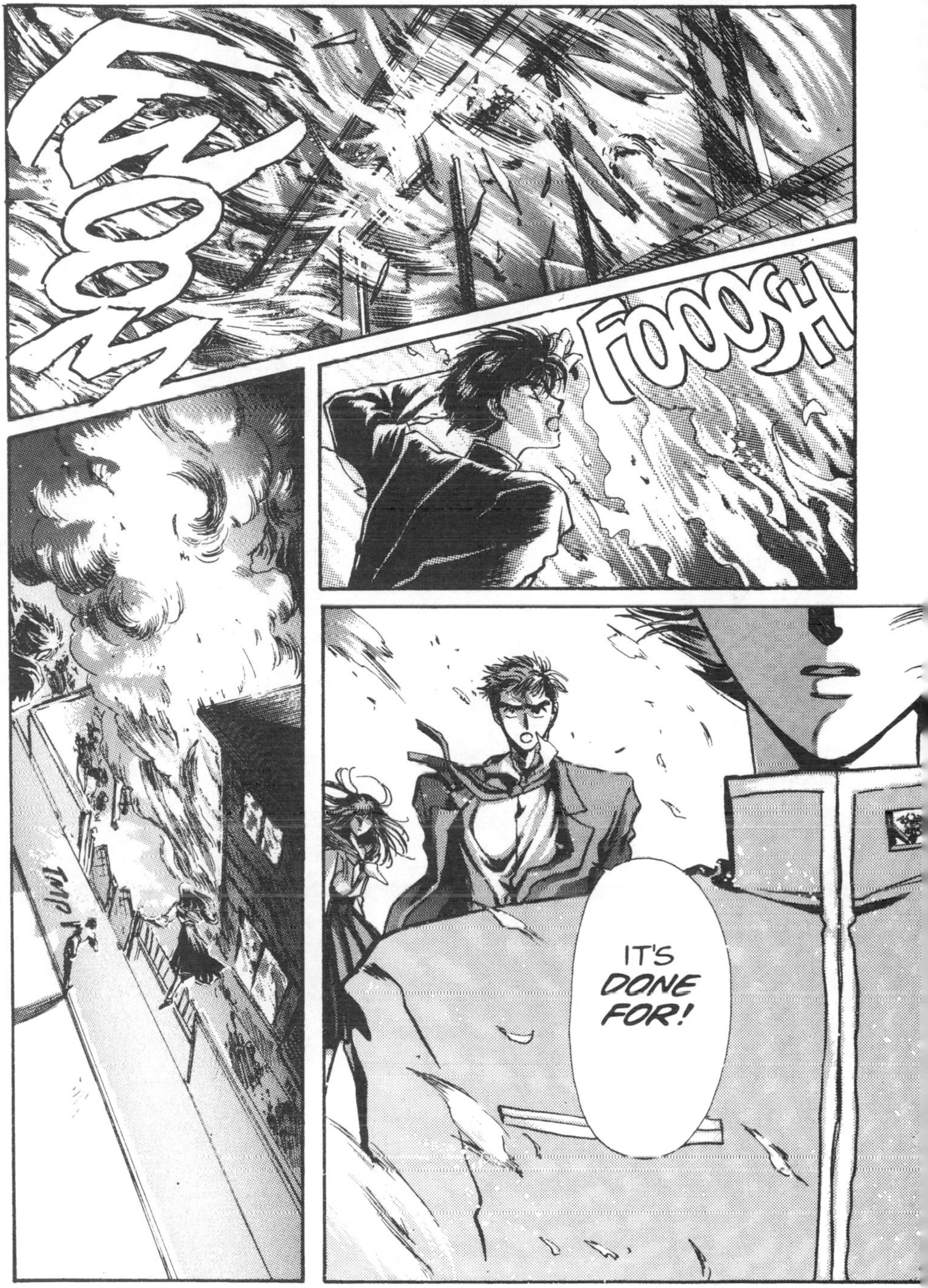
BOOM
FOOOSH
IT'S *DONE FOR!*

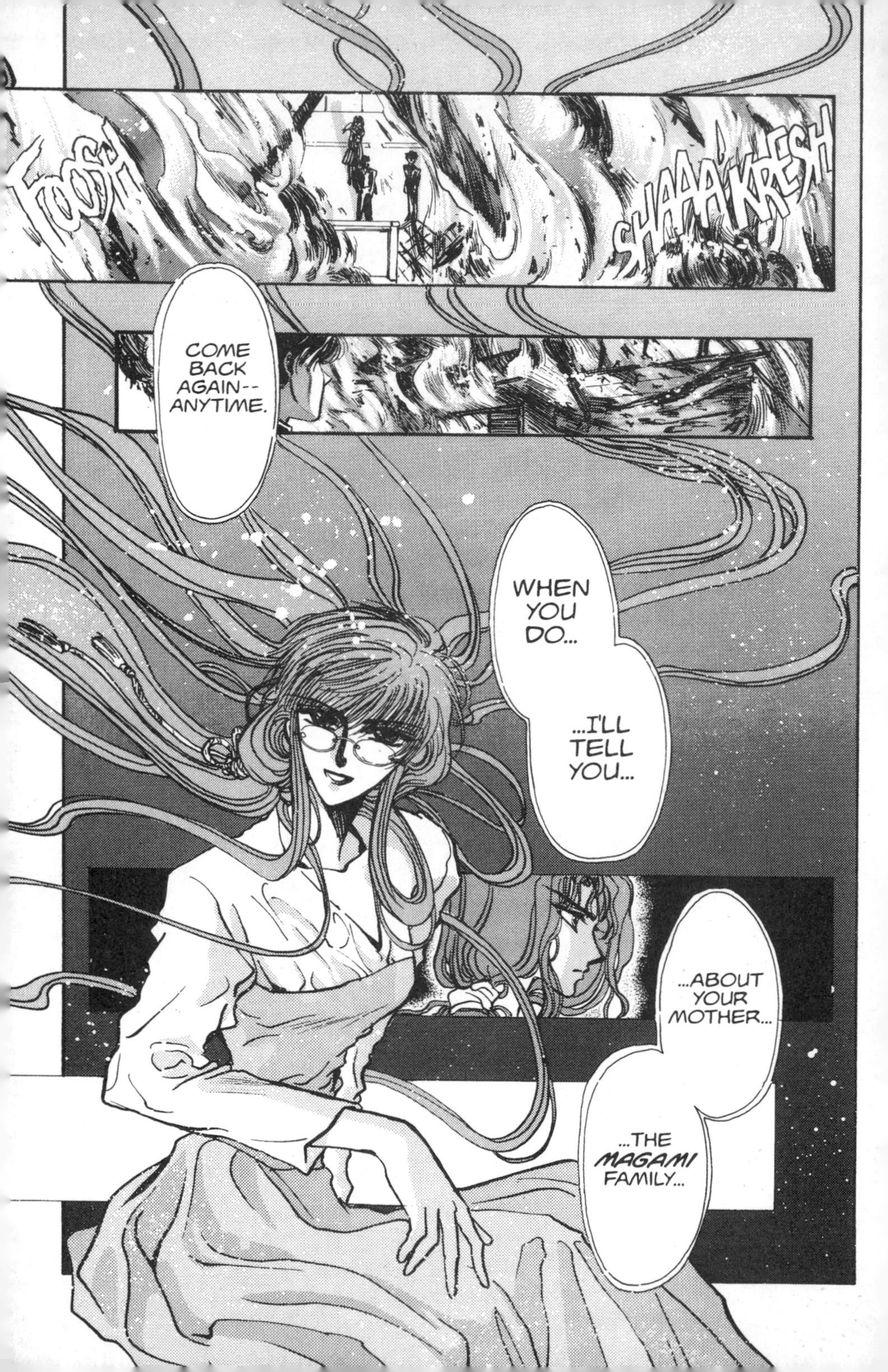
SHAAA KRESH
FOOSH
COME BACK AGAIN-- ANYTIME.
WHEN YOU DO...
...I'LL TELL YOU...
...ABOUT YOUR MOTHER...
...THE MAGAMI FAMILY...

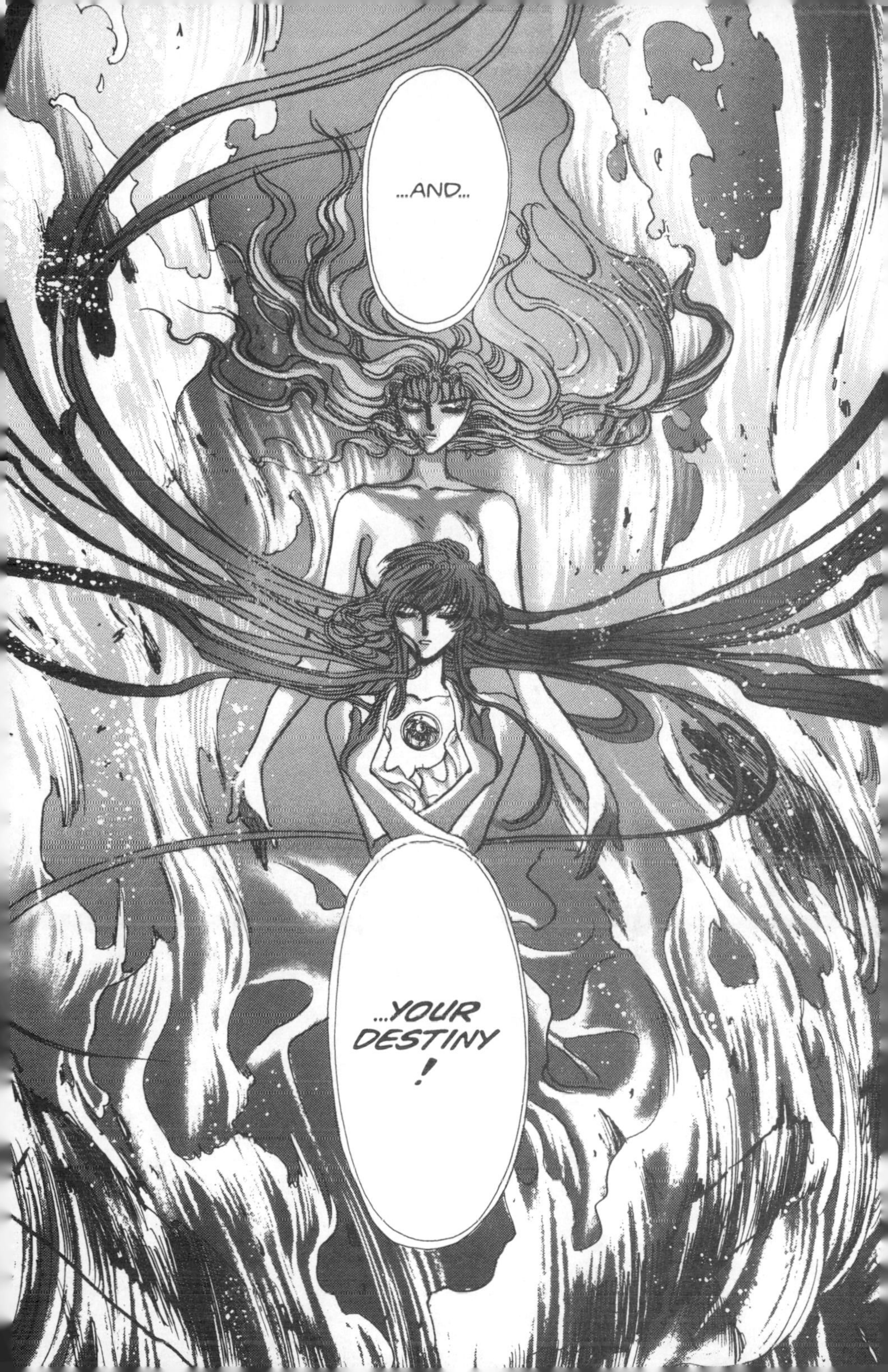
...AND...
...YOUR DESTINY !

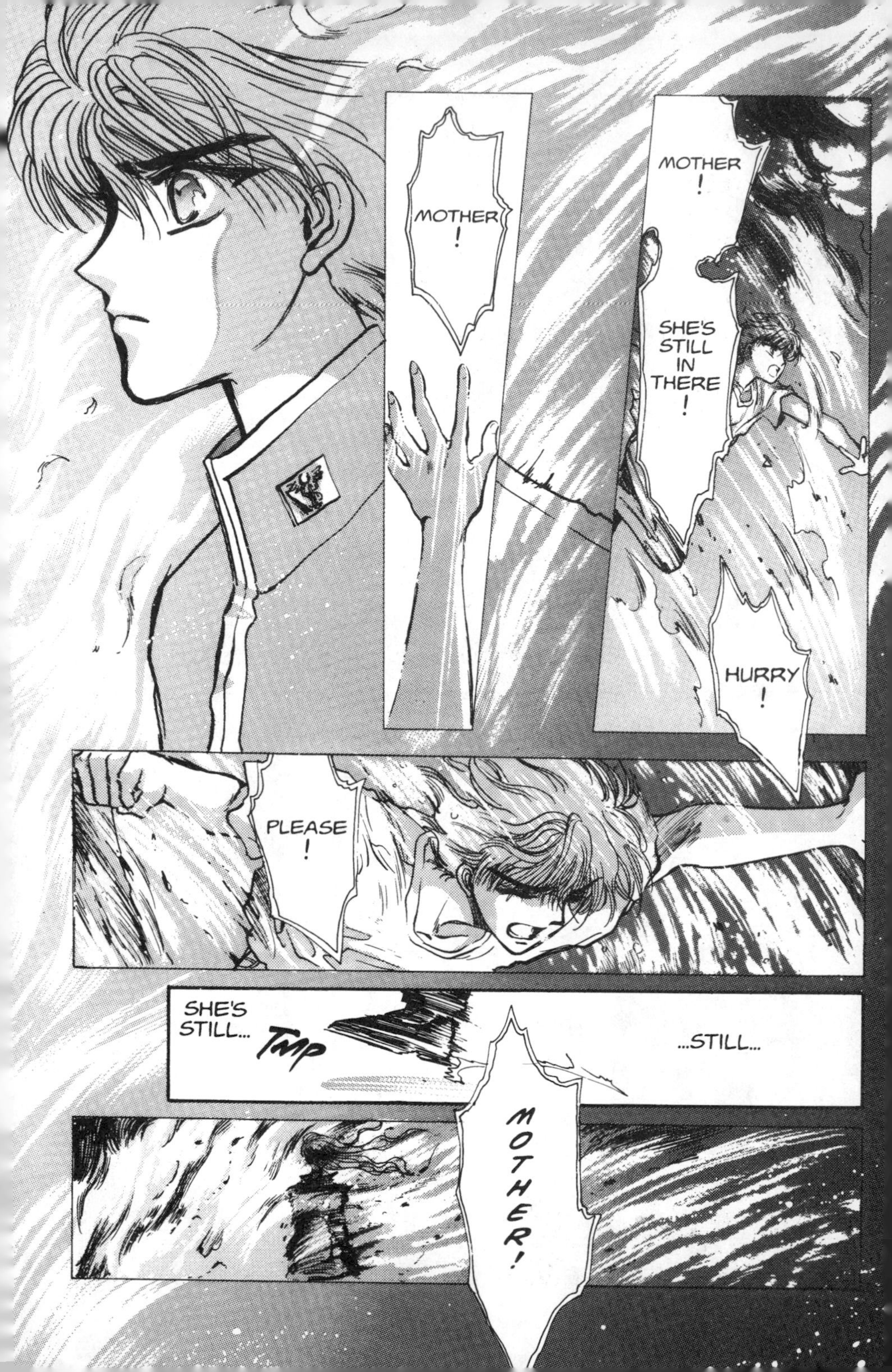
MOTHER!
MOTHER!
SHE'S STILL IN THERE!
HURRY!
PLEASE!
SHE'S STILL...
TMP
...STILL...
MOTHER!

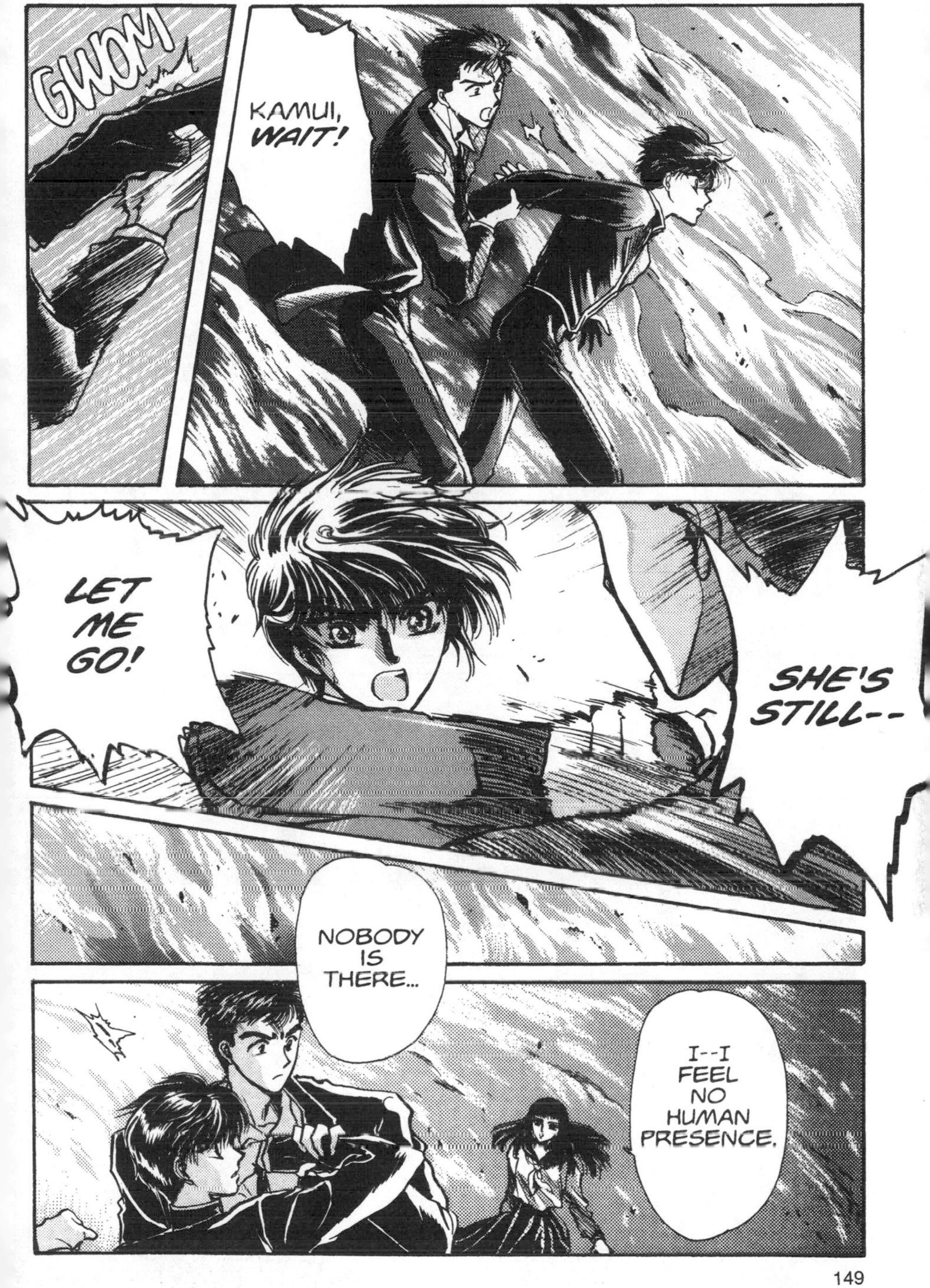
GWOM
KAMUI, WAIT!
LET ME GO!
SHE'S STILL--
NOBODY IS THERE...
I--I FEEL NO HUMAN PRESENCE.

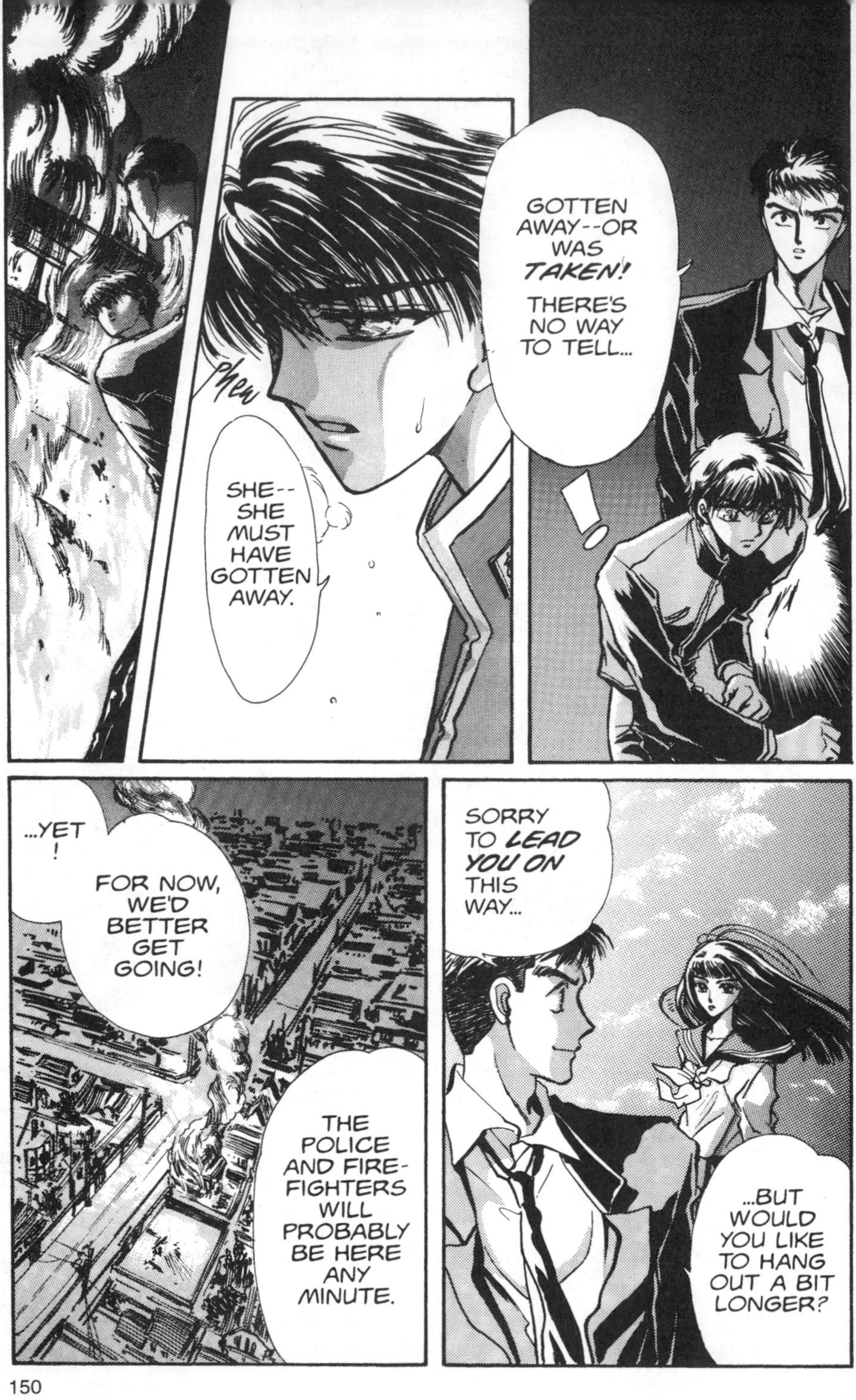
Phew
SHE-- SHE MUST HAVE GOTTEN AWAY.
GOTTEN AWAY--OR WAS TAKEN!
THERE'S NO WAY TO TELL...
!
...YET!
FOR NOW, WE'D BETTER GET GOING!
THE POLICE AND FIRE-FIGHTERS WILL PROBABLY BE HERE ANY MINUTE.
SORRY TO LEAD YOU ON THIS WAY...
...BUT WOULD YOU LIKE TO HANG OUT A BIT LONGER?

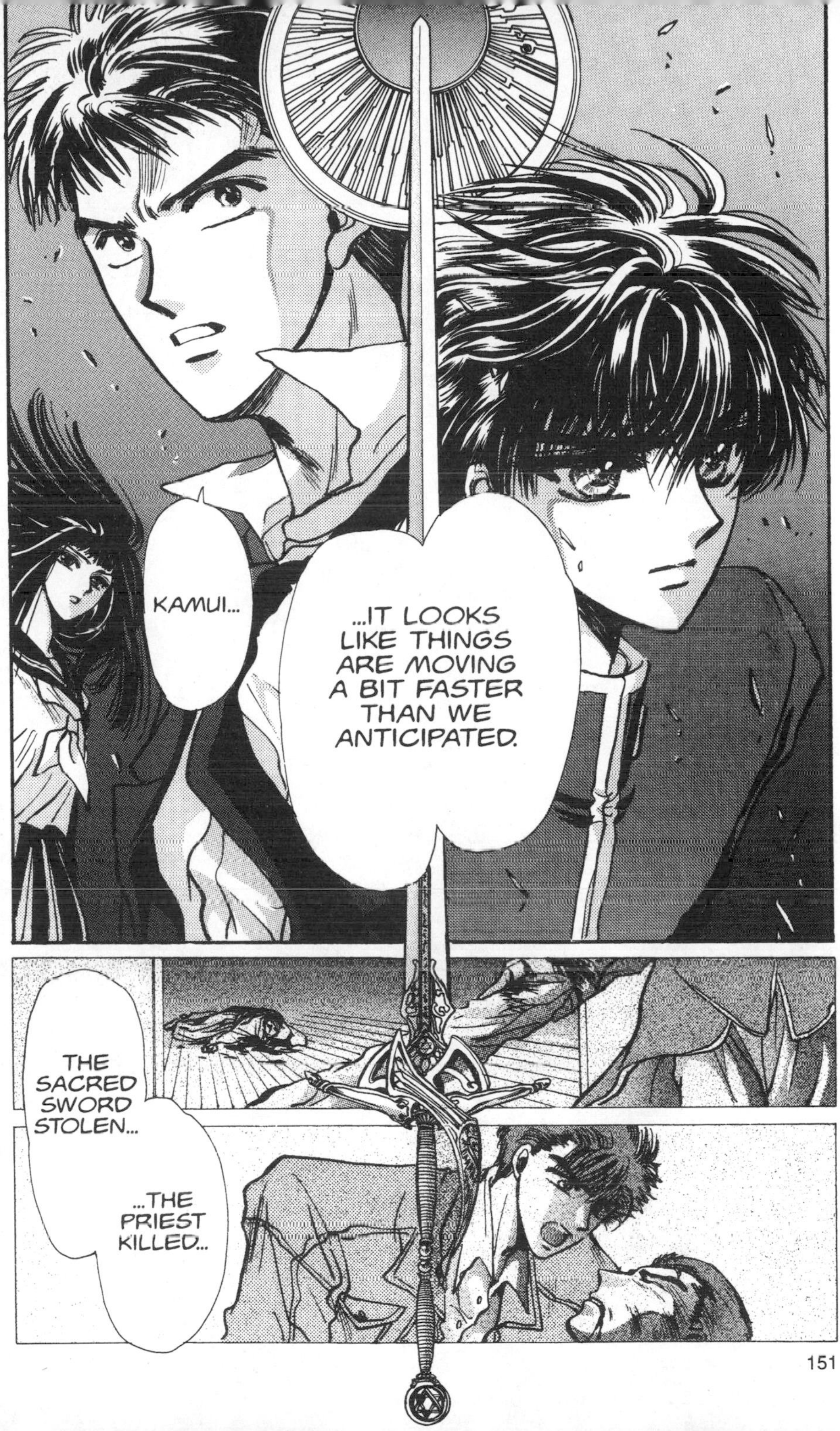
KAMUI...
...IT LOOKS LIKE THINGS ARE MOVING A BIT FASTER THAN WE ANTICIPATED.
THE SACRED SWORD STOLEN...
...THE PRIEST KILLED...

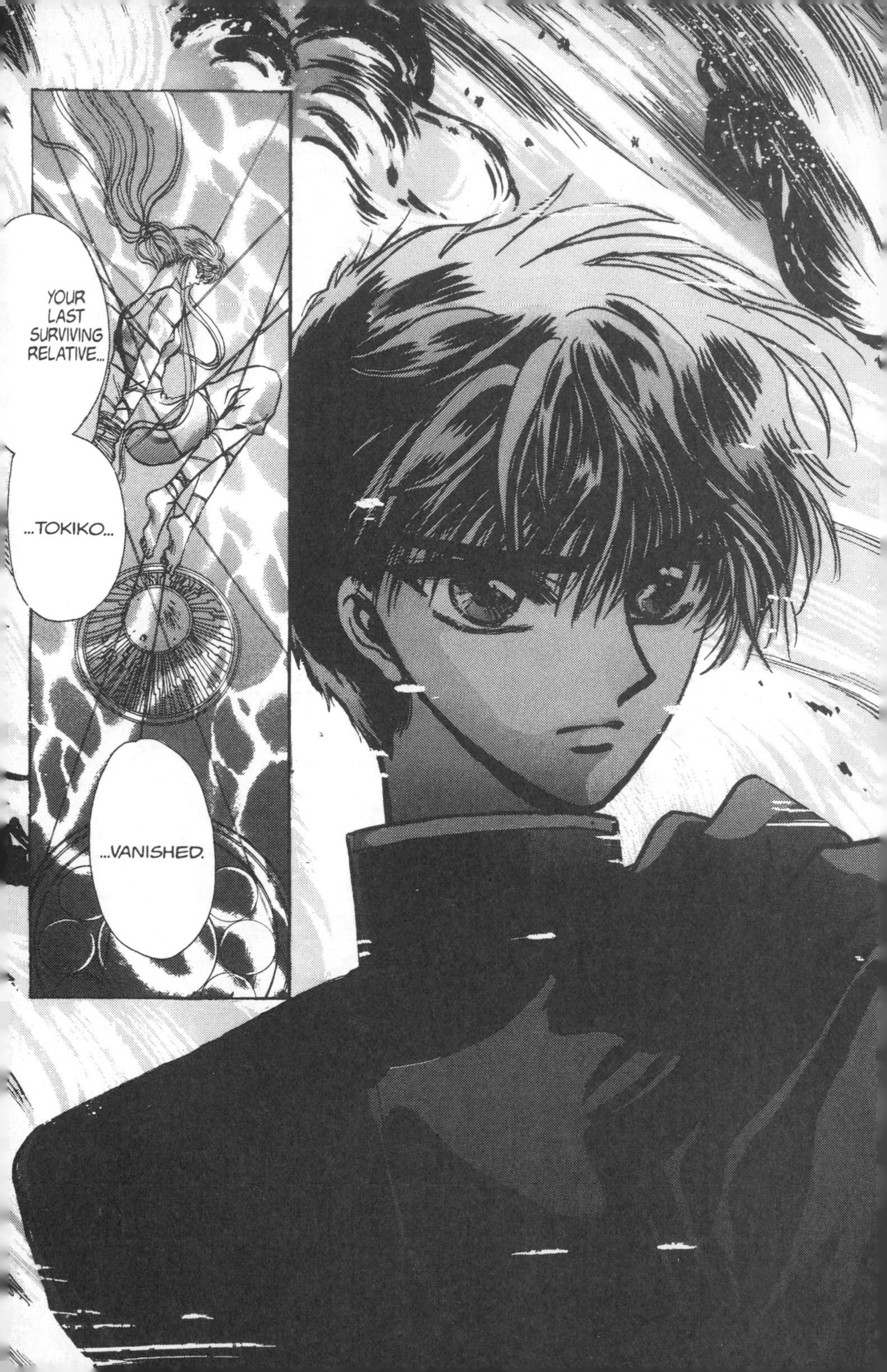
YOUR LAST SURVIVING RELATIVE...
...TOKIKO...
...VANISHED.

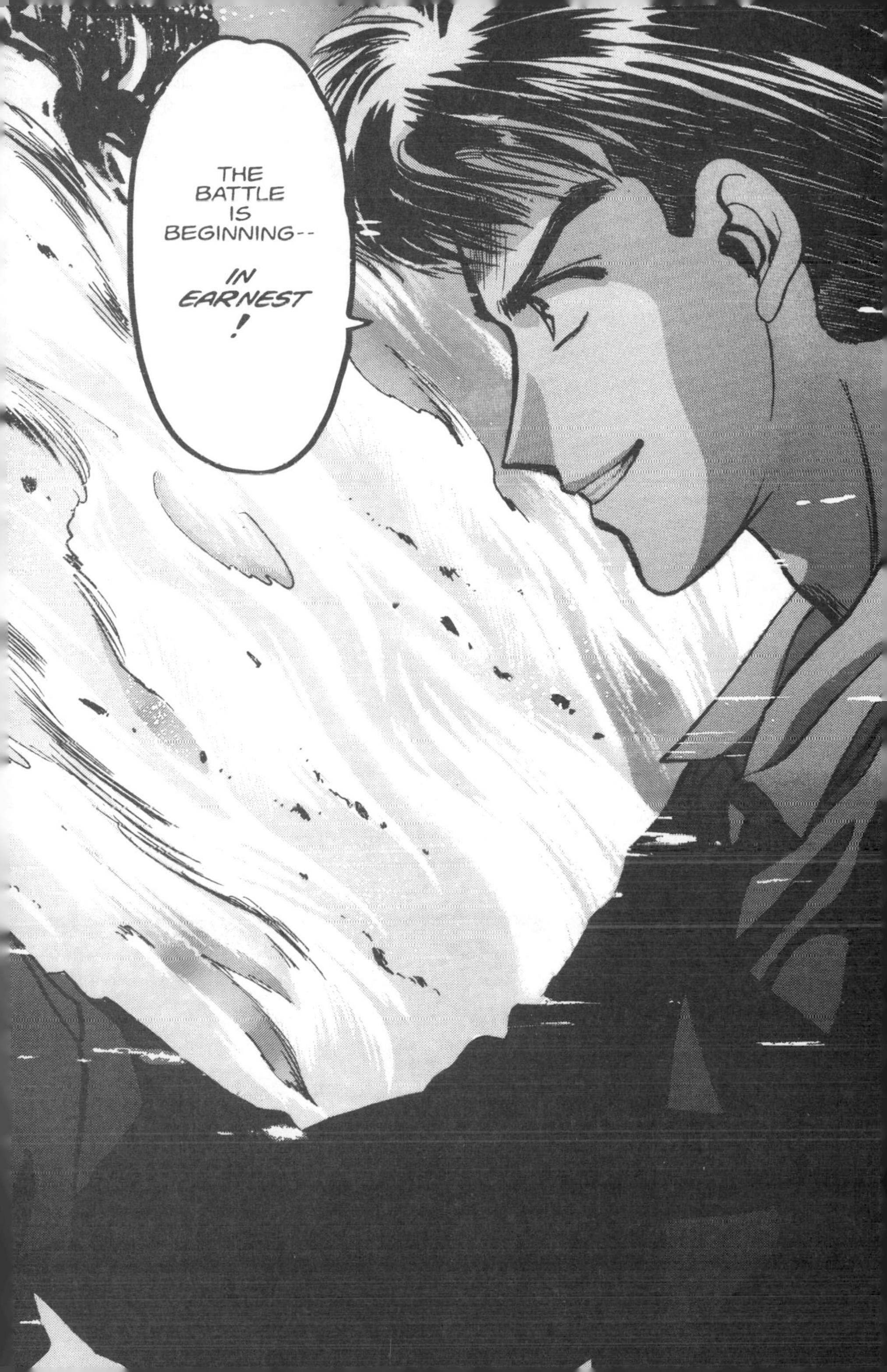
THE BATTLE IS BEGINNING-- IN EARNEST!

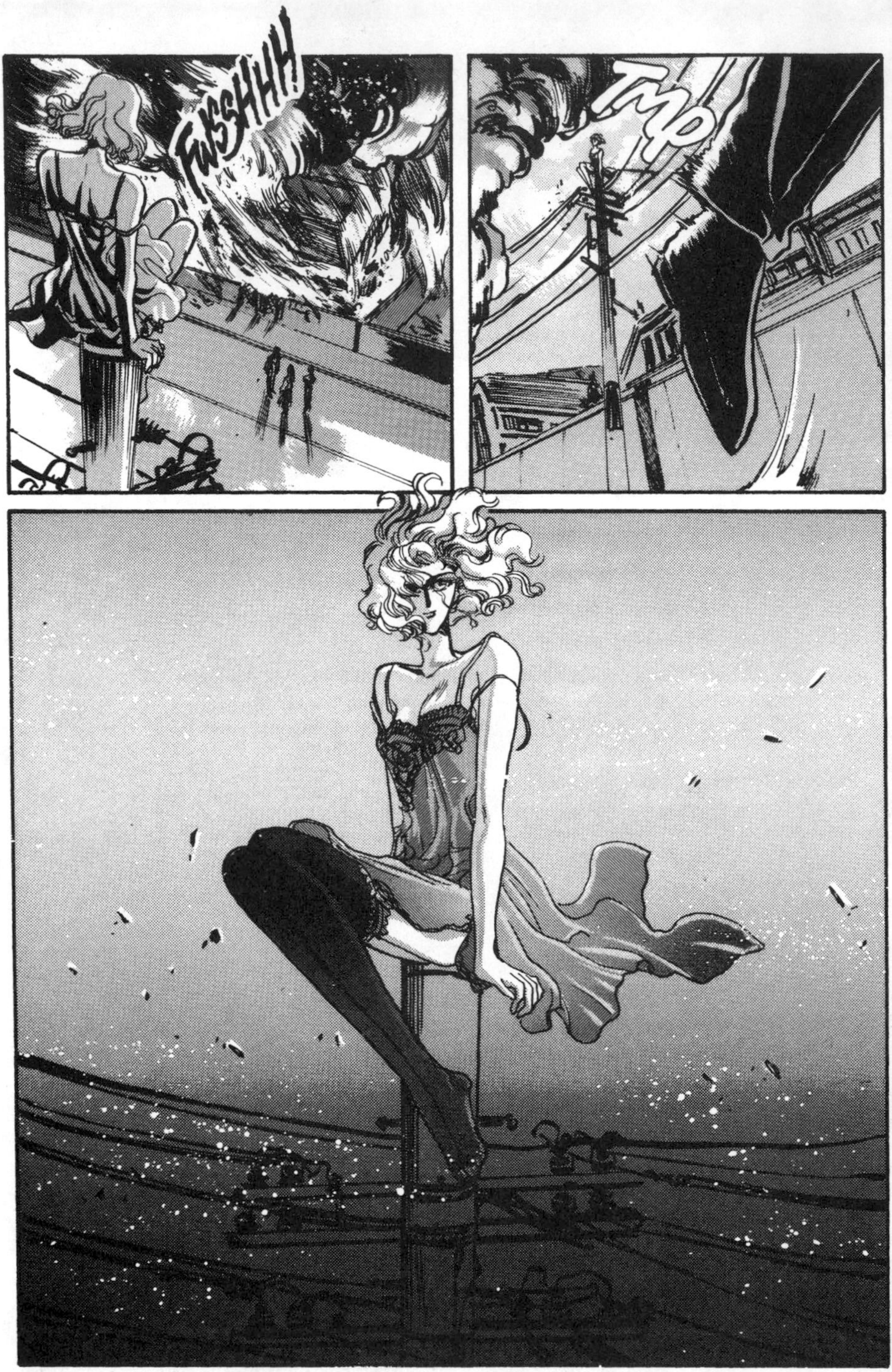
FWSSHHH!
TMP

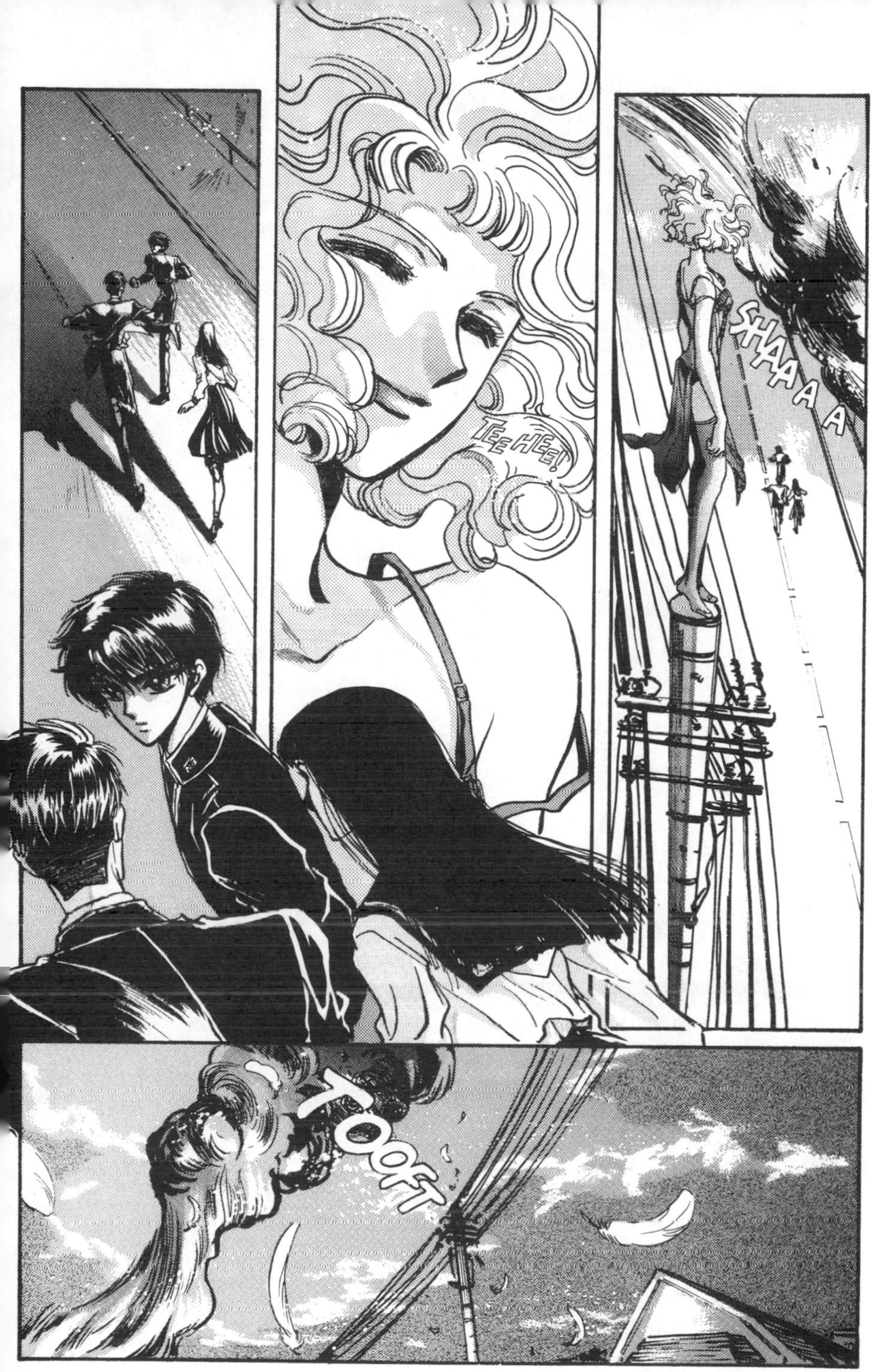
TEE HEE!
SHAAAAA
TOOF!

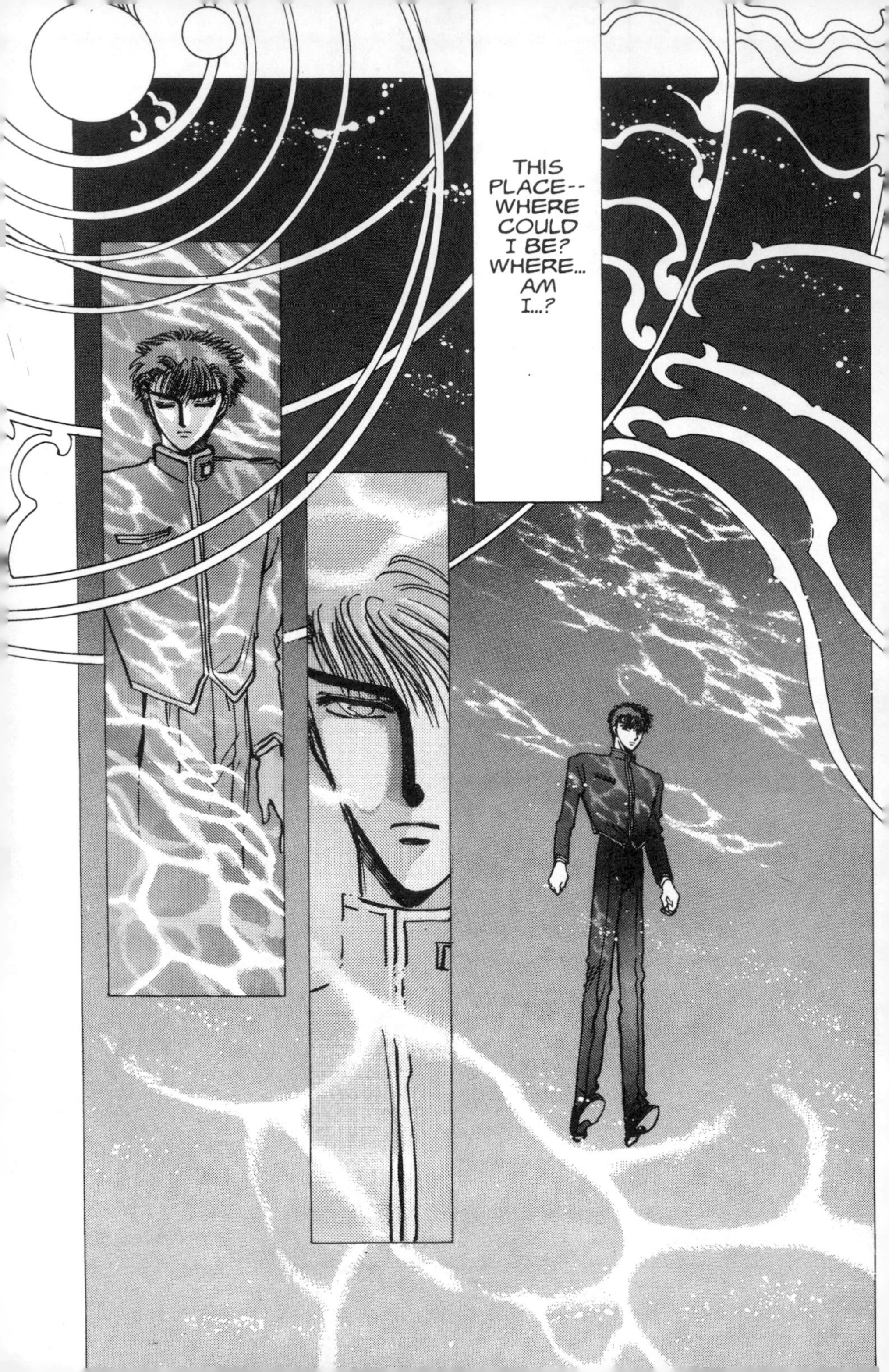
THIS PLACE-- WHERE COULD I BE? WHERE... AM I...?

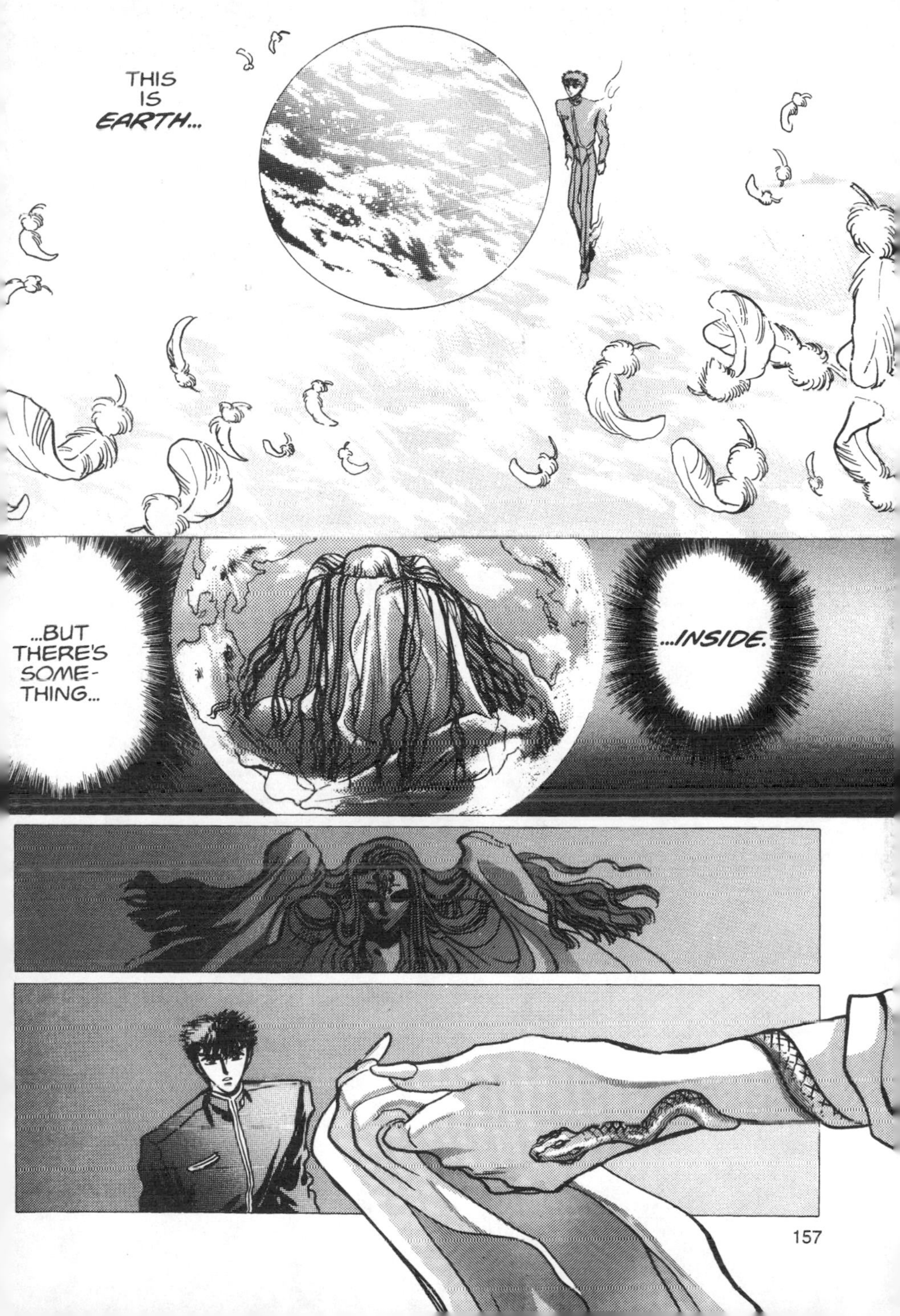
THIS IS EARTH...
...BUT THERE'S SOME- THING...
...INSIDE.

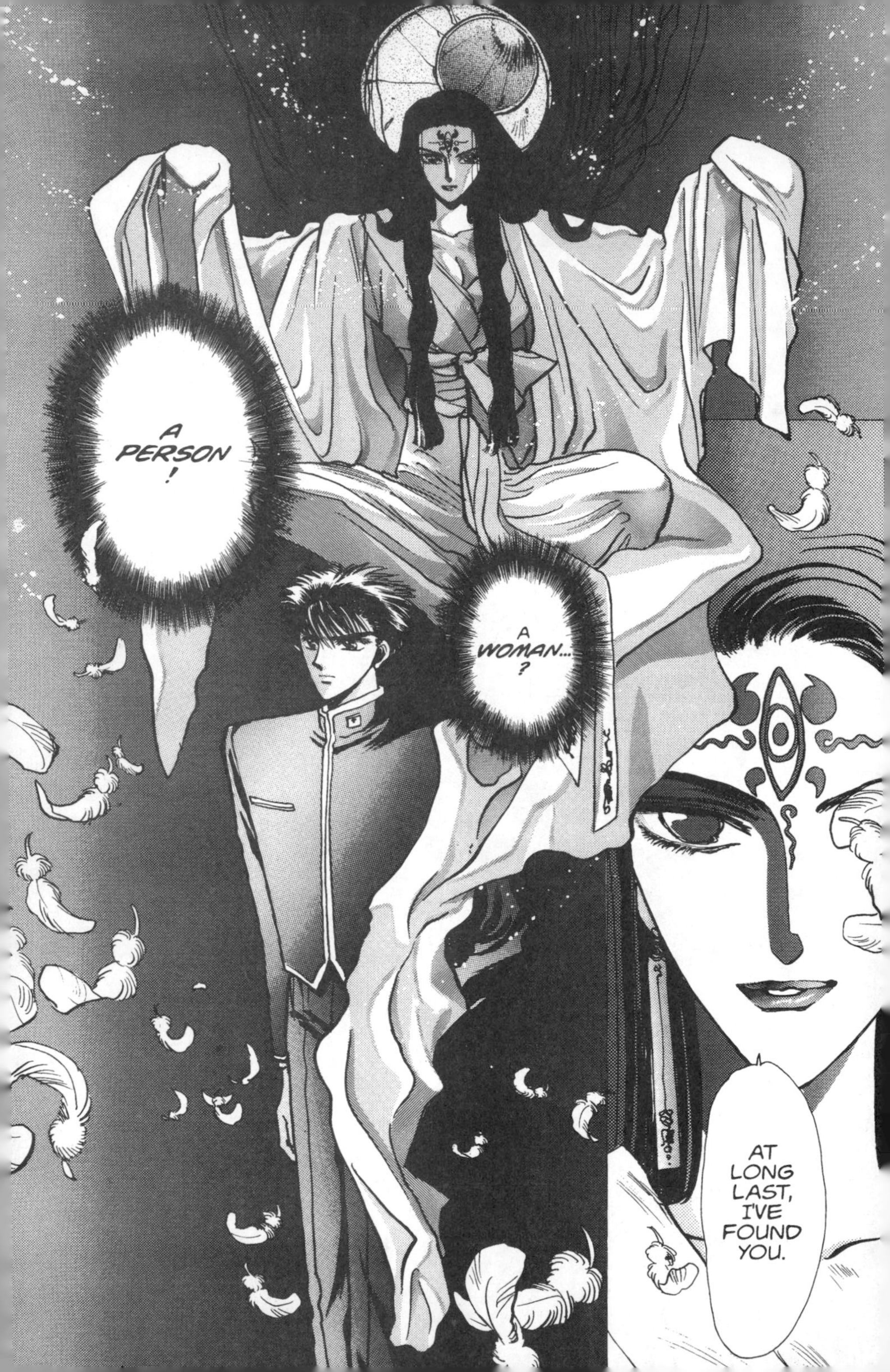
A PERSON!
A WOMAN...?
AT LONG LAST, I'VE FOUND YOU.

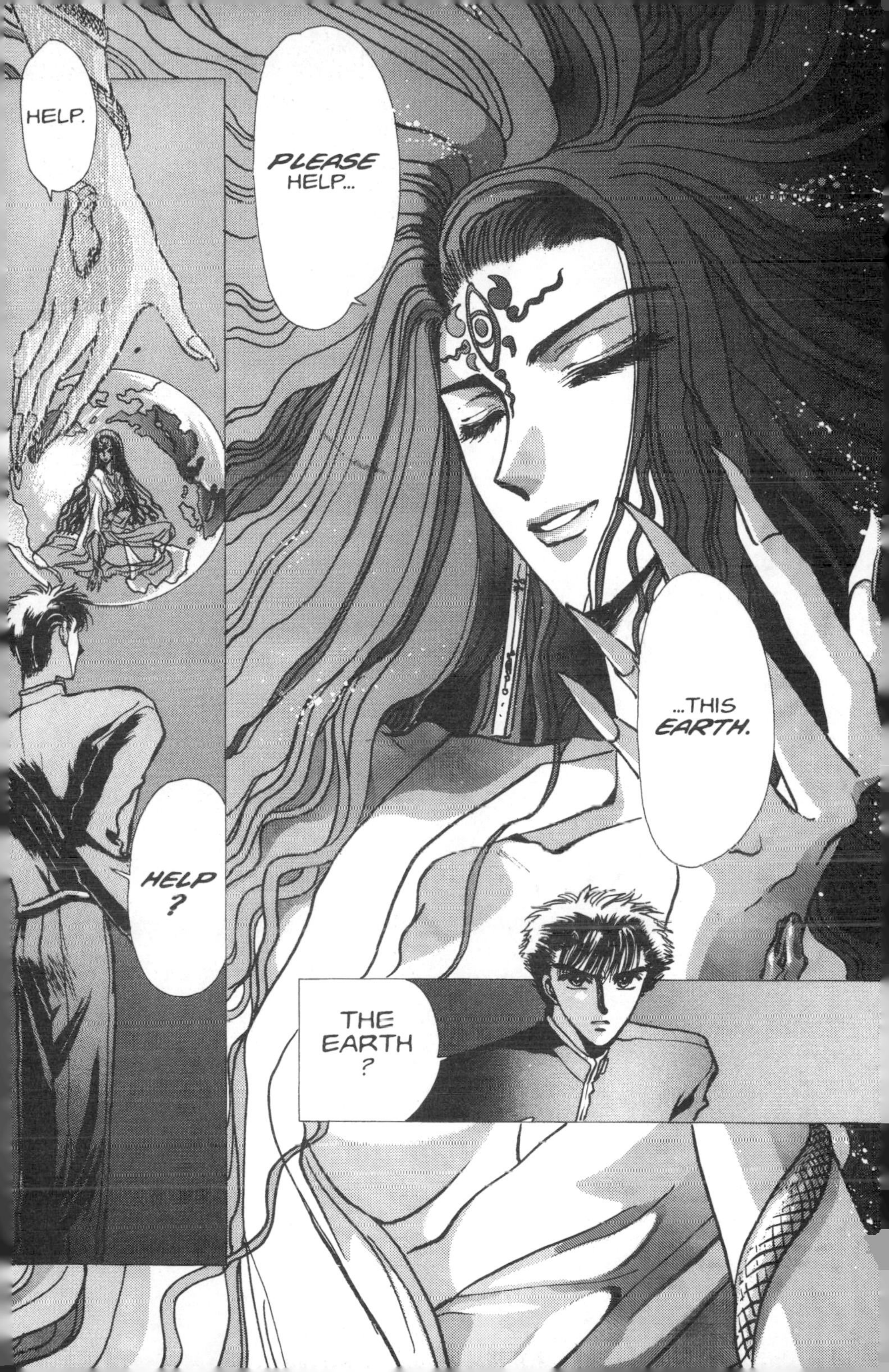
HELP.
HELP?
PLEASE HELP...
...THIS *EARTH.*
THE EARTH?

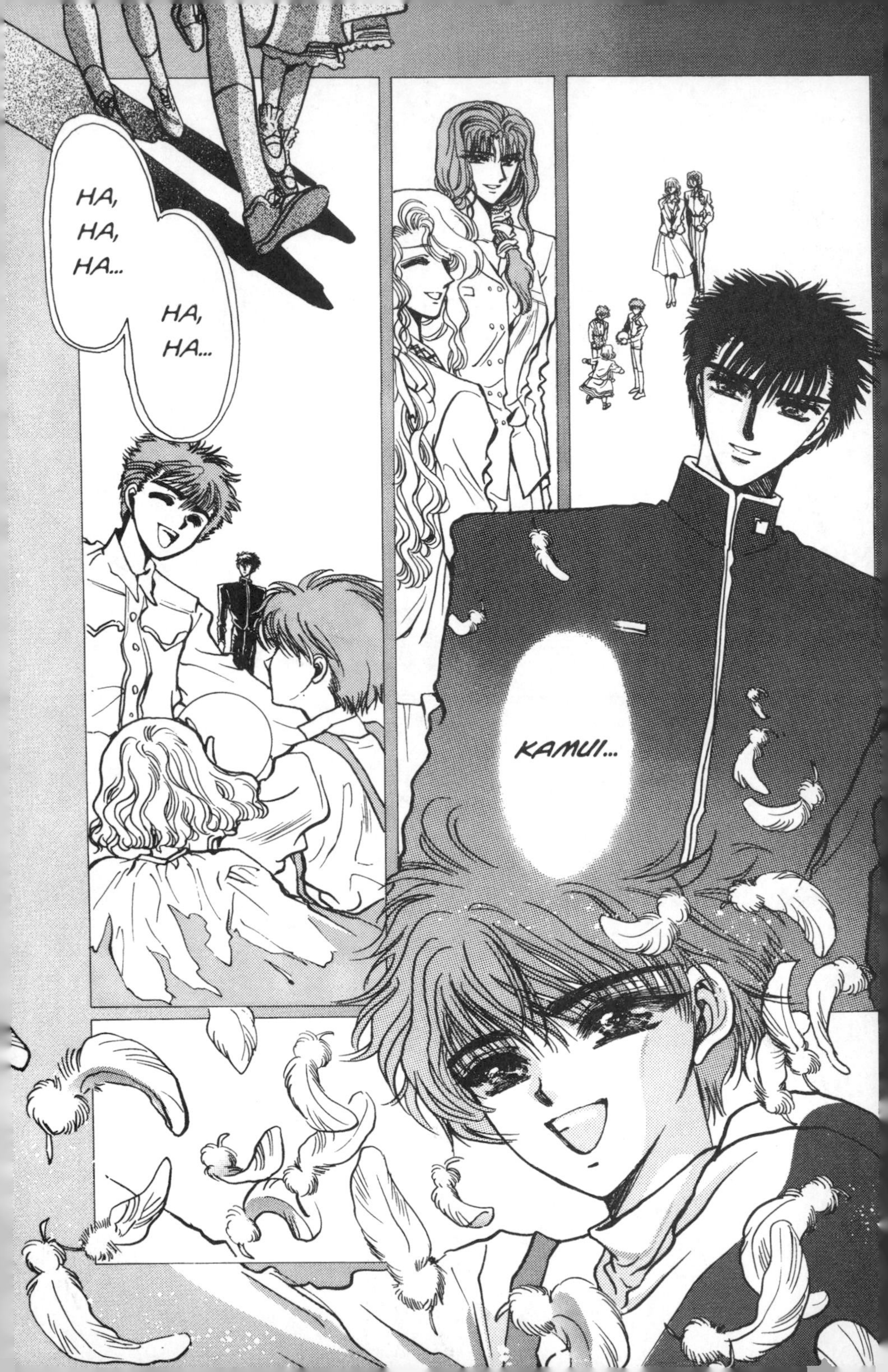
HA, HA, HA... HA, HA...
KAMUI...

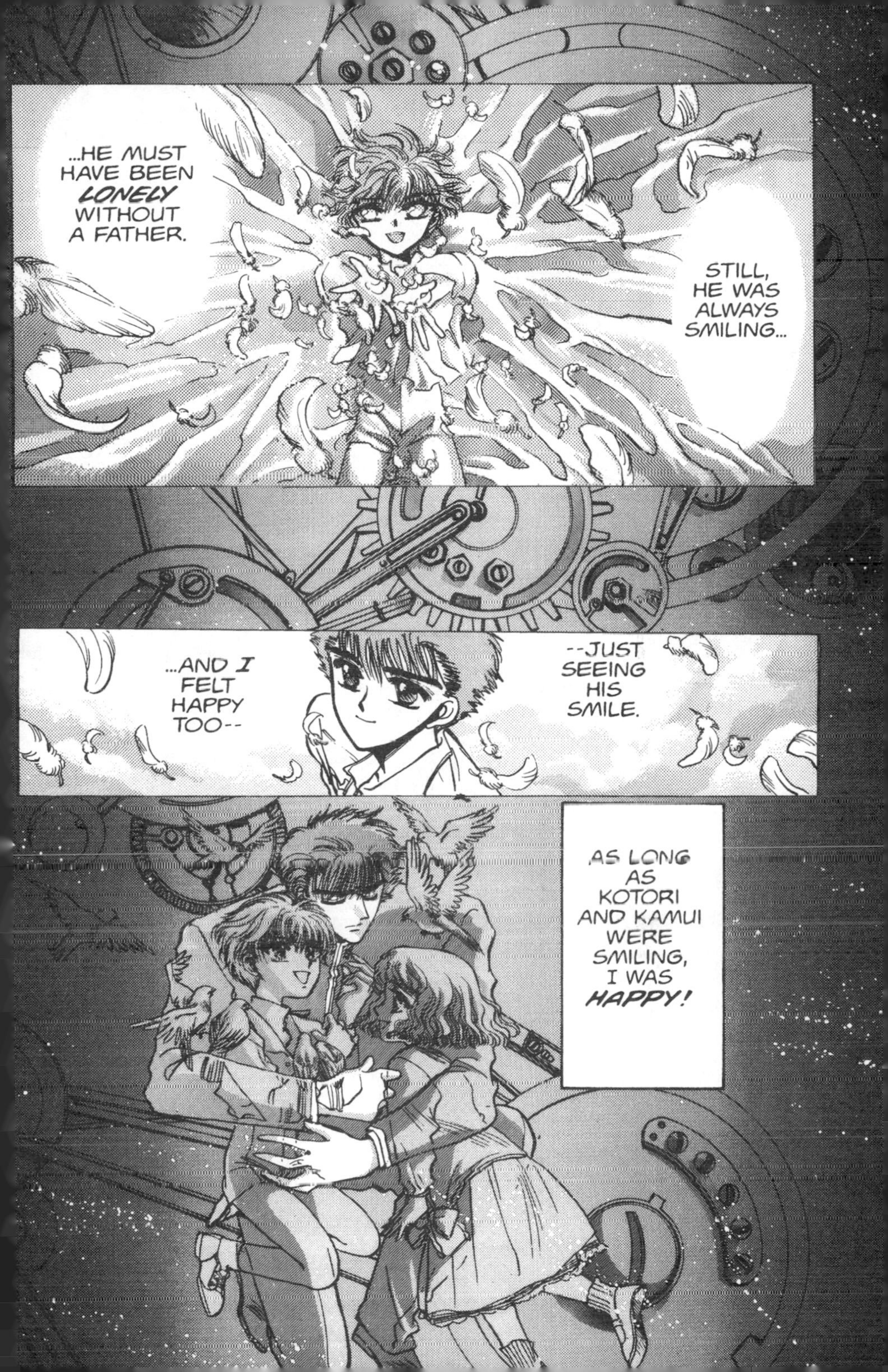

...HE MUST HAVE BEEN *LONELY* WITHOUT A FATHER.
STILL, HE WAS ALWAYS SMILING...
...AND *I* FELT HAPPY TOO--
--JUST SEEING HIS SMILE.
AS LONG AS KOTORI AND KAMUI WERE SMILING, I WAS *HAPPY!*

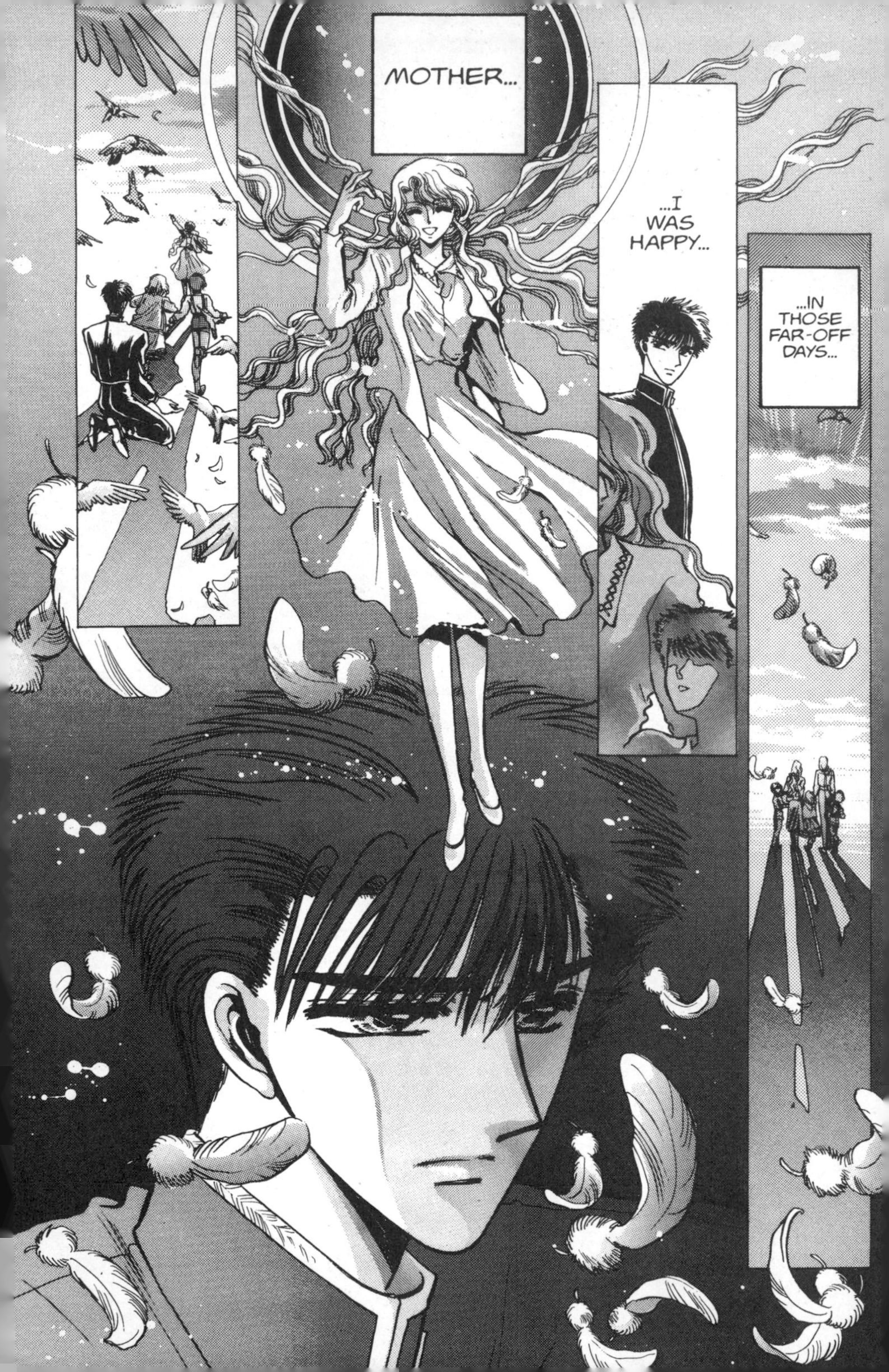
MOTHER...
...I WAS HAPPY...
...IN THOSE FAR-OFF DAYS...

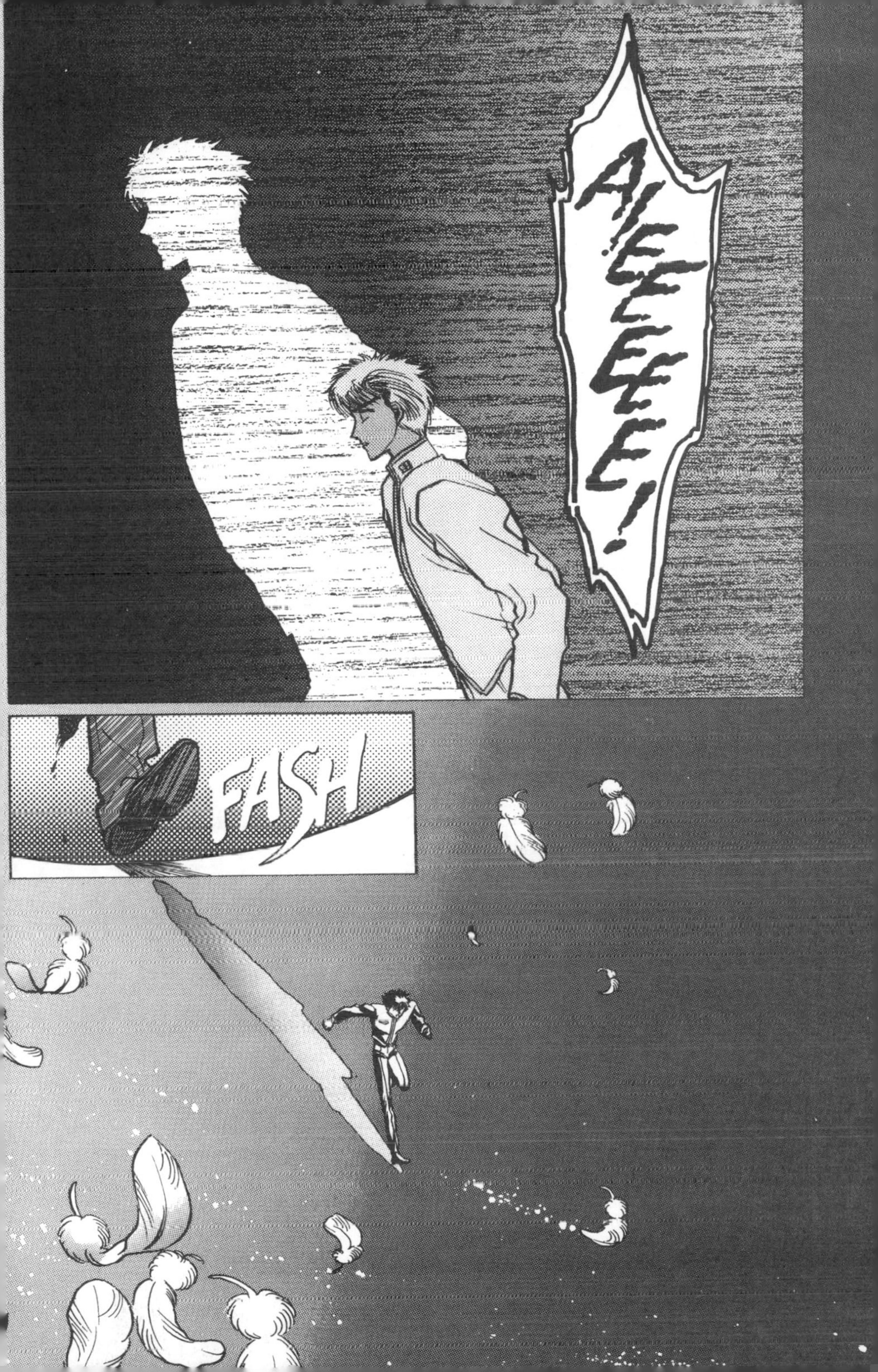
AIEEEEEE!
FASH

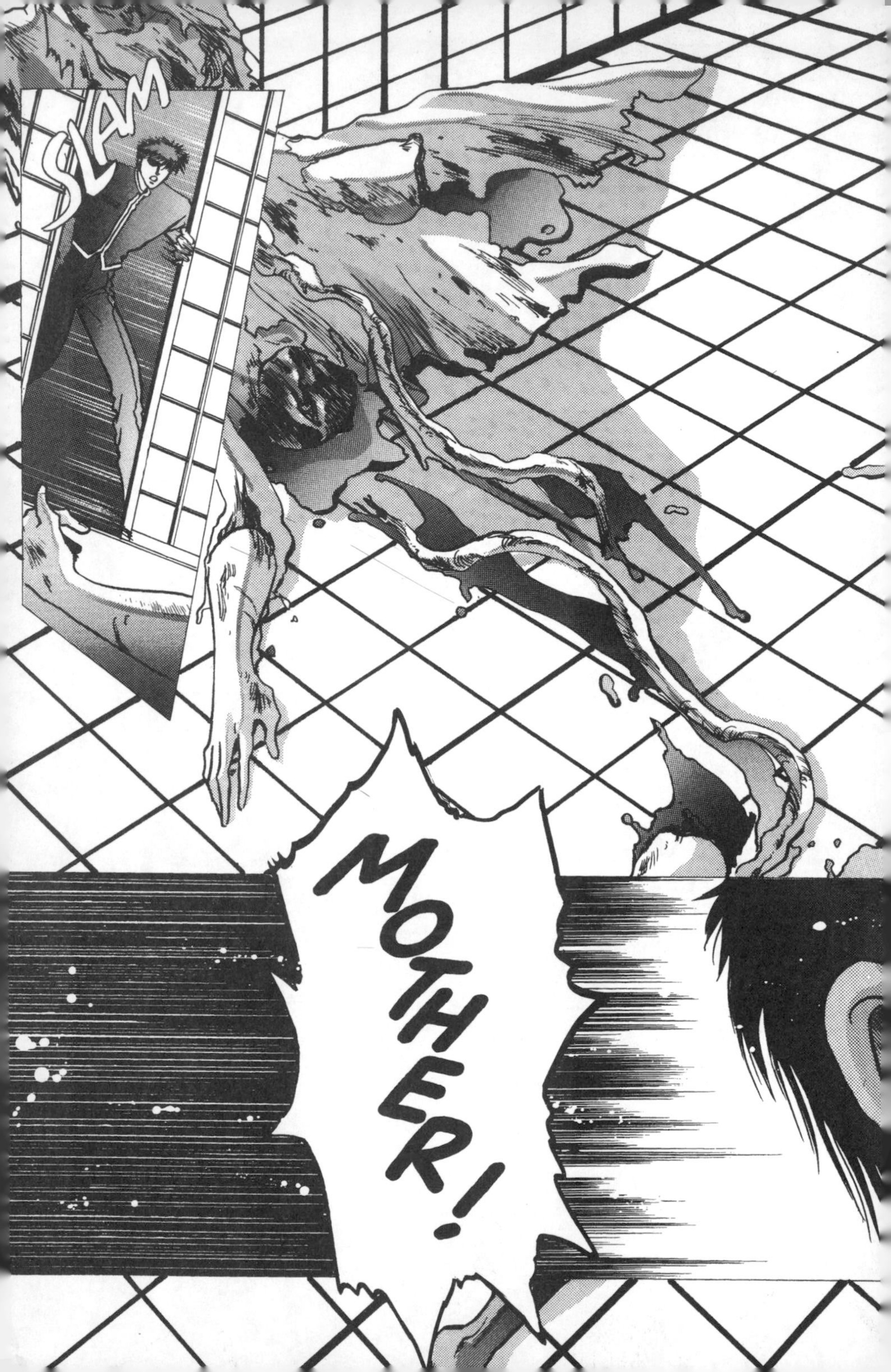
SLAM
MOTHER!

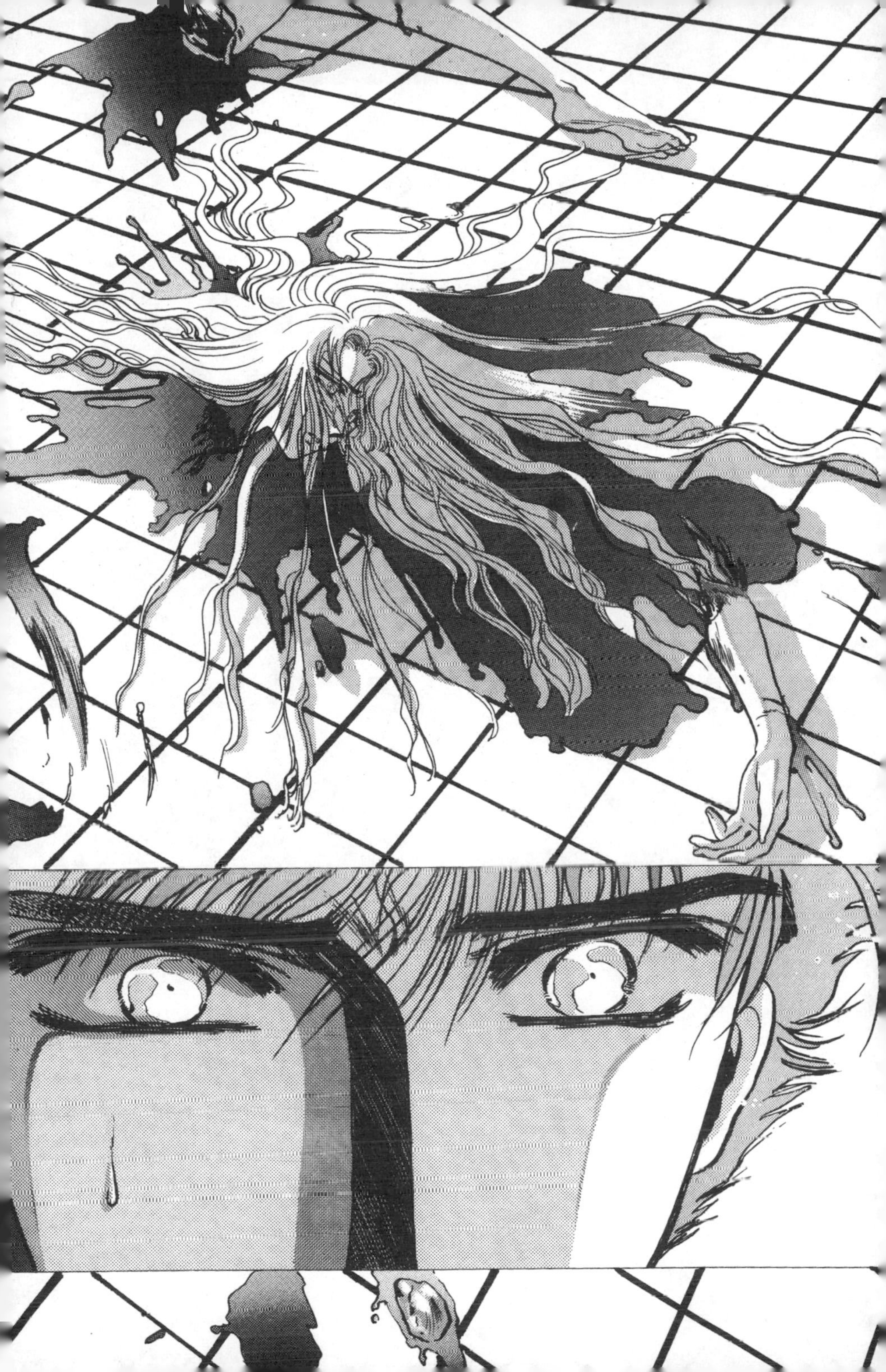

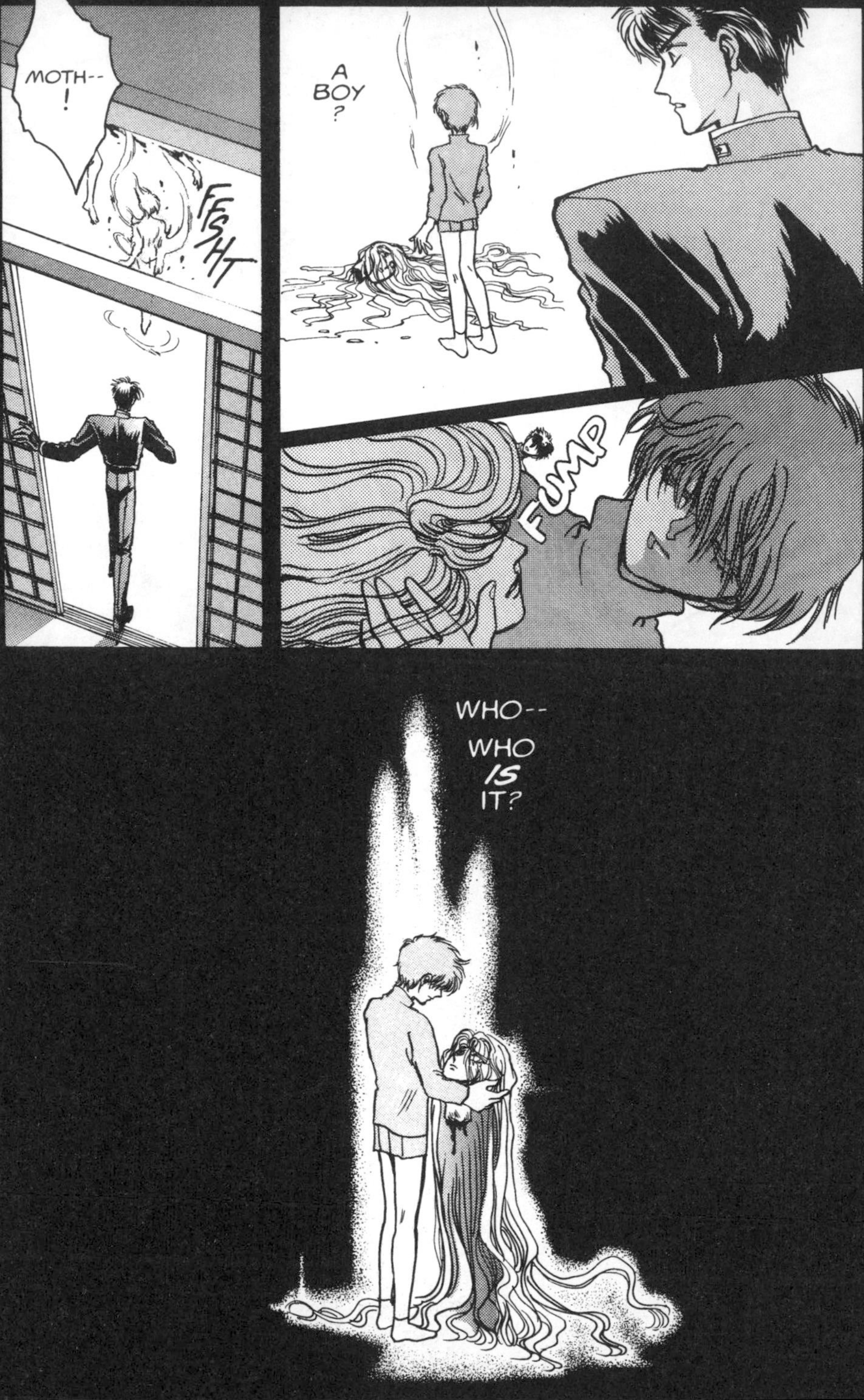
MOTH-- !
FFSHT
A BOY ?
FUMP
WHO--
WHO *IS* IT?

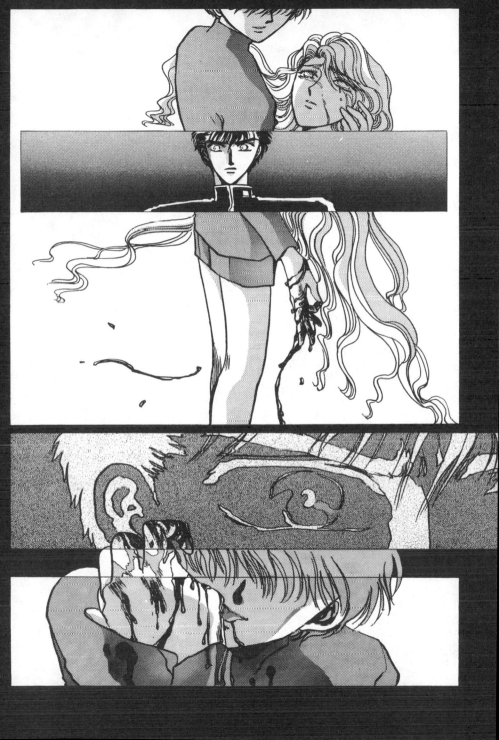

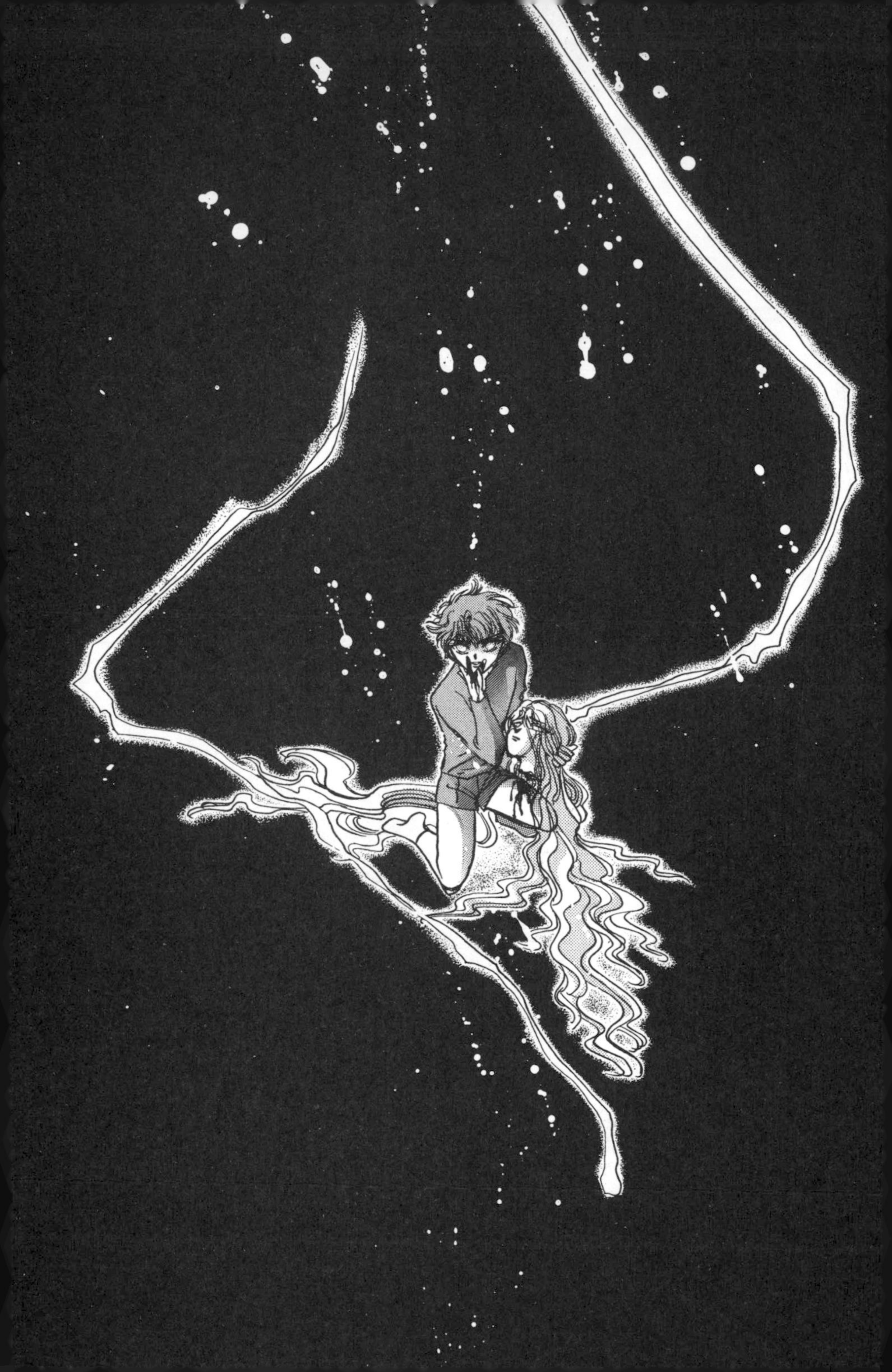

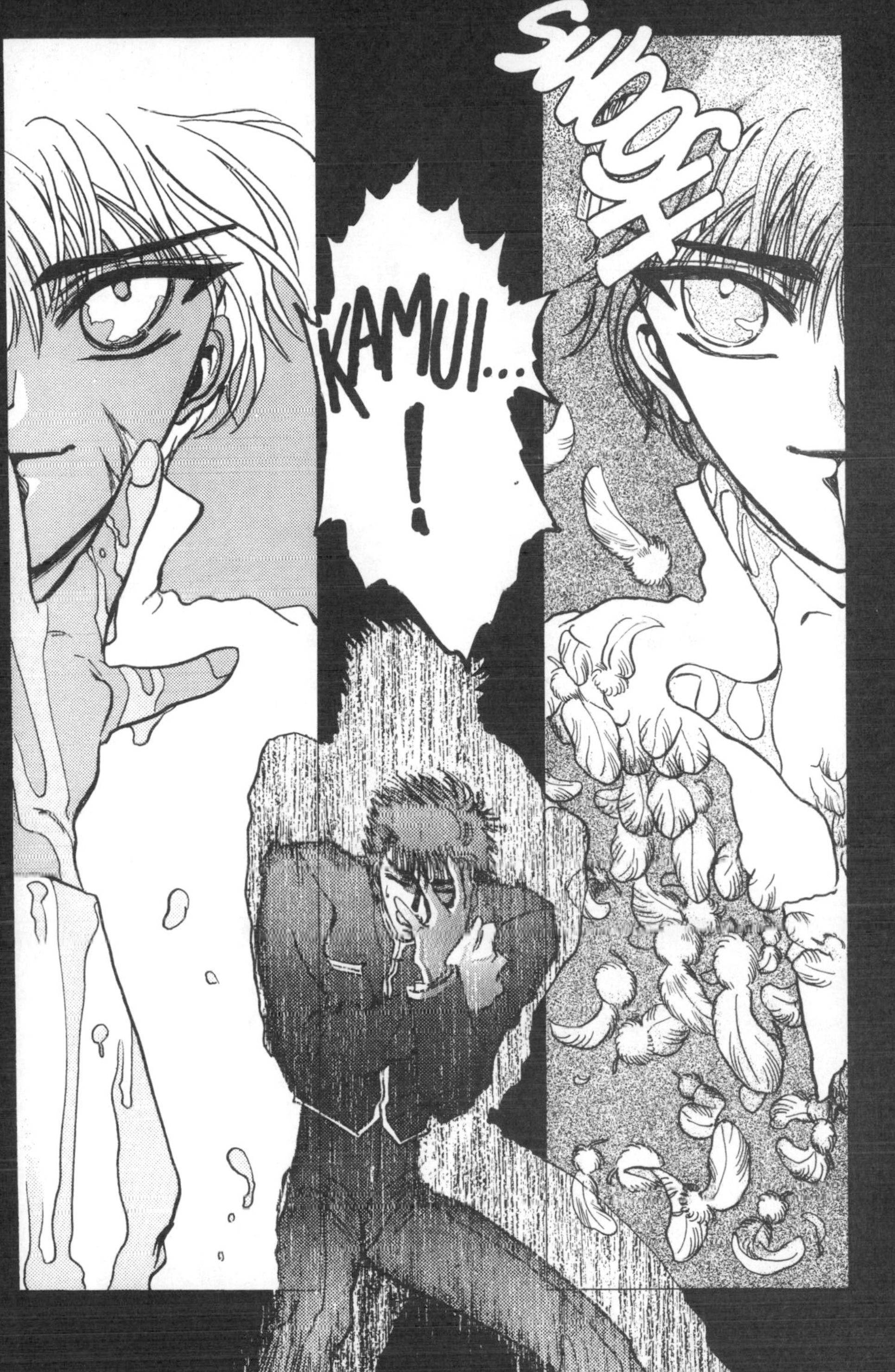
KAMUI... !
SHOOSH

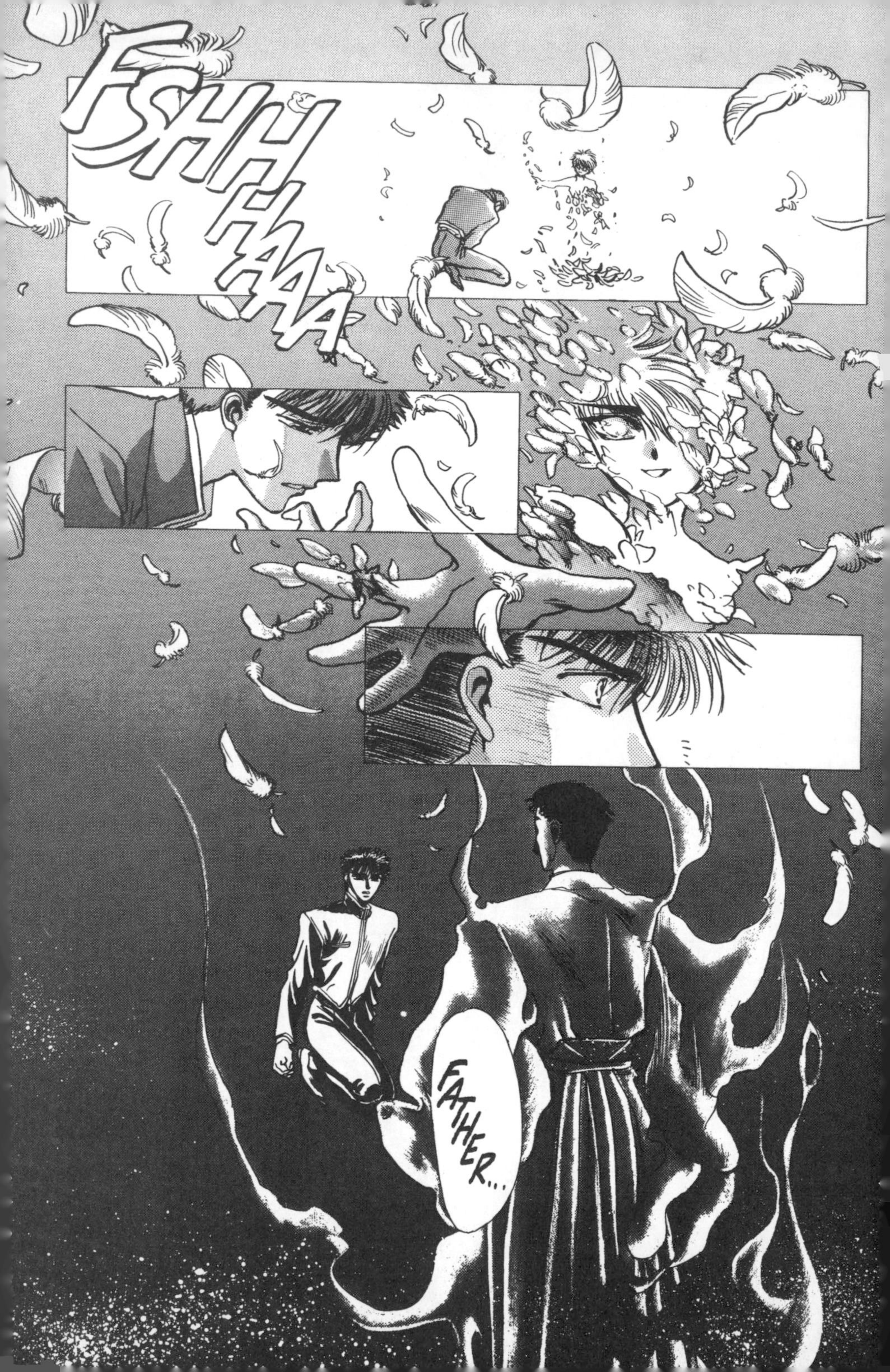
FSHH HAAA
FATHER...

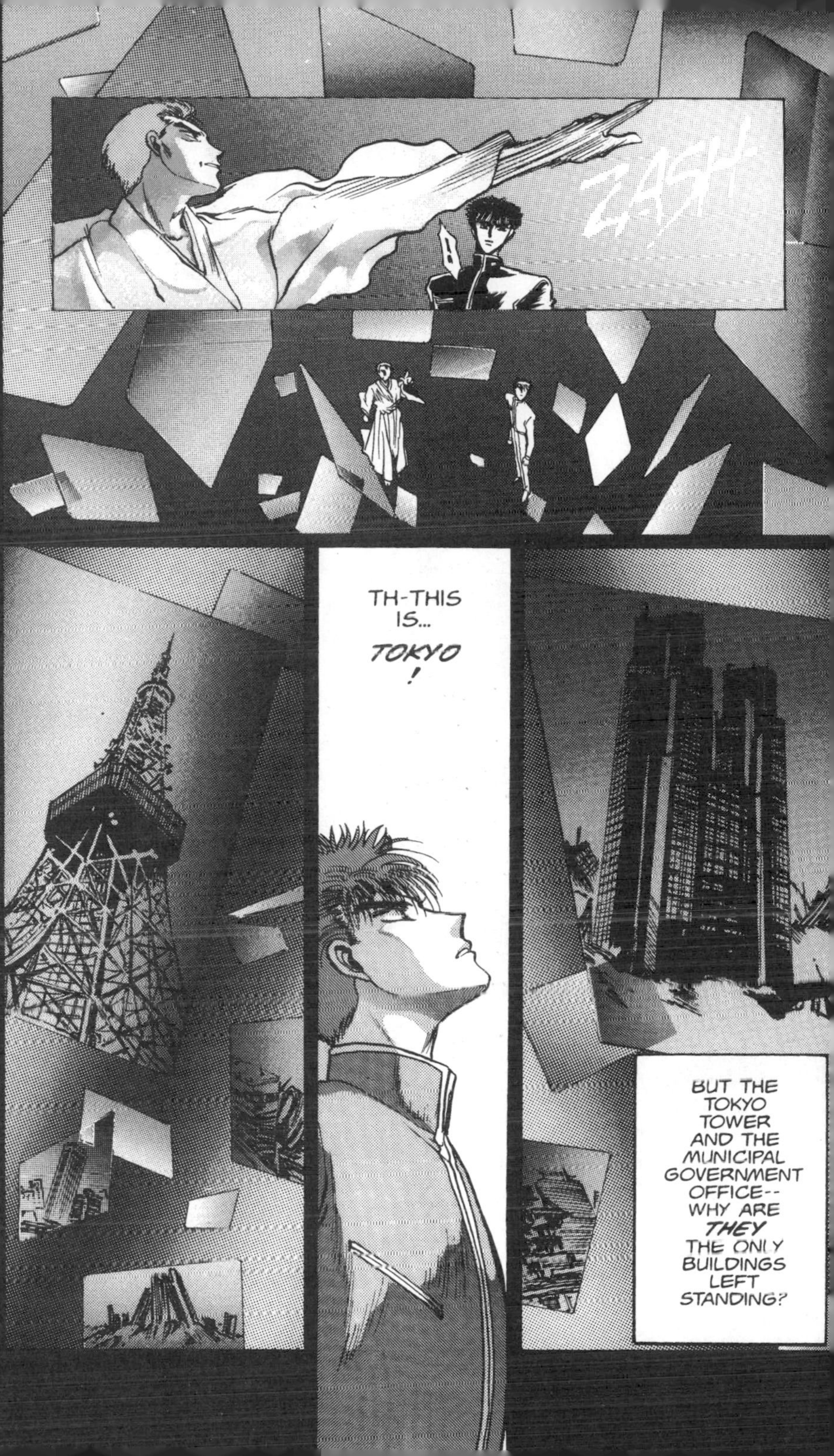
ZASH
TH-THIS IS... TOKYO!
BUT THE TOKYO TOWER AND THE MUNICIPAL GOVERNMENT OFFICE-- WHY ARE THEY THE ONLY BUILDINGS LEFT STANDING?

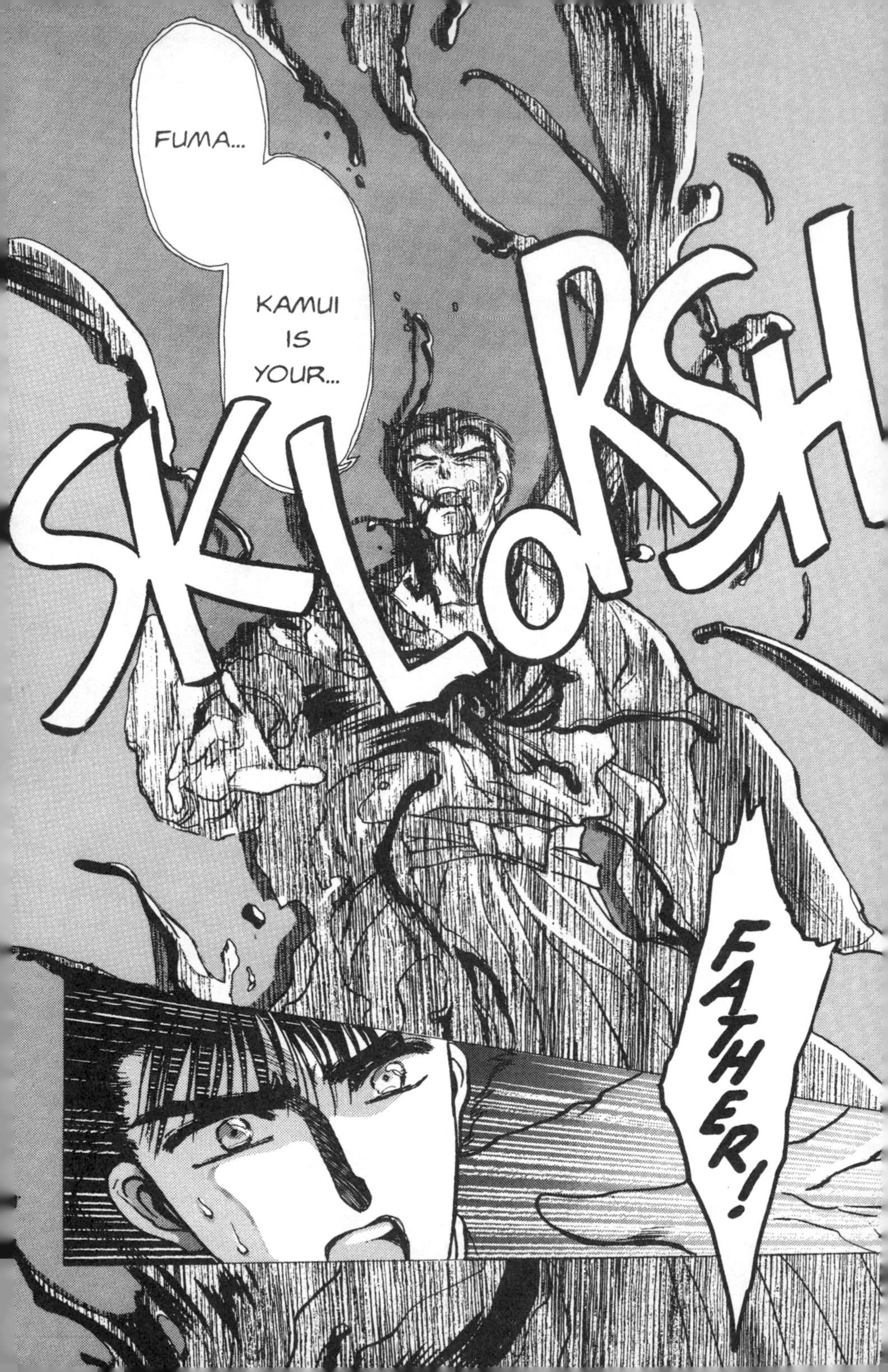
FUMA...
KAMUI IS YOUR...
SKLORSH
FATHER!

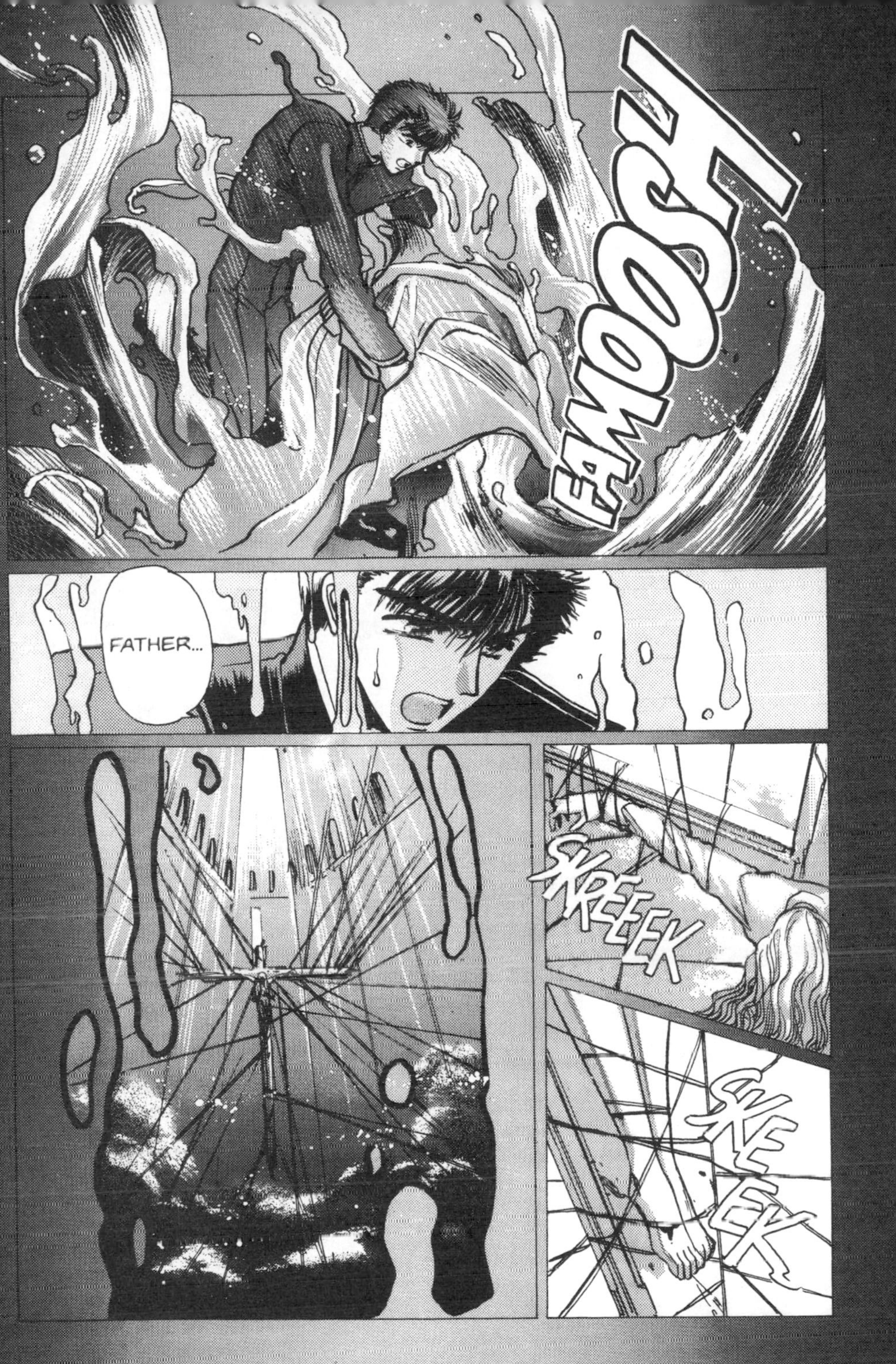
FWOOSH
FATHER...
SKREEEK
SKREEEK

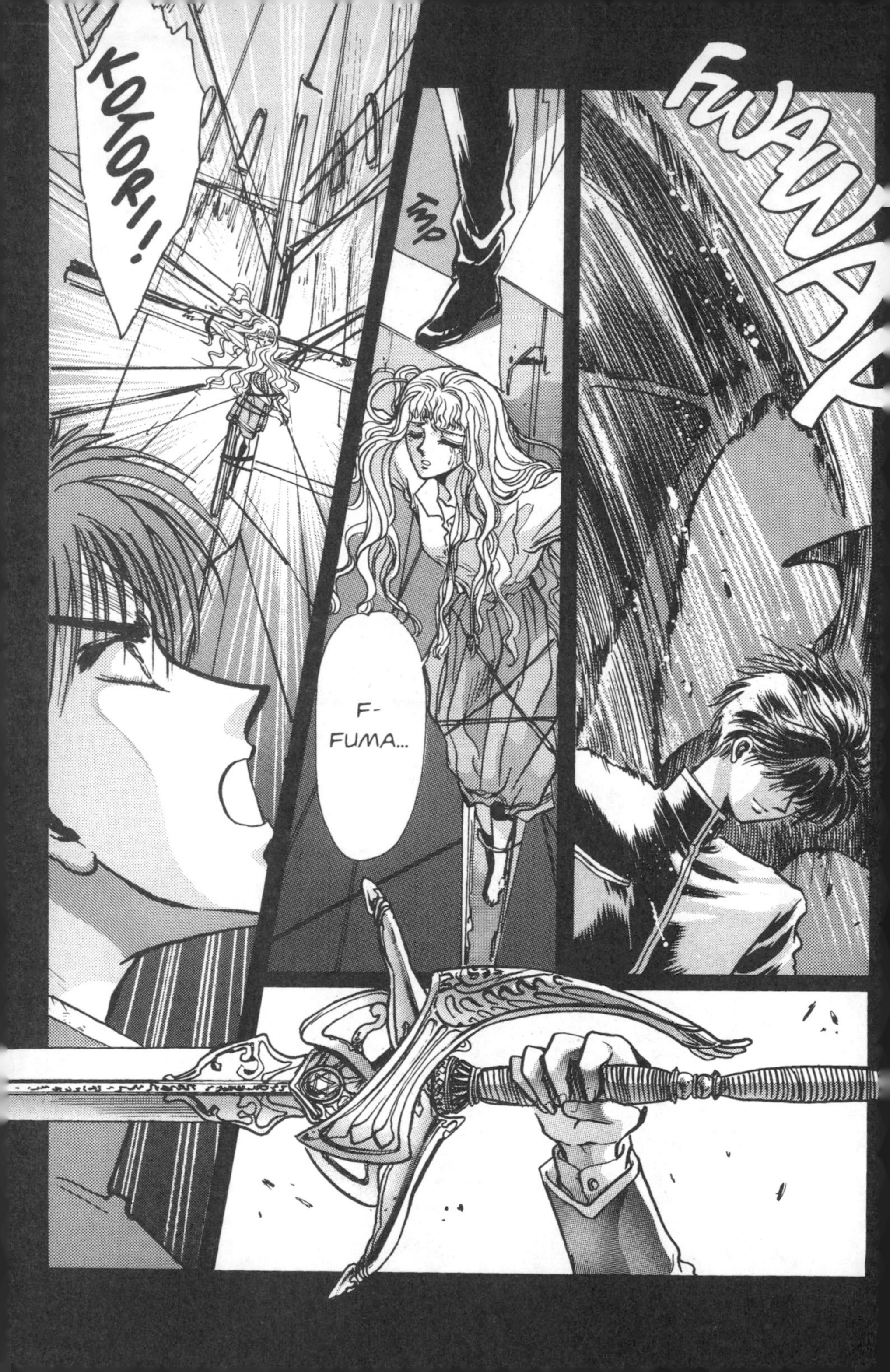
KOTORI!!
TMP
F-
FUMA...
FWAAAP

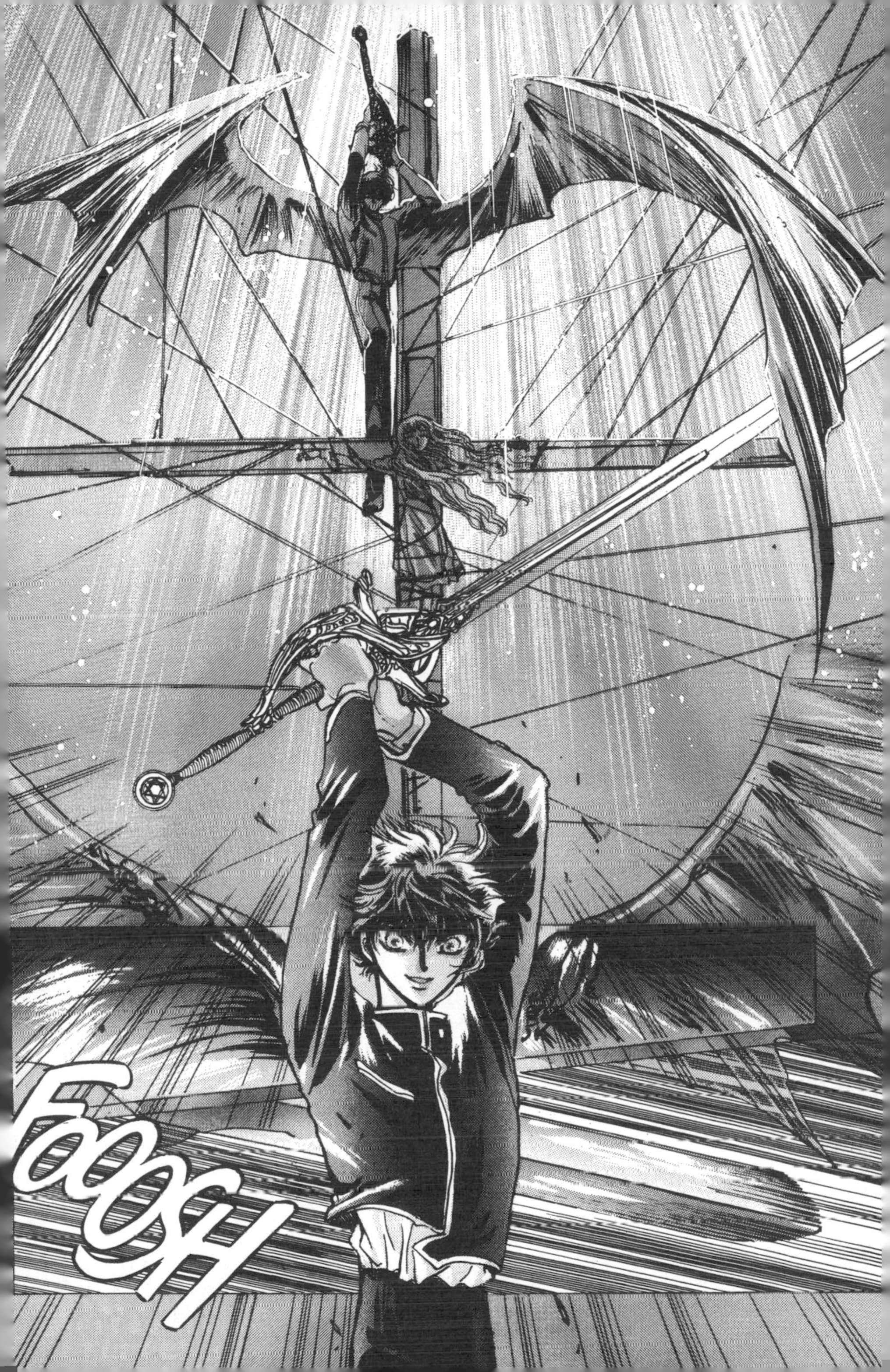
FOOSH

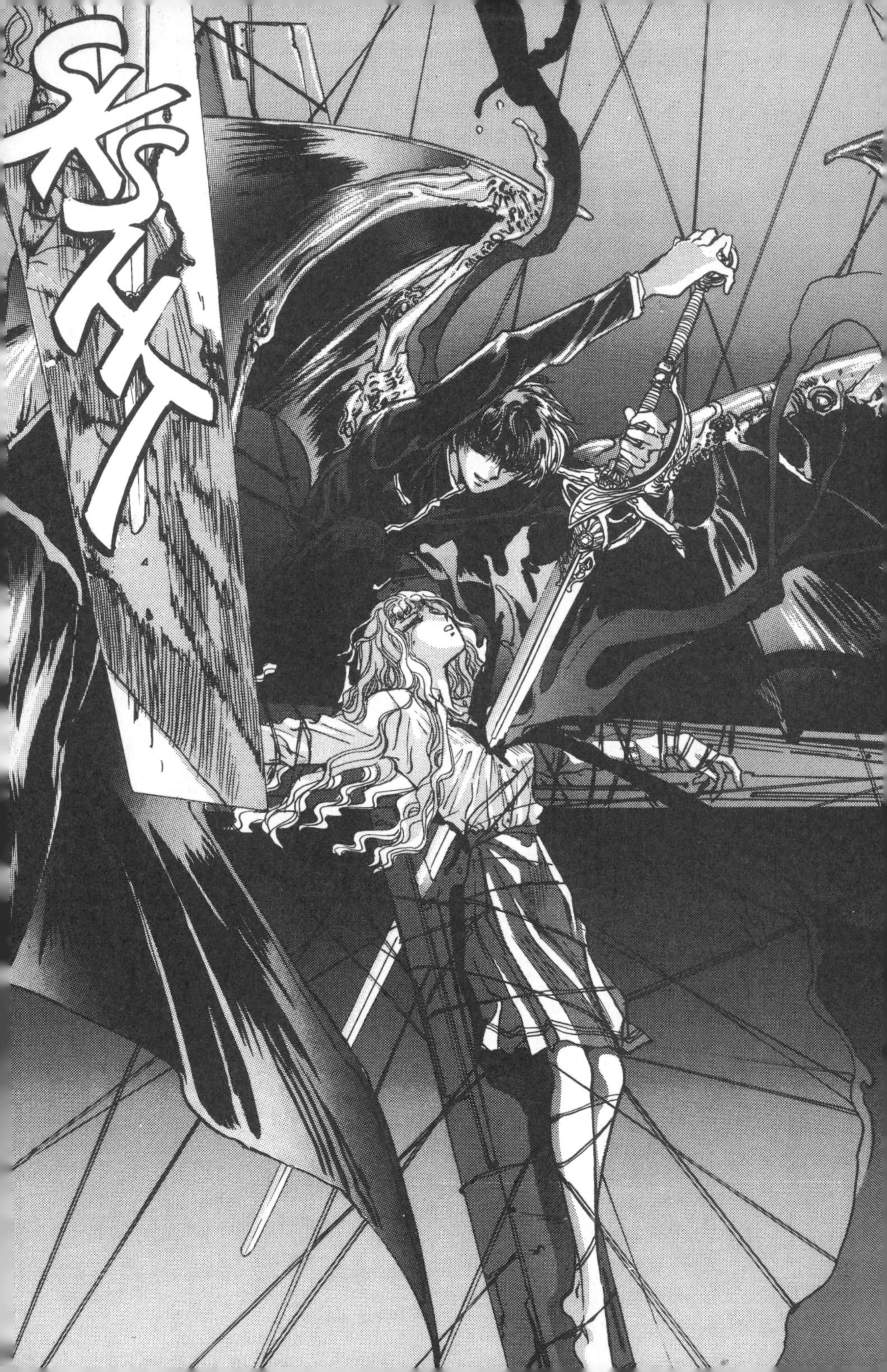

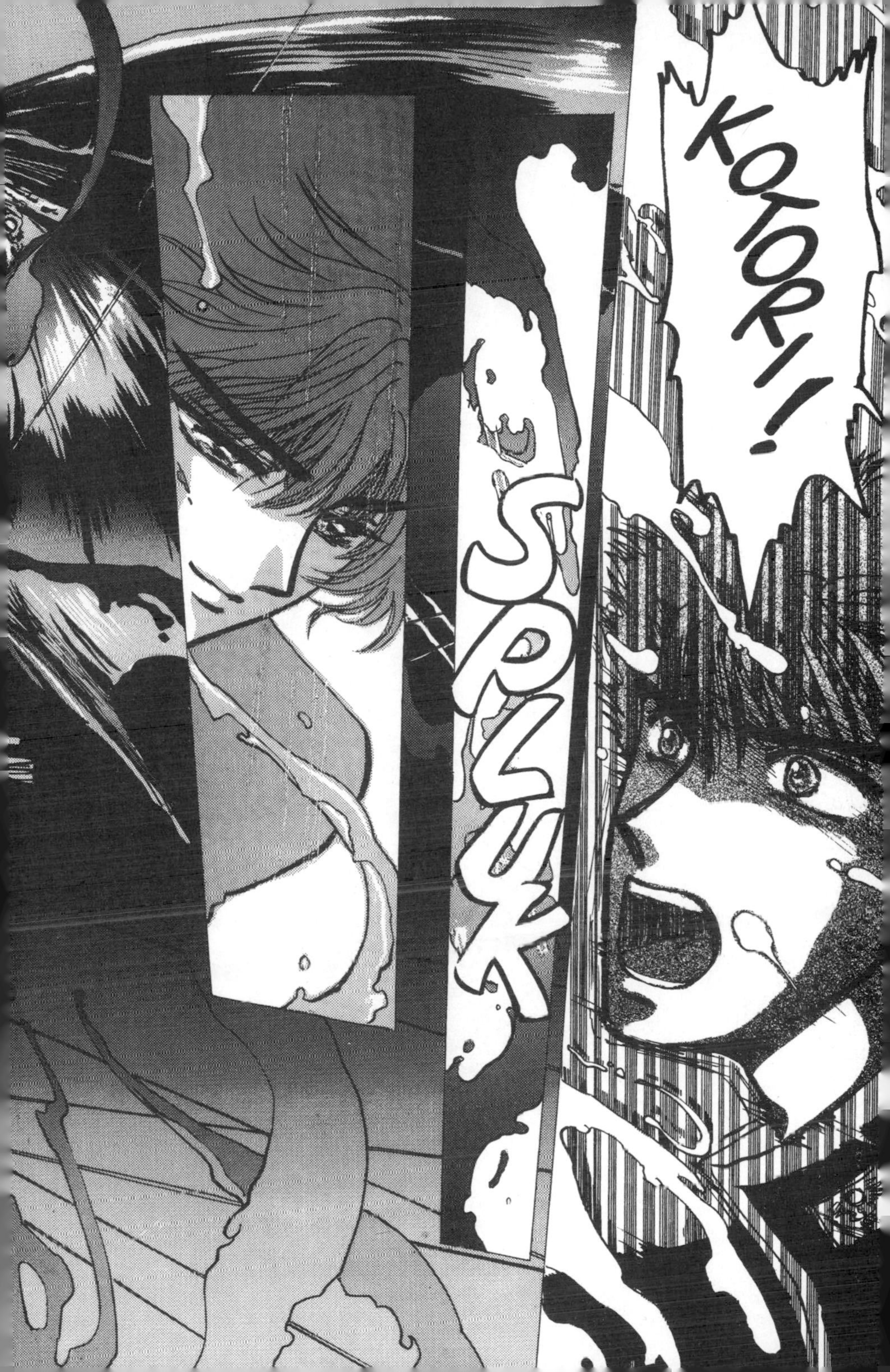
SPLUK
KOTORI!!

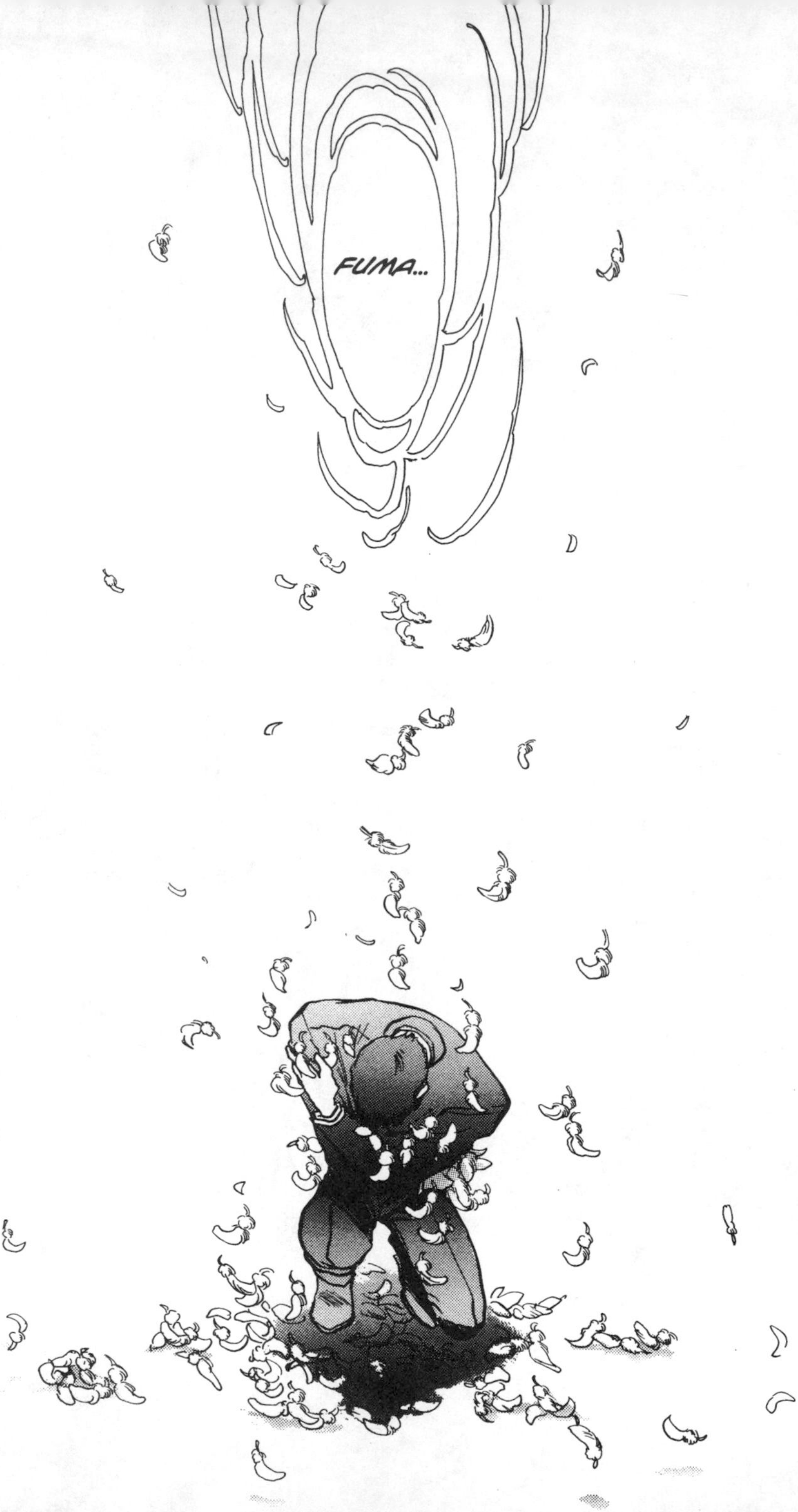
FUMA...

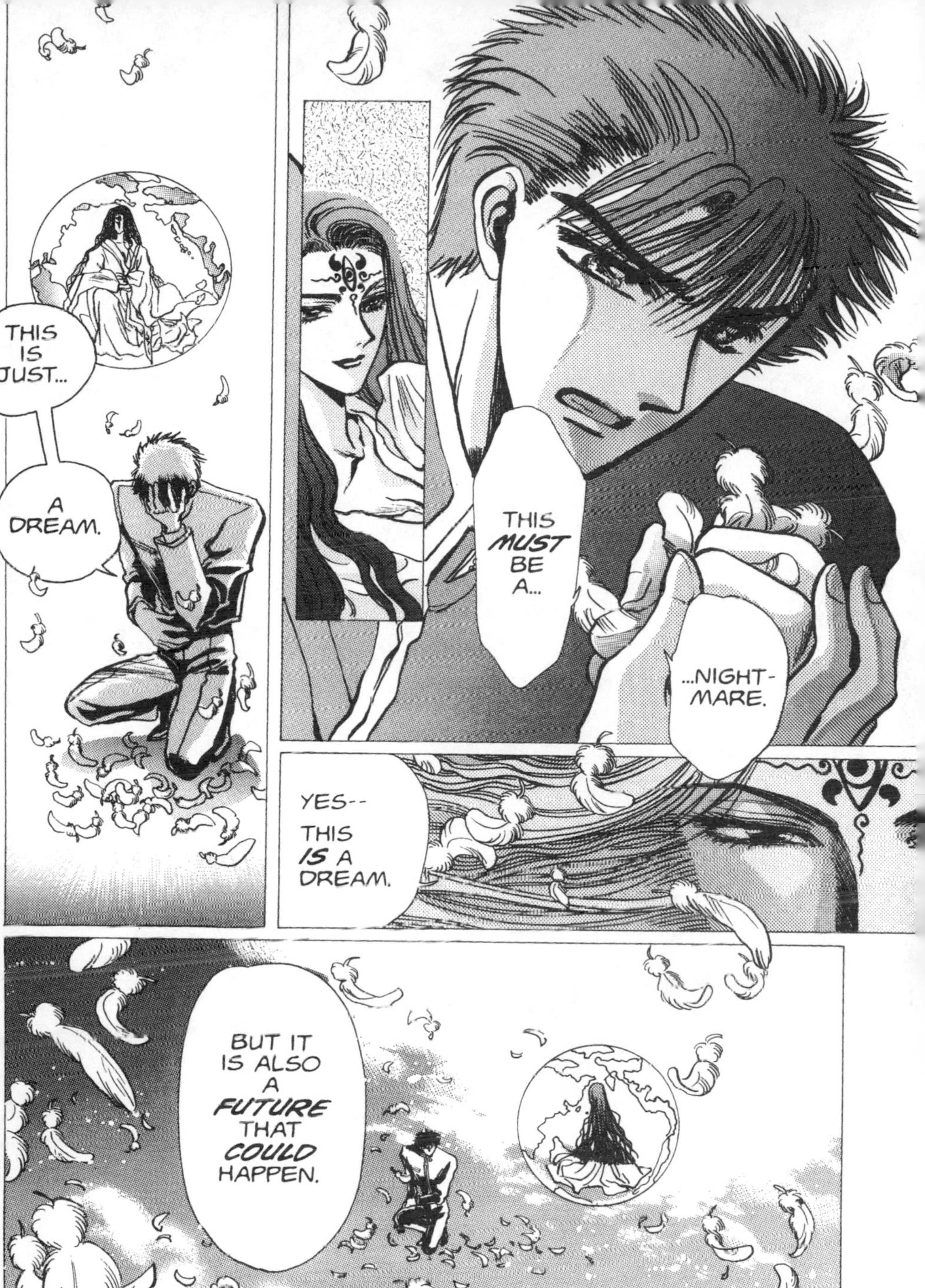
THIS IS JUST...
A DREAM.
THIS *MUST* BE A...
...NIGHT-MARE.
YES-- THIS *IS* A DREAM.
BUT IT IS ALSO A *FUTURE* THAT *COULD* HAPPEN.

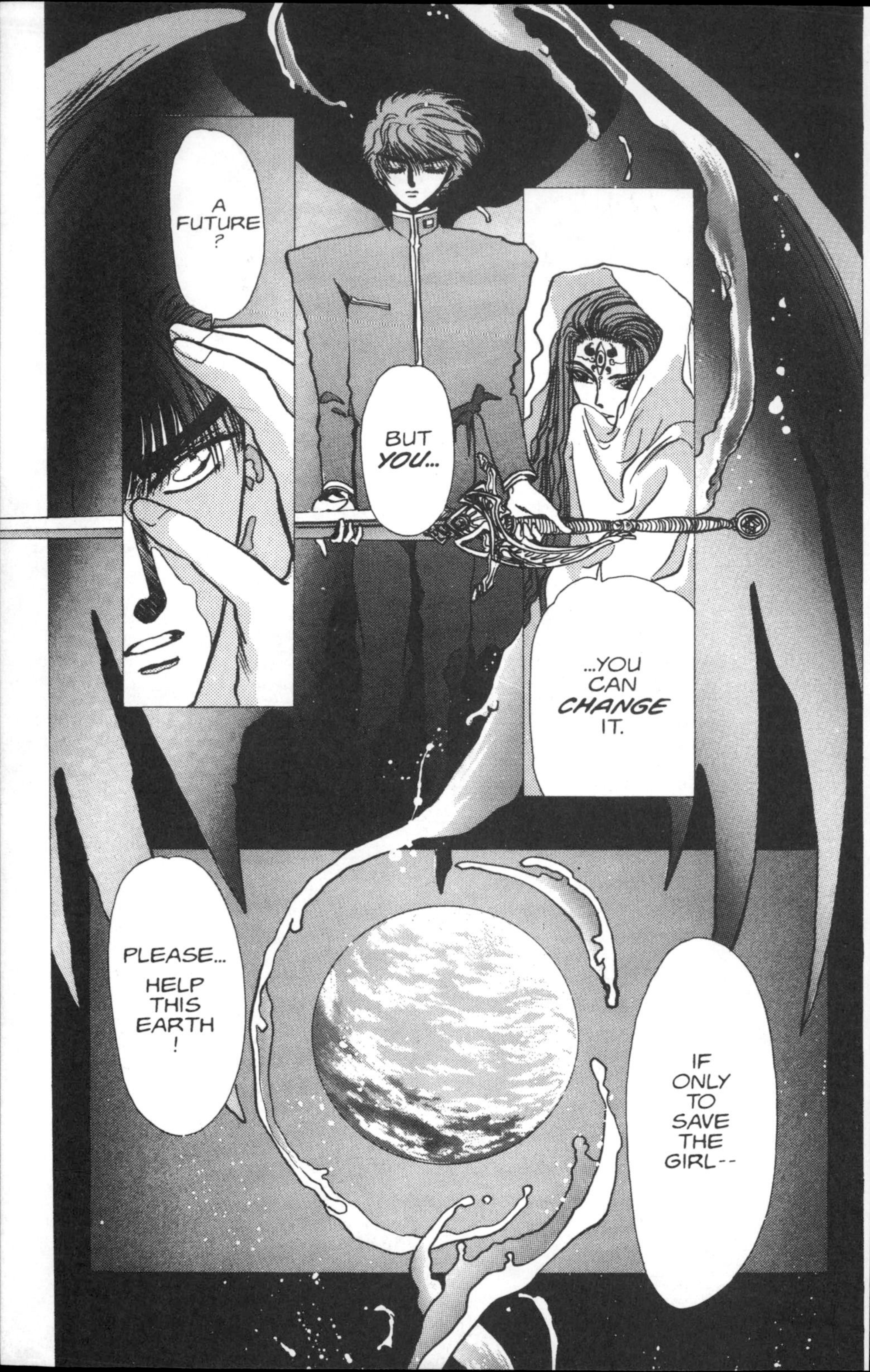
A FUTURE?
BUT *YOU*...
...YOU CAN *CHANGE* IT.
PLEASE... HELP THIS EARTH!
IF ONLY TO SAVE THE GIRL--

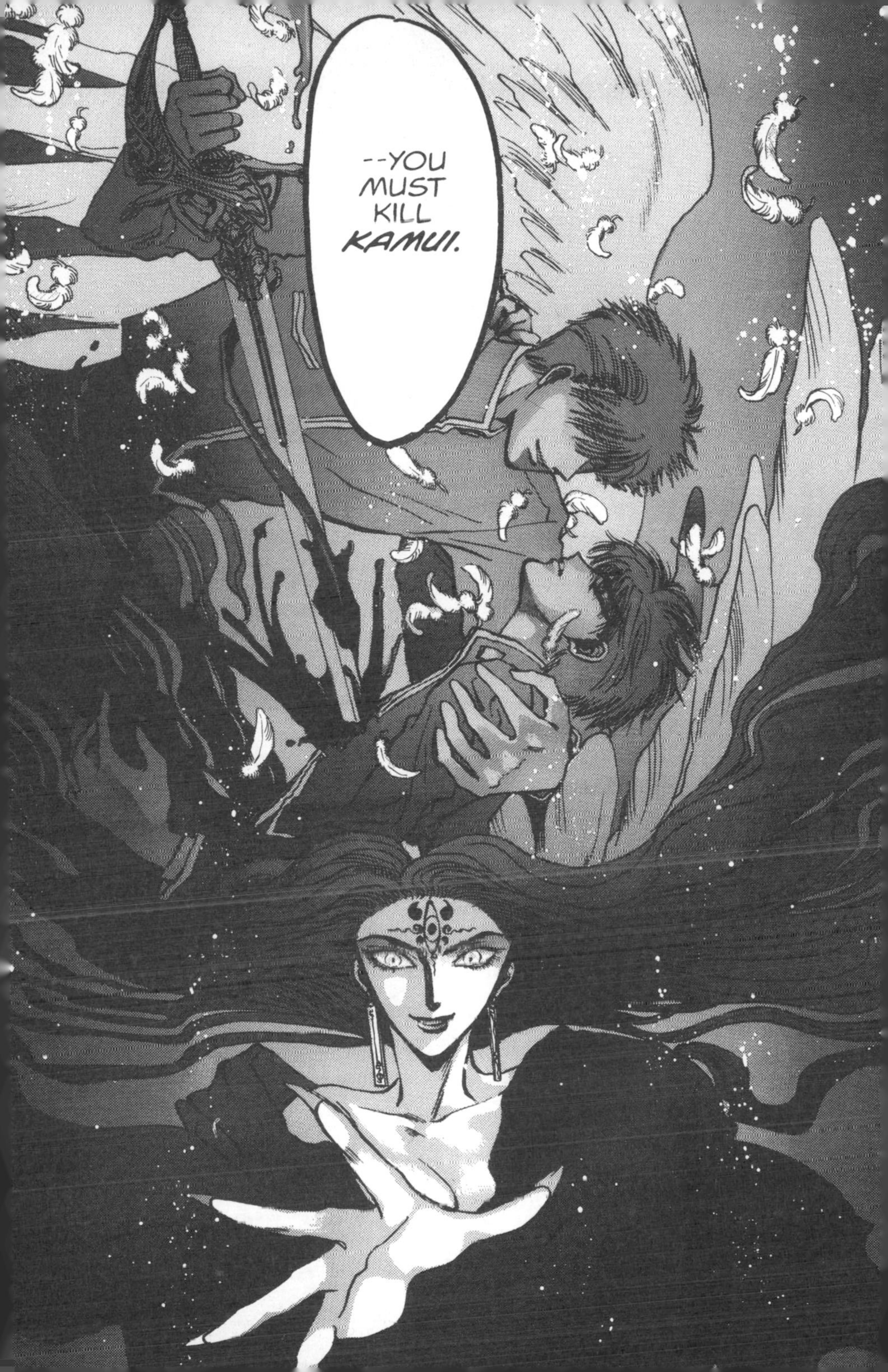
--YOU MUST KILL *KAMUI.*

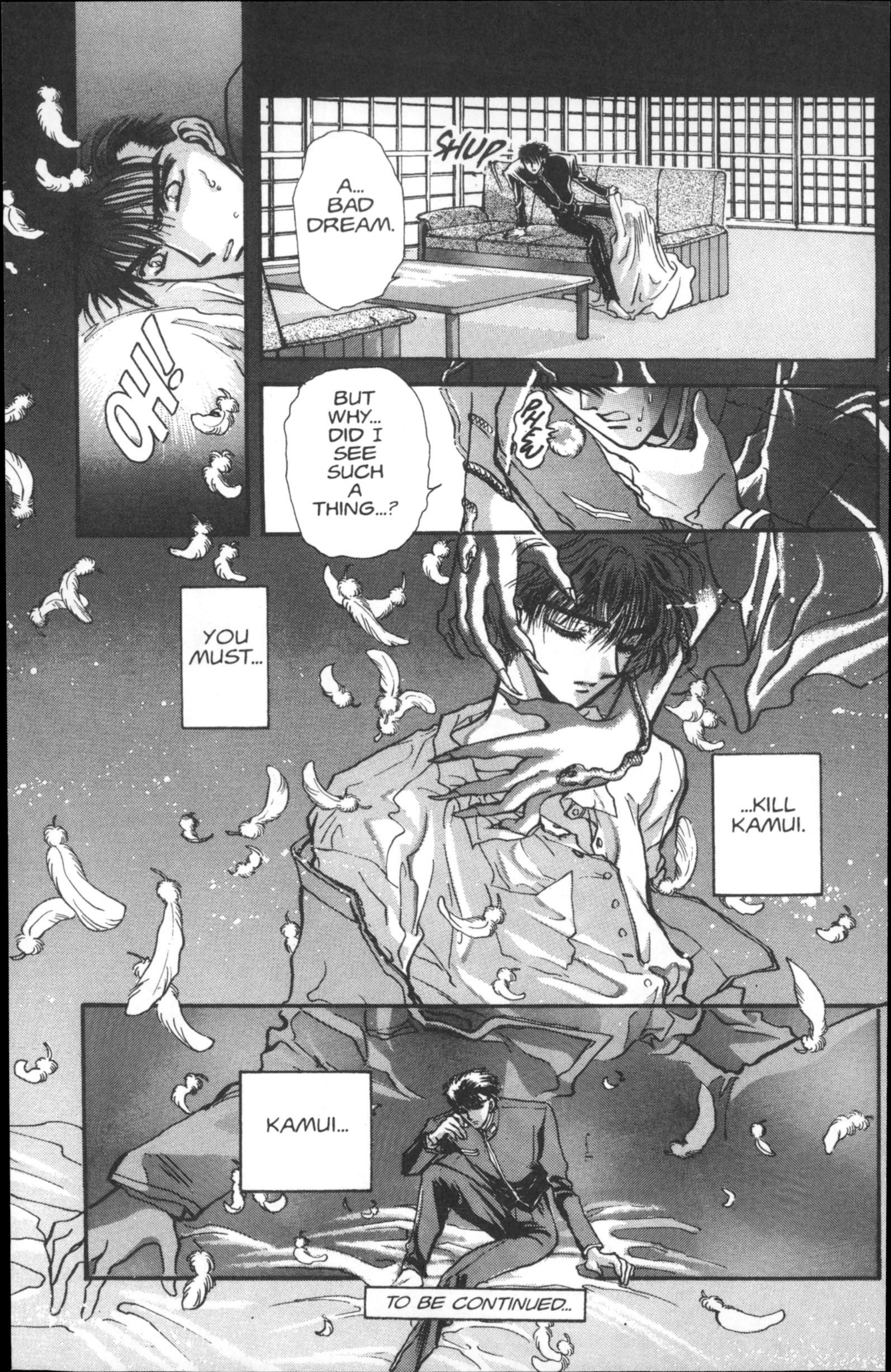
OH!!
SHUP
A... BAD DREAM.
PHEW
BUT WHY... DID I SEE SUCH A THING...?
YOU MUST...
...KILL KAMUI.
KAMUI...
TO BE CONTINUED...